VIALLI

A DIARY OF HIS SEASON

Also by Harry Harris
Ruud Gullit: The Chelsea Diary
The Ferguson Effect

VIALLI

A DIARY OF HIS SEASON

Harry Harris

ORION

First published in Great Britain in 1999 by
Orion Media
An imprint of Orion Books Ltd
Orion House, 5 Upper St Martin's Lane,
London WC2H 9EA

A CIP catalogue record for this book
is available from the British Library

Typeset in Great Britain by Selwood Systems, Midsomer Norton
Printed and bound by Butler & Tanner Ltd, Frome and London

To Linda, a true Blue

Special thanks to Chelsea chairman Ken Bates, chief executive Colin Hutchinson, and Gwyn Williams for their co-operation. Many thanks also to the expert photo selection from the *Mirror* picture desk: John Mead, Greg Bennett, and editor Ron Morgans. Finally, Orion editor Simon Spanton deserves recognition for his perception in recognising the charisma of Luca Vialli.

CHRONOLOGY

1964	Born on 9 July, Cremona
1981	Makes debut for local club Cremonese
1984	Transferred to Sampdoria for £1.8m; wins first medal a year later in Italian Cup
1985	International debut v. Poland
1991	Wins championship with Sampdoria; top Serie A scorer with nineteen goals
1992	Transferred to Juventus for world record £12.5m; plays last game for Italy v. Malta in December, falls out with coach Arrigo Sacchi
1996	Plays last game for Juventus, leading them to European Cup win; days later moves to Chelsea free under Bosman ruling
1998	In February becomes surprise choice for manager when Ruud Gullit leaves Stamford Bridge; within three months leads Chelsea to League Cup and Cup Winners Cup; scores hat-trick in 5–0 Worthington Cup win at Arsenal in November.

PLAYING CAREER

Sampdoria (1984–92): 85 goals in 223 games
Juventus (1992–96): 38 goals in 102 games
Chelsea (1996–98): 36 goals in 74 games
Italy (1985–92): 16 goals in 59 games

HONOURS AS PLAYER/PLAYER-MANAGER

Sampdoria: Serie A title (1991); Italian Cup (1985, 1988, 1989); Cup Winners Cup (1990)
Juventus: UEFA Cup (1993); Serie A title (1995); European Cup (1996)
Chelsea: FA Cup (1997); League Cup (1998); Cup Winners Cup (1998)

Introduction

Luca Vialli wanted to become a Chelsea legend. He has done just that.

In his quest to win the title for the first time in forty-four years, Chelsea lost a mere three games in the Premiership, finishing third to qualify for the Champions League for the first time in the club's history, and Vialli became the first Chelsea manager for nine years to top the table, taking his team to the summit just before Christmas in his first full season. He was the first to do so as a player-coach, although he conceded the dual role was highly stressful: 'When Ruud Gullit left and I had the chance to take over, it all happened so fast that when they made the offer I accepted it immediately. I must admit, in retrospect, that I'm not sure whether I would have been able to accept one of my team-mates moving above me to become player-manager. Mostly, that is because of the type of person I am. Admittedly, the figure of a player-manager is a delicate one, and all at once I had a thousand different responsibilities as well as a thousand different preoccupations. In my entire career I have only ever met one other player, Toninho Cerezo at Sampdoria, who seemed capable of being a player-manager but, after a trial period, I found a way to organise myself.' He quickly accepted the multitude of extra problems, abandoned much of his golf, returned to smoking, departed from his childhood sweetheart (who returned to Italy), and underwent fits of depression before, during and after every game.

When Vialli was named player-manager of Chelsea it was greeted with derision in Italy. Serie A bosses with years of experience scoffed at the notion that a thirty-three-year-old, no matter how successful as a player, could be trusted with a Premiership side. Former AC Milan manager Fabio Capello said: 'It's like giving the keys of a Ferrari to an eighteen-year-old.' Scarcely ten months later, Vialli's Chelsea won three cups – as many as they had won in the previous twenty years – and challenged for the Premiership.

It was perhaps no coincidence that Capello's analogy involved a teenager and a Ferrari: Vialli's privileged background is well documented. He is the Italian equivalent of a toff, and that does not sit too well within Serie A quarters, where the roots of the game, as in England, remain working class. Capello sent another barb Vialli's way, while addressing a seminar on management at Milan's prestigious Bocconi University: 'Managers should not be players, they shouldn't even train with the players. The idea of managing while playing makes so little sense, it could only happen in England. Those two only played because they named themselves in the side and refused to substitute themselves.' He did not name names, but, given the Italian audience, it was clear that the phrase 'those two' referred to Vialli and Gullit. Luca's response to Capello? 'I didn't ask for the job here. If people on the Chelsea board thought I was right for it, either by watching my behaviour or taking into account my experience, then I think I can drive the car.'

Chief executive Colin Hutchinson had, of course, sounded out Vialli's credentials in Italy before he succeeded Gullit. Vialli had worked as a player under Enzo Bearzot, Giovanni Trapattoni and Marcello Lippi, as well as Gullit. Lippi enthused: 'There is only one thing you need to know about Luca and that is he was born to leadership just as a baby is born to his mother's breast. He will take to management as naturally as a baby suckles from its mother. People who know him well know that he has a pedigree, and the bigger the challenge, the more he rises to it. Never once did he attempt to hide from any task.' Attilio Lombardo also issued a glowing reference at the outset of Vialli's managerial career: 'He is a clever person, a gifted player and has a sober personality. So he has a combination of qualities that will enable him to succeed.'

The title was Luca's priority as he set out on his first full season in charge, but merely contesting the championship was a new delight for long-suffering Blues supporters. Remember the last time Chelsea won the title? There was a national dock strike, the Warsaw Pact was signed, Newcastle beat Manchester City 3–1 in the FA Cup final, and Tony Bennett was number one in the charts with 'Stranger in Paradise'. That was May 1955. But Chelsea's squad had plenty of experience of winning League championships – Ferrer had won five in Spain, Petrescu four in Romania, Desailly two in Italy and one in France, Vialli two in Italy, plus one each from de Goey, Le Saux, Goldbaek (in Germany), Di Matteo (in Switzerland), Babayaro (Belgium), Zola and Kharine; when Laudrup was around, he added another six – so things looked good for Luca.

Also in 1955, V-neck sweaters were at the top of the fashion charts, so Luca has already brought a flavour of that decade back to the Bridge. The style police are on constant red alert with Luca's V-necks, brown tie-up brogues and those huge knots at the top of his loosened tie. 'I go shopping everywhere, but mainly in Italy. I have my own tailor in Cremona and a few shops where I go and get all my stuff. I haven't really got round to shopping here. There is nowhere in London yet, but I cannot tell you where I get my sweaters. It is a secret.' Now with a sportswear sponsorship, there was definitely no need to: Robe di Kappa polo shirts, sweat shirts and accessories are everywhere.

Luca is more particular when it comes to his appearance on the field. Kit man Aaron Lincoln said: 'Footballers are a very superstitious breed, so it's absolutely vital that they have everything. You have to be meticulous, and there are lists of lists. Dennis has still got his lucky vest, although he hasn't worn it that much. Doobs liked to have a new pair of socks and a new vest for every game. Franco and Ed de Goey have their shirts specially tailored. Frank Leboeuf has some extra bits and pieces too. It's basically the foreign players who have more kit. The biggest nightmare would be to forget a player's boots as they're the most personalised items. Luca's boots are funny because they are dated on the bottom. If an apprentice wants to learn how to look after his kit, all he has to do is look at Luca. The man is immaculate.'

ES magazine's Allegra Donn was afforded the privilege of an 'at home' with Luca in his luxury house in Eaton Square. 'Spacious and totally unpretentious' was how she described it in a fascinating article, the feature set up through the Scottish-based franchise of the Kappa sponsorship: some football mags and books on interior design on the large coffee table, pale beige sofas, a replica of his friend Jean Alesi's Formula One driver's helmet on the mantelpiece; videos vary from a full set of *Friends* to action movies and Hitchcock's *Strangers on a Train.*

On a normal day, Luca is woken up by his alarm clock at 8.40 a.m., has coffee, toast and jam, and drives his Jaguar to the Harlington training camp with Simply Red, Morcheeba or Cafe Del Mar on the sound system. 'I love the elegance and the swiftness of English motors, and Mick Hucknall is my absolute musical hero.' Michele Padovano, a former Juve team-mate, introduced him to Cafe Del Mar. 'I'm not a discoverer of music,' Luca said. 'I always get there late, but when I like a CD I listen to it until it exhausts me.' Training finishes at one p.m., he stays on until three p.m., and is back home in time for a late lunch. 'Then I spend the rest of the afternoon making phone calls or watching videos I need to see for work.' Then a massage at home or at the Peak Health Club, or another English lesson.

In the evenings he takes in a movie, with a portion of sweet popcorn and a Diet Coke. 'Either people don't see me or they don't always recognise me; in any case they let me get on with it. Back in Italy, all that was impossible.' A pizza down the King's Road, perhaps drop in at Friends, Roberto Di Matteo's new restaurant, or San Lorenzo's. Sundays he rarely leaves the house. 'It's really my own time to unwind. I stay in bed, watch TV. I don't even get the papers.' Unattached after a twelve-year relationship with his home-town sweetheart, he has more time to himself. 'I love beautiful women, and if I go out with a girl that's another time to forget football.'

Luca came to London for a new experience rather than the hackneyed reason rustled up in some of the tabloids that foreigners are mercenaries. Not only did he amass a personal fortune from his soccer exploits in Serie A, he came from a well-heeled family from Cremona, in northern Italy, where he lived in a sixty-room castle. 'I was thirty-two, and at my peak. Football had enriched me, so rather than a lucrative contract, I was searching for a new life experience.' More dosh was on offer at Ibrox, but he chose west London – ironically, among the multitude of reasons was the manager, Ruud Gullit.

Most important to Luca was that he discovered a new release to mix again with the life of the city rather than to hide from it. 'It was like a celebration. The first time I took a walk in Hyde Park, I felt an incredible burst of adrenalin. Even a simple visit to the supermarket was something I hadn't been able to do in Italy since becoming a professional footballer. London has given me a freedom I had lost for a very long time.' However, there is a very strong impression that once he found his favourite haunts and got to know his way around, visits to Sainsbury's – well, the Harrods Food Hall – became less frequent. Now, if he is too busy to go to his favourite restaurant, San Lorenzo, they come to him, a takeaway of the most expensive pasta in town. There is even a dish on the menu named after him. 'There was a plate of pasta named after another Italian player, so I asked Lorenzo one day if I could have one too. We were off to play at Old Trafford, and he said, "You win and I'll put your dish on the menu." We did.' Penne alla Vialli is made with tomato and fresh mozzarella, his favourite. 'Have you tasted the mozzarella at Harvey Nichols and at Harrods? It's excellent.'

Luca found a new identity. From blond to bald, and virtually everything in between, he discovered that he liked being a manager as well as a player; whatever his task he took it on with conviction and dedication. 'I may not be as talented as Zola is, but I work hard and dedicate myself to what I do.' A month before he arrived in London, he took up golf 'because I knew it would a great thing for me to do here'. Cricket? He still hasn't got a clue. But he threw himself into English lessons – more than 200 hours of private sessions. 'Though,' he laughs, 'someone did tell me the other day that I should ask my teacher for a refund.' He was very happy in London. 'In Italy football is the main sport, and every town has just one team or a maximum of two teams, so you get too much attention. In London there are lots of teams as well as other important sports like cricket and rugby, so there are many champions and you're not the main focus. English fans are great because they have a lot of respect. You're never hounded.'

Eight years ago, during pre-season training at Sampdoria, he wore a jersey with a message on the back: THE BEST-LOOKING. THE SEXIEST. THE STRONGEST. THE SMARTEST. THE BEST. VIALLI. It was supposed to be a joke, a self-deprecating jab at his own status as Italian football's golden boy, yet there were some who failed to see the humour in it then, and continue to feel he has been handed success all his life. Capello, for instance: 'Vialli is doing well and I heartily congratulate him. I think he's bought himself a very strong side. He probably overpaid a little for most of his players, but many of them are quite good.' Capello did praise Vialli's impact as a tactician, though: 'I was there when Chelsea played Real Madrid in the European Super Cup and I've watched them a number of times on television. You can see he has a tight, effective side, and a very Italian one at that. By this I mean a club whose first priority is not allowing goals. A side that takes a one-goal lead and then puts everybody behind the ball. It may not always be entertaining, but it is very Italian.'

Juventus manager Marcello Lippi, a key influence on Vialli's career, agreed. They speak two or three times a week, although Lippi is quick to point out he does not offer advice: 'Luca is his own man. We exchange thoughts and ideas, we compare notes, but he does not need me to tell him what to do. With his players, he has a knack for being appreciated. Some like him, some don't, but I think everybody respects him. And he is very ambitious. He never does something just so he can say he's had a crack at it. If he takes something on, he does so because he wants to excel and he won't rest until it's done. The bottom line is that Gianluca is a winner who won't accept anything less than 110 per cent. I know it sounds like an awful cliché, but in his case it's the truth, and he's been that way for as long as I've known him.'

Lombardo, who knows a thing or two about playing and managing, having had his own brief stint at Palace last year, added: 'At Sampdoria he was a natural leader.

I remember him getting furious in training if a team-mate slacked off during drills. He would get angrier than the manager, and he was just a twenty-five-year-old kid. But nobody resented him because they knew how badly he wanted to win. What amazes me is the way he can absorb criticism and turn it into something positive. Earlier this year, when the press were giving him a hard time, he responded not for himself, but for the club and the players. As far as he's concerned, the more he's criticised the stronger he gets.'

On 18 February 1999, Luca celebrated one year in charge. Already he has become the club's greatest collector of silverware. Luca reflected: 'I wouldn't say it's the silverware or anything like that. Now I have credibility as a manager, which wasn't the case in the beginning. Now when people look at me they know I can do the job and do it quite well.' Yet there was a time when he thought about leaving the Bridge, not long after arriving as the captain of European Cup winners Juventus. Injury and illness left him bewildered on the bench under Ruud Gullit for five months with only a two-minute cameo appearance in the FA Cup final. He departed for the Far East tour to review his future. 'I don't like to leave things undone. When I signed for Chelsea I was delighted, it was a new challenge for me. I just wanted to make an impact. As I said in one of my first interviews, I wanted to be a legend. I didn't want to leave after such a difficult year without trying to change everything. I was really upset with the way things had gone, but was determined I could change things.' In the Far East he spoke with Colin Hutchinson. 'He told me to stay calm and that in life you always get what you deserve. So I went on holiday, worked hard, and came back with confidence.'

Hutchinson had already spotted managerial potential; it wasn't long before it would be realised. Vialli succeeded Gullit with the team still second in the Premiership, in the quarter-finals of the Cup Winners Cup, but precariously entering the Coca-Cola Cup second leg with Arsenal. 'I'm not sure there was a trigger point,' said Hutchinson, 'but right from the time I went to Turin to sign him only twenty-four hours after he'd lifted the European Cup, from various conversations I just got a gut reaction.' He explained why the job was offered to Luca after the acrimonious departure of Ruud: 'In everything he does as a player he's ultra professional. He's a thinker about the game. He's also got that single-minded streak.'

Vialli had already been sounded out about taking the job, so it was hardly a shock when it was offered, but he recalled: 'I took about forty-eight hours to make up my mind. You have plenty of ideas. They come to you straight away. They had been in the back of my mind for ages because I always thought about football a lot, about what I would change, and not just at Chelsea. I had the situation quite clear. The most difficult part of the job was to handle the pressure, to change my relationship with the players, to put into practice my ideas and to make the players get my messages. It was a new situation and I hadn't had time to prepare mentally. It was a shock for the players too. For them, everything changed from one day to the next.'

A bold Juve-style 4–3–3 formation overcame Arsenal, but after a few setbacks he reverted to 4–4–2 and stuck with it. He adopted Gullit's rotation system, and while he has not been on the bench he has left himself out more than Gullit did.

Hutchinson observed: 'To his lasting credit, how he's kept himself so fit as a player with the pressure of management I don't know. He's probably fitter now than in his first season. That's all part of his will to win.' Vialli relied heavily on his back-up team: 'I couldn't have done it, and I couldn't do it now, without the vital help of Gwyn and Ricco, with whom I have the closest working relationships, and the other members of the staff. And the players showed understanding and enthusiasm straight away.'

On his relationship with his manager, chairman Ken Bates said: 'Well, I'm probably the only chairman in the league that gets called El Presidente by the manager. I remember after the Oldham game that he decided to polish his shoes with a rag, then I put my shoe in front of him and he got on and polished mine. I like having a good relationship with the manager, but I don't impose myself and I give him his space.'

Luca had no worries about fielding a starting line-up with eleven foreign players. 'I don't care whether the eleven players I start with are foreigners or not. I don't look at the passports of the players when I pick the team. I just want them to be successful. Of course I need the players to speak the same language on the pitch, but they speak English. When you are young and part of such a successful team you should be happy. You can learn from the experienced players. Maybe I'm wrong, but I don't think the supporters care too much about the fact that there are not enough English players in the team. They just want to see the Chelsea flag flying high.'

Vialli is very much the antithesis of Gullit. The dreadlocked Dutchman was accused of being aloof, arrogant, a loner when it came to decisions; Vialli consulted, took advice, and went socialising. He even offered his players quality champagne *before* his first match in charge, that vital semi-final against Arsenal. Gullit chic replaced by Italian style, but from dreadlocks to the slaphead, this was still a team of foreign superstars and there were clear differences in style between Gullit and Vialli that Franco Zola analysed: 'Ruud was very important for me. He asked for me to come here and I am thankful for that. Without that chance, my career would not have been the same. Ruudi was more free, he leaves more space for players to play. He leaves more to the imagination. Vialli is more of a perfectionist; he is more serious and organises everything.'

But it wasn't long before Luca appreciated the need to distance himself from his former team-mates, even though he was still a player. It led to a great deal of what Vialli described as loneliness in the job. 'It is quite hard for me because I think I am quite an open character. I like to share jokes and take the mickey out of the other players. I think it is nice that they can do the same, but now, in my position, and with all the decisions I have to make, I understand that I am not so popular and some of the players might be, not angry, but a bit upset with me. This is part of the job, something that has made me feel a bit lonely sometimes, but, as Alex Ferguson said, if a manager wants to socialise with the players, good luck to him. I think that is a bit extreme, but it is a difficult situation.'

The new Caesar had the backing of the club's Brutus. Rix said: 'He is not so egotistical that he thinks he doesn't need help from anybody. He doesn't only ask me. He asks the players and other members of staff, trying to glean what he can off players.' This type of support is important to Luca; unlike Gullit, he has no coaching certificate, only a policy of co-operation. 'An open, honest rapport is the key to a successful team. I will let my players know why I make decisions as they need to know why a manager is doing something. They might think I'm wrong, but I want to have my conscience clear. Even if they think I'm wrong, I think they will respect my decision. Players can't go on the pitch and do a job unless they want to do the job for you. They have to play for themselves but also for their manager, to care about him. They will care if you treat them the right way.'

That theory was tested within weeks of the start of his first full season in charge, with one of the world's top stars, Brian Laudrup, in open conflict with Vialli's rotation system – precisely how Vialli reacted when Gullit stuck him on the bench. The nuances of management began to hit home. But subject to Vialli's tactical wishes, Rix was really in charge on match days (now it's Ray Wilkins); team-talks, substitutions and dressing-room confrontations were Rix's domain. When Petrescu bolted down the tunnel after being taken off against Vicenza in the Cup Winners Cup semi-final first leg, Rix said: 'In front of all the boys I said, "By the way, Dan, you ever bloody look at me again and spit on the floor and I will come over and punch your face in." His bottle went a little bit and he muttered under his breath. But Luca looked at him and said, "If you've got something to say, Dan, say it. Say it now, come on. Why do you think you were brought off? You were brought off because you weren't performing. It's not because we don't like you. If you don't perform you don't play." I put my head on the line and I got Luca's backing, so fair play to him.'

Vialli's £12m investment in overseas signings since the Cup Winners Cup triumph over Stuttgart in Stockholm – Laudrup, Desailly, Casiraghi and Ferrer – sent Chelsea's wage bill soaring to £23m a year, and some had to go as he wanted a squad of twenty. Vialli's backroom summer signing – fitness guru Antonio Pintus – was just as important. Vialli explained: 'If you are a professional player you have to look after your body, stay in and have the early nights. When you reach the top the satisfaction is so big, so great, that it pays you back for all the sacrifices.' Pintus, who knocked Juventus into shape, has a diploma in the Science and Techniques of Training, and spent twelve months in France qualifying for a doctorate in physical education. Print-outs and charts measure the players' heart-rates, weight, body fat, blood pressure and speed test times. Pintus said: 'The players here are fit – but they could be fitter. It will be important for them to keep consistent levels of fitness during the season, with each player working on individual aspects tailored to suit their own needs.' Chelsea also extended their rehabilitation team: John Kelly, a full-time masseur, joined in the summer from West Ham, with physio Jim Webb under head physio Mike Banks.

The ambition to mount a convincing championship fight was increasingly dependent on a willingness to shoulder a colossal wage bill to attract the big foreign stars. Desailly was a key signing for a team which the previous season had lost fifteen League games and conceded forty-three goals, yet still finished in fourth position. Liverpool were desperate to sign the French World Cup winner, but he refused even to discuss a move to Anfield. Manchester United considered Desailly, but blanched at the £40,000 plus per week wages and opted to pay PSV Eindhoven £10.75m for Jaap Stam, a record for a defender.

Desailly made a slow start, blamed for Dion Dublin's headed goal in the opening-day defeat at Coventry, but he soon became a major influence in midfield and an even bigger barrier in defence. His arrival was a coup for Chelsea and turned them from a team with defensive liabilities to more solid stuff. The man mountain said: 'For me it was not difficult to return from the World Cup because I changed club, I changed country, I changed culture, I changed everything, and it's a new experience for me. It could have been really difficult to return to Milan because I remember the first season there. It was beautiful, everything was beautiful, but after a while, it was a routine. Psychologically, yes, sometimes when we started the training at Chelsea it is true it was not so easy, but after a game with everything in the stadium, it is okay and I am happy. It was not a lot of money for Chelsea because my contract was big in Milan, and I still had two years left. The thing is I wanted for myself new emotions. I spoke to Frank Leboeuf before I signed and Frank recommended Chelsea to me.'

With so many high-profile world superstars, the arrival of Albert Ferrer was overlooked. Yet he had enjoyed superlative success with a long spell at Barcelona. The media interest from Spain was enormous, in contrast to the lack of enthusiasm from the domestic press. He said: 'I have a phone call every day, it seems, from people in Spain who want to know how I am going, wanting to know about football in England. People in Spain think English football is very strong but not so intelligent. I know that there are many good players here and the football is very tough. It will be hard for me, but I am confident.'

Ferrer planned to move to Datchett in Berkshire, where Gus Poyet lives. They converse in Spanish, but his Italian has proved very useful. 'Italian is very similar to Spanish, so sometimes in English when I don't have the words, I try it in Italian.' He doesn't hang around the training ground, eating in the canteen or chatting with his mates; he is straight off home, and has settled in well. 'When I came here I was living in Gloucester Road. I was looking to live near Gus, but now I am living in Chelsea Harbour. It is very good there. My wife [Genny] is here and when I'm two days away to play then it's better for her to stay in London. When we made the decision it was difficult for her. I'm doing the same thing more or less – playing football; she has her family in Barcelona, but we are happy here. It has been a good decision.'

The downside of this expansion was that supporters had to contribute for the privilege of watching the latest foreign influx of world stars. The glossiest luxury goods catalogue in the UK? No, not Harrods or Harvey Nichols, but the new Chelsea Football Club Official Merchandise Brochure. From gold jewellery to bed linen, adult luggage to infant wear, golf balls to frying pans, the catalogue offers consumers the opportunity to live the total 'Blue' lifestyle. There are two collectors' items that are absolutely irresistible: a £295 'limited edition' print of the whole FA Cup-winning 1997 squad, featuring the enlarged portrait and actual signature of Ruud Gullit; and a flask of 'CFC One' scent 'for men and women' to ensure that owner Ken Bates's vision for Chelsea pervades even those most romantic moments.

As one of the catalogue's T-shirts declares CHELSEA WOMEN DO IT BETTER!, can we conclude that they are more fragrant too?

But it wasn't all sweet smelling for Vialli, for he suffered the same dilemma as his predecessor. More than most Premiership managers, he knew how despised the rotation system was; it cost Vialli and the Dutchman a lifetime's friendship. During the long winter months of the previous season when the Italian was constantly used and then banished to the bench, the coldness between the two men became so intense that Vialli sometimes even declined to sit in the dugout with Gullit. It almost moved Vialli to tears at times – especially on the kind of occasion when Wise displayed a cheer-up message on his T-shirt during a match when Luca sat dejectedly the bench. On one occasion – a London derby at Tottenham two seasons ago – Vialli spent the whole game either standing or sitting as far from Gullit's touchline seat as possible, once even retreating to the players' tunnel. But the scars no longer pain him enough to prevent him inflicting similar hurt now that he has the final say on which of his glittering array of players gets to wear Chelsea's first-team shirt.

Where it was once Gullit imperiously ignoring the plight of the dejected Vialli, now the once much-loved Italian was forced to make such stars as Flo, Laudrup, and even Zola suffer the dreaded rotation system. Vialli had to endure the critical chanting of fans demanding the appearance of Flo or listening to their annoyance whenever he substituted Zola.

But Vialli's determination to clean up Chelsea's act and turn them into winners was not just restricted to on-the-field compliance. Mobile phones in the dressing room and hotel dining rooms, for instance, are outlawed; anyone who is late for training, or who sits down to a pre-match meal wearing a baseball cap, is automatically fined; card schools are permitted, as long as money doesn't change hands. Double training sessions became the order of the day. Vialli demands patience and understanding from them all, insisting that because of the fiercely physical stresses of English football and the intellectual demands of European competition, he needs a depth of choice. 'Competition for players is very vital. And while it is sometimes difficult to keep every player happy if he is not playing week in, week out, I do not want to sell any of my players because any manager in England would like to manage Chelsea when we talk about strikers. But goals are not everything to me; they are not the only thing I look at when I judge a striker. I like to look at what they do in other ways, when they are not scoring: how they react to others, how they connect. Of course, it is difficult to keep everybody happy, but if you are a player you can use the frustration you feel when your chance comes. Sometimes, I make up my mind, but then I see how training goes, who we are playing, what injuries we might pick up, and that can change it all again. But it is a nice problem for me. It is better than to have only eleven players to choose from – that would be a bad problem.'

And Vialli also knows the importance of laying the foundations for the future, signing two teenager Italians, Luca Percassi and Samuele Dalla Bona. Percassi and Dalla Bona's adventure began last spring when Mick McGiven, Chelsea's reserve team coach, went to Bergamo, near Milan, to watch Atalanta against Udinese in a youth league match. Atalanta, who were on their way to the youth league title, won 3–0 that night, and right-back Percassi and central midfielder Dalla Bona made an impression that eventually brought them to the Bridge. Both players are former schoolboy and Under-18 internationals expected to have big futures in Italy, but they agreed five-year contracts with Chelsea.

Percassi, whose father was an Atalanta player in the seventies, said: 'We do not know if it is a traditional Chelsea policy going around Europe scouting or if it is something new to do with Vialli being the manager. In Italy, now, it is quite a common thing for teams to go abroad and sign foreign young talents. Players from Ghana and Nigeria are already flooding in. This is the way football is moving. Maybe for the people now it is a difficult concept to accept because we are in the beginning of this process and we have been brought up under national flags, but I am sure that my children and my grandchildren will find it a natural concept.'

The chance to live in London was a decisive factor in luring them away from Serie A. They share a flat in Lancaster Gate. Dalla Bona said: 'Chelsea, without any doubt, are the most famous team in Italy and one of the best in Europe. They have great aspirations. They want to win trophies and carry on winning them. They are working hard to achieve the success and we feel proud to be part of them. For us, joining Chelsea was more than a dream and we think that we have been very lucky to have been able to do so.'

Percassi found the transition from Italian football easier than Dalla Bona. The stylish right-back likes pushing forward and soon adapted to the tempo and speed. After three months in the reserves, he made his first-team debut. 'The unforgettable first time,' as he put it, 'was in the fourth round of the Worthington Cup at Highbury against the champions of England. Chelsea were three up already with seventeen minutes to go when Graham Rix, very relaxed, tells me to go in and take my usual position as right-back, asking Dan Petrescu to move forward more like a winger. In that moment I thought, That's it, it's happening!' Chelsea won the match 5–0.

Problems with Dalla Bona's transfer kept him back. A central 'creative' midfield player, who always looked up to Frank Rijkaard of AC Milan, he took time to adjust. 'In my role of central midfield player, it is very important to learn immediately how to adapt to the new pace and tempo. Things are getting better every day. At the beginning I have honestly found it a bit difficult to adapt. The speed and the physical approach to the game here are such that there is not a lot of time to think with the ball at your feet. The delay in my transfer did not help – there is nothing better than a competitive match to learn and adapt to new situations.'

But in June 1998, Vialli's deep thinking, preparations for and theories about the game, and his *modus operandi* on and off the pitch, had barely been tested. His first full season under the spotlight at Stamford Bridge would provide a truly searching examination.

June...
June...
June

The Rock wants to win the Champions League with Chelsea ... it's four world-class players in eleven days

MONDAY, I JUNE

As a player, Luca Vialli was a bit of a rebel. He stole the odd fag when in dispute with Ruud Gullit. He gave one interview wearing nothing more than a pair of hip sunglasses, flip-flops and his birthday suit, a look he described as 'naked, but wicked'. Transformed into the Boss, he issued an ultimatum on clean living and healthy eating at Chelsea: 'Without a doubt you have to make sacrifices if you want to be successful. As teenagers you may start going out looking for girls, getting drunk, smoking cigarettes and going to nightclubs. But if you are a professional player, you must behave differently. You have to look after your body, stay in and have the early nights.'

So the playboy club once graced by Osgood, Hudson and Cooke was no more; banned, with good cause, were cream in the players' coffee, butter on their toast and dunking a perfectly healthy sprig of lettuce in greasy, calorific mayonnaise.

Nor would Vialli be seen dead eating one of the pizzas advertised on TV by his predecessor. An Italian chef was installed in the canteen at the training base near Heathrow.

There were fifteen reasons for Vialli's puritanical purge, these being the number of Premiership defeats Chelsea suffered last season – far too many to sustain a credible title challenge. 'Now we have proved ourselves to be a great team in cup competitions, at home and abroad, the title is what our supporters really want – and that is a huge challenge. We have made great strides as a club over the past two or three years, but winning the championship is what would really lift the image of Chelsea in Europe. I would love to qualify for the Champions League and compete with the strongest teams in Europe on a regular basis – but if you want to be the best, you have to prepare like the best.'

Vialli's final transfer moves were under way, with chief executive Colin Hutchinson embarking on a whistle-stop tour to complete four world-class signings in eleven days. A deal for record £5.4m signing Pierluigi Casiraghi was concluded at a meeting in London on Thursday, 28 May. Originally Lazio asked £7m and Chelsea offered £4.5m; then, Lazio president Sergio Cragnotti arrived in London at the end of May with the hidden agenda of trying to sign Roberto Di Matteo. Hutchinson said: 'I told him Di Matteo wasn't for sale. He said every player has a price. I told him not this one.' A deal for Casiraghi was agreed, and the next day the player flew in and signed.

Then Hutchinson travelled to Paris for a three-hour meeting with Marcel Desailly. The hunt for Desailly had been a long and exhaustive one, going back close to two years. Hutchinson and interpreter Gary Staker had spent three days around the Italy–Paraguay game towards the end of the previous April on a transfer mission, meeting AC Milan officials. They wanted to keep him then, but would resume talks at the end of the season. Milan representatives had come to London on 8 May, and met at Chelsea Village; over a meal at the upmarket Irish restaurant Arkles, Milan offered several players, but Desailly was the only one on Luca's list. In Paris, his agent made it clear he was aware of interest from Liverpool, Atletico Madrid, Real Madrid, Lazio and Manchester United. Having just returned from the pre-World Cup tournament in Morocco, and about to depart for a friendly in Finland, he asked for a week to think it over after a financial deal was agreed. Hutchinson said: 'It was a big decision as to whether he really wanted to leave Milan. Even though they had had a bad season they are one of the biggest clubs in Europe. But he wanted it sorted out before the World Cup.'

TUESDAY, 2 JUNE

Dennis Wise's suspension for two bookings in the Cup Winners Cup was lifted. He was free to play in the Super Cup. Dan Petrescu, red-carded in the final, was banned for two games, missing the Super Cup and the first tie in defence of the Cup Winners Cup.

THURSDAY, 4 JUNE

Desailly said yes. A meeting was arranged for the following Tuesday, inside France's World Cup headquarters.

SATURDAY, 6 JUNE

Hutchinson flew to Copenhagen to complete the signing of Brian Laudrup at lunchtime. A pre-contract had been signed the day after winning the Coca-Cola Cup semi-final against Arsenal on 19 February. The day Laudrup's contract expired, 31 May (Scottish contracts end a month ahead of England), Rangers were still demanding £6m compensation. The very day he became a free agent he was signed. It was a hard battle. Hutchinson said: 'All the uncertainty and speculation had to be removed, his mind freed of all the politics so he could go and concentrate on the World Cup. It is now up to Rangers what they want to do. Six million pounds is outrageous. We have spent a lot of time with solicitors taking advice and the case is with the European Commission.'

SUNDAY, 7 JUNE

Hutchinson flew to Spain having ascertained Barcelona would sell Albert Ferrer, who played in Barca's victorious team over Luca's Sampdoria in the European Champions Cup final of 1992. Hutchinson recalled: 'We'd been looking at various right-backs, and I got a hint that he would be available. I threw his name at Luca. He knew him and said straight away he would take him.'

MONDAY, 8 JUNE

Hutchinson agreed the £2.2m fee after six hours at the Nou Camp, but they insisted on the agreement being written in Spanish, so it had to be translated.

The two clubs signed. Then Colin dashed off. 'I got a flight with fifteen minutes to spare, got a taxi to Chantilly where Spain's base was, and received permission from their coach, Javier Clemente, to see him. When I got in, I briefly met the player and was surprised because I was told he didn't speak English, but he gets by with a little bit.' As the players trained in the early evening, Colin had to wait a further three hours until after the players had dined. It wasn't until midnight that Ferrer signed. 'I got Luca on the mobile. Luca spoke in Italian, he spoke in Spanish, and they seemed to understand each other. He was delighted to be coming.' And Colin had the satisfaction that his mission was unknown to the media. 'The beauty of it was that we completed that one without anyone knowing. One of our strengths is that we're able to tie these deals up quickly.' He then jumped into a taxi bound for Paris, a two-hour journey costing £80.

Back at a more sedate pace in west London, new fitness coach Antonio Pintus began house-hunting in London and talks with physio Mike Banks. Vialli had restructured the set-up with head conditioning coach Pintus arriving from his old club Juventus; Ade Mafe was appointed as his assistant. 'I have athletics and football at heart, but athletics is my mother,' said Pintus. He had joined Juve in 1991 and was their number two for many years, working with Vialli. 'I remember Vialli with curls. In Italy I think Vialli is known like Ronaldo, maybe more. He's won everything. Number one for him was intelligence. Without the quality of intelligence you'll be a zero. He is one of the most intelligent players I've ever known. Second, he has great motivation. His high levels of physical fitness and technical play have been important. Put that all together and you have a great professional.'

In his limited English, and partly in Italian, he continued: 'The first problem with me is to get to know each player individually, to know their surroundings, to know English football and then the characteristics of their football. Once I know this, depending on the history of each player, I'll make a programme for each one. I need to get together with the medical staff, know everyone's individual problems.' His priority was to upgrade and extend the Harlington gym, in tune with Vialli's mission to increase stamina and fitness for the final stages of games when the team was often beaten in the past.

Jim Duffy became the new youth team coach as Chelsea prepared their Youth Development Academy which would include the two teenage acquisitions from Atalanta, Percassi and Dalla Bona.

TUESDAY, 9 JUNE

In the morning at his hotel Colin met up with Desailly's agent. Hutchinson then headed out to France's training camp, with permission from Aime Jacquet, with club doctor Millington, and Banks.

The camp was an hour's drive outside Paris. The four-year contract was signed in a huge, empty marquee – the press facilities. Bernard Lama, who shared the same agent, popped in. Leboeuf described Desailly as a 'monster' in the French team; now Milan's 'Rock' was a Chelsea player. Twice he spoke with Vialli about his role within the team during the prolonged negotiations. Desailly said: 'My first position is defender, then after if Chelsea need me I can play midfield. Luca knows I can play midfield. When I played against him in Juventus, that's how I played.' He also felt that Casiraghi would be a big influence in the new Chelsea team. 'He's a strong player and a good player. When he plays and has only one occasion he can score the goal. In England I think it is always a stronger defence, but he is a player with a lot of heart to take on the defence.'

Closeted away in the World Cup camp, he had no idea that Ferrer had been signed the night before. 'Really?' He was delighted. 'I know him as a player. This is good. I'm really happy. He's a good player, he's strong, he's quick, he scores goals, he gives the ball to the attack, and then with Casiraghi and Laudrup, the new players, I think Chelsea's going to be a strong, strong team. They have won the Cup Winners Cup and they are growing, and I'm happy to be at the beginning of the growing, and I hope that in a few years we win the Champions League. For me this is the ambition.'

Mission accomplished, the delighted Chelsea contingent returned to London via the Channel Tunnel late that afternoon. Gwyn Williams and Pintus flew to Holland to book facilities for the pre-season tournament at Ajax, only to discover police concern over a clash with the Gay Olympics. Despite an option to return to Nigel Mansell's hotel complex in Devon, the squad booked a Dutch training centre at Zeist. Williams explained: 'Luca trained in Zeist with Sampdoria and thinks it's excellent for developing players in pre-season.'

WEDNESDAY, 10 JUNE

The World Cup kicked off. Chelsea were represented by eleven players spanning ten nations – better than the total number participating in the club's *entire* history, which amounted to eight over forty-four years. The tournament was a major issue regarding the timing of the pre-season. Those reaching the final would need two weeks' break. As soon as anyone was knocked out they were to contact the club. The few who didn't go would begin pre-season training the day after the final.

FRIDAY, 12 JUNE

Premiership fixtures were announced, but the computer cocked up: all games following Euro ties were away instead of at home. The same for Newcastle. Protests failed.

MONDAY, 15 JUNE

Pierluigi and his wife Barbara arrived in London to start flat-hunting. For Casiraghi, his arrival at the Bridge meant meeting up with old chums. He had played a season with Luca at Juve, 'when he had hair. He was younger then. When Luca was playing in Italy in the last few years he was the best forward in the country. He's a very strong personality. He, Baggio, Mancini and Del Piero are the most technical and gifted players in the last ten years of Italian football. He was a fantastic player at Napoli and Parma, but coming to London he has found real roots and he's become an even better player. I've asked him and Roberto about the lifestyle in London, of course.' And his game? 'I'm an athletic sort of player. I like to play with the ball in the air and I like to play as part of the team, a team game. Chelsea have already done quite a few wonderful things in the last few years, so we want to better this, to become one of the best teams in England and Europe. To do that you have to win things like the Premier League and play in the Champions League. This must be the aim of all the players and fans.'

FRIDAY, 19 JUNE

Danny Glanville was the first of the summer sales. He joined Leeds for £1.6m, rising to £2m depending on appearances.

MONDAY, 22 JUNE

Virginie arrived in London to start her search for accommodation for the Desaillys and their three children on the day Super Dan became the first Chelsea player to score in the World Cup finals, the second to score against England (Zola was the first). Poor Graeme Le Saux!

For Denise Summers this was a hectic period behind the scenes at the Bridge. There is no end to her talents in helping the new players find accommodation. Actually, Denise joined the club in November 1994 to handle the payroll in-house. 'I also sort out any problems the team have, from finding a home to shortening curtains. When I joined, Chelsea didn't have anyone doing general personal duties – Gwyn Williams would have been responsible, and still is, though to a lesser degree now. I can arrange everything: finding the right property, schools for children, logging on with utilities, organising mobile phones.' Laudrup was problematical. 'One of the most difficult negotiations was for his property. We protect the identity of the player until the last minute. Once the landlord realised who wanted the property he became very difficult to deal with. We did secure the property, but almost lost it at the last moment because someone else had put an offer on it.'

It's not unusual for Denise to receive night calls from players in distress. 'I've had a call on a bank holiday weekend from the Poyets to say their telephone wasn't working.' Now, that would be an emergency for talkaholic Gus!

'I've even turned up at the airport at five in the morning with a new set of keys for Frank Leboeuf after his landlord had changed the locks in his absence,' she recalls. 'I've arranged permanent residency for Dmitri Kharine and I've been doing the same for Dan Petrescu. People forget footballers live on that edge that makes them so supreme, so brilliant on the field, but the smallest thing, something we would consider so insignificant, can just knock them over that edge. Roberto Di Matteo's curtains were driving him mad and knocking him over that edge, because they were too long. I went to his house with a friend to shorten them. The bonus for me was that it was a Sunday afternoon and Chelsea were live on TV. So we sat in front of his TV watching the game while taking up his curtains.

'Zola came to London in November and was alone in a hotel to start with. He came close to that edge too. He was very down without his family.

'I never forget too that the wives are as important as players. When the Leboeufs first moved in, boxes and boxes of stuff had been delivered. Betty Leboeuf was all by herself and didn't know where to start. She phoned me and I went with my sister-in-law and helped to unload and unpack. We were there until nine that night.

'Generally, if I can't help I know someone who can. The Leboeufs needed someone to help with French schools, and my ex-sister-in-law, Chantal, is French but had lived here for a number of years and was well acquainted with schools, so I introduced her to them. She proved to be the ideal person to assist them. Things snowballed and they became very good friends, and now she is almost like an English agent for them.'

Language is one of the major headaches. 'I was particularly pleased with the English tutor I found for Gianfranco. He didn't just want to learn English, he also wanted to understand English, which meant picking up all the little quirks and colloquialisms of the language. I think he's done exceptionally well on that count.

'One of the strangest things I've done was also one of the most delightful. Class 2B from a school in Havant had sent in a tape for Zola of a song they had written to the tune of the Kinks' 'Lola'. I was so smitten listening to them singing this song that I sent it to Gianfranco. He wanted to thank them and paid for them and four teachers to come along to a match.

'I try very hard not to be intrusive, to do just what they want and no more. I don't want to take over or make them dependent on me. I just want them to be comfortable and happy and try to make sure life is easier for them until they get to grips with it.'

July...
July...
July

Welcome Prince Charming of Denmark et al ... farewell the fiery Welshman

SUNDAY, 12 JULY

France won the World Cup, with Frank Leboeuf and Marcel Desailly lifting the precious trophy, but Luca Vialli was deep into his own plans for the new season after a summer break. 'I had a great holiday. I think we had a great season, but also a very tiring season, and we needed to get away. I did that. Obviously I was on the phone to Colin Hutchinson quite often because there were a lot of things to organise – new players to try and bring in – but I didn't think so much about football, more about how to relax.' Usually Luca maintains his fitness regime during the summer with plenty of running, cycling and love-making. 'It was pretty much the same as last year with the training, but no love. I am a single man now. I didn't get too much chance to do that sort of exercise. I just wanted to relax.'

During the summer break there was a chance meeting with his chairman. 'That was a funny moment because the first person I met before I got on my boat in Portofino was the chairman. It was the first time we'd met since we won in Stockholm. We had a toast and a joke. Then we met again in Monte Carlo.' Luca dispelled the rumour that his boat is three times the size of his chairman's. 'That's just his joke. Out boats are nearly the same.' He continued: 'I would like to thank the chairman, but also Colin Hutchinson and Gwyn Williams with regard to signing players because they acted quicker than anybody else in England. When we want to do something at Chelsea, we're very determined. This is good for me as manager. The club are always behind me, helping me and making life easier.'

Luca studied the World Cup from the perspective of his own players' welfare. 'Of course Desailly and Frank Leboeuf are going to be on cloud nine when they come back, but I think after twenty-five days on holiday I would hope they are motivated enough to do even better in England. To have eleven players at the World Cup was a wonderful feeling as a manager, but now it's a bit tricky at the start of the season without these players, but I think we've got enough experience and enthusiasm to cope. If they want to win I think our team is good enough to be the best in England. But you need a bit of luck. We don't want to have any regrets next May, but we can't say for sure we are going to win something because as I said before you have to be a bit lucky. But at the end of the season, if we've done our best then nobody can blame us for anything.'

Vialli was aware that expectations were at the highest ever. 'There is enormous pressure on us and I think that football is very important, but we must think that it is just a game and we should learn to enjoy it a bit more. You go up, you go down, and sometimes people then concentrate on the not-so-positive, but it all helps to sell newspapers.'

MONDAY, 13 JULY

A group of sixteen started training. Mark Hughes completed his £650,000 two-year deal to sign for Southampton. He had rejected overtures from West Ham, Leicester, Bolton and Sheffield Wednesday to move to the south coast.

Hughes, thirty-four and the first player this century to win four FA Cup winners' medals, was frustrated at Chelsea's squad rotation system and the summer signings of Laudrup and Casiraghi. 'Obviously last year it wasn't ideal. I played a reasonable amount of games but there were four forwards and two places. So when Chelsea were involved in discussions with other strikers, something had to give and I felt it was time to move on. As a professional footballer you want to play week in, week out, and that simply wasn't happening. I left Manchester United because I didn't feel I was getting the amount of games I deserved. Last year there were quite a few foreign players at Chelsea, and when they bought two more I felt it was a case of last in, first out, which meant it was me. They are always in the market for big players because of the size of the club, and I accept that.'

Manager David Jones insisted there was no automatic first-team place for Hughes at The Dell, even though he left because he felt he was underused. 'I accept Mark just wants to play football, but there is no guarantee that he is going to get a regular first-team place here. He will have to compete with the other strikers I already have, but signing him certainly puts us in a healthier position.'

FRIDAY, 17 JULY

Steve Clarke was appointed to Vialli's coaching team. His playing days virtually over, he was rewarded with a promotion after over eleven years on the playing staff, becoming player-assistant coach in the final year of his contract. He played 421 games for Chelsea, the fourth-highest figure in the history of the club. But the thirty-four-year-old was unlikely to get many chances, with the Foreign Legion taking almost all the places on the team-sheet. 'If everyone is fit and well then I know I won't be in the side. But that is not to say that I can't contribute as a player. Hopefully we can carry on winning the trophies and I want to be part of that.'

WEDNESDAY, 22 JULY

Team Laudrup comprised father Finn, an international star in his own right, brother Michael and wife Mette. Ironically, 'travel' was a focal part of their relationship as the husband–wife partnership organises trips for Rangers fans from Denmark to Scotland to watch him in action. They have a travel business based in Copenhagen. No doubt, then, one would expect the Laudrups to travel well.

Mette is a major influence in the Life of Brian. In many ways it is an unusual combination as Mette is seven years older. Initially, that caused difficulties in the very close-knit Laudrup family household. Brian was happy to admit to the crucial role his wife played. They married in 1989, the same year in which he moved from Brondby to Bayer Uerdingen just when his career began to take off. 'I met my wife very early in my life but, although I was quite mature, the age gap was a little bit too much for my parents at the beginning. Then they changed. We got married when I was nineteen and now they love her more than anything else. But I firmly believe that this difference in age has been very important to me throughout my career.

'I was raised with football, so I've been used to interviews and television exposure since I was a little boy, but Mette's experience of life has proved invaluable. The many times I was really down and couldn't see a way out of things, she has been there to support me and help me react to situations. She talked me through a very bad knee injury in Germany. Then, when I was having a horrendous time in Italy, she told me I would get through it. I don't want to offend any woman, but not many players could say they can go back home and really talk about football like they do with another man. I can with Mette. She has seen football for so many years and knows what's good and bad. I love this woman very much. I've always said that football is a short career. I've played the game since I was five, but I hope our marriage will last fifty or sixty years. It comes above everything else.'

Mette was right about Italy, but not before Laudrup and their children – son Nikolai and daughter Rasmine – had been forced to face angry crowds in Florence, a campaign which ended with Mette having to secretly get them out of the country.

Laudrup had joined Fiorentina from Bayern Munich in 1992, but relegation left him a marked man in the eyes of their supporters. They openly voiced their hatred of him, and for a fortnight, Brian, Mette and the children were forced to hide away in a hotel room until the anger of the fans had subsided. Mette recalled: 'We had to smuggle the kids out of Italy because the fans were so mad after the club had been relegated. There are a lot of divorces in football, but if ever it was going to happen to us, then it would have been in Italy. Things were very hard then, but we stuck together.' Laudrup finally quit Italy for a less stressful life with Rangers four years ago. Both he and Mette soon began to feel at home.

Brian's move to the Bridge coincided with plans to dismiss Gullit. Brian and his family unwittingly found themselves caught up in the crossfire after he had spoken to Vialli and Zola while the Dutchman was still in charge. It was Zola's assurance to Laudrup that his family would love London which eventually convinced the Dane to turn his back on a queue of twenty other clubs, including Ajax, where his brother was playing, Copenhagen and Manchester United. Zola said: 'Brian feared his wife and children would be dragged into his football life like they were at Fiorentina. The pressure there was intense, but I assured him that in London you are left alone.'

Laudrup also wanted to nail the criticism that the Premiership is little more than a retirement home for money-grabbing mercenaries. 'The Premiership is one of the most demanding leagues in the world and any older players coming here thinking they'll have an easy time would be stupid. A lot of good players have come to England over the past three or four years and they've helped turn it into a very good league, up with Italy, Spain and Germany. But while I'm sure the English players have learned from the foreigners, as they have in Scotland, people tend to forget that it works both ways. It means the mixture is right. If players want to just pick up the money they should go to Switzerland or somewhere like that.'

Chelsea's reputation as the most European-style side in England had been a major factor in overturning his decision to sign for Ajax. 'The way I would like to play is obviously a Continental, technical style, and if a team like Chelsea have more foreigners they are more likely to play that way. But you only have to look at the trophies they won last season, the Coca-Cola and the Cup Winners cups, to see they are one of the best sides in England. With the players the club have added it looks exciting for me. I am ambitious and I've come here because I want to win the League.'

The World Cup had represented a golden opportunity for Laudrup to prove that the paucity of the opposition was not the only reason he shone in Scotland, as he took Denmark within a whisker of knocking out Brazil, only to lose their quarter-final 3–2. 'I was just pleased to be able to show what I could do at the World Cup. Some people have said, "Well he can do it in Scotland, but can he do it at the very top level?" I think I proved I could.'

Chelsea would surely gain from his decision to quit international football after the World Cup because he wanted to finish at the top. He would not be one of the legion of players leaving regularly with their national teams. 'I can use all my energy now for Chelsea. When there are international games, there will be only five or six players back here, because all the other players are away, so I think Mr Vialli is rather pleased that I will still be here.'

Laudrup admitted to making a big mistake in his attempt to emulate some aspects of his fiery father's game. 'When I was younger I was a bit like my father. He was a very temperamental person who was forever slaughtering other players on the pitch. Dad was very lazy, but a tremendous player. If the ball wasn't coming accurately to him he would stand and yell at people. I must have tried to copy that because if I didn't play well or my colleagues didn't perform, I would scream and become hysterical. I could be quite hard to work with. My mother watched me one day when I was thirteen and later told me not to try and copy my dad. She said it was the worst thing I could do because she couldn't stand him on the pitch!'

Fascinating observations ...

THURSDAY, 23 JULY

The summer spending spree was over. Vialli spent more than £12m in two months assembling a team capable of mounting a serious challenge for the title. Luca said: 'We don't want anyone else. At the moment we have twenty-five first-team professionals and that is probably too many according to our plans. So we are not looking to sign anyone else. We will have to wait and see what happens once the season starts but, fingers crossed, and depending on injuries, we won't need to bring anyone in.'

Vialli needed to trim his squad, but some were not for sale. Roma tried to lure away Flo with an audacious £9m bid; Zola was wanted by his home town club Cagliari. Vialli insisted: 'It is normal that plenty of offers come in, but we want to win something this season. We have got a great squad with great players, especially up front. Flo had a marvellous World Cup and Chelsea received plenty of offers for him from lots of clubs. We don't need money, we need good players, so at the moment we are not thinking about selling Flo or any of our top-class players.'

Desailly hoped to have the same effect on Chelsea as countryman Eric Cantona had on Manchester United. 'Eric transformed United so it would be nice to think I could have the same effect on Chelsea. It's too early to say whether we will be the main challengers to Arsenal, but it wouldn't surprise me when you look at our players. I know Gianluca is after the championship. That's what he wants more than anything else. He is a manager who has a burning desire for more success. I want to win honours with Chelsea, and if I didn't think I could do that, then I wouldn't have come to Stamford Bridge.'

FRIDAY, 24 JULY

There was a friendly at Northampton before the squad flew to Holland to take part in a three-way 'round robin' tournament against Vitesse Arnhem and Atletico Madrid. Wise picked up a thigh injury in training.

Vialli was confident his World Cup winners had not lost their hunger for success and would return to England determined to land the title. Unlike Arsene Wenger, he did not feel his French heroes would have any problem rediscovering their appetite for the Premiership. 'I know that Frank Leboeuf and Marcel Desailly are used to winning things, so I don't think their attitude will change. I hope that after one week they will be perfectly tuned in. I am sure they will be ready, but if they do struggle a little bit at the beginning, we will look after them, and if they need physical or mental rest, we will help them.'

Vialli's main task before the start of the season was shaping a championship-winning team out of his multinational squad. When the World Cup players joined their team-mates for the pre-season tournament in Holland, there were only two weeks before the start of the season. Vialli said: 'It could be a problem because we haven't got a great deal of time to train together and to try things. But when you have got great players like Desailly, Ferrer, Laudrup and Casiraghi, you don't need to explain too many things to them. You just have to make them physically and mentally fit, then it's up to them.'

Vialli reiterated his aim to be fit to play throughout the season. At thirty-four, and with four world-class strikers, many felt he would give up playing. 'I am not joking when I say I am available for selection. I want to keep myself as fit as possible, but I hope Casiraghi is going to score thirty-five goals this season to keep me out. He will need some rest during the season and I hope I'll still be able to wear my Chelsea shirt with skill, ability and passion. It is going to be a difficult season with Arsenal and also Manchester United, who do not normally fail twice in a row, but we have a better team than last season and want to finish in a better position.'

Casiraghi was settling in with his new team-mates, enjoying living in London.

Zola believed his proven striking partnership with Casiraghi for Italy would unlock the door to the championship. They were stunned to be left out of the World Cup squad after both scored vital goals in the qualifiers. They had watched the final on television at Zola's London house, and were looking forward to spearheading the club's challenge in order to answer their doubters back home. Zola said: 'I have played with Casiraghi many times and there is a wonderful understanding between us. I think we can do well because we both have a point to prove. I am quite sure we are good enough to win the League. The favourites are Manchester United, Arsenal and Chelsea, because we have something more than the others. It is going to be hard, but if Chelsea can stay at the same level then we have a chance.

'Being left out of the World Cup squad was a huge disappointment, it was very painful, one of the worst moments in my career. I thought it was only a matter of form and that I would definitely get back in, particularly when I scored the winning goal in the Cup Winners Cup final. I thought Maldini would take notice, but he didn't. He said it was because of my poor form and the fact that I had been having a difficult season, but I knew I was in perfect condition, both mentally and physically, when the squad was chosen. Last season was difficult for me, though; I knew I wasn't playing well and was struggling. But now I have turned my disappointment around and being left out of the squad has made me even more determined to make this season my best ever with Chelsea.'

As to his future, Zola said: 'Of course I am staying. I am really happy here and I have no thoughts of leaving. My intention is to respect my contract to the end. I have settled well here, my family have settled, and there is no reason for me to leave.'

The arrival of two new front players, despite the departure of Hughes, continued the debate over the rotation system. Zola said: 'We have had a discussion about it. It is good to rest sometimes, but my opinion is that it is also good to play continually, because only by playing can you find yourself. But I understand that the idea of the coach is to have a large squad and rotate players to have a team in good condition all the time. I am not playing against the other strikers at Chelsea; if I play well and give my best performances then I expect to play. But if someone else plays better then they deserve to be in the team ahead of me. There is no reason to say there is anything wrong with the system. Of course we all want to play all the time, but the team is the most important thing.'

TUESDAY, 28 JULY

Fitness coach Antonio Pintus introduced much more stretching and plyometric work to strengthen the players' legs. Training sessions were twice a day. In the secluded training camp in Zeist, the card schools helped kill the time between these exhausting sessions. Zola, Casiraghi, Poyet and Petrescu, the latter still displaying remnants of the yellow streaks the Romanians bleached into their hair at the World Cup, converse together in Italian as they play cards. 'You are a terrible, terrible player,' Wise says, chastising Zola. Wise's banter is relentless. He continually reminds the foreign legion that Vialli wants them to learn English. 'Cut out that Eyetie stuff,' he admonishes them, mid-hand. 'You know, Gianfranco don't do too bad. It's funny to hear him tell you: "I'm going down the apples and pears and getting into my jam jar to go down the rub-a-dub".'

It is a decade since Wise was a spiky-haired youngster pocketing an FA Cup winners' medal as a founding member of the Wimbledon Crazy Gang. 'Funny looking back, but I used to meet Vinnie [Jones] down the caff about quarter to ten each morning. We'd have sausage, egg, bacon, beans and a fried slice, then go training.' Wise is now a devout convert to the dietary plan decreed by Vialli. His belief in Vialli's vow to deliver the title to Stamford Bridge for the first time in forty-three years was absolute. 'Luca's an intelligent man. He was nervous when he started and that was understandable, because everything was on his shoulders. The whole season could have collapsed, and I think the worry got him down. The way he was going on, he'd have gone totally bald!' Vialli's hyper behaviour had prompted coaches Graham Rix and Steve Clarke to quietly counsel him when the three of them holidayed together in Bermuda at the manager's invitation in May. 'They just told Luca to calm down, and already it is noticeable that he has a milder attitude to the job.'

Rix eagerly awaited the entrance of Desailly to the Chelsea camp after the defender's holiday following his World Cup triumph. He said: 'I know how long Luca was trying for Desailly. He already looks a snip at the price. All four players we have signed are world-class, and I am excited about what we are doing. We now have twenty players capable of playing in a Premiership team, so the skills of the management team will be severely tested to keep people from getting restless.' Wise entered the debate. 'Everyone at the club has to stick together, suffer the disappointments without rocking the boat. It is the only way we are going to win the championship. Luca probably knows the basis of his side, but some players may have to rotate and, obviously, there will be suspensions to cover. Alex Ferguson has shown how it can be skilfully done at Manchester United.'

The size of some Chelsea players' salaries had not destabilised the dressing room, according to Wise. 'We are all well paid. You do the best for yourself that you can, of course. But I think all of us know this is now a club that wins major trophies, including the championship. That's what interests us most. I cannot look outside of United, Arsenal or Chelsea for the next champions.'

The only hitch in the training camp was the pinched nerve Laudrup sustained in his back. He deserted room-mate Wise to fly to Copenhagen to consult his own doctor.

Seventeen-year-old Italian triallist Luca Percassi, with six Italy Under-16 caps, was signed on a five-year contract in London.

WEDNESDAY, 29 JULY

Typical day at Zeist: breakfast by nine, training at ten, finish by one for lunch at 1.30. Bed soon after. Up at 4.30, training at five. Finish around seven. Dinner at 8.30. Bed.

THURSDAY, 30 JULY

Controversy was ignited over snubbing home-grown talent when the club beat off a queue of the world's top clubs to sign seventeen-year-old Finnish wonderkid Mikael Forssell, considered the best prospect in Europe. He signed from HJK Helsinki on a five-year deal. Forssell was not scheduled to arrive until November because HJK needed him for their European Champions League qualifier against Metz. Forssell scored four goals for Finland's Under-18 side against Lithuania on Wednesday. Ajax, Inter Milan, Liverpool, Bayern Munich, Sampdoria and Rangers all wooed the young goal-scoring sensation.

Forssell said: 'I could not believe the number of clubs that wanted me. It was very flattering. I have seen a lot of English football on television and when my parents and I visited London, Chelsea felt right for me. I met all the players from the youth team to the big names, and everyone was so welcoming. It will be marvellous to learn from watching and working with players like Gianfranco Zola, Brian Laudrup and Tore Andre Flo. It is a dream chance.' Forssell, who speaks four languages, was still at college in Helsinki and would continue his studies in London. He had played for Finland's full international side in a practice match against France in May – and scored against Leboeuf.

PFA boss Gordon Taylor argued that home-grown youngsters were being squeezed out by Chelsea's big-name foreign signings. He told Radio Five Live: 'If I was a parent of a young, talented footballer, I'd think twice about letting them join Chelsea. You can see a club where they are not bringing in the young lads and you just wonder whether they are going to get opportunities. They have just sold Danny Granville to Leeds and they have the most foreign players of any team now. I can appreciate Chelsea supporters will say they won the Coca-Cola and European Cup Winners Cups last season, but how many Michael Owens and David Beckhams are missing chances because clubs are reluctant to give kids a chance and buy foreign internationals instead? It is nothing personal against Chelsea; I am merely stating facts. Manchester United and Liverpool have been prepared to introduce kids, but I can't see the likes of Jody Morris at Chelsea getting many opportunities.'

Colin Hutchinson hit back: 'I think what Gordon Taylor has said is unhelpful and unprofessional. No fewer than nine home-grown players made their first-team debuts for us last season, and that's a record any club would be proud of. When Ruud Gullit was here, he said that anyone who was good enough would get their chance, regardless of age or where they'd come from. Gianluca Vialli has continued that policy. It would be nice for great players to come through the ranks, but it does become more and more difficult, not only for our home-grown products but for others from the English market, to be better than what we've already got.'

Youth development officer Bernie Dickson said: 'Look at the team of last season. It variously included Mark Nicholls, Jon Harley, Nick Crittenden, Jody Morris, Andy Myers, Michael Duberry, David Lee, Eddie Newton, Frank Sinclair and Graeme Le Saux, who we bought back from Blackburn but was developed here. So how can anybody say that home-grown players don't get a chance here? As for wondering about where the next Michael Owen is coming from, we just might have him. Our youngster Leon Knight scored thirty-five goals for the Lilleshall School of Excellence team last season and they're talking about him in the same terms as Michael. He has the body and ability of a Brazilian. He strikes the ball like a pro with both feet, he is quick, great in the air, and can score goals as well. If we don't give boys like him what they want, and need, then they will go. Leon could have left when he was fourteen, but we haven't lost one yet – they all want to nail their colours to the mast here. I defy anybody not to be excited when they turn up at the training ground and see Luca, Gianfranco Zola and Brian Laudrup. The kids watch them, and after training they spend half an hour or more practising free-kicks, without being asked. The way to learn is from watching the masters, and that's what we're teaching them to do here now.'

Bates also attacked the union leader: 'The trouble with Gordon Taylor is that he rushes into print without checking his facts. I think he should stick to what he is paid to do and stop interfering in other people's business. It is nonsense to suggest this club has no youth policy.' Bates pointed out that Taylor had conveniently forgotten the club had a dozen players who had come through the youth ranks, and four players had been on recent duty with the England Under-17 squad recently; they had also sold over £5.5m worth of home-grown talent over the last few seasons, including Muzzy Izzet to Leicester, Graham Stuart, now with Sheffield United, and Sinclair to Leicester for £2m.

Vialli was convinced there was still a bright future at Stamford Bridge for the large number of young home-grown players coming through the ranks. 'This is going to be an important season for players like Jody Morris and Mark Nicholls. They're going to play certainly a few matches, maybe more, and I know they can do the job, improve, and be part of Chelsea's future. When you're young and you're part of such a successful team then you have to be happy because you can look at the more experienced players and learn from them and grow to be a better player.'

FRIDAY, 31 JULY

Bates won a public apology and 'substantial' undisclosed libel damages over newspaper allegations that he cynically planned to replace Vialli with Terry Venables or George Graham if Vialli failed to win the Premiership or a cup. The High Court heard the *Daily Mail* had alleged that, even before Vialli's first game as player-manager, Mr Bates, in cynical disregard of his contract with Vialli, had been planning his replacement. Publishers Associated Newspapers and journalist Jeff Powell accepted the allegations were false and should never have been published. They agreed to pay damages.

It was widely reported that Frank Leboeuf wanted talks so he could earn World Cup winner's wages. Chelsea condemned an attempt to set up a move to Liverpool as a possible attempt to force a rise in Leboeuf's salary. He was on £16,000 a week, but wanted to match the £25,000 paid to his team-mate and fellow French defender Marcel Desailly following his night of triumph in Paris on 12 July. The club confirmed they were contacted by a London-based business associate of Leboeuf's, Chantal Stanley, to be told that Liverpool were prepared to pay £7m. Chief executive Colin Hutchinson insisted Leboeuf was staying, despite doubts whether he would play in Vialli's planned flat-back-four defence; 'It might be some under-hand dealing to try to get Frank a new, improved contract.' Leboeuf's agent in France, Philippe Flavier, said Stanley had no right to handle transfer dealings for Leboeuf, but added: 'I would like to talk to Chelsea about a new deal for Frank. We have an agreement to speak about such matters and it could be done very soon. Maybe within the next fifteen days. We have a good relationship with the club and we do business in the correct way. And I must stress that Frank's heart is at Chelsea and there is no way he wishes to leave. But he is now a World Cup winner.'

Chelsea were quick to snuff out links with Liverpool and Blackburn. Hutchinson said: 'I've spoken to Blackburn and they assured me they had made no approach and are not even interested in the player. Liverpool are different. Frank's agent said that Liverpool were ready to offer £7m, but we've never considered selling Frank, so there is no price on his head. I asked the agent to contact Frank yesterday to ascertain whether he wanted to join Liverpool or was happy to stay at Chelsea. The message came back that he wanted to stay at Chelsea.'

August...
August...
August

What a start ... defeat on the opening day of the season at Coventry with Zola on the bench ... but another trophy, the Super Cup, beating Champions League winners Real Madrid

SATURDAY, I AUGUST

Vialli had no qualms about the distinct possibility of making history fielding the first team without a single Englishman. The season after Arsene Wenger became the first foreign coach to lift the Premiership, Vialli could emulate the triumph without a single domestic player in his starting line-up. He could pick eleven World Cup internationals from ten different countries as well as Jersey-born Graeme Le Saux. Michael Duberry, Dennis Wise and Jody Morris were the only other Englishmen seriously involved. Vialli said: 'Yes, we could field a team of eleven foreign players. Would that bother me? No, not at all. I know I've got twenty-five players but I don't care if somebody comes from Italy or England. I just want the best team on the pitch and to get a result.

'For top players like Marcel Desailly and Frank Leboeuf, to come to England it means that something has changed at Chelsea, but also in England. Now all the most important players want to come to Italy or England because they are the places to play. Over here you can earn good money and you can enjoy yourself because the supporters are always very enthusiastic. It's still a great challenge to show that you are good enough to play in England. That's because in England there's a style of football a bit different from the way we play on the Continent. So, if you are good in the Continent, and you are good in England, it means you are a very good player, a complete player.'

A 5–0 win was recorded over a weak Go Ahead Eagles from the Dutch top flight. Nicholls scored the first half's only goal, then Flo got two, Zola the fourth and Le Saux a penalty with twenty minutes to go.

SUNDAY, 2 AUGUST

Four players were not on the club's new list of squad numbers. The absence of numbers for Bernard Lambourde, Andy Myers, David Lee and Paul Hughes – despite spare numbers at fifteen, eighteen and twenty-one – heightened speculation they would be allowed to leave if the price was right. Clarke switched from six to the available four. Desailly was the new six, Casiraghi took the number nine shirt, and Ferrer seventeen. Lambourde's number seven shirt was given to Laudrup.

Lambourde had failed to win a regular first-team place since joining the club for £1.5m from Bordeaux, and his chances diminished further with the arrival of Desailly. Lee, who lost his first-team place after injury and was told he would be given a free transfer at the age of twenty-eight (Wimbledon and Oldham enquired), managed less than a handful of games last season after recovering from a broken leg. Myers, one of the few Chelsea successes from the youth team ranks, was unlikely to figure. Hughes, though, enjoying an impressive loan spell at First Division Norwich, was a surprising omission after emerging as one of their most talented prospects.

Even Michael Duberry had to fight for a place. He knew there were not many in the Premiership boasting two World Cup winners ahead in the starting line-up. 'Let's be honest, I am the least fashionable name at Chelsea, but that can work in my favour because there is no pressure on me and few expectations. Marcel Desailly has arrived and we have all seen how good he is. But I have played well in pre-season and I am feeling good about myself. Now my ambition is to give Luca Vialli a headache when he is picking the team. Marcel and Frank can compete among themselves with me. It is no good for me if I am going to be on the bench week in, week out. But I am not even thinking about leaving as some people have suggested. I have not lost my way. I want to stay in the side and work hard. It has got to be my aim to succeed.'

Duberry stormed on to the Premiership scene under Gullit two years back when he earned sparkling reviews. There were predictions of England caps, but despite a few Under-21 appearances, Duberry has yet to win senior international honours. On his day, he can be as good as any defender around. He has enormous strength and good pace, but he is sometimes let down by a lack of concentration. Nobody is more aware of this than himself, and he knows it is the one aspect of his game that he must improve. Duberry reckoned the new competition would help him develop a mean streak – and maybe he could then start thinking about England honours. 'We always know we will score because we have so many talented players,' he continued. 'But we have a tendency to give away cheap goals. We have got to become harder as players and more difficult to beat as a team.'

Vialli had yet to decide who would be his first-choice goalkeeper.

MONDAY, 3 AUGUST

The whole squad was finally getting back together. Luca and Pintus introduced a ghetto-blaster to pre-season training, expecting all the rhythmic work to pay off. The trio who lasted to the World Cup final weekend also resumed training. De Goey joined up in Zeist, while Leboeuf and Desailly reported to Harlington for fitness work under the supervision of Ade Mafe, who flew back from Holland especially to begin their pre-season.

At the Bridge, 3000 tickets were sold by postal application for the opening game at Coventry; the remaining 1000 went on sale to personal callers at the box office and were sold out by closing time.

Vialli's costly summer collection were preparing to go on show in Arnhem against Atletico Madrid in the Gelderland tournament.

TUESDAY, 4 AUGUST

Atletico Madrid 4   Chelsea 0

Wise was sent off after clashing with Atletico's Carlos Aguilera, who was also dismissed in Arnhem, and it left him sweating on the referee's report. A flare-up nine minutes from time resulted in players from both sides surrounding the Chelsea captain, who stamped on Aguilera, one of several incidents in a bad-tempered second half. Wise was in deep trouble. The Dutch FA would pass on the details to their English counterparts. FA spokesman Steve Double said: 'The Dutch FA would be within their rights to forward the report to us. It doesn't always happen, but if it did, it could lead to a suspension. If we are notified by a national association we are obliged to act upon it.'

Vialli said: 'It was a pity that Dennis was sent off. It shouldn't happen in a friendly match. Dennis is a very hot-tempered player and he doesn't like being beaten. It was a challenge between two players and the ref sent him off, but I think it is better he gets sent off here rather than later in the Premiership. I do not think his sending-off will affect any Premiership games. Hopefully nothing will happen, but if there is a way to appeal we will. But I am not concerned about Dennis – he is a winner.'

Two first-half goals from Juninho effectively turned the game, and the only consolation was that new boys Casiraghi, Desailly and Laudrup were not involved.

Ferrer was the only one of the summer buys to start the game, and he was handed the difficult task of marking Juninho, the target of a failed bid from Aston Villa that week. An unforced error by Duberry proved expensive as Juninho was allowed to slip past Kharine before slipping the ball into an empty net. Juninho accepted another simple chance less than two minutes later when Serena opened up the Chelsea defence before laying on a tap-in. Atletico were by far the better side and were gifted a third goal seventeen minutes from time when Kharine allowed a twenty-five-yard free-kick from substitute Oscar Mena to squirm past his body and into the net.

Moments earlier, Vialli had made a triple substitution with Petrescu, Lambourde and Mark Nicholls replacing Di Matteo, Sinclair and Flo.

Arrigo Sacchi's team put a gloss on the victory when Vladimir Jugovic, a recent £3m signing from Lazio, slipped the ball past the hapless Kharine. With Flo labouring, Zola ineffectual and Vialli keeping himself on the bench, it was left to Poyet to offer the main threat up front for Chelsea. He went closest to pulling back a goal three minutes after the restart when he headed over from Le Saux's cross. Nicholls had one of Chelsea's better chances in stoppage time, but he screwed his shot wide of Molina.

WEDNESDAY, 5 AUGUST
Flamengo 0   Chelsea 5

Playing like this, the player-manager was going to have difficulty finding excuses to leave himself out. Vialli opened the scoring after fifteen minutes with a glorious flying header. Petrescu launched himself to head the second, and Poyet and Di Matteo also scored before half-time. Vialli's superb dummy set up Poyet for the third goal; Di Matteo scored from thirty yards. Flamengo had Marcel Pimentel sent off just after the interval for fouling Vialli, and Petrescu got his second fifteen minutes from time. The boss was one of seven changes from the side spanked by Atletico Madrid in the Gelderland tournament. He was obviously in no mood to hang up his boots.

Hitchcock flew home with a nasty ulcer behind his eye.

THURSDAY, 6 AUGUST
The squad flew off to Sicily.

Attilio Lombardo, thirty-two, turned down a move to Chelsea because he believed he had a better chance of an international recall with Terry Venables at Crystal Palace. 'Luca Vialli wanted me and I was tempted. But Terry arrived and things changed. With his guidance I can make the Italian team again. How many clubs have the luxury of a boss like him? He has coached Spurs, Barcelona and England. His experience is amazing.'

But the capture of another Italian, Dalla Bona, one of the most promising youngsters in the Italian game, caused deep unrest back in Italy. There were allegations that unscrupulous agents had urged him not to sign a professional contract with his old team, turning his back without offering any kind of explanation, the boy bursting into tears in front of his old coaches. Dalla Bona was the brightest prospect in Atalanta's youth system, captain of the Italian Under-16 side. Realising his immense potential, Atalanta had offered him a five-year professional contract.

'Chelsea and their agents acted like cowboys,' said chairman Ivan Ruggeri. 'I'm disgusted by this whole affair. At his age, Dalla Bona is not allowed to have an agent, yet he left for England with Alessandro D'Amico, who happens to work for Claudio Pasqualin, Vialli's agent. Is this just a coincidence? If I could, I would take legal action, but I can't, because the laws are inadequate. UEFA or the European Union needs to step in because this is a serious threat to football.'

The reality is that the rules had changed. Atalanta had offered him a contract which would have paid him little more than £200 a week – a decent enough amount for a seventeen-year-old, but a pittance compared with what he could make at Chelsea. Hutchinson said: 'Dalla Bona was recommended to Chelsea. We watched him in Italy and with the Italian youth squad in Scotland. He asked for a trial with Chelsea to get a feel of English football and find whether he could settle in London.' Hutchinson also stressed that although Chelsea came out on top this time, next time, it could be one of their prospects who walks out on his YTS deal to join the likes of Real Madrid or Juventus. He said: 'We were given undertakings that Dalla Bona was entitled to sign professionally for a club outside Italy. We worked within the framework of current regulations and have done nothing wrong.

We can understand Atalanta's annoyance at losing such a prospect, but since Bosman the game has changed. We have lost players because of the Bosman ruling.'

Dalla Bona was sure he had made the right move. 'This is a great opportunity for me. Every day I am learning something new. I'm getting a flat in Bayswater with Luca Percassi. They tell me a lot of young people live there and there are a lot of different restaurants. I haven't tried Indian yet but I've had Chinese food.'

FRIDAY, 7 AUGUST

There was a furious Ken Bates broadcast on ClubCall, a rebuff of a *Daily Mail* article that several stars were for sale. Clearly the *Mail* were determined to upset the chairman! Newspapers reported that Duberry, Petrescu, Sinclair, Kharine, Morris and Hughes were listed in a clear-out aimed at trimming the club's massive £23m-a-year wage bill.

In the evening the last pre-season game against Parma, in Palermo in front of a tiny crowd was ruined by appalling rain. De Goey played the first half and made two good saves. Parma twice took the lead, Poyet and Vialli equalised. Babayaro gave a particularly good performance on the left side of midfield.

Back at the Bridge, season ticket sales closed with over 18,000 bought and £13m in the bank, a new record.

SATURDAY, 8 AUGUST

The squad flew home after thirteen days away. The flight was late departing; the delay included forty minutes on the runway waiting for a hailstorm to pass.

MONDAY, 10 AUGUST

For the first time the whole squad trained together in the same place at Harlington. Lunch in the local hotel was followed by bed, then an afternoon training session at four p.m. Ray Wilkins brought his children, all dressed in Chelsea gear, to see the training session and set up a game of golf with Luca.

TUESDAY, 11 AUGUST

Vialli welcomed the decision by a legal prosecutor to interview the Roma coach at the centre of a drugs controversy tearing apart Italian football. Czech-born Zdenek Zeman caused a storm with interviews with several newspapers and the news weekly *Espresso* which accused a number of Italian stars, including Vialli and Juventus striker Alessandro Del Piero, of using performance-enhancing substances to improve their physique. Zeman claimed: 'There are suspicious muscular explosions which began with Vialli and ended with Del Piero.' He was ordered to appear before Turin judge Rafael Guariniello to give evidence as to why he accused the two strikers of using 'too many pharmaceutical products'. Vialli's agent Andrea D'Amico said the Stamford Bridge manager was 'delighted' that Zeman was forced to explain his comments.

At the heart of the controversy was the use of creatine, a 'wonder' pill widely used to improve muscle growth. However, doctors say overuse of the dietary supplement could lead to liver and kidney failure and users have complained of muscle cramp, dehydration and nausea. Although Vialli and many other footballers – including Glenn Hoddle's England team – admitted using vitamins and dietary supplements including creatine – under a dedicated team of experts who administered it scientifically – Zeman did not specify which 'products' he was referring to, leading to the widespread belief that he meant illegal substances. D'Amico said the accusations by Zeman were 'extremely hurtful' to Vialli and the involvement of the prosecutor was welcomed as he had the authority, under Italian law, to decide whether there was any truth in the claims. D'Amico said: 'What Zeman said was nonsense. Why did he pinpoint only two players as having exceptional muscle growth when he could have chosen hundreds of other footballers who are much bigger? Gianluca has never done anything illegal in his whole career and it is absurd to suggest otherwise.'

Having at first refused to dignify the charges with a reply, Vialli gave a frank response. He angrily said Zeman was a 'terrorist trying to destabilise the soccer world'. Del Piero instructed his agent to sue for libel; Juve said they too would sue Zeman for what club president Vittorio Chiusano described as 'an underhand and ambiguous form of defamation which cannot be tolerated'.

Vialli continued: 'It's a good thing I was in England and not in Italy when all this happened. Who knows, maybe by now I would have already beaten up Zeman. At Juventus, where they are a lot more open-minded than he is, they've studied and found new ways to train and that's why they're ten years ahead of him and every other club. In Italy it's very difficult to admit that clubs who win do so because they're simply better than the competition. Just watch, when Juventus stop winning, they'll say it's because they ran out of drugs. This kind of nonsense infuriates me.'

Zeman's allegations had hurt. 'The worst part was that they were insinuations, not straight accusations. He mentioned my name and Alessandro Del Piero's in the context of an article about illegal performance-enhancing drugs. It's difficult to defend yourself when that happens because if you deny it, people think you have something to hide.' Indeed, according to an Italian saying, denying a false accusation simply serves to spread it further. 'Zeman's words reached England as well. One paper published a photograph of me with my shirt off. It was upsetting, but nothing compared to what the lads at Juventus will now have to face from opposing fans. It's not an easy thing to live with, the taunts and the suspicion, when your only fault is having trained harder and better than others.

'I went back and looked at old pictures of myself when I was eighteen, nineteen years old. Sure, I was thinner, but even back then doctors told me I had a propensity to build muscle mass. And besides, if you're a professional footballer and you train hard every day, it's perfectly normal for your body to thicken and build muscle. Take people like Marco Van Basten or Ruud Gullit – compare them at eighteen and twenty-eight. They look bigger as well.'

His reputation as a health freak was seriously misguided as well. 'I hate working out in the gym. Lifting weights is boring and it doesn't even yield exceptional results. Sure, my muscles might seem big and powerful but I'm not that strong. There are many less well-built players who can lift much more than I can.'

He did admit that in addition to creatine he had thought about taking amino acids: 'I collected a lot of information about them and I seriously considered taking them, but I realised the drawbacks outweighed the benefits in my case. But it should be stressed that amino acids are not illegal – you can buy them in any health store.' Vialli refused to respond directly to Zeman's allegations other than to say: 'If someone has made a mistake, they must pay for it, but I am not going to be the one who pays for anything because I have done nothing wrong.'

WEDNESDAY, 12 AUGUST

The first training ground practice match involving the team took place. Casiraghi and Flo paired up front with Zola and Vialli on the other side.

Title contenders Arsenal and Chelsea faced the prospect of losing their French World Cup stars for up to a month between December and January because the world champions were scheduled to play in the Confederation Cup in Mexico. The tournament was derided by Bates as a 'Mickey Mouse exercise', but it had full FIFA status and, should France coach Roger Lemerre insist, the clubs would have to release players such as Emmanuel Petit, Patrick Vieira, Nicolas Anelka, Marcel Desailly and Frank Leboeuf as early as two weeks before the 6 January kick-off date. FIFA was aware of the massive disquiet, bordering on rebellion, among Europe's leading clubs at the idea that their star players could be plucked away like this. In Germany and Italy, tensions were running high, although the problem was eased to some degree by their winter breaks. The Premiership has no such respite, and the domestic programme is at its most fierce during those two months when games come thick and fast and FA Cup replays add to the stress.

One Chelsea player unlikely to be troubled by national call-ups was their former Barcelona star Albert Ferrer, one of six players dropped from the Spanish squad for their opening European Championship qualifier in Cyprus. The twenty-eight-year-old defender was paying the penalty for Spain's pitiful World Cup performance when they went out at the group stage.

Kharine was informed that he'd been recalled to Russia's squad for the first time since Euro 96.

THURSDAY, 13 AUGUST

The first pre-match press conference of the new season attracted eighty journalists and camera crews. Vialli knew the board expected nothing less than the title trophy at Stamford Bridge for the first time since 1955. 'I've got no excuses now. We've got the team we were looking for at the start of the summer and bought the best four players who were available. We have to win something. I'm desperate for us to start on the right footing because I know it could be vital by next May. Maybe I'm not good enough to help Chelsea win the championship, and if that's the case there's nothing I can do about it as long as I give it my best shot. All I'm looking for is for the players to do their best. If we do that, even if we don't win something, I will be happy.'

Vialli asked his players to learn from the lessons that had cost them so dear in the League the previous season. 'Certainly we have to be more solid than last season when we lost fifteen games. If only seven or eight of those games had been draws we'd have been second in the Premiership and in the Champions League this season. It is vital that we stop giving goals away cheaply like we did last year.

Of course we want to play nice football and I think we're still capable of that, but I have asked the players, first and foremost, to concentrate. That's why I've brought in Marcel and Albert, because they will make us more solid at the back.' Vialli stressed the point about Desailly. 'He's really keen on playing in England, and he wants to work hard and prove to Milan, I think, that he is still good enough to play in Italy for a great team like AC.'

All four newcomers were already out of hotel limbo and seemed to have settled in well, but Desailly knew it would be difficult to gel straight away. 'We have to be intelligent because we don't know each other really on the field. But we are all intelligent players and everyone knows they must play at their best, so I see no reason why Chelsea cannot challenge for the championship. We have to be careful everyone just does the best he can in his position and doesn't try to do too many things too quickly. If we can start like this we'll pressurise, we'll grow and slowly we'll come up at the top.'

Sinclair passed a morning medical and joined Leicester for £2m, rising to £2.5m depending on appearances. He probably wouldn't be Vialli's last rearrangement of the furniture: 'Sometimes you have to make sacrifices when you know it is vital for the team. But it is always up to the players because I am not going to force anyone to stay at Chelsea if they are unhappy. I respect their wishes all the time because, if I didn't, I would be a selfish manager. If they want to move, it's up to them. I try to be frank with the players so they know the situation and can decide what to do. Of course I can try to convince somebody to stay if I think it is good for me, him and the club, but if he definitely wants to leave then there is nothing we can do apart from help him to find a good club. It is a free world. Economically it was a good move for Frank, and I am prepared for others to leave.'

Sinclair became the third first-team squad member to leave in the summer, following Granville and Hughes. He advised other clubs to look at the Chelsea reserves as a recruiting ground; 'With sixteen or seventeen internationals in the squad it's going to be especially difficult for youngsters and home-grown players to get in the side.' Sinclair, who went to the World Cup finals with Jamaica's Reggae Boyz, added: 'I couldn't wait any longer. At twenty-four, it is no use to my career just sitting around week after week. I could have stayed at the Bridge. Vialli made that perfectly clear. But I am not the sort of person who likes to be inactive. Leicester are a good club and now I can look forward to an immediate debut against Manchester United in front of 55,000 Old Trafford fans. It might seem I'm stepping down, but career-wise it's a step up because I'll be playing in the Premiership rather than sitting on the bench or in the stand at Chelsea.'

Coventry away was fast becoming a bogey fixture. Last season's first-day defeat had stunned fans. Vialli suggested a more cautious approach: 'I'm going to ask the players to concentrate for the whole game. We lost 3–2 to Coventry last season; we were in front twice and then in the last five minutes they scored twice. If they don't score at all you have a great chance to win the game.' With all his players fit, he initially named a squad of twenty-three for the opening-day game, yet five of them eventually did not even make it on to the bus. Vialli remained confident his squad believed that his rotation system would give them all a chance at some stage, and that continued success would convince them all to stay put.

He was under some stress, though, even at this early stage of the season: 'I've had a tough time in the last two or three weeks. First of all being player-manager is exciting but very demanding. Sometimes I put myself too much under pressure. I like the perfection. I am never happy. I can't chill out, even though Rixy makes me laugh all the time. But also this doping thing in which I've been implicated in some way by a very frustrated manager. I didn't need it and didn't deserve it. But if you're always in the front line you have to handle it.'

Wise was congratulating the World Cup winners. 'We've had to make the dressing room door bigger for Frank 'cause he can't get his head through.' He anticipated another successful season. 'We've signed some quality players again. It's gonna make competition for places very tough, and I think that's great. It's sad to say goodbye to some players who have done well, particularly Sparky, the Ledge, Frank and Danny. Hopefully they'll also do well for their new clubs 'cause they really were great Chelsea lads.'

FRIDAY, 14 AUGUST

Scandal in the morning papers! Graham Rix was under police investigation for allegedly having sex with a fifteen-year-old girl.

The squad was announced – no Petrescu, who was given permission to leave early for international duty.

I tipped Chelsea for the championship in the *Mirror*. Harry Redknapp felt the title wasn't difficult to predict. In the *Sporting Life*, Harry said: 'It is impossible to look beyond the first four teams in the betting for the Premiership, and I reckon Manchester United have the all-round strength to regain their title. There is no doubt that Arsenal, Liverpool and Chelsea will give United problems, but the return to action of Roy Keane should tip the balance. Chelsea have often been talked up in the past but I really think that they now have a team capable of a sustained challenge for the title. Luca Vialli is a nice, friendly bloke and I wish him all the best. He's been a great player, and there is no reason to believe he won't achieve plenty as a manager as well. Brian Laudrup is a superb player and Marcel Desailly proved in the World Cup that he is one of the best defenders in the world. Some people may feel that the side will take time to gel with so many new faces at the Bridge, but good players can always play together and the Blues should have no problems.'

Gary Mabbutt believed Chelsea looked the most formidable team. His reservation was whether the team could bed down sufficiently in the first season. He argued: 'Arsenal did it last season with a reshaped team, but history tells us that this is the exception rather than the rule.'

Andy Gray, in his *Sunday Mirror* column, observed: 'Chelsea to me are a fascinating unknown quantity. I just can't wait to see how it pans out. It's a little bit like throwing up a jigsaw from a cup and wondering whether all the pieces on the table will fit together nicely, or will they all be disjointed and not fit together at all? It's not quite the same situation, but I remember Harry Redknapp at West Ham about two years ago. He went for what we all termed his League of Nations team. He signed all these foreigners, and Harry freely admitted it was the worst thing he did and he quickly got rid of them within twelve months. They are all great individual players that they have signed, I wouldn't argue with that. But individuals do not win you the league. The question Gianluca Vialli and the players have to answer – and everyone will be asking it – is are they good enough to go through the thirty-eight games consistently enough to win the League? I look at Chelsea and I see an amazing Cup bet because of the talent they have.'

Chelsea planned to unveil their new all-white change kit at Coventry, but Premiership bosses ordered them to shell out on a new set of yellow shirts. They claimed that both Chelsea's traditional blue and the new white shirt would clash with Coventry's latest sky blue kit. Chelsea were forced to play in a hastily launched all-yellow strip to the disappointment of the 20,000 fans who had bought brand-new white away shirts. Two seasons ago at Highfield Road, Chelsea had been similarly forced to change their away kit at the last minute. They ended up playing in Coventry's change kit, and losing 3–1.

Bates pointed out that the net expenditure on players for the new season was £8m as the sales of Granville, Hughes and Sinclair helped balance the books. 'For different reasons we were sorry to lose all three players, all of whom in their different ways have given us excellent service, but for every new player we bring in, somebody has to leave, and our departing players have made good personal career moves so everybody should be happy. It is generally acknowledged that we have probably the most exciting squad in the country and when it settles in we will be a force to be reckoned with. We have had a very busy time, but very productive; many clubs decided to go shopping after the World Cup, we decided to do ours beforehand. Other clubs who left it late either paid through the nose or missed out altogether.'

SATURDAY, 15 AUGUST

Coventry City 2   Chelsea 1

Chelsea fielded a starting line-up of eleven internationals for the first time in its history. Altogether there were thirteen international players, speaking eight languages, and costing £34.5m to buy and £1m a month to keep. The result was one goal and no points.

That was Chelsea's balance sheet from Highfield Road when the first results of the season were released; money may talk, but it does not necessarily make sense. Chelsea were no slackers, but their work-rate lacked the edge that came from Coventry's fear of what might happen if they eased up. City have good players, but only Hedman, who had an outstanding game in goal, George Boateng and the goalscorers, Dion Dublin and Darren Huckerby, would have a chance of making even Chelsea's squad.

Within three hours of the final whistle, Vialli had fled the country. After watching his team of expensive stars start the season losing to unfancied Coventry, it's no wonder the Chelsea boss did a runner! In fact, Vialli left Highfield Road in a hurry because he had a plane to catch. 'Gone to watch a match on the Continent,' said Rix.

Self-destruction in the first sixteen minutes of the season raised immediate doubts about Chelsea's claim to be serious title challengers. Last season, defensive errors had proved fatal to their ambitions of lifting the title, and those same frailties were still present, despite Vialli's investment in fresh talent. Desailly discovered that trying to keep tabs on a team of eager beavers like Coventry can be a whole lot more difficult than facing Brazil. First, after ten minutes, he was left for dead when Dion Dublin's flick-on from a long kick freed Darren Huckerby's pace to lob keeper Ed de Goey. Six minutes later it got even worse as Dublin beat Desailly in the air to head City's second from Noel Whelan's free-kick. In terms of an introduction to the English game, this was about as harsh as it came. Desailly confessed: 'For me, the opening twenty minutes were very difficult. I cannot pretend otherwise. I was at fault. I need to understand what happened. I must not make such mistakes again. I will not make such mistakes again.' Leboeuf declared: 'Marcel and myself will talk together to put things right. The World Cup is gone. Our task now is to be together in the Premiership and form a partnership which makes it difficult for opponents to score. Against Coventry, it went badly in the beginning. Marcel is unhappy, I am unhappy. We must talk.'

Swedish full-back Roland Nilsson sympathised: 'It will need at least ten matches before Desailly and the rest are properly integrated. You don't get the measure of English soccer in just one game, I can tell you that for sure from personal experience. The first ten clubs you play against will hit you with ten different tactics. It can be quite bewildering, and one moment's hesitation can be fatal. In addition, there is no other country where the football is so fierce. It is harder, faster and more determined, so Chelsea's newcomers should be warned.'

To be fair, there was nothing wrong with Chelsea once Coventry's goal rush subsided, in fact plenty that was right. Wise and Poyet began to run midfield, and the Sky Blues were pushed back. Poyet scored with a superb thirty-seventh-minute header, meeting Wise's free-kick, while Casiraghi proved a constant threat and might easily have grabbed a hat-trick, forcing three excellent saves from Hedman with a twisting header, a close-range thrust and then a shot fired expertly on the run. But, to chants of 'Eng-ger-land, Eng-ger-land', Coventry held on.

A victory for England? Not quite. Significant roles were played by Scandinavian, Dutch and Scots, while a pair of Belgians wait in the wings. Coventry defender Richard Shaw said: 'Casiraghi looks the business. His experience and range of movement enable him to lose you in a split-second.' Add the brilliant Laudrup and Chelsea's attack force could be capable of inflicting major damage. Laudrup was missing through injury, but there was still no place for Zola. It was a sign of how deep the quality goes in the Chelsea squad that he was restricted to a fourteen-minute cameo performance.

Coventry manager Gordon Strachan, exultant in victory for a Sky Blue line-up boasting not a single new face from last season, admitted: 'Chelsea have better players than us. My players always work hard. They possess a spirit which cannot be beaten by any other Premiership club. Against Chelsea, packed with world-class performers, they had to go to the extreme of effort to pull off such a good result. Worried? Of course I was worried. But someone once told me, "Get your first goal, your first point and your first win as quickly as possible, son." And we've finished with the complete set from taking on one of the very best teams in the country. That's not so bad, is it?'

Bates said: 'As Rixy said, we did start our season fifteen minutes after everybody else, but a final score of 6–2 in our favour would have been a better reflection of possession and chances. I am sure the setback was an early lesson which was well learned.' Wise said: 'We fell asleep twice and got caught on the hop. We played so well. Gigi was extremely good, but sometimes when you're a striker you need luck. Apart from those two goals we didn't give them any chances, we did quite well. We started off like that last year, of course, except last year we gave them three chances. This year we've got to make sure we sort the problems out. We mustn't lose concentration.'

When Poyet scored, a five-year-old girl, seated with her father in an area reserved for home fans, stood up wearing a Chelsea shirt and waved a Chelsea flag almost as big as she was. A Coventry fan nearby spewed forth a torrent of abuse and demanded stewards throw the interlopers out. With the intervention of his friends an uneasy calm prevailed, though the terrified little girl kept the flag down from then on. Leaving aside the foolishness of the parent – and the near certainty that Stamford Bridge would have been equally intolerant – the worrying aspect was the weakness of the stewards who were even more reluctant to intervene when the same Coventry fan later picked a fight with a fellow City supporter over the merits, or otherwise, of Whelan.

A caller to Six-O-Six demanded the sacking of Kenny Dalglish barely a hundred minutes after Newcastle's opening game. Chelsea were due to meet Newcastle the next week; whoever loses will be the season's first 'crisis club'. No wonder both were reported to have requested 'further information' following an approach from the proposed European Super Leaguers.

SUNDAY, 16 AUGUST

Petrescu's future was on the line. Vialli told him he was surplus to requirements. Petrescu said: 'Chelsea want to sell me. Vialli has told me I will not be playing in the first eleven this year. I will leave if I can find a club to join.'

A devastated Petrescu was back home in Bucharest attempting to sort out his future. Vialli would accept around £2.5m, with Ajax interested. Petrescu had sought an extension to his current contract when he returned from World Cup duty, where he scored against England in the group stages, but Vialli told the versatile player he was not guaranteed a place following the signing of Ferrer. Hutchinson said: 'We became aware last week that Ajax were interested in him and he expressed the view that if the deal could be progressed, then he would like to go there. We will not stand in his way, but Ajax have not yet made a formal bid to us and have not yet come to the negotiating table.'

Petrescu has made almost a hundred appearances since moving to west London from Sheffield Wednesday, and was a first-team regular last season, but didn't even figure in the eighteen-man squad which travelled to Coventry. Hutchinson insisted the club was under no financial pressure to trim their large squad.

MONDAY, 17 AUGUST

All was revealed about Luca's mystery disappearance from Highfield Road: he had to testify before prosecutors in Turin in the Zeman case. He emerged tight-lipped from his hearing. 'It went really well, but I can't say anything,' he said, before climbing into a car and speeding off.

Thirty-eight Chelsea Village flats had gone on sale, and all but four had been sold, including one to Martine McCutcheon.

TUESDAY, 18 AUGUST
Poyet took over as captain as Chelsea appealed unsuccessfully to the FA about the three-match ban for Wise's dismissal during a pre-season tournament. Chelsea asked for a rethink because the tournament organisers implemented their own punishment and because the respective associations in Spain and Brazil took no action against their players sent off in Holland. The FA insisted the ban stayed and Wise missed the next three Premiership games – all at Stamford Bridge – against Newcastle, Arsenal and Nottingham Forest. 'Poyet will take over because he has the character and ability to make an excellent captain,' said Rix. 'He is well respected within the club and by the other players.'

Babayaro went for the latest scan on his troublesome foot. Good progress was shown on the union of the bone, but there was still some way to go.

WEDNESDAY, 19 AUGUST
No rest day this week.

David Rocastle dropped in, his season finished in Malaysia where his team finished third in the league and runners-up in the cup.

Chelsea launched a scathing attack on Forest manager Dave Bassett for daring to make public 'non-existent' bids for Flo and Duberry. Hutchinson was furious when he spotted on Teletext that Chelsea had supposedly turned down a bid from Nottingham Forest to exchange Pierre Van Hooijdonk for Flo, and Vialli had considered a £2.5m bid for Duberry. Bassett said: 'Flo is a player I admire greatly and he would have been an ideal replacement for Van Hooijdonk. Unfortunately, Chelsea weren't interested in taking Pierre.' Hutchinson said: 'It must be the silly season or David is being a bit mischievous, but the idea of swapping Flo for Van Hooijdonk is beyond the point of being ridiculous. I'm a bit disappointed in him. We had a quiet word after the Coventry game and he said that he would like to talk to me about players available at our club and that he would give me a call. He did not call, and he did not mention any names. And I am sick of saying that Flo is not for sale. If he was moving he would have far more of a choice than the City Ground!' As for Forest's bid for Duberry, Hutchinson added: 'It's garbage. Again I am tired of saying Duberry is not for sale, and if he was I would stress we would not sell at £2.5m in today's market. That is laughable as well.'

Hutchinson also announced that any proposed deal with Ajax for Dan Petrescu had fallen through without an offer being made by the Dutch club, although other offers would be considered for him as he still wanted to leave. 'Dan is obviously at the age where he's looking perhaps for a final contract. He's held discussions with Luca, and they've mutually agreed that if the right club came up, Dan would like to move.'

Petrescu was only one of a number of players – Newton, Lee, Myers, Lambourde and Kharine – available. Hutchinson did not discuss names, but he told ClubCall:

'There are some players within the squad we would be prepared to let go, and that's something we deal with on a day-to-day basis. Luca has always said he wants a smaller squad than we have operated with in the past, and there are players who don't see any prospect of getting into the first team and obviously want to play first-team football, and a few of those may at some stage go.'

Leboeuf played for France, conceding a penalty from which Austria took a 2–1 lead, after which he came off. The game finished 2–2. Kharine played the second half for Russia in Sweden, not conceding as his team lost 1–0. Flo and Petrescu faced each other in Norway's goalless draw with Romania.

THURSDAY, 20 AUGUST

Vialli had a special training session on defending. Leboeuf volunteered to participate even though he only got to bed at 5.30 a.m., flying straight home after his international. Duberry trained alongside him with Desailly in midfield.

Lambourde was added to the squad numbers at twenty-one.

FRIDAY, 21 AUGUST

Desailly's home debut loomed. 'I have no image of Newcastle at all,' he said. 'I wasn't in the Champions League when they were last year. Only when Ginola went there, I saw some of them then. But I know their ground because I played there in Euro 96 and it's a lovely stadium.'

Chelsea had lived with the burden of 'no silverware' between 1971 and 1997, and Steve Clarke pointed out the similarities with Newcastle: 'Newcastle haven't won anything because they've lacked good enough players. When they had that big lead in the Premiership a couple of years ago they didn't have the players to last the whole season. Like Chelsea, they've pretended to be a big club, but big clubs win trophies. In the last two years we've become a big club. What they are is a very well-supported club.'

Dalglish could also comfortably field a side of players from nine different footballing nations. One of his many imports – Newcastle included fourteen nationalities on their books – was Laurent Charvet, the French defender who was on loan to Chelsea. Wise said: 'Chav is back after his loan here, playing centre-half now for them. He did well for us; we were disappointed to see him go. He was one of the lads. His English was getting better and he was a nice fella.' Leboeuf added: 'Every time he played for Chelsea everybody was astonished by his performances. I really think he did well. Chelsea decided not to keep him and that was a pity for me. But he really deserved to be at a good club. I hope he does very well, except this match I hope he does very badly!'

SATURDAY, 22 AUGUST

Chelsea I   Newcastle United I

Newcastle fans looked on enviously as Wise showed off the European Cup Winners Cup and the Coca-Cola Cup before kick-off. In nine months' time the home fans were hoping to see Wise doing a lap of honour with the League trophy, but after collecting just one point from six, the team did not appear to be familiar with the script.

With so much talent on show from every part of the globe, it was depressing to discuss sweat rather than polished football. But it was that sort of match. Apart from a superb interchange of passes between Zola and Poyet that led to Babayaro's goal, there was more perspiration than inspiration. With the mighty Marcel having been given a rude introduction to the Premiership in the heart of the defence at Coventry, the Frenchman switched effortlessly into midfield to cover for Wise. Duberry got his big chance, but slipped at the crucial moment when Shearer's long-distance cross picked out Andersson. 'Sloppy' was the Vialli verdict on the goal, but he said: 'I can't blame the players for the goal conceded, because every-body worked very hard. For the first forty-five minutes they had only one chance and they scored, and of course we could have avoided the goal. But when you play against great players like Shearer they take advantage of everything.

'In the future we have to do better. When you play a weaker team, on paper, they put in extra effort to show Chelsea are not unbeatable and to get the headlines in the newspapers. That should give us an extra boost, an attitude that "to beat me you have to kill me" and not give anything away cheaply. We can improve. In two seasons we have won three cups, which means we are not as bad as sometimes people say. But we have to do better, especially in the Premier League.'

The most disappointing aspect of the performance was the lack of goals from a team that had managed more than a hundred last season. Under Gullit there were the trademark defensive blunders, but the forwards usually outscored their opponents. Vialli had two more forwards, as well as two additional defenders, yet there was no perceptible difference.

In his shirt sleeves, with a jumper around his waist, Luca had been on the bench only as the coach. He still wanted to be considered one of the players, but his apperances were going to be staggered. 'It depends on my shape, how I feel, and the condition of my other strikers. But I will always be available and will try to keep myself fit.'

Referee Uriah Rennie booked two Italians for diving: first Pistone after eighteen minutes when he fell after a challenge from Di Matteo, and then in the last minute Casiraghi for trying to win a penalty. Leboeuf was also booked, for protesting about the defensive wall as Zola lined up a free-kick. He had taken the captain's armband from Poyet, who had been substituted for Petrescu. Leboeuf was furious. 'I just told him to put the wall the distance it should be. I don't want to criticise, but if I'm not allowed to speak when I am captain, then what is the point of a captain on the field?' Leboeuf has been part of the Chelsea revolution from the start, but he conceded: 'I am very disappointed because I thought we deserved a penalty. It was very clear.' His old French pal Charvet made the tackle. 'He was lucky.'

Petrescu made it clear he was willing to stay after receiving a standing ovation from fans when he came on as a fifty-seventh-minute substitute. 'It was a very good reception when I came on and the fans were great when I was warming up as well. I have a good relationship with them and I was very happy with it. I would be more than happy to stay at this club because I love the place.' He wouldn't hang around forever on the bench, though. 'If I go a long time without playing then maybe the manager with Romania won't pick me, and that would be a problem because I love playing for the national side. I will have to wait and see what's going on and make a decision after that. I think I have a chance of getting back in the Chelsea team and if I get the chance I will try my best to stay in.'

Kharine was desperately unhappy. 'Unfortunately, who will be the main goalie was decided not on the football pitch but outside. Two days ahead of the opening game I was told Ed de Goey was to be number one and that I was not even substitute. The sooner I quit, the better. Although my contract doesn't expire until the end of this season, I won't wait that long. I'm thirty and can't afford to be sitting on the bench. I want to play very much and must support my family. I'd like to stay in England or, if not, play in Scotland.'

MONDAY, 24 AUGUST

Italy's top anti-drugs investigator was planning talks with Vialli, Di Matteo, Zola and Casiraghi. Ugo Longo, who headed an inquiry by the Italian Olympic Committee (CONI), had been expecting the Stamford Bridge Italians in Rome, but CONI officials had no reply to their faxed invitation. 'At this stage, it might be down to me to go to London and meet them,' admitted Longo, who was interviewing a series of top sporting figures.

TUESDAY, 25 AUGUST

Flo missed training with a heavy cold; Wise and Di Matteo went home early with the same symptoms. Le Saux trained after being substituted suffering from one.

Luca took part in the most extraordinary line-up of star personalities since the BBC's famous 'Perfect Day' pop video. *EastEnders* star Martine McCutcheon, comedian Harry Enfield, globetrotter Michael Palin and chat show queen Ruby Wax, plus Vialli, were among the ten-strong cast in the Beeb's latest promotional film. Just ninety seconds long, the show was part of a £1m advertising campaign to tell viewers about digital TV. The commercial, in the shape of a virtual reality journey, also starred author Salman Rushdie and dance music king Goldie. Like the 'Perfect Day' video, which featured stars such as David Bowie and Elton John singing Lou Reed's classic, the stars waived their fees.

Dennis Wise attended the premiere of the British-made feature *Lock, Stock & Two Smoking Barrels* along with his old mate Vinnie Jones at London's Virgin Haymarket Cinema. Earlier, he had complained bitterly of being singled out with the pre-season incident in Holland because of his poor disciplinary record. 'I hope the FA are treating all the players who got sent off in friendlies the same. It's funny how the Spanish FA didn't hit the fella I got sent off with. I have been given a three-match ban despite the fact I was suspended for the next game in the tournament.'

THURSDAY, 27 AUGUST

Ruud Gullit was back as boss of Newcastle in place of Kenny Dalglish. Vialli turned up at Heathrow airport, bound for Monte Carlo and the Super Cup clash with Real Madrid, quickly changing his Italian silk tie to Chelsea's blue stripes, oblivious to the Gullit appointment. Had he been in a different part of the airport he would have bumped into Gullit as he arrived from Amsterdam on his way to talks with the Newcastle directors. By the time the squad reached Monte Carlo, it was the talk of the trip.

The Chelsea contingent could not believe the gamble their old boss was taking by accepting the Newcastle job, but there was no animosity from Vialli. Wise believed he would replicate the success story at the Bridge. But trust Bates to come up with the most cutting and whimsical comment of them all: 'I wish him well. I hope he does well. Are there direct flights from Newcastle to Amsterdam? As for a million pounds a year, I couldn't believe he's come so cheap, but perhaps the cost of living is cheaper up there! And I wonder whether he asked netto or gross?'

Chelsea's press conference in Stade Louis II was hijacked by the shockwaves of Gullit's re-emergence in the Premiership and the rivalry between the Dutchman and the Italian. Vialli said: 'I've got nothing against Ruud. I wish him all the best for the season. Having said that Kenny Dalglish is a great person and a great manager and it's a shame if he's been sacked.' Vialli didn't stay too long. He quickly got fed up with the questioning from an allegedly drunken reporter, and walked out grim-faced, saying: 'How many cup finals have you played in?'

Next, Desailly and Leboeuf faced more slurred questions from the same journalist dressed in shorts and T-shirt. Leboeuf, vexed by his French colleague being asked about Dion Dublin and the goal he scored, glared and said: 'Have you been to Jimmy's Bar?' I passed a note to Gwyn Williams. On it I had written 'dress code' as a comical reference to the journalist's attire; he responded by writing 'breathalyser test'.

Real Madrid had refused to take part in the UEFA press conference in the bowels of the stadium because of the lack of air conditioning.

Zola laughed when it was suggested that Gullit might buy him again. 'I'm happy for him. It is good that a man like him is back working with a team, but joining him? I don't think it is possible. I have a contract at Chelsea and I like to respect it. I'm too tied to that contract, but also I'm very attached to Chelsea and Chelsea's supporters. I'm happy to stay at Chelsea and give them my heart.' Leboeuf, the subject of transfer speculation since returning as a World Cup winner, said: 'It's good every time a manager wants you, but if he wanted me he would have to ask Chelsea and I don't think Chelsea would let me go as I'm on a three-year contract.' Leboeuf was very close to Gullit, and expressed his amazement that his old friend had signed for Newcastle. 'I'm from Marseilles in the south of France, and there's no way I could put up with that weather or that kind of life. I went to see David Ginola a year ago in Newcastle and it was so cold we stayed in and watched TV. It's not just about the football, it's about your lifestyle. I didn't expect to see Ruud at Newcastle, but it's a very good thing for Newcastle. I just wish him a very enjoyable life there and I want him to have good results and good games – except against Chelsea.'

Back to the Super Cup. The big question was, could Laudrup play in the same formation as Zola, who came off the bench to score within seconds the winner against Stuttgart in Stockholm? Zola said: 'Why can't two beautiful people play together?' If they can't then Zola won't be happy with a place on the bench for any length of time this season. Just ask Vialli and Gullit!

New Italian boss Dino Zoff dumped a dozen of the World Cup stars in his first squad since taking over from Cesare Maldini, for the European Championship clash with Wales at Anfield. Despite the fact that Di Matteo and Casiraghi were on stand-by, Zoff overlooked them. The squad was greeted with surprise in Italy. AC Milan defender Alessandro Costacurta and goalkeeper Gianluca Pagliuca were axed, and three uncapped players were summoned.

FRIDAY, 28 AUGUST

Morning at St James's Park, and a press conference to unveil Ruud Gullit as successor to Kenny Dalglish. The fans gathered outside, awaiting Gullit's coronation. Gullit described his new job as 'a great honour'. He said: 'I played here a couple of times and the atmosphere was really incredible. The most important thing is that the stadium has got to be hell for the opposition. I will put everything I have in my grasp into making this club successful and giving the fans something to cheer about. I want to win. I must win. I have won things all my life and I am going to Newcastle to be successful. And I hope we can play some really sexy football.

'There was no heavy negotiation with Newcastle. They wanted me, I wanted them. I did not put a gun to their head. There was no crazy money talk. The only discussion we had was that I be allowed to do the job my way. I had to have that assurance. And this time I want my own people around me. I do not want a repeat of what happened when I was at Chelsea.'

Just twenty-four hours after the departure of Dalglish, the autobiography of their former boss was already off the shelves at the St James's Park club shop, replaced by dreadlock wigs. Even legendary Jackie Milburn had his statue crowned in the braided hairpiece in a celebration which bridges generations but is still a million miles and pounds away from Wor Jackie's bygone era.

Gullit was offered the biggest bonuses in football to bring the silverware to St James's Park. He will almost double his money – the salary is just under £1m a year gross – if he can finally end the misery of the Geordie fans. Gullit accepted a 'modest' salary by his own high standards, but the pay-related success deal would make him by far the biggest earner in the managerial stakes in the Premiership. Top of the league is Luca Vialli at £1.4m a year – but he is still a player as well as the Chelsea coach – next is George Graham at £1m a year, followed by Alex Ferguson at £800,000 plus big bonuses. Gullit earned £1.2m a year as a player at Stamford Bridge and took bonuses of £250,000 for bringing the big prizes to the club for the first time in a quarter of a century. He was kicked out when Chelsea claimed he was demanding £2m a year net, which amounted to £3.6m a year gross.

At midday in Monte Carlo the draw for the Cup Winners Cup was made. Chelsea were pitted against Helsingborgs of Sweden.

FRIDAY, 28 AUGUST

Real Madrid 0   Chelsea 1

The Super Cup was not around for the 1971 Cup Winners Cup team to play for, as it was only introduced as a competition in 1972. So this was the club's first go at the trophy, and at the end of an amazing day, Chelsea collected their fourth major cup in a whirlwind sixteen months. As the fans paid homage to Vialli, no one could forget that the first trophy, the vital breakthrough, was delivered when Gullit was in charge.

With twenty of the players who were on show in France at the World Cup, more was expected of this confrontation between the Spanish champions and the club from along the Fulham Road. But Vialli opted to leave out Poyet, with Wise deployed wide to curtail Roberto Carlos. Leboeuf held the defence together, and on his home territory in the south of France was my man of the match, making one particularly vital tackle on Raul after the young Spanish striker had eluded Duberry, and even hitting the post with a curling shot in the second half. From a Zola cross Babayaro miscued from six yards, and then Real came close to the opener just after half an hour when Roberto Carlos lined up for one of his famous long-range free-kicks. Sneakily, Fernando Hierro took just two strikes and whipped the free-kick over Le Saux at the far end of the wall, the shot swerving five yards before striking the inside of the post, with de Goey hurting himself in the dive.

First Vialli sent on Poyet, and then, as Laudrup stood by the touchline awaiting his first appearance for his new club, to replace Zola, Chelsea created the break-through. Casiraghi headed on and Poyet opened up the defence for Zola, whose shot was blocked, but he had the exceptional technique to regain possession and control and teed up the ball perfectly for Poyet to shoot into the far corner from just inside the box. The players embarked on yet another of their goal-scoring celebration routines, standing on one leg in a circle.

When Duberry pulled back substitute Fernando Morientes, Madrid coach Gus Hiddink pulled off half his jacket in frustration. This was Vialli's first encounter with a Dutch coach, but it wouldn't be his last.

Vialli singled out Leboeuf for his 'outstanding performance'. 'I don't normally single out individual players, but I'm going to make an exception tonight as we have won a cup. Frank Leboeuf was outstanding. He was great in defence, and when he got the opportunity, he went forward.' He did admit that his side had been somewhat fortunate when the referee delayed Laudrup's introduction from the bench to replace Zola. 'We were ready to make a change and put Brian Laudrup on for Gianfranco Zola but the referee didn't see. Gianfranco got involved and allowed Gustavo to score.

'We didn't perform as well as we could have done, especially in the first half, but this is still a learning process and we are making progress match by match. Looking at the whole situation, I'm very happy. We can still improve a lot, but to win three cups in the last six months is a great achievement for this club, the supporters, the players and the staff.'

Wise, Laudrup and Desailly stayed on in France for a few days; the rest arrived home at three a.m.

SUNDAY, 30 AUGUST

Gullit watched from the directors' box in disgust and frustration as his new team went down 4–1 to Liverpool.

Gullit was in open conflict with his old club over the appointment of Steve Clarke, whose arrival at St James's Park was held up by disputes over cash: Chelsea sought a six-figure transfer fee for their longest-serving player, and there was a disagreement over money owed to him. Gullit suspected it was always going to be tricky to prise away any player or member of staff from the Bridge after his acrimonious departure, but he hoped the club would reward Clarke with an easy passage to a high-profile coaching position in the Premiership.

Clarke had brought forward his retirement as a player to concentrate on stepping into coaching. He had celebrated his thirty-fifth birthday on Saturday, and said: 'I had already decided that this season would be my last as a player. It means now that my last game was in the European Cup Winners Cup final. That's not a bad way to bow out. I have been coaching since the start of the season. I found out that Ruud wanted me during the Super Cup in Monaco.

'It was Ruud who first spoke to me about coaching. He sat me down during pre-season a year ago and said I should think about moving into that side of the game. He was the first one to put over the point that I had something to offer. When Ruud left, Gianluca Vialli must have seen those qualities because he offered me a coaching job.

'Newcastle is a top-class club, the facilities are first-class, and the players are class. Their attitude in training since my arrival has been excellent, but to be honest, I am not surprised. I'd expect that of players at a club of this stature. I'm excited and looking forward to the challenges ahead.'

The hold-ups over the appointment were soon resolved, and Clarke signed a three-year deal. Newcastle paid £160,000, to include the money he was owed as part of his contract at the Bridge. 'As soon as Ruud phoned me last Thursday,' Clarke continued, 'straight away I said yes, and it was just a matter of sorting things out from there. It was obviously difficult to leave because twelve years at one club is a long time and I've made a lot of friends and have got some great memories of the place. But in football things move on.' Freddie Shepherd confirmed the club had paid a compensation fee: 'We have agreed to pay them a nominal fee in the form of compensation and would like to thank them for the amicable way they negotiated. They recognised this was a great career move for Steve and did not stand in his way.'

Vialli said: 'Clarkey has gone to Newcastle after twelve years of loyal service at our club with an outstanding attitude. Of course he's a loss, but sometimes when a chance comes, when the train passes, you have to get on it without thinking too much about the future. I wish him all the best. He's a smashing character and he deserves the best.' Wise chipped in: 'I'm sad to see Clarkey go, he's been a good friend and I'll miss him. But Newcastle as assistant to Ruud is a great job for him. Good luck, Clarkey.' Rix also offered him his best wishes: 'Steve will be a huge loss. This season Luca and I had provided him with a place on the management team. We wanted to use him in a year or two's time, in some capacity, and we thought it would be an ideal situation with him still being available as a player, being on the inside and learning management skills. But this opportunity has come up and you know he has got to go.'

The Bridge hierarchy were a little cooler. Bates said: 'Steve Clarke has followed Ruud to Newcastle. We wanted him to stay at Chelsea, learn his trade and come up through the ranks in our management team. However, the offer of becoming an immediate number two and jumping in at the deep end proved irresistible to him, so despite having a year left on his contract we could not, in all fairness, stand in the way of such a loyal servant. We will miss you, Steve, and wish you well – but not too well.' Hutchinson added: 'He was adamant he wished to move on. We understand his reasons. His playing days at Premiership level are over. He wants to get to the top in management. We could have been bloody-minded and blocked his chance, but that would have been totally unfair to a man who has given us twelve years' tremendous service. I believe Steve will become an excellent manager. Who knows, one day he might return to the Bridge.'

David Mellor wrote in the London *Evening Standard*: 'Steve Clarke has gone to Newcastle as number two, and jolly good luck to him. But perhaps instead he should have been stuffed and put in a case at the Natural History Museum as the last of a kind of professional now lost to our game. Today they're all mini-Ronaldos. No sooner do they arrive at a club than they're itching to get away to an ever bigger pay day somewhere else. On average players will be with a club for two or three seasons. A Stevie Clarke, who stays put for more than a decade, is as dead as a dodo. Steve was a great servant of Chelsea Football Club. A solid right-back and determined central defender, he was also that pearl beyond price, a good dressing-room man, a player the young chaps could look up to, part of the cement that bonds a squad together. Most of us hoped he'd work his way up the coaching ladder at Stamford Bridge. But Ruud Gullit's nobody's fool. He saw Clarke's strength of character and has given him his big break. And knowing Steve, he will seize it with both hands.'

MONDAY, 31 AUGUST
Gwyn Williams flew out to the Rasunda Stadium to watch Cup Winners Cup opponents Helsingborgs draw 1–1 with Stockholm.

September...

September...

September

*Super sub Flo to the rescue ... from
eighteenth to seventh in the table*

TUESDAY, 1 SEPTEMBER

There was sadness as Steve Clarke said his goodbyes at the Harlington training camp before heading off to the north-east to join Ruud.

The summer flu bug lingered on. Le Saux was unable to cope in the second half against Newcastle and came off. Vialli was ruled out of the Super Cup because of it, and it affected his training. Flo missed three days of training but made the Super Cup squad. Wise and Di Matteo trained gently. Laudrup was also affected, and missed training. Physio Mike Banks said: 'There's very little we can do to manage this. They all had slight temperatures and the best policy is for them to go home and rest so we can minimise the spread.'

WEDNESDAY, 2 SEPTEMBER

Just seven months earlier Jim Duffy resigned as Hibs manager while his team went into freefall and, ultimately, to the First Division. Having swapped Easter Road for the Fulham Road, Duff worked an eleven-hour day, six days a week. He had started on 1 July with just thirteen kids for the first week. 'That was ideal because that gave me the chance to get to know them and vice versa. That was just as well, because on my first day some of the youngsters asked if I was Frank Leboeuf! I'd like to think that my outstanding ability at five-a-sides made them think of Frank, but it's more likely to have been my shining dome. Even so, it's still an improvement on Lee Hurst, the other guy I'm mistaken for.

'In the last week our kids have had Dan Petrescu and Brian Laudrup working with them and that's given everyone – me included – a boost. The first team also train twice a day but they go to bed for a sleep between sessions and their second work-out finishes at six. The coaching isn't all that different, but the level of ability obviously is. You can do courses and study manuals until you're blue in the face but that doesn't compare with watching the likes of Gianfranco Zola and Pierluigi Casiraghi at work. The movement and runs they make are an education in themselves and that's something I've already attempted to pass on. I've worked with enthusiastic players before, but never with guys who have the style I see here on display every day. I make a point of staying back until they've finished, then help tidy up. By the time the dressing room is cleared it's eight o'clock and I'm knackered. That's not a complaint, though.'

After years of working on shoestring budgets, the attention to detail in England has impressed the former Dundee boss. 'At Chelsea, every aspect of our young players' lives is taken care of by the club. They get their breakfast in the morning – cereal, yoghurt or fruit – and Vialli has brought a chef from Italy just to cater for their lunches. Again, it's all healthy stuff like pasta. He prepares those meals and also the players' diet sheets so that they have a high carbohydrate content as well as lots of protein. Each player is examined and has his own individual requirements. Some have vitamin tablets along with their food, and there are always high-protein drinks instead of water at training.

'I have a three-year contract with Chelsea and, although you can never tell in football, I can't see myself walking away from this fabulous place. The facilities couldn't be better anywhere and everyone, from Vialli down, has helped me fit in and feel relaxed. The pressure here is all on the top team. I'm out of the firing line and that'll do me for now.'

Petrescu won his seventy-seventh Romanian cap in a 7–0 win over Liechtenstein in their first Euro 2000 tie.

THURSDAY, 3 SEPTEMBER

After eight years at the club Wise was presented with the Player of the Year award at the Novel Hotel dinner. Zola stood on a chair heckling as his captain received the award: 'Please! Stand up, will you?' Wise called up all his team-mates on stage for a round of 'Singing in the Rain'. Zola was obviously in a mischievous mood; as Poyet received the Chairman's Award, he shouted: 'Hey! Speak-a-da English!'

FRIDAY, 4 SEPTEMBER

Gus was the victim of the stick brigade at training next morning for winning the chairman's prize. 'Now I have a new name: Ken Bates's son. Every player call me his son! I was surprised. I knew I don't win Player of the Year, I don't have to speak, I can stay quiet with my friend Albert. And then Ken Bates says, "Say something!" I think, No, no! But it was great.'

Poyet had to adjust to the new regime under Vialli. 'My position has changed. For seven years I play in front of the midfield diamond. When I came to England with Ruud Gullit, I play the two or three first games in front. But we had a lot of problems because I go forward, Robbie goes forward, Dan Petrescu goes forward – it was only Dennis Wise in midfield! So we change my position to the left. I think I play good on the left, but now this season, Luca changed me because we play with Bab on the left. I am naturally right-footed and it's similar on the right, no more responsibility, but I need to play more as it is different team-mates with me there.'

SATURDAY, 5 SEPTEMBER

Le Saux was part of the beaten England team in Stockholm. Kharine returned for Russia to win his thirty-eighth cap, and Leboeuf was part of France's 1–1 draw in Iceland. Petrescu won cap number seventy-eight in a draw with Germany in a friendly in Malta.

SUNDAY, 6 SEPTEMBER

Flo and Norway suffered a Euro 2000 setback, losing 3–1 to Latvia.

MONDAY, 7 SEPTEMBER

Mark Nicholls' mother died after a long illness. Vialli said: 'He dedicated his goals to her against Coventry last season when she was already poorly. Gwyn and Graham have told me how much his parents have supported him down the years and it was wonderful that Mark responded on Monday by coming and trying to train with his friends. We sent him home because it was very upsetting and he and his family have our thoughts at this time. He's a wonderful boy and she would be very proud of him.' Mark was moved. 'It meant a lot to me, Luca, Graham and Gwyn and all the boys turning up at my mum's funeral.'

All the players were available to begin the countdown to the Arsenal clash, except Flo, who returned from Norway during the morning. Ferrer limped out of the session after turning his ankle in a tackle with Babayaro.

TUESDAY, 8 SEPTEMBER

Rix felt Chelsea would never have the full respect of the Premiership until they won the League. While Arsenal were the finished article – their gleaming trophy cabinet could testify to that – Chelsea were still the great pretenders. Rix said: 'Arsenal and Chelsea both won two trophies last season, but they got the one we want. This will be the first indicator of where we really stand against them this time. If we want to be remembered as a great team by our peers, then the Premiership is the thing. We finished fourth last season and we were looking to do a lot better, but there was a shift in football power with London clubs taking over from the north.'

Arsene Wenger branded some of soccer's expensive foreign imports as 'cheats'. Wenger even accused Vialli of diving during a Coca-Cola Cup tie. He said: 'That was a particularly tough game for him. He had taken over from Ruud Gullit and was determined to make an impression. Arsenal and Chelsea were London's top teams last season and every match was a derby with a purpose. They were certainly exciting to watch! But I would book any player who acts, and also those who pick up a ball after committing a foul and then throw it back when they've walked away. It stops the flow of the game.'

WEDNESDAY, 9 SEPTEMBER

Chelsea 0   Arsenal 0

Vialli emphasised in his programme notes that the Premiership title had become a priority: 'For the thousandth time, I would like to underline that this is just the starting point of the future of this club. We have to keep improving. There are still so many things to reach. We must keep our feet firmly on the ground and play like we haven't won anything. That is the secret, I think, after winning something.'

London's most combative fixture claimed another victim as Lee Dixon became the third player to be sent off in successive Chelsea–Arsenal matches. He was dismissed for two incidents involving Le Saux, as the capital's title challengers slipped further off the pace. Arsenal did move up to fourth, but they had won only once in four games, not scored in three, and had two players dismissed. Chelsea were faring even worse: from one game fewer they had two points, two goals and were rooted in the relegation zone.

There was profound disappointment at Stamford Bridge after the team failed to take advantage of thirty minutes' playing against ten men. While Steven Lodge was right not to give a penalty for Keown's inadvertent handball from Le Saux's cross, he might easily have given one when Vieira sent Casiraghi crashing in the box. Vialli said: 'I would say it was a penalty, but I don't like to argue with referees because they do their best and they can't see everything. The referee said he didn't see what happened. He did his best, and next time maybe we will get a penalty.'

Despite the involvement of nineteen foreign players, including seven Frenchmen, the match was characterised by the typical close-quarters foot-to-foot combat of an English local derby rather than a graceful display of continental skills.

Last season's four encounters had reaped two red and twenty-six yellow cards and it took only five minutes for the first of last night's seven yellows to arrive, Keown going through the back of Casiraghi. Tackles flew, the midfield was congested, and time on the ball a rarity. Of the 'flair' players, Zola initially coped best, linking well with Di Matteo and finding space where none seemed available. After twelve minutes he was given too much room to manoeuvre and, from twenty yards, curled a shot towards the far corner which Seaman did well to tip over. From the corner, Lambourde volleyed wide.

Chelsea then assumed a measure of control, but Arsenal were content to defend deep and watch them pass the ball ineffectually in front of them. As the half closed they broke out, Bergkamp playing a one-two with Parlour before being stopped by a fine Duberry tackle. Anelka also went close.

The exchanges raised the temperature, and Dixon and Le Saux were booked for a contretemps just before the break with the dispute continuing into the tunnel.

The fifteen-minute cooling-off period had little effect, with Duberry booked for a foul on Anelka within minutes of the restart. The game simmered – temperamentally, at least, if not in terms of the football. Then Le Saux galloped down the left touchline, Dixon missed his tackle, and off he went.

Arsenal pulled in the wagons in familiar style. They survived the two penalty scares, watched Poyet flash a header just wide, Casiraghi shoot over and Seaman save well from Babayaro. They might even have stolen the game when Bergkamp surprised de Goey with a shot that the off-balance goalkeeper cleared with his feet.

Vialli observed: 'They are a very strong team and they defend very well. We tried everything, but we kept our shape very well despite all the players wanting to go forward and crowd the box. They are so strong and sometimes a bit lucky, so it was very difficult to win.'

Dixon was furious with the England wing-back – who went flying over his ill-judged sixtieth-minute challenge – and mimed a 'diving' gesture to the referee. Words were exchanged as he walked away from Le Saux and left the field. Dixon made a bee-line for Arsenal's team bus after the game to avoid being quizzed by reporters, but the Chelsea star said: 'I can't say what he said to me. It wouldn't be right. But it all started from late in the first half when we were both booked just because he flew off the handle. He went down, but I didn't touch him and told him to get up. I guess I insinuated that he dived, but he didn't like that and his reaction got us both booked. In the second half his tackle was definitely a foul on me, but only the referee can decide whether it's worthy of a second yellow, and obviously he thought so.'

Despite lifting two cups, Chelsea had managed only six Premiership wins since Vialli took over from Gullit in February. 'We were disappointed not to win but I'm pleased with our performance. We are improving all the time. We should be scoring more goals, but I know that things can change very suddenly and soon we are likely to go bang and get quite a few. There comes a certain time in a season when you decide what you really want most. Last time we decided to put everything into winning the Coca-Cola Cup and the European Cup Winners Cup; now our aim is to win everything we can.'

Vialli admitted new boys Laudrup and Casiraghi were still off the pace. The Dane, who had not played a full game since the World Cup clash with Brazil on 3 July, said after being substituted after less than an hour into his full Chelsea debut: 'I've got some work to do yet to reach my best again. For now it is just good to be involved, and I'm hopeful I'll go from strength to strength.' The two newcomers' age was not a problem, Vialli insisted, 'not when a player has quality. Look at the Arsenal defence. They are all getting older but not any worse as far as I can see. And I'm satisfied I also have a great squad now that is capable of winning everything we want. Every competition is very tough in the English game and, while I don't know if it can be done, we certainly have the capability to do it. All that is preventing us producing our best at the moment is the fact that so many of our players are still to reach their best shape again. But I can see clear signs of an improvement from game to game.'

Desailly also sensed that Chelsea were making progress despite some negative vibes. 'It was interesting to see one of the biggest teams in England and to play against them, and we showed that Chelsea can do something in the championship this year. We, of course, would prefer to win, but we dominated all the game and you can see that now we have been here one month all together, we know how the other players are playing and we are becoming like a team. We were maybe not like a team at the beginning, but now we are strong because there is quality and there are some physical players.' Marcel was not surprised by the pace of the game; 'I was more surprised when we played against Newcastle and Coventry because they just want to play in the air.'

THURSDAY, 10 SEPTEMBER

Give or take an odd bit of carpet, the new gym opened, two-and-a-half sizes bigger than before with lines of impressive new machinery – a major step for Luca's fitness regime.

It was back to the drawing board as Luca sought his first League win of the season against Forest. His forward line was given a tactical shake-up to improve on just two League goals from three matches, from Poyet and Babayaro. He said: 'It's become difficult to play killer balls because the penalty area is quite crowded. We have to sort it out and maybe change something about the way we play attacking football. But my players are good enough to change. It's difficult at the moment because all the teams who come to Stamford Bridge first of all want to defend, to get at least one point. They are not too worried about playing football, they want to play counter-attack. For some strange reason we're not scoring as well as last season, but it's not something to worry about, it's football.'

Antonio Pintus was the key, as Vialli took a sideways swipe at his predecessor: 'In my humble opinion, when I took over I thought that physically we should improve a lot. We think we can improve on everything but especially the physical side, and we want to be physically the best team in England. Now we aim to do things better. We have great players with great skills, and if we can run faster, for longer than the opposition, and can be organised tactically, then we can win all our games.'

Vialli had also noticed an improvement in young defender Michael Duberry – 'I think he's made up for his earlier mistakes and he's improved.' The twenty-two-year-old had muscled his way back in, and said: 'There is no reason to go. I've got to play my best and hope it is good enough. If not, I'll have to raise my standards. I've never thought of leaving and I'm going to stick with it, fight for my position, because there is no other club I want to be at.'

Zola was among the honoured first six footballers to enter the 'exclusive club' of the FA Premier League Hall of Fame, as the foreign stars dominated the nominations. One player was chosen from each season the Premier League has been running – Dane Peter Schmeichel, Frenchman Eric Cantona, England's Alan Shearer and Les Ferdinand, Italian Zola and Dutchman Dennis Bergkamp. They were selected by a nineteen-strong panel of football experts chaired by Sir Geoff Hurst. He said: 'I hope and believe that the players inducted will act as role models to the young fans, who are the future of our sport.' The Hall of Fame, based at London's former County Hall, was due to open in March. It offered fans a celebration of English football from the past and present – and into the future. Zola, who was chosen for the 1996–97 season, thanked the members of the panel, who included World Cup legend Sir Bobby Charlton and a number of journalists, for voting for him. From a training session at the Chelsea ground, he said: 'It is a great honour for me to be voted. Thank you, Geoff Hurst and all the others, and I am looking forward to seeing the opening in March 1999. It is such a great honour to be there.'

Questioned about the fact that only two English players were selected, Sir Geoff said: 'One thing we looked for was excitement which got us up out of our seats. I don't think we have produced enough top-class English players recently, but players like Michael Owen and Rio Ferdinand might be included if you turn the clock forward six years.'

An appointment was made a little later for Zola to model for his Madame Tussaud's-style wax work. He had to stand frozen like a statue while casts were made of various parts of his body. Backed up by computers and cameras, the Zola look-alike was created so that the Italian could be immortalised in County Hall.

Zola had just as important a date on the training ground with Leigh, twelve, and Jodie, nine, who suffer from a blood disorder known as sickle cell disease. Jodie, a mad Chelsea fan, had suffered a stroke in February. The family went on a stadium tour, and community officer Gareth Jones arranged for the special meeting with the girls' heroes, Gianfranco and Luca, at Harlington.

FRIDAY, 11 SEPTEMBER

Vialli's programme notes for Saturday's game stressed: 'We are still not in the best position in the table. In fact, at least I can say we can't do worse! We can just improve. But we do have to look on the bright side. I felt happy straight after our draw with Arsenal. The attitude of our players was outstanding, and they played with quality and skill, but also were solid and concentrated for ninety-five minutes.'

Petit prepared his Saturday morning column in the *Mirror*. The subject was Le Saux. 'I have two nasty cuts on my right ear which will remind me of Chelsea – and Graeme Le Saux in particular – for some time. They are the result of Le Saux's foot scraping across my ear ... I am, as you can imagine, not very happy about it at all. Anyone watching will have been struck by how furiously I reacted after the incident.

'Well, that was understandable – it hurt me a lot at the time. Don't get me wrong on this one. I am not whingeing or moaning about it. I know that football is a very physical game, particularly here in England, and even more so in London derby matches. And I love that, I really do. But I like to think that there is a line within which all players must stay ... And I have been around long enough to know all the professional tricks that go on, things that the fans can't spot from their seats in the stands and are sometimes even missed by the TV cameras. It is my instinctive belief that is what happened to me in this incident. And I can tell you that when Le Saux came to see me after the match I didn't want to talk to him and told him to go away and leave me alone.'

SATURDAY, 12 SEPTEMBER

Chelsea 2   Nottingham Forest 1

Vialli performed a role reversal that threatened his impartiality. The call for Flo reverberated around the Bridge, but Vialli cocked a deaf 'un to the voice of the people. Instead, the £10m-rated Norwegian striker was stuck on the bench. Casiraghi continued to labour in front of goal, full of running, bundles of hard work and energy, but not a single goal yet. A slow start for the club with only four goals in their opening four games – surely Flo deserved a chance?

Vialli said: 'If you want to be part of a great team these are the rules. I didn't set them up. Because I consider us to be a great team we can't have just eleven great players and nobody else on the bench. They know where they stand, they might play all of a sudden, and it is up to them to be ready to cope with it. They are reasonably mature and don't mind sitting on the bench. At the moment there is no problem at all about that.'

Flo suffered in silence, no doubt eased by a double-your-money wage packet to ward off approaches from several clubs.

Fortunately one Italian was on top of his game. Zola scored the fastest goal in the Premiership, after just twenty-four seconds, with Casiraghi hassling a defender into an error. Zola wanted to repay the favour and help under-pressure Casiraghi to open his Chelsea account. 'Personally I would like to do my best to give him the right ball to score. It is the best way to start a game with a goal so quickly and I took advantage of the work Casiraghi did. He is working very very hard but not scoring goals. I know it must be a bit frustrating. All I can say about him is that he is such an important player because he works so hard for the team.' Zola, too, had suffered a dip in goalscoring form, but he might have had a double hat-trick if it hadn't been for Dave Beasant. 'I spoke with the goalkeeper afterwards and told him next time my shooting will be better. It was like a good training session for him.' Zola felt he wasn't striking the ball cleanly, 'but I congratulate him on his performance'.

Chelsea created so many chances it could have been double figures by the time Forest's Jean-Claude Darcheville scored in the sixty-eighth minute after Poyet had headed in the second in the thirty-fourth minute from a Zola corner headed on at the near post by Desailly, and then Babayaro at the far post. Suddenly Chelsea went to pieces. Steve Stone and then Darcheville had shots saved. An equaliser would have caused a bad reaction from an already stunned Chelsea crowd, but Vialli's team held out for their first win. Laudrup came on for the final couple of minutes, Lambourde replaced the tiring Poyet, but there was no sign of Flo.

SUNDAY, 13 SEPTEMBER
Niedzwiecki flew to Sweden to spy on Helsingborgs. They conceded a last -minute goal to leaders Hammarby, and failed to go top.

MONDAY, 14 SEPTEMBER
Ferrer and Di Matteo returned to training.

Luca dined out at Scallini's in Walton Street, just behind Harrods, one of the finest Italian restaurants in town and a favourite haunt of the footballing fraternity. Room-mates Petrescu and Poyet enjoy a night out at Scallini's. Dan's idea of a good night out is 'three hours in Scallini's to eat and then to a nightclub, Cafe De Paris'. The Petrescus live not far away in Chelsea Harbour. His idea of a bad night out would be 'going to the pub'.

Another favourite with the players at the time was Roberto's restaurant in the Fulham Road, La Perla. Babayaro said: 'My idea of a good night out is with Rob to Cafe De Paris or his restaurant, 'cause I don't have to pay no bills. He pays it all. Anywhere!' Celestine lives in a semi in Chiswick on his own. 'My friends all come around whenever they like and they do the cooking, or we eat at an African restaurant.'

Luca's favourite pasta is at San Lorenzo's in Beauchamp Place. With so much emphasis on food under Luca's regime, it's little wonder that Norwich director Delia Smith should name one of her recipes after the Blues' boss: Pasta Vialli. Delia's *How to Cook: Book One*, published by BBC Worldwide, contained this unusual tribute to Luca: 'This recipe is my adaptation of one I ate in the famous San Lorenzo Italian restaurant in Knightsbridge, which is apparently a favourite with the Chelsea Football Club players. This particular dish is named after famous Italian star player and manager Gianluca Vialli.'

TUESDAY, 15 SEPTEMBER

Zola was in sparkling form again in training, fully recovered from the misery of missing the World Cup. 'There was no reason to leave me out. I was one of the players who had contributed and done well in the past and I helped the team get to the World Cup. It was only a question of fitness. Okay, I wasn't in the best of form at times last season, but towards the end I was playing quite well and I showed my fitness was back. Now I'm not thinking about Italy; at the moment, I don't know if I want to play for them again. I do know that I'm ready to challenge again. I'm rested, recovered, and I have a lot of revenge to take in what is a very important year for me. I want to make this my best season.'

Zola was helped by the new fitness trainer. 'It's similar to work I used to do over in Italy, but there is also something new in what we are doing here, and I have to say, it's extremely effective. You can see nobody's got muscular problems so far, except Brian Laudrup in the first few days' training, so the work is good, the job is good and it's giving results.'

Zola was also discovering the subtle differences between Gullit and Vialli. 'The manager is asking more from the strikers, because in his opinion the defensive action starts from the strikers and he is asking us to work more when the opposition has got the ball. He is asking us to help the team to defend better so it is more work to do for us. But we are doing it with passion and I think we are coping with it very well.'

No team had ever successfully defended the European Cup Winners Cup, and among those who had tried and failed were Vialli and Poyet. Vialli was a runner-up with Sampdoria in 1989 and a winner in 1990, so he knows the pitfalls of defending a European trophy. 'There are two problems. When the opposition play against the holders they put in extra effort and make life very, very difficult. And you might not have the same hunger or anger – or both – having already won. This might be the challenge for our team.'

After training the players studied videos of the Swedish side. 'When you don't know one player from the other team you have to be careful,' Desailly said. 'Sometimes they have surprises.' They would try to hold out for a goalless draw or snatch an away goal on the counter-attack. Vialli said: 'We know enough about Helsingborgs not to be unaware of the problems they can cause us if we don't approach this game in the right way. Basically they will come here and play 5–4–1. They are very solid and will defend quite deep to keep a clean sheet. We have to make sure they don't score, for it will be much more difficult for us to turn the match around in the second leg. They might be part-timers, but because we are the holders of the trophy, every team will want to try and beat us even more. We will need all the support we can get.'

WEDNESDAY, 16 SEPTEMBER

Laudrup highlighted the frustrations of Chelsea's rotation system. He had made just one start, and only came on as an eighty-ninth-minute substitute during the win over Forest. After only five weeks at the club he made his feelings known to Vialli. 'I have been to a meeting with Vialli and the other forwards at the club. Vialli said that he regards us all as stars and that actually each of us should play every single time, but he would not give any guarantees to any of us. His message was that none of us can feel secure of a spot in the starting line-up, and of course that's a new situation for me that I have to get used to. I didn't like the same system at Milan, and the big danger is that some players might never find the right rhythm.'

Chelsea had failed to find their rhythm so far. Laudrup put that down to a lack of playing time for the team to gel together, and was desperate to get as much match practice as possible to prove his worth. 'I need all the playing time that I can possibly get right now because it was a big problem in my League debut that my team-mates didn't know me and I didn't know them. I was criticised for my debut, but please notice I played in a strange role in right midfield which is not my favourite space at all. I think that Vialli has already seen that the best space for me is as the free runner behind the forwards, like I played for Rangers and Denmark. Physically I am fit, but I lack a bit in timing and only playing big matches will help me now.'

Vialli had an almost full squad to choose from for the Helsingborgs match, with only Petrescu missing through suspension. Wise was available again after his three-match ban.

Preparations were complete for the opening of the club's first satellite to the Megastore in Guildford the following morning.

THURSDAY, 17 SEPTEMBER

Chelsea 1   Helsingborgs 0

After a disjointed display, flawed by much more than the mere missing of chances, Vialli justified his controversial rotation system with great reluctance. He switched to a 4–3–3 with Kharine in for the injured de Goey for his first start of the season, Desailly in defence, Wise returning, Laudrup starting and Vialli himself partnering Flo in attack, with Casiraghi relegated to the bench. 'There is no policy here about the strikers,' he insisted. 'I've got twenty-two players and plenty of matches this season. I don't want to end up in January with the situation where I have players injured and no replacements. It is about more than just eleven players. I have to make changes and I don't want to keep explaining this. The decisive time in the League comes in March, April and May and the way we do it nobody will be too tired.

'I am happy with this win because in Europe the standard of all the teams has improved and it is now a lot more difficult to see matches in which one team beats the other four or five nil. They will play with passion in the second leg and will try to catch us out from corners and set-pieces.'

Vialli made seven changes from the side that beat Forest, intent on rotating his squad in order to avoid fatigue. He picked himself for the first time since the opening day of the season. Zola did not even make the substitutes bench. His reshaped team once again struggled to live up to its billing. Possession was not an issue, though, as Chelsea dominated. According to Vialli, the failure to add to

Leboeuf's first-half penalty was a combination of the goalkeeper's endeavours, bad luck and a lack of composure in front of goal. But with Laudrup, Casiraghi in the second half and Vialli himself, fate and a part-time goalkeeper should not come into it.

How Casiraghi managed to keep the ball out of the net from three feet is a mystery. Di Matteo was more unfortunate when his second-half header was turned round a post. Chelsea saw plenty of the ball, but only once in the opening fifteen minutes did Sven Andersson have to make a save – a good one too, to keep out Vialli's header. Laudrup enjoyed himself starting a game for only the second time this season. The flicks, feints and darting runs were all there. But operating a flat back nine Helsingborgs simply got men behind the ball when defending, and sought out the jet-heeled Magnus Powell as early as possible when attacking.

If the goals did not flow as expected, there was no surprise at the first Chelsea name to go in the book – Wise (just back from suspension and promising to clean up his act), for an ugly lunge on Stig Johansen.

The team looked as if they didn't fancy it much, and judging by the attendance, neither did the Chelsea faithful. If Chelsea were expecting an easy night with which to begin the defence of the Cup Winners Cup, they were disappointed, because of the 17,714 spectators who turned up a good number wore Swedish colours, hoping for another night of gloating against English opposition. The club had contemplated concessionary prices, but abandoned the idea, as a five-pound reduction would have needed a 6000 crowd improvement just to break even. There had already been a lot of resentment over the increased season ticket prices, tickets which didn't include the European games.

FRIDAY, 18 SEPTEMBER

No game until Monday, so Vialli gave everyone a day off.

Luca didn't expect Chelsea's season to warm up until the winter. He became irritated by the bombardment of questions about his continual rotation of the squad and the decision to make seven changes for Helsingborgs that backfired.

Vialli planned more changes as his team sought their first away win of the season.

Chelsea had won only one Premiership game, but Vialli was not concerned. 'I am one of the managers who believes that the season starts seriously in December, January and February, and that's when we can be at our best. Look at what Arsenal did last season. In December, they were something like fifteen points behind Manchester United, so the decisive part of the season, in my opinion, starts then. Hopefully, when other teams are perhaps going down, we shall be improving.'

Vialli recalled de Goey and Zola, and Casiraghi was restored to the line-up with Flo relegated to substitute. Flo had dislocated two fingers in the game against Helsingborgs, but was fit to play. Petrescu also returned after serving a two-match suspension.

When asked how Zola felt about being dropped for the Helsingborgs game, Vialli simply replied he hadn't asked his former international team-mate. But Zola remained focused on assisting those players who had returned jaded from the World Cup. 'It was the same for me when I came back from Euro 96. It's very difficult at the beginning of the season because the other players are fitter than you and you need time to get back. The team can help them to get back quickly and we will support them when they are in difficulty.'

SATURDAY, 19 SEPTEMBER

Over £7000 worth of business reported in the Guildford Megastore; at one stage 500 people queued round the block. The opening day did £2000 of business. Chelsea's merchandising empire was in full growth.

SUNDAY, 20 SEPTEMBER

Speculation intensified that Flo was being lined up as a partner for Shearer. Flo's agent, Gunnar Martin Kjenner, told Norwegian newspaper *Dagbladet* that Gullit had been given the all-clear to make a bid if Chelsea were willing to sell. The figure quoted was 113 million kroner, which translated to £9.2m.

After training, the squad flew to Manchester at 4.30 p.m., only to sit on the runway for an hour waiting for take-off clearance.

MONDAY, 21 SEPTEMBER

Blackburn Rovers 3   Chelsea 4

At virtually any other club, Flo could be guaranteed a starting place in the next game after this match-winning performance – but not at Chelsea. Flo came off the bench with twelve minutes remaining at Ewood Park and scored twice in the final eight minutes to give Chelsea a stunning win after they had trailed 3–2 – the first time Chelsea have won at Ewood Park in the League for twenty-two years, and the highest score in forty-five games between the two clubs.

Vialli reflected on an incredible game, perhaps the defining moment in the early part of Chelsea's season. 'I attended one of the most exciting and amazing matches in my career, certainly in my career as a manager. It was gripping. At the end of the evening I must admit we were a little bit lucky, but we worked really hard to get the three points.'

Flo did more than anyone to make that happen as he celebrated his fiftieth Chelsea game. When Vialli was asked if Flo would start in the next game against Middlesbrough, he replied: 'No, not necessarily. Goals are very important but they are not the only thing I look at when I judge a striker. I look at what he does during a game, his dribbling and his running off the ball and things like that. It's their whole game I have to judge to get the whole picture. Gianfranco and Gigi did very well for seventy minutes at Blackburn and I would have to agree if you said they were our two best players on the pitch. They worked their socks off, caused all sorts of problems; Gianfranco scored a terrific goal and Gigi won a lot of important battles. It is a good headache to have, though.' Vialli was adamant he was not interested in selling Flo or any of his star names. 'No way, we can't let any of our strikers go. It's difficult for me to make a mistake when I pick from Gianfranco, Tore, Pierluigi and Brian. All of them are great and I think every manager in England would like to manage Chelsea when it comes to strikers.' So how will he decide on his strike pairing to face Boro? 'I'll draw lots,' he joked.

Blackburn's night started badly when record buy Kevin Davies reported sick with tonsillitis, giving Martin Dahlin a rare start. It was clear Flowers was in for an uncomfortable night from the moment Zola beat him with a twenty-five-yard free-kick after fifteen minutes. Flowers could have been distracted by Stephane Henchoz's insistence on guarding the goal instead of lining up in the wall as Zola prepared to take aim. Flowers flapped helplessly on his haunches as Zola curled the ball David Beckham style into the top right-hand corner. It didn't help, either, that Celestine Babayaro had embarked on a decoy run to catch Flowers' eye as well. And there was further misery for Flowers in the fiftieth minute when he needlessly conceded the penalty that gifted Chelsea their second. Flowers was on full alert at the sight of Zola trying to zip round him. He should have watched calmly and guided the ball over the by-line, such was the danger to his goal, but inexplicably he dived to extend a gloved hand which caught Zola's boot, and the Italian went tumbling in the box. Referee Peter Jones didn't flinch from pointing to the spot, and Leboeuf easily drove the ball home. Then the double in four fearsome minutes from substitute Flo finally finished Flowers off. The final whistle saw him trudge off, head down, with his white towel thrown over his shoulder.

But Blackburn had twice come back, and had actually taken the lead before Flo entered the field along with Laudrup as substitutes for the outstanding Zola and Casiraghi. Dahlin found himself in a tight corner in the twenty-second minute but somehow managed to force the ball across to Sutton who gleefully wrong-footed his old team-mate Le Saux, rolling his shot into de Goey's opposite corner for Blackburn's first goal. Blackburn drew level in the fifty-eighth minute when Flitcroft caught Leboeuf napping once more. He somehow managed to hook the ball back into play from the touchline, and Perez pounced for an equaliser.

Nine minutes later Perez was sent off for his part in a bust-up with Le Saux, who was also told to leave the field. Perez had been booked for a foul on Le Saux only three minutes earlier. Le Saux, who had refused to shake hands with Perez, was aggrieved that his shirt had been tugged, and he lashed out with a forearm smash which left the Blackburn man flattened, holding a bloodied nose. Referee Jones instantly showed the red card to Le Saux, and waited for Perez to finish having treatment before sending him off in disgrace too. Vialli tried to defend Le Saux's petulance, under pressure from the fans' reaction to the way he left Blackburn a year ago, and from the snappy tackles of Perez. 'In Graeme's opinion the referee exaggerated it a little bit. He did not think anything was wrong. All the matches in England are very physical and quick with plenty of tackles, so sometimes you get in trouble. Graeme is such a fair player.'

Duberry brought down Dahlin in a seventy-ninth-minute lunge, and up stepped Sutton to slam Blackburn back into the lead, but four minutes later the Flo show began. Fellow substitute Laudrup appeared from nowhere to cross for Flo, who poked the ball past a stranded Flowers to make it 3–3, and then Flo raced clear with three minutes left, lucky not to be penalised by a linesman's offside flag. Flowers came, then stopped in his tracks as he became unsighted in a rush of bodies. Flo stuck the ball into the bottom corner for an amazing winner. In fact, Flo could have ended up with a hat-trick when Laudrup picked him out once more in the final seconds, but Flowers' instinctive one-handed save kept the Norwegian for once at bay.

Blackburn manager Roy Hodgson saw red over the match official's handling of the game: 'If this was Old Trafford or Stamford Bridge the referee would not have got out of the ground. Perez was sent off for the misfortune of putting his nose in the way of someone else's elbow. The penalty was unlucky too. Gianfranco Zola is very good at that; a keeper like Tim Flowers isn't going to pull him down in the area. Once again I feel somewhat aggrieved that a good performance has brought zero points.'

Chelsea's win took them level with Manchester United, looking upwards again, while Rovers were locked in the bottom three.

TUESDAY, 22 SEPTEMBER

Vialli was dismayed by his players being labelled greedy mercenaries in the *Gazzetta dello Sport*, and fed up at seeing his selection policy constantly questioned.

Normally the most relaxed of managers, he let his true feelings emerge in his home country's sports newspapers. 'I wish the media would concentrate more on our merits. I can't find out the root causes why, but it is a fact that we are not getting the credit we deserve. The media have stuck an unpleasant label on us. Whenever they talk about Chelsea they call us a team of multi-millionaire mercenaries and say none of us can speak English. We don't deserve that at all. We are a squad of world-class professionals. We are in London because we like it here, but also to take our work seriously. We are not a circus.'

Le Saux's old pals at Blackburn were furious that his forearm smash into the face of Perez had left him with a swollen, bloody nose. Le Saux's an avid *Guardian* reader off the pitch, an art collector and university graduate with a refined Channel Islands background that makes him a founder member of soccer's culture club. Once he pulls on a shirt, though, Le Saux can turn into Mr Nasty. He has only been sent off twice in his career, but he has been booked thirty times in 160 Premiership games. He broke two fingers landing a left hook on to team-mate David Batty's chin during their pitch bust-up in Moscow three years ago while both played for Blackburn. Blackburn's Garry Flitcroft said: 'You don't go round punching people. When you go into a tackle you have to show the aggression then. He deserved to get sent off for punching someone like that. But he's such a nice bloke off the pitch. A great lad. He has such a different personality when he steps out on to the pitch. OK, he got stick from the crowd because of the way he left us, but you have to put up with that. Sebastien [Perez] didn't say much, but he was down in the dressing room. He just got dressed and went. He was gutted.'

Despite these controversies at the club, this was a day off. Wise went for a scan on his knee injury, but it showed no ligament damage.

In the evening it was time for Luca to unwind with his players. 'I went to see Simply Red. I had one of the best nights of my life. They are my favourite band and they sang my favourite songs of the last ten years. I was dancing, singing and looking back at my youth. They brought back great memories. So I feel much better now!'

Then it was dinner at Michael Caine's restaurant, The Canteen, in Chelsea Harbour, organised by Dennis Wise. The bill, with little change from a grand, was paid by those late for training. Dennis the Menace ensured that 'Casi, Franco and

Frank' all paid up. Wise said: 'Franco got clamped. He still thinks you're allowed to park on double yellow lines. Not only did Franco have to pay for his clamping, but for our meal as well. That'll teach him to be late.'

WEDNESDAY, 23 SEPTEMBER

Supporter Felicity Harris turned up at the training ground with a cake she had baked for Dennis, but the skipper insisted she present it to Luca and birthday boy Antonio Pintus. After gym work and before outdoor stretches she carved up some cake and handed it out, then made a speech congratulating the players on their win at Blackburn, followed by kisses for the scorers.

More food later that evening. The new Venetian resturant Canaletto opened in the East Stand in the Chelsea Village complex. Luca and his Italian contingent were present at the special charity gala dinner (guests were charged £1000 a ticket) in the presence of the bald Italian ambassador – a soul-mate for Luca! Richard Attenborough also attended. The Italians signed a shirt which was auctioned for £4600. A cheque for more than £20,000 was on its way to the Venetian Peril Appeal.

Luca gave his chairman the perfect plug for the new venture. 'An Italian restaurant with Italian food, Italian chef, and Italian style. It's another part of Italy being brought to England. As someone involved closely in the club, I'm happy to see the transformation of Stamford Bridge getting further and further towards its end.'

THURSDAY, 24 SEPTEMBER

Mick McGiven flew to Helsingborgs to see them lose at home by two Malmo penalties.

Petit's *Daily Mirror* column all but wrote off Chelsea's championship chances. 'Chelsea have many fantastic players, and I believe they will do well this season, but when I read that Brian Laudrup is unhappy not being in the team, when I see the team change every game, and that Marcel Desailly is a defender one week and a midfielder the next, I know it is not the recipe for a championship success.'

FRIDAY, 25 SEPTEMBER

Vialli chose the eve of his side's clash with Middlesbrough's cosmopolitan clan of Teessiders to respond again to snide remarks about the lack of Anglo-Saxon blood in Chelsea's dressing room. His anger had been fuelled by Hodgson's insinuations about Zola's dive for a penalty; then Forest manager Dave Bassett accused Vialli of being 'touchy' over his foreign contingent.

Vialli raged: 'After the way we came back from 3–2 down with six minutes to go at Blackburn, I know my players possess the famous fighting spirit everyone talks about in England. We have won four trophies in less than eighteen months and I think my players deserve more respect for their achievements. But too much of the talk about Chelsea is about our so-called millionaire players and lazy foreigners, a team which plays nice football but is not tough enough or good enough to compete in the Premiership. It is wrong to generalise about players like that. I know most people over here think English football is the best in the world, but it's important for the game that some foreigners come over here and raise the overall standard. It's not right to think that, because they are foreigners, then there must be something wrong with them – either they must be cheats, lazy, fat, mercenary or have the wrong attitude because they are crazy. I don't like it when a player of Gianfranco Zola's ability is called a cheat.'

Poyet and Ferrer attended the pre-match press conference, Gus keeping the media amused by hiding under the table when Albert complained about not having been able to get him on the telephone for advice about England before moving!

Wise was recovering faster than expected from his knee injury.

Gullit dropped any notion of trying to sign Flo, knowing the wisdom of not pushing for any players at his old club. 'I won't be moving for Tore,' he said. 'But then I won't be trying to sign any other player from Chelsea either. It's just my own principle. I don't want to give anyone a reason to say I demolished the team I built at Chelsea.'

SATURDAY, 26 SEPTEMBER
Chelsea 2   Middlesbrough 0

In his matchday programme notes, Luca stressed: 'I don't know anything about our record at home to Middlesbrough and I don't care. I just want to beat them and keep this good run going. Everyone knows it won't be easy. We've played so many matches in a short time and they have all been quite physically and mentally demanding. Middlesbrough have a very good team with some great individual players.' He made the point that to ensure the win at Blackburn wasn't a 'waste of time' the team had to make it count in this game.

Also in the programme Zola declared his intention to score by lobbing the keeper, and he was as good as his word, supplying a sublime finish to Poyet's pass. Zola was again proving indispensable after being axed for Chelsea's only defeat of the season, their opening-day blow-out at Coventry. He said: 'It was something I knew was going to happen some day. I'd been looking forward to executing a goal like that and now I've done it. That moment completed a very good game for me.' Zola sent a special message to twelve-year-old fan Dale Franklin, who had sent him a hand-made woollen doll, complete with the number twenty-five on the back. 'Since it arrived three weeks ago I haven't stopped scoring. I'll have to make sure I pack it with my luggage when we go to Sweden.' Vialli couldn't praise Zola enough: 'Franco is a very proud man with incredible enthusiasm. He always wants to be the best.'

On his Middlesbrough debut in last season's League Cup final, Gazza was lucky to stay on the pitch after trampling on Zola and Wise in a violent cameo as substitute. And of eight yellow cards dished out by Birmingham referee Mike Reed today, only Gascoigne's gratuitous hack at Zola in first-half stoppage time truly smacked of malevolence. Zola, the perfect gentleman, forgave Gazza his crass indiscretion, shaking hands on the final whistle and adding: 'Gazza was only trying to get the ball but he found a wall in front of him. Me! He apologised for the challenge after the match and we were friends again. There is nothing wrong with being passionate and aggressive on the pitch, and though he plays it hard, he is not nasty.'

That foul summed up Gascoigne's afternoon of frustration as Chelsea's all-star team took the ball off him as easily as candy off a baby. On one of the rare occasions he threatened any damage, Zola tracked back to dispossess him and, when the Sardinian wizard was speeding into Boro's box a few seconds later, poor old Gazza was miles adrift, puffing over the halfway line.

Chelsea, who were keen to buy Gazza when Hoddle was in charge at the Bridge, witnessed the awakening of Laudrup's season. It was his cross, forty-three seconds after the restart, that the otherwise faultless Gary Pallister glanced expertly past his own keeper to give Chelsea their second goal.

MONDAY, 28 SEPTEMBER

Wise returned to training, but his knee was still troubling him.

Europe's leading professional soccer leagues boycotted January's controversial Confederations Cup in Mexico. 'The professional leagues have decided that they will not take part,' said Jean-Marie Philips, director of the Belgian professional soccer league. 'We know it may have consequences, sanctions ... [but] we'll go all the way ... there will be no players from European leagues who will be made available for this competition. We're not declaring war on FIFA. It's the clubs who pay the players and who will have to make them available with all the inconveniences that poses.' The only 'spontaneous candidacy' from Europe had come from France, Philips said. 'We replied cynically, but with a bit of humour, that in any case the French championship would not be hampered because the players who would take part compete in Italy, England, Germany or Spain. Other countries would suffer.' The French League said it might reconsider its decision.

TUESDAY, 29 SEPTEMBER

Stamford the Lion found! The club mascot had gone missing after the Forest game, believed stolen, and the theft was reported to police. It turned up in a cardboard box outside Sky TV's Isleworth headquarters addressed to Tim Lovejoy, presenter of Sky's Saturday morning football show *Soccer AM*, and a Chelsea fan.

An important stage in Luca's fitness regime was the opening of the massive new gym in the second week of September. Vialli explained the move in greater detail: 'If you think about modern football, you need players with skill and fighting spirit. As a manager I felt we needed to improve on our fitness. I don't want to be paranoid, but it was something that needed doing. So we have now our new fitness coach, Antonio Pintus, who is working alongside Ade Mafe. They are getting on well together – almost too well off the pitch! And we have improved our facilities by extending our gymnasium. It is bigger, has more machines, and has more room for players to work out. It's easier to work on our fitness now. And the way in which the players have approached the physcial part of training has been spot on, and that helps our two fitness coaches big-time. It's important that the players do what we tell them to do, but it's even more important that they believe in it. At the moment they have seen the advantages that improvement of physical condition can bring them, and they have had some good results. I'm happy to be listening to the players after a few matches into the season saying that they could go for even longer at the end of a game, they could keep running for longer at the same speed. As we say in Italy, they have the spring that makes you work.'

WEDNESDAY, 30 SEPTEMBER

Luca pitched in to the Paolo Di Canio row. The Sheffield Wednesday midfield player had retreated to Rome after being charged with misconduct by the FA over the referee-shoving storm, and had been threatened with an Eric Cantona-length ban. Vialli claimed his countryman was a victim of double standards, inferring that the witch hunt against Di Canio had racial undertones, as well as accusing Sheffield Wednesday boss Danny Wilson of undermining the player's temperament by branding Di Canio 'a fancy dan'.

Vialli, without defending Di Canio's actions, felt the outrageous shove on referee Paul Alcock had been greeted with hysteria compared to a similar incident involving England midfielder David Batty last May, when Batty was handed an extra one-match ban for manhandling FIFA official David Elleray in Newcastle's defeat at Blackburn. 'No one talked about that. He was given a couple of extra games' ban and that was that. Now people are talking about nine months, a life ban, no more games in England. Because he was English, and Di Canio is not English, they are treating the two cases differently.'

This was the Vialli sequel to his earlier claim that his cast of foreign stars were not shown enough respect. He believes foreign players can get a raw deal. 'Maybe it's the English attitude, but over here foreigners are treated differently sometimes. We talk too much about the bad influences they bring English football and not enough about the positive aspects. If you want to be fair, you have to look at everything that is relevant. Di Canio was put under pressure by his own manager, who kept saying he was not tough enough to cope with English football. When you are put under pressure by someone that close to you, you can end up reacting the wrong way.'

Zola also had a point of view: 'He made a mistake and he should be punished. But sometimes there are a few seconds out there when you are not in control. That happened to him, and I know he is sorry for it.'

But Vialli had a more pressing worry than Di Canio's treatment: Casiraghi had gone 607 minutes without a goal. 'I can't even remember the last goal I scored in competitive football,' Casiraghi groaned. 'All I know is that it was for Lazio towards the end of last season, which is a long time ago. But the manager has said he will not judge me on goalscoring alone, which is just as well – although I do feel I am contributing to the team in other ways. We are unbeaten since the first day of the season, which means we must be performing well as a team and doing something right. Of course, with every match that passes and I haven't scored, I pray, please let it be next time.'

Brian Little issued a timely warning for Vialli ahead of the second leg with Helsingborgs. The Swedish team had knocked out Aston Villa two seasons before. 'They are charming people. But don't be fooled by all this part-time stuff. Helsingborgs are very professional, very careful, and know exactly what they are doing. It might be a small, quiet fishing town but they revel in beating English sides. Our football is very big all over Scandinavia, and to get the better of an English club is a prize to be had. The first thing we found when we got to their ground was that they had made the pitch a lot smaller to make it that much more difficult for us to find a way through. Would little part-timers do that? I don't think so.'

Vialli gave a late fitness test to skipper Dennis Wise, who missed the win over Middlesbrough with the bruised knee sustained at Blackburn ten days earlier.

At Malmo airport the players were fascinated by Marcel's new gadget, a portable video machine.

Chelsea were roared on by five coachloads from their own Swedish supporters' club who were making the 400-mile trip from Stockholm.

October...
October...
October

'Reserves' inflict biggest win at Highbury for seventy-three years ... the end of Aston Villa's long unbeaten run with a Luca hat-trick

THURSDAY, I OCTOBER

Helsingborgs 0   Chelsea 0

Vialli's 'Euro' attack drew a blank as the player-manager selected himself and Flo, leaving out in-form Zola, Casiraghi and Laudrup, and it nearly backfired. Chelsea scraped through against a team composed mainly of students. Not surprisingly, Chelsea looked disjointed.

Casiraghi's removal to the bench gave Flo a rare chance, but his service from the flanks was poor. Vialli's decision to pick himself was more predictable. His six goals in the Cup Winners Cup last season had catapulted him to third in the club's all-time Euro scoring charts. But his only contribution in this game was a monotonous propensity for straying offside. In fact, it was twenty-three minutes before a shot was registered, and even then Di Matteo's left-footer carried little venom.

At the back, acting skipper Leboeuf looked out of sorts, especially in the air, and from the Swedes' sixth corner of the night Chelsea enjoyed a lucky escape. Anild Stavrum, the leading scorer in Swedish football, teased de Goey with a wicked corner kick and Peter Wibran – whose goal had put paid to Villa in the UEFA Cup in 1996 – stabbed his shot against the foot of a post. That, briefly, gave Helsingborgs the scent of an upset, and when Leboeuf made a complete hash of clearing his lines, Magnus Powell's first-time shot fizzed alarmingly close to the same upright. As Vialli and Flo made little headway, Poyet wasted the holders' best chance of a goal. The Uruguayan midfielder rose unmarked to meet Di Matteo's corner, but headed tamely wide.

Vialli offered no excuses, but he was unrepentant, denying his selections were a symptom of his club treating Europe as second-rate. 'There's no way you can win anything if you're not solid, so I'm reasonably satisfied we did our jobs tonight. We know we can play much better, and we hoped Helsingborgs would come out more so we could get behind them. But we were not positive enough on the edge of the box. We always try to play our best team. This is an important competition, and we still want to do well in it, especially as we are the holders. But we do have another big match at Liverpool on Sunday.' Vialli had fluffed a chance to make the tie safe in the very last minute; he joked: 'I miscontrolled the ball and I hope to do better next time – if the manager picks me!'

Ruud Gullit's Newcastle crashed out of Europe in Belgrade.

Flo finally set a price on his Chelsea career by threatening to quit to safeguard his international place. The Norwegian World Cup star, who had yet to start a Premiership game this season, expected to be dumped back on the bench for the trip to Liverpool. 'Obviously there may come a point when I'll have to consider my position,' he said. Only the indulgence of new Norway coach Nils Johan Semb stopped Flo demanding clarification of his place from Vialli. The twenty-five-year-old striker had been in regular contact with Semb about his frustrating bit-part among Vialli's expensive assembly of Euro-stars. So far, Semb has tolerated Vialli's pick-and-mix tinkering at the expense of Norwegian football's golden boy, but the ceasefire may not hold out much longer.

Flo, a £300,000 signing now valued at a modest £25 million by Ken Bates, warned: 'Luca tells me I am a good player, but he has gone out and picked other strikers. I've got to accept that, but I've been talking to the Norwegian coach about it. He says the situation is okay for now and told me to fight my way back into the side. But I don't know how long that can go on for and we'll just have to wait and see if I can manage to get a starting place. I would prefer to be Chelsea's number one striker than go anywhere else, and Luca says I have a good future here. But I haven't started a Premiership game yet this season and, of course, I want to be involved in those as well.'

While Vialli's all-Italian partnership looked sure to get the nod for the Liverpool game, his French foreign legion was facing its biggest test yet against Michael Owen. Graeme Le Saux admitted that Owen's tilt at his French team-mates and Chelsea's ability to shake off the ring-rust from the goalless excursion to Sweden would be key areas. 'Michael is a difficult player to harness and that will be one of our priorities. He's so quick out of the blocks that, even if you give him only half a yard, he could be gone. We have only a few days to get the fatigue of a long haul to Sweden out of our system, and that may give Liverpool an advantage because they have had more time to recover since their game on Tuesday night.'

The team travelled home from a different airport an hour away, and there was a delay, so out came the cards. Luca, Ed, Graeme and Kevin got in a few games in the corner of the tiny airport.

FRIDAY, 2 OCTOBER

Successful times again for Zola. He was presented with the *Evening Standard* Footballer of the Month award. The only downside was a kiss from Dennis Wise for the photographers as Zola posed with his handsome bronze statuette and magnum of Moët Chandon champagne.

Zola was so committed to the Blues that he shelled out for an artificial plywood wall so he could carry on practising free-kicks at the training ground. The old row of dummies had taken too much of a battering and Zola, who practises around

150 free-kicks a week in training, was having a replacement built. 'It's going to cost around six hundred pounds and Franco is willing to pay for it,' said Gwyn Williams. On the field, Roberto organises Chelsea's defensive wall. 'The manager gave me that responsibility,' he said. 'I have to be in touch with the goalkeeper and he tells me where to put the wall. The goalkeeper decides how many go in it. The manager has decided before the game who goes in it, so we all know. It depends who is playing, but usually we try to put the same people in so we get used to it straight away. Apart from me, we have tall guys in it to stop the ball going over us. It's always a big fight from the point of view of opponents standing in front of you. You have to be strong. It depends who is taking the free-kick whether we jump or not. Some you know like to take it over the wall, so you jump; if someone touches it to the side you'll need someone to run out of the wall. You have to be determined. If the ball is hit at you strongly, it does hurt sometimes!'

Chelsea were handed another Scandinavian mission in the second-round draw against Danish dark horses FC Copenhagen. Chelsea switched venues for the first leg.

The Blues had been due to travel to Denmark on 22 October, but Brondby were due to face Manchester United at home in the Champions League the night before, and both Danish clubs use the same stadium so they agreed with the Danish club that the game would be played instead at Stamford Bridge. Only 17,714 had turned out for the opening tie at the Bridge against Helsingborgs, and Wise wanted better support to answer the critics who had devalued the tournament. 'I don't know what some people want. We beat a very good European team, but all we hear is that the Cup Winners Cup doesn't matter any more. I don't remember anyone saying that when Arsenal or Manchester United won the thing. We had it when we won the FA Cup and the Coca-Cola Cup as well, and it was the same in Europe. It's almost as if the press don't want Chelsea to win trophies. The British press should get more behind the British teams in Europe.' Wise was unhappy too with criticism over the first-round win. 'We know we didn't play well in those two games, but we never looked like conceding. Not playing well and winning 1–0 is the sign of a good team when someone else does it. I bet Newcastle wish they had got a boring 0–0 in their game against Belgrade.'

Dennis might not be as well travelled as some of the international stars, but he has learned from Chelsea's foreign imports. 'I used to come in and have my sausage breakfast and Ruud couldn't believe it. Now I know how important proper diet, proper exercise, preparation and so on is to a footballer. It's not really making you play better, it's about making you fitter and more able to play the game for longer. I know it's doing me good and might put a couple of years on the end of my career. Don't worry, I still believe in the get-stuck-in way of doing things. Chelsea's improvement is mostly down to the standard of foreigners that have come over here. They've improved us and they've improved themselves as well. The place has taken off thanks to Batesy putting his money where his mouth is and building a great team and a great stadium. It would be a disaster to let it slip now.'

SATURDAY, 3 OCTOBER

Flo was axed again from Sunday's game. He'd scored a total of seventeen goals from twenty-five starts and twenty-six sub appearances. Casiraghi, on the other hand, had failed to open his account.

Chelsea travelled to Merseyside less than three days after their return from Sweden, an exact repeat of last season, when Chelsea returned from their first-round second-leg victory at Slovan Bratislava early on Friday, played at Anfield on the Sunday, and were promptly demolished 4–2. This time, with Leboeuf and Desailly starting to give the side the solid backbone boss Vialli has been crying out for, they travel with more hope, although Liverpool have had an extra two days to recover from European exertions.

The Blues had not lost since the opening day of the season, despite failing to find top gear. Le Saux said: 'Even in the League, we've already noticed that sides coming to Stamford Bridge are defending very deep against us. That's something that any good side has to cope with, and it's up to us to have enough guile and skill to open up teams. We're winning games, but still not quite punishing teams in the way we should. It would be frustrating if we were losing or drawing games, but as long as you're winning and creating chances then that's the key.'

Liverpool, with only one point and seven goals conceded in their last three Premiership games, had been bitterly disappointed that Desailly turned them down for Chelsea and the bright lights of London. Boss Gerard Houllier said: 'Liverpool had an interest in Marcel, but I know his agent very well and he preferred to go to London for family reasons. I gave him his first cap when I was in charge of the French team. He is a good footballer. He's strong, quick, comfortable on the ball and good in the air. He can play in midfield, but I believe he is better as a central defender. I think Chelsea will play Marcel alongside Frank Leboeuf in defence to try and stop Owen, and I'm excited about the confrontation of our strikers against France's World Cup-winning defensive pair. It will be like a match within a match.'

SUNDAY, 4 OCTOBER

Liverpool I   Chelsea I

Casiraghi's first Premiership goal could be the start of something big, according to Vialli, who has stuck by his £5.4m record signing through a troubled spell during which he has looked like an expensive flop. Vialli was clearly delighted by Casiraghi's first strike, saying: 'Pierluigi was playing really well, was working hard, doing a lot of things for the team, making great runs. Unfortunately he couldn't score. Now, after what happened this afternoon I hope and believe he will be in the scoresheet more often. Strikers are always measured on the amount of goals they score, so for him to get his first one in England will help his confidence.'

Anfield was a lucky ground for Gigi: he scored twice there for Italy against Russia in the Euro 96 finals. And he certainly showed a cool head today. Di Matteo's long ball from virtually the halfway line arced gracefully over the Liverpool defence, to allow Casiraghi to gallop like a young colt towards the goal. The forward may not have scored all season, but his touch had not yet deserted him. It was exquisite as he brought the ball down in one movement, cruising into possession, took the ball round the onrushing David James and calmly angled it into an empty net.

Phil Babb injured himself colliding with a post as he tried to scoop the ball away. The Irishman lasted just two more minutes before he was replaced by Dominic Matteo, clearly hampered by the injury. At another stage Casiraghi even tried an ambitious shot from forty yards that flashed inches wide.

But all Chelsea's good work was undone by Jamie Redknapp's late equaliser from a free-kick won by the effervescent Fowler, who was dragged down on the edge of the box by Leboeuf. Vialli said: 'I can't blame Ed for that because Redknapp is very good at free-kicks. The draw was a fair result as Liverpool worked really hard in the second half. To give them credit, they kept trying, trying and trying.'

With Babayaro away on international duty, Vialli had reverted to three at the back for the first time, and Chelsea had exerted a vice-like grip on much of the game. Chelsea last played the system in the 3–1 defeat at Leeds the previous April. After the four at the back all season, it was a surprise switch, but Rix explained: 'We decided Owen and Fowler were the danger men and the best way to combat them was to go man-for-man marking, leaving Frank Leboeuf as free as possible as often as possible. Fowler had a couple of half-chances but never got a shot in at Ed de Goey, and Michael Owen did nothing. That's all credit to Michael Duberry and Albert Ferrer. He was outstanding. Barcelona tended to play with three markers and a sweeper, so he'd done man-marking before. I'd asked Gus about it and he'd told me he was capable of doing that.'

The strategy, hatched by Luca, was to play three up, spearheaded by Casiraghi, with Laudrup supporting on the right, Zola on the left. Rix continued: 'It was basically 3–4–3. We said to Brian and Franco, while you've got freedom when we've got the ball, you've got a certain amount of responsibility when Liverpool have it. They needed to block off their full-backs. Then everyone else could do the rest behind them.' But as the game progressed it became increasingly 5–3–2, with Petrescu and Le Saux alongside the back three, first Zola dropping deep, then Poyet. Rix explained: 'Liverpool are no mugs, you have to treat them with respect. McAteer likes to push on and Heggem, when he came on, launched himself forward. I was delighted. Graeme got near to Leonhardsen and Dan to Berger. We worked really hard, defended well and tackled well.'

Albert Ferrer was named Man of the Match.

MONDAY, 5 OCTOBER

In-form Zola and Di Matteo hoped for recalls against Switzerland in the Euro 2000 qualifiers, but Zoff ignored them, along with Casiraghi, leaving Chelsea a refuge for Italian discards. Zola was again disappointed, but Casiraghi didn't really expect a recall: 'No, not now. I think they want to do a national team for the next World Cup and they want young players.'

Whatever disappointment Casiraghi felt was tempered by the relief of his first goal for Chelsea, ending 618 minutes of famine. 'Although I was often playing as a lone striker up front against Liverpool, and it was hard work, I enjoyed myself and we can be happy with our performance and a point. I felt well physically, and now also mentally I feel better. The ball was at an angle and it was not very easy. Because it was my first goal in the Premiership – I wait six or seven matches for it – I was very happy so I went to the Chelsea fans. It is different in Italy: the people, the fans, are not near the pitch, so this is the first time I touch them. I've always wanted to do it. It's very nice.' He had already been dubbed the new Hughes. 'I hope I can play like Mark Hughes. I love Mark because he was a very great player. I saw him when he played in Manchester and so I know him very well.' A month earlier Gigi would have struggled with such an interview, but his English had improved appreciably. 'Now I want to speak better because now it is not very good. I started to learn in Italy at the school, but only one hour a week, you couldn't learn English very well. I am very happy playing in London and with Chelsea. London is very nice so I have no problem.'

Le Saux was ordered to calm down by Hoddle after his tunnel flare-up with England team-mate Paul Ince. Hoddle said: 'I have spoken to Graeme about it and he has to calm down. I am not too much concerned about what happened although we need to make sure it doesn't happen in the future. If it happened down the tunnel at Wembley then I'd deal with it. But I've not spoken to Paul and until then I won't know all the ins and outs.' Later it would emerge that there was no punch-up with Ince. Informed sources suggested that Ince started it by mouthing off and chasing up to Graeme, who responded in kind.

Le Saux's boot deal with Adidas came to an end; the sportswear firm wanted to concentrate on the game's youngsters. He was playing with the brand logo on his boots blacked out. An Adidas spokesman said: 'So many of the top players think there is a bottomless pit of money. This is not true. Graeme was brilliant for us but we have decided to place our future with the new lads coming through, players like West Ham's Joe Cole.'

TUESDAY, 6 OCTOBER

UEFA decided to axe the Cup Winners Cup and expand the Champions League in an attempt to avert the formation of a European Super League. The executive committee of European football's governing body agreed to merge the Cup Winners Cup with the UEFA Cup and enlarge the Champions League to thirty-two teams from the 2000–01 season. UEFA's new proposal offered £370 million, with the winners pocketing between £27.5 million and £37 million. The details of the new formats and the crucial financial rewards for teams would be officially announced at the next executive committee meeting in December in Jerusalem. It was expected England could have three teams in the Champions League: the Premiership winners and runners-up (automatically), with the third-place side having to qualify.

Manchester United, Arsenal, Liverpool and other major European clubs admitted they held discussions with Media Partners International about the proposed league, which promised huge pay-outs from TV revenues for the clubs taking part. UEFA had reacted quickly to quell the breakaway, with general secretary Gerhard Aigner addressing a meeting of the twenty Premiership chairmen last month. He assured the clubs that UEFA was willing to restructure its competitions and, more importantly, would do so in such a way as to bring in more money for the clubs. That brought an assurance from the Premiership chairmen that all talks on the subject would in future be conducted collectively through the Premier League, as well as a 'unanimous' objection to a breakaway, with most clubs apparently keen to stay under UEFA's jurisdiction.

MONDAY, 12 OCTOBER

Laudrup's patience with Vialli's rotation system was stretched thin. 'When I first discussed terms with Chelsea in February, nobody told me about this system. I don't like it. Whenever I play and feel as though I have done well, I don't know if I will play the next game. What I need to maintain a good level of fitness is to play all the time.' Laudrup was not allowed to play reserve games in case he picked up an injury. 'I have experienced this kind of thing before, of course. Five years ago, when I was at AC Milan, the coach, Fabio Capello, also rotated his players and I hated it. Yet now the same thing is happening to me at Chelsea. I was always brought up to believe that if you have a team that is winning, you stick with those players until something goes wrong.'

Laudrup had already had one clear-the-air meeting with Vialli after he and Zola were left out of the starting line-up for the European game with Helsingborgs. They had confronted their manager and were promised that they would be selected for the Premiership clash at Anfield. 'Of course I can understand it if players who get tired are given a rest, or if the team is changed around because of pressure of matches. But it is still early in the season and no one should be feeling physical or mental strain right now.' Most annoying of all for Laudrup was the knowledge that Vialli's system generally applied only to the forward players. 'One of the worst aspects is that when you sit down for the announcement of the team you know that seven or eight of the players in the room are pretty sure they will be playing. They are defenders and most of the midfielders. But it is very difficult when you build yourself up for the game all week and then, only an hour before kick-off, you are told that you are not playing.'

Vialli was clearly miffed by such moaning. 'I'm a bit unhappy about the limitless articles in the newspapers about our rotation system. I have warned the players what the media are trying to do with us, that they try to help make the atmosphere unrestful. We have to be clever, mature, and despite it being difficult sometimes to keep all our feelings inside. I say to the players, let's talk to each other rather than publicise disappointment or unhappiness. Atmosphere, spirit, inner strength, desire for victory and cleverness are more important sometimes than tactics, technique and fitness. We need to keep this in mind.'

TUESDAY, 13 OCTOBER

Lambourde was on the look-out for another English club as he saw no way of breaking into Vialli's side when even superstars like Flo couldn't get in. Lambourde had started just once this season, against Arsenal, and had only seen first-team action sixteen times since his £1.6m move from Bordeaux. He said: 'It's impossible for me to stay on the bench for another two years, which is the length of my contract. I would like to stay in England, why not? If another club is interested and there is a good deal then I would listen to what they have to say. But I suppose it's hard for me to complain when the likes of poor Flo are also sitting on the bench. It's disappointing bearing in mind what I had hoped for originally, but there is nothing I can do in the meanwhile except work hard and do my best.'

Jody Morris won his first cap in two years for England Under-21s when he came on for the last fifteen minutes in the 1–0 win over Bulgaria at Upton Park.

WEDNESDAY, 14 OCTOBER

As England beat Luxembourg 3–0 with the pressure on Hoddle, most of Luca's players were away on international duty. 'We needed and deserved a weekend break,' he said. 'It has allowed us to recharge our batteries, to wind down a little, but also to train as hard as ever. We should be able to cope with the number of important matches we have to play in a short space of time. Unfortunately – or fortunately; I don't know which way I should be feeling – we've had many people away with internationals and they haven't had a break at all.' Some players returned the next day, but some only the day before the next match, leaving only Friday for training with the entire squad. 'Sometimes I think it's difficult for the manager when he gets the whole team just a day before a game. It's a bit strange. It's difficult for the player too to switch focus. Fingers crossed, we can all cope with the situation now and in the future.'

Chelsea have always jokingly said that their tiny players like Zola and Wise should be able to double up as jockeys. So what better than for the football club to buy a few horses and start a racing club? Zola and Wise posed alongside Frankie Dettori at Ascot to launch the project. Zola went racing for the first time at Ascot last month, taking his wife and two children along with him. He loved every minute of it, despite being surrounded by autograph hunters as he made his way from the paddock to the stands. Wise has long been a fan of racing and, in particular, the talents of Dettori, even if all his efforts to convert the Arsenal fan have failed. Wise became a director of the racing club, and was genuinely excited about the project. 'It's great for our fans. If they support the racing club like they do the football club we'll have some terrific horses and some good fun.'

Speaking the same language is always a help, and Gianfranco got on famously with Frankie, who agreed to ride for the club as often as he could. Both their families hail from Sardinia, but it was the soggy winners' enclosure at Ascot which hosted the first meeting of the two Italian sporting legends. The two men, who share a similar height and superstar status, hit it off big-time, according to the man who introduced them, Gary Pinchen, a director of Chelsea Village plc, the holding company of the football team. 'They both wanted to meet and Frankie was riding for me that day so it seemed the ideal opportunity. They got on really well. Gianfranco must have signed about two hundred autographs but he had a fabulous time.'

The plan with the racing club was to involve 2500 Chelsea fans who would own six horses between them for a two-year fee of £200. It's the idea of Gary Pinchen and Alan Shaw, who as company secretary at Chelsea Village was already planning a number of racing-related events at Stamford Bridge. Pinchen has had horses in training for years, including one in partnership with Wise that can only be described as useless – and that's being charitable. One of the first horses was called Frank Leboeuf.

THURSDAY, 15 OCTOBER

Wise a future coach at the Bridge! Vialli envisaged him as the perfect replacement for Steve Clarke. Wise told his boss he wanted to concentrate all his efforts on winning more trophies as a player for this season at least. At the age of thirty-one he had two more years on his playing contract. 'I have always been interested in becoming a coach but I've got a few playing years left in me. I love it at Chelsea and I want to see my career out here. I was happy when I signed my latest contract and I'm just as happy now. I've won four cups in fifteen months and I think there are more to come.'

Vialli and Wise have been friends ever since the Italian arrived in London. Vialli has never forgotten how Dennis persuaded him into staying when he was left on the bench by Gullit.

FRIDAY, 16 OCTOBER

Luca was concerned about the tidal wave of cash sweeping through the English game, making it more difficult to motivate players. He frequently gave team talks to nearly a dozen millionaires and he believed the huge financial rewards in the game can make some players lose their hunger. Looking ahead to the game with Charlton – whose players, with the exception of Yugoslavian keeper Sasa Ilic, were entirely from the home countries – he contrasted the two clubs. 'On paper there is no question, we are better than them, mainly because I have got so many internationals at this club. But if you look at their record, they managed to get draws at Arsenal, Liverpool and Newcastle and I think Charlton are a very good team. What has impressed me most is their attitude. This does not surprise me because money does not always bring you happiness. You cannot buy the team spirit and you cannot buy the motivation. You may be a team with no money, but if you have young, intelligent, motivated players, a good manager and a crowd who back you all the time, and if you believe in yourself, you can do a good job.'

While ability is important, Vialli always checks out a player's character before he buys him. A good character with limited skills always gets his vote ahead of a wonderfully gifted individual who lacks intelligence. 'If a player is intelligent,' he said, 'he will do a good job, but if he isn't, it will not be good for team spirit. You don't just look at the way he plays but at the way he behaves on and off the pitch.'

Less than a week after Paul Gascoigne had gone into a drying-out clinic, Vialli also spoke about the drinking culture that surrounds the domestic game. He believed players should be allowed to decide themselves how much is too much when out for a few drinks. Vialli pointed out that smoking is a problem in Italian football, while you rarely see an English player with a cigarette between his lips. When it comes to boozing, though, the English are in a league of their own. 'It is all to do with the culture. We smoke a lot, while in England somebody might like a few drinks. Sometimes it happens that somebody might drink too much. But we are all human beings not robots, and we can all fall into temptation, although we should set an example. It can be very difficult when you are under pressure to behave the way people want you to. Sometimes people deserve a little understanding.'

Vialli still believed English football looks after its young stars a lot better than in

Italy, despite the drinking culture. He is impressed with the Professional Footballers' Association's efforts to educate young players who fail to make it or are forced to retire due to injury. There is no such consideration given to the educational needs of young players in Italy. 'I like the way English players grow up, but I would like to see them all go to school. It is always bad to see somebody at the age of twenty-one or twenty-two who is not good enough to play football but unable to do anything else either. From my point of view, it would be nice if they had something else. There comes a time when a player must decide what to do.'

Annual pre-tax profits were £2.1m, up from a £0.4m loss. There was no dividend, but shares rose 1.5p to 79p. Less than half the turnover now comes from football. Bates waived his consultancy fee – £120,000 a year – taking a salary for only two of the last ten years. The club pays £6.6m annual interest on a £75m Eurobond loan to pay for the construction work on Chelsea Village, and the commercial enterprises were 'essential' to meet the debt. In a statement accompanying the financial results, Bates said: 'We are committed to building the strong squad necessary to compete at the highest level in Europe on a continuing basis by judicious purchases of top-quality players. This has been evidenced by our results through winning major cup competitions and finishing fourth in the Premiership last season.'

The opening of the 160-room hotel and the Megastore, plus the acquisition of travel firm EDT, had boosted the company's turnover by almost 300 per cent, leaping from £23.7m in 1997 to £88.3m for the year ended June 1998. But Bates was frustrated by the slow progress in the public inquiry before he could rebuild the West Stand. A roof and two more tiers, including lavish facilities for 6000 to have lunch prior to the game, would generate potential revenue of £2m per full house, making Chelsea the richest club in the country. Bates commented: 'Council officers involved with Chelsea have put their personal prejudices in front of proper rational decision-making, which is a total disgrace. I'm confident the inquiry will go our way because the council case is based on emotion rather than logic.' A Hammersmith Council spokesman countered: 'It's outrageous for Bates to make personal attacks when you consider the huge amount of individual and collective work that has gone on here to help Chelsea.'

In the wake of BSkyB's £623.5m bid for Manchester United, the club was also one targeted by potential media companies, but Bates insisted: 'Somebody has put us up for sale along with Liverpool and Arsenal, but we're a little bit different here. Although we're a public company, the majority of the shares are still kept in a few pockets and those pockets are in no hurry to cash in and make a quick buck. Maybe it will be to our advantage having an alliance with one of the big media groups; on the other hand it may be to our advantage to be independent and sell our wares where we want. There's the Harding stake which is up for sale, and maybe somebody will take that and become our partners – there's every possibility. We just have to make sure we do the best for Chelsea, not the best for me, not the best for some media mogul.'

SATURDAY, 17 OCTOBER

Chelsea 2   Charlton 1

Vialli stressed the dangers of underestimating Charlton in his programme notes, but Charlton were tougher than perhaps even Vialli imagined. Chelsea were – well, average.

Before the match the big screen flashed up the image of a Chelsea crest superimposed on a Union Jack. The Charlton fans responded with taunts. During the game Charlton captain Mark Kinsella had a crash course in playing one of the country's most highly rated sides, although by the end of the game he and midfield partner Neil Redfearn were convinced the title would be heading back to Old Trafford: 'The only team that well and truly battered us was Manchester United. Of all the teams we have played so far, they are definitely the best. They keep possession better than other sides and that's what makes them so special.'

Nonetheless, Chelsea opened the scoring after sixteen minutes when the wonderful Zola played a telepathic ball through to his fellow countryman Casiraghi, who was upended by Ilic inside the area. The Charlton keeper was a little lucky only to be shown the yellow card, but Leboeuf showed less mercy than referee Steve Dunn. Ilic went off shortly before half-time with what looked like an extremely serious injury following a collision with Casiraghi and team-mate Richard Rufus. He was taken to hospital, but thankfully the injury was only a concussion.

Physio Mike Banks observed: 'I went to attend Casi first of all and didn't realise that the keeper was unconscious. Casi had bruising below the knee but just needed a few minutes to get over the pain. Then I turned my attention to the keeper. Jimmy Hendry, Charlton's physio, was there with a doctor and seemed extremely worried, getting him in the recovery position and calling for a stretcher. It was only then that I realised he must be unconscious at the very least. One of their players asked me to look at Rufus and he'd injured his leg just above the knee. It was his knee that had collided with the keeper rather than Gigi's. There was quite a commotion in the medical room at half-time, but it seemed that Ilic had recovered by then and was speaking fluently in English. Our doctor, Hugh Millington, organised a precautionary brain scan and X-rays of the neck and skull at Charing Cross Hospital, and thankfully we were informed a couple of days later that apart from a few loose teeth Sasa was doing fine.'

Up to that point Zola had been the chief architect of most of Chelsea's good work, but after the break it was a different story. Charlton equalised in the fifty-eighth minute when Danny Mills took a long throw-in from the right. The ball was not cleared and Eddie Youds was in the middle of all the bodies to slam it into the bottom left-hand corner from ten yards. And Charlton had the best of the play thereafter. Amazingly, the team packed with foreign stars beat the typically English side at their own game in the final few minutes: a corner by Wise was met at the near post by Poyet, whose header flashed past substitute keeper Andy Petterson.

Vialli conceded: 'If we had drawn we would not have been able to complain. We played poorly, but our spirit was right and that is why we won.' At least the form of Poyet, the rugged goalscoring Uruguayan, was encouraging, with nine goals in thirty Chelsea appearances. 'Gus is a very good player in the air and the timing of his arrival in the penalty area is always very good,' the boss said. 'I pick him as much as I possibly can because he is the sort of player any manager would want in his side.'

Despite the knock-down from the Charlton camp, there was plenty of optimism bubbling just under the surface at the Bridge. Babayaro backed Chelsea to win the Premiership title after they moved into fourth position in the table with their fourth win in five games, unbeaten since their opening-day defeat at Coventry. They were just six points behind leaders Aston Villa with a game in hand. The Nigerian said: 'I think we can still win the League if we continue playing the way we are. We haven't been doing so bad and hopefully we can go out and show the people we can still do it.'

Vialli had restricted himself to a relatively conservative two changes, but the decision to sub in-form Zola had been greeted with howls of disapproval from the fans. Vialli joked: 'Maybe I'm going to make an application to the FA to change the rules about how many players we can field, and then everyone will be happy!'

Wise began his comeback as a sub, but he got a booking straight away. 'I thought it was a terrible decision. In fact, I don't know what I was actually booked for. I assume it was for throwing the ball away, but I actually looped it back over the Charlton bloke's head to where the foul was committed. If I'd hoofed the ball away I could understand it. Maybe he booked me for the handball, but I thought I was fouled then anyway. Whatever it was, we won and we've got to keep our results going.'

The players were delighted to see a young fan, Charlotte, in the players' bar. Wise said: 'She's Chelsea mad, and Robbie and I went to see her in hospital a few weeks ago when she'd had an operation for a hole in the heart. She came to see us and had written me a lovely letter.'

SUNDAY, 18 OCTOBER

Leboeuf spoke at Oxford University. In the oak-panelled splendour of the Oxford Union debating hall, he answered questions in front of three hundred attentive students, which he flatteringly described as 'the elite of England'. He brought the house down when asked if scoring a goal is better than sex. 'I think sex is better – but it's difficult for me, my wife is here.' Putting on the style with his elegant frock coat, chic suit, shirt and colour-coded matching tie, he added: 'It is a great honour for me, as a Frenchman. I am very flattered. But I was very nervous. Playing in front of eighty thousand is much easier.'

Later Frank confessed to a passion for ancient civilisations and a desire to return to education. 'When I was at school I wanted to continue my studies but I was given an ultimatum and told to concentrate on my football. You have to make a lot of sacrifices to be a footballer. Now I read lots of books about Egypt and the Mayans in Mexico. I really like history. Maybe I will take the time to return to studies when my career is over. I will have the time, and maybe I could come back to Oxford and study.'

Inevitably, Leboeuf's comments about Beckham, Riedle, referees and the Murdoch take-over of Manchester United made the headlines. He gave a frosty reception to the Sky bid and claimed the prospect of a European Super League was 'a nightmare' for his sport. 'Man United is the biggest club in the world, and Rupert Murdoch doesn't know anything about football,' he said. 'Fans can't afford to go abroad all the time to watch AC Milan or Barcelona. Nor do they want to. It would be very bad for players, too. I played fifty games last season, and in the Super League I'd play ten or fifteen more. Players need to rest. Those who want the Super League to come true will ruin the game.'

Of his ongoing personal war of words with Beckham, he said: 'He told me I had big ears. He's too arrogant. He's got a lot to learn about football. But I think very soon he will be one of the best players in England.'

But the most controversial issue was his comments on Riedle. In ninety minutes of questioning the quietly spoken, elegant Frenchman fended off the attacks of the undergraduates accusing him of setting a poor example by trying to get Karlheinz Riedle booked. 'I don't believe I made contact, so if he goes down he's cheating.' He had brandished the imaginary card at the referee over the Riedle incident, and added: 'Referees need help, firstly from players, who must accept they're humans. But they must become professionals like us. Why are they only amateurs? You have to be prepared in football, so they need to be able to have videos for penalties and offsides to help them make the right decisions.'

Gerard Houllier was outraged by Leboeuf's comments. 'Frank has lost one good opportunity to shut up. The first rule is that professionally they should respect each other. And one professional who deserves respect is Karlheinz.' Co-manager Roy Evans was equally angered by the accusation: 'Frank Leboeuf should look after his own problems. He has got nothing to do with this club. Karlheinz has been a fantastic professional for many years. He has won everything, and Frank Leboeuf should take a leaf out of his book.'

MONDAY, 19 OCTOBER

Thoughts turned to the match against the Danes in the first leg of the second-round clash at Stamford Bridge. Vialli said: 'We need a better performance. The most important thing in Europe is not to make any mistakes.'

Wise was getting frustrated: 'I've been out a long time now and it's been driving me mad. Without me we've beaten Middlesbrough, gone through in Europe and drawn at Liverpool, so you lot don't really need me around at the moment! All the same, I just want to get back and play.'

Chelsea Village announced profits of £2.1m for the year ending June 1998.

Players' salaries leapt by 60 per cent.

Nick Crittenden joined Plymouth on a month's loan. His grandfather lives just five minutes from Fratton Park.

TUESDAY, 20 OCTOBER

Vialli got tough. Well, toughish. It certainly came across as a disciplinary stance – at least, the papers were full of Vialli's threats to fine, drop or even sell players who undermine him by complaining constantly about the rotation system.

Laudrup's dissatisfaction was repeated in the English papers this morning, although it was the same interview given some time ago – and now the Dane was back in the side on a regular basis. Vialli accepted Laudrup's explanation that it was an out-of-date interview that had been regurgitated, but it still left Vialli open to questions on the media open day to preview the Cup Winners Cup tie. 'I understand complaints,' he said, 'but I want players to explain to me their complaints. If they don't change, I will make them change.' When reminded that he had rebelled against Gullit using similar tactics, Vialli added: 'What I did as a player is different to what I expect as a manager. When you are a player you only think of yourself. As a manager I must think of the team. Players will be allowed their say, but their views should only be positive. I have to protect the spirit and atmosphere of the team.'

As for the tie against FC Copenhagen, Laudrup said: 'Their problem is inconsistency. They'll turn it on against Brondby one week, then lose to some small team the next.'

Eddie Newton was ruled out for almost two months when it was discovered he had suffered a hairline fracture on Friday during a reserves match against Spurs. His leg was in a special boot, and Vialli said: 'It's a terrible blow to him and the club, but to me it only emphasises that we need a big squad to cover situations like this and players must accept it. He is the first and I hope the last seriously injured player this season. Despite him not having played very often this season, he is always a player we can rely on. Eddie never lets you down.' It was bad timing, because Chelsea had a gruelling schedule ahead of them: eight games in twenty-four days. Vialli admitted: 'It's a big loss for us with so many games coming up. Eddie is a very hard worker in midfield and he's going to be out for at least a month and a half. I hope we can cope without him until he's ready and fit again to join us.'

Vialli had Le Saux available again after he missed the win over Charlton through suspension. He was serving a three-match ban, but the suspension did not apply in European competitions.

WEDNESDAY, 21 OCTOBER

Luca was shocked on the day before the Euro tie to pick up the *Evening Standard* and discover the headline YOUR TIME IS UP, the article suggesting that, with Bates's agreement, Vialli would retire as a player in the summer of 2000. It went on to say that the move to restrict Vialli's career was an attempt to avoid a repeat of the Gullit affair. Bates said in the paper, 'He has a player's contract until the end of next season and then he is on a manager's contract until 2001. We did that to avoid what happened with Gullit. Once his playing contract runs out the salary won't be the same as what he received as a player and a manager.'

Vialli told close friends in the Italian media: 'I learn something every day in the press. It is amazing how they can create something to try to stir trouble. I'm not aware of a new contract. I only know I extended my contract for two more seasons when I took over as a player-manager on top of my remaining season and a half, which means it covers me until 2001. It is a contract that has a number of variables which can work either way, but there is no indication as to when my playing career must end.' He might have been a shade peeved to start with, but he showed he has a sense of humour when he concluded: 'It will be a pity anyway because I'm so good now!'

Laudrup had spent the last week back in his native country. Of FC Copenhagen, he warned: 'Don't be fooled by them. They are actually a good side. I've played with some of their players and I've told the boys that in my opinion they are certainly a stronger side than Helsingborgs. They will make it difficult for us because they want to do well against Chelsea. Copenhagen know if they win it'll be a great night not only for them but for Danish football. They are a typical Scandinavian side who can run all night and make life difficult for opponents.'

Jakob Kjeldbjerg, once an accomplished central defender at Chelsea until a knee injury forced his retirement in 1996, now of Channel TV3 in Denmark, had no doubts that Laudrup would be the pivotal influence. 'He is the mega-star in Denmark and I know the Copenhagen players respect him so much, almost to the point of awe, that he could destroy them. As a club they have been very spoiled, indulged, over the years. You see, they play in the national stadium in the capital city and they have this tradition of glamour about them. That has resulted in inconsistency and underachievement. In many ways you could almost call them the Chelsea of Danish football. Both clubs have tended to underachieve over the years, although that has changed at the Bridge recently. Copenhagen can be a useful side on their day, but, when you look at the respective teams and then throw in Brian Laudrup, I just believe that Chelsea will be far too strong over the two matches.'

Vialli knew it was going to be tricky, and he was planning to put out his strongest side. In his programme notes Luca called for more goals than his side had managed against Charlton; however, he pointed out: 'I can assure you all they are much stronger than Helsingborgs. I am sure it will be the same kind of game as at Helsingborgs. They'll wait for us in their half and counter-attack. We have to be patient, imaginative, and keep our heads cool but our feet as warm as possible! And we must increase our percentage of goals.'

The press ad for the Chelsea–Copenhagen tie was even more controversial than the Cup Winners Cup tie involving Newcastle when David Batty was dressed up in stockings. The ad showed Hoddle asking Shearer why the TV wasn't on. The England striker replied, 'Have you ever thought it could be down to you?', the question Shearer was alleged to have put to his manager in a dressing-room altercation after the Luxembourg game.

THURSDAY, 22 OCTOBER

Chelsea 1   FC Copenhagen 1

'Scary ride?' was the first question for Luca in the post-match press conference.

'What is this "scary ride"?' he asked, looking extremely puzzled. The Italian contingent attempted to find a suitable Italian equivalent. The boss quickly got the point and tried to explain away how the holders were thirty seconds from a massive Cup Winners Cup upset when Desailly's first goal for the club saved them. His curling fifteen-yard shot off the post came in the nick of time to preserve the Blues' impregnable run at Stamford Bridge. The Frenchman admitted afterwards: 'We are in trouble. We've got to go over to Denmark for the second leg and get a result, which won't be easy. Copenhagen are not a great team, but they are a strong team.'

Copenhagen coach Kim Brink was furious that four minutes of stoppage time had been played even though neither trainer went on the pitch all night. 'I was very surprised, but I guess Chelsea were 1–0 down and they got a bit of a bonus as the home side. It makes me sick to think we came so close to becoming the first team to win a European tie here, and it doesn't make me feel any better about the equaliser. But there will be forty thousand people cheering us in the return leg and, psychologically, this is still a great result for us.'

Vialli gave a charitable assessment. 'A 1–1 draw is better than a 1–0 defeat and we still have a good chance of going through to the quarter-finals. I was delighted with the players' spirit tonight and I have nothing but praise for the way they stuck to their guns. As holders, we are finding that opposition teams put in a little extra effort, which doesn't help. But we are good enough to win the second leg and go through, as long as we play the same way in Denmark. Although we didn't always enjoy good fortune in front of goal tonight, we can't complain about our luck. We scored in the last minute against Charlton, and we've done it again. On the whole, we've got what we've deserved this season.'

Vialli refused to blame Desailly, for passing across his own eighteen-yard area, and Wise, for failing to control it, in the defensive shambles leading to Bjarne Goldbaek's eightieth-minute strike. He added: 'We could have done better there, but I've played football long enough to know that we are all human enough to make mistakes sometimes.' Certainly Desailly was in no mood to accept the blame. 'I don't feel responsible for the goal. Maybe I should have just kicked it away. The pass was good for Dennis but he didn't control it. Maybe we didn't give him enough information that he was under pressure. At the end we were a bit tired. But I want to win this Cup because at Milan we did not win it. I said to myself, "You have to try to do something to help the team", so I went up and I had the opportunity and I'm happy that I've done it.'

As expected, Chelsea were in control for most of this tie, but none of Vialli's expensive collection of forwards could manage a breakthrough in a season where the glut of goals has dried up. Chelsea have a proud record of twenty-five European ties unbeaten at the Bridge stretching back forty years, but they couldn't have come closer to surrendering it. Zola was in imperious form, again the instigator of most of the creative moves (in the first half he struck the inside of the post when he whipped a shot from just on the edge of the area that took a slight deflection), but the other forwards were luckless. Laudrup was barracked mercilessly by the travelling Danish fans. Referring to his exorbitant wages, they sang: 'You only play for the money'. Laudrup struggled to make much headway against his compatriots, despite Vialli's verdict that he played well, befitting a world-class performer, creating chances for himself and others. But for the third European match in a row, Chelsea's embarrassment of riches in attack had failed to hit the target.

Copenhagen's twenty-one-year-old striker David Nielsen was scathing about his opponents: 'We didn't even expect to score at Stamford Bridge. But we've shown they are just human and, when they come to Copenhagen for the second leg, it will be one of the biggest games in the city all year.' Keeper Michael Stensgaard pointed to the fact that while Chelsea's players individually had 'unbelievable skill', 'Maybe they weren't efficient enough as a team.'

The second anniversary of Matthew Harding's death was largely ignored. The expected minute's silence never materialised. But managing director Colin Hutchinson did pen a heartfelt tribute in his programme notes. Hutchinson wrote that club staff would remember Harding 'in our own personal and different ways', but Bates deliberately did not devote a single word of his column to the memorial.

FRIDAY, 23 OCTOBER

Vialli ordered his first-team squad to report for training at 10.15 a.m., half an hour earlier than usual. The boss wasn't pleased.

In defence in Europe, back in midfield in the Premiership – Desailly, the mainstay of the French defence, was involved in his own little rotation system. He still needed to steady himself after the heady excesses of the World Cup, but he was increasingly concerned with more mundane matters: settling his wife and three children into the family home in Surrey, the launch of a new line of clothing, perfecting his English and adding another League title to his priceless collection of medals. The French call Desailly 'hautain', which in English means haughty. 'It's the way I talk,' he said. 'It's not me. When you see me on the television you may think I'm very sure about myself. That is not the right image. I am a nice, family man, a good father. I'm a simple guy.'

In training, Desailly rarely joins in the japes. He changes in the quietest of the dressing rooms opposite Poyet, another studious professional. The neatness of movement in Desailly is surprising for someone who weighs twelve and a half stone and stands well over six feet. His greatest friend, Didier Deschamps, referred with some awe to Desailly being 'au sommet de son art' – at the height of his powers. Desailly smiles at the compliment. 'I was under pressure because of what I had said, but I was one hundred per cent sure I would have a great World Cup. In France, people saw only the image of a Milan team losing. I was disappointed that they were doubting me. I had nothing to prove to them, just to myself, because soccer is my passion as well as my profession, and I like to do it well. Winning is beautiful. That's why I say you have to give of yourself, because when you succeed it is so beautiful.'

Ghanaian-born, his African roots remain strong: his mother has recently moved back to Accra, his brothers live there, and in Seth Adonkor, a half-brother, who was killed in a car crash fifteen years ago, Desailly carries a permanent reminder of another life. Desailly refused to dedicate his World Cup victory to his memory, saying that Seth was always with him so there was no need, but his pre-match ritual involved a conscious assimilation of all the many influences channelled into him. 'I like to have a quiet moment and to realise the chance of being in front of a lot of people and expressing yourself through your passion. I try to take some positive things from the African mentality and from the French and European mentalities. My homeland is France, but I like to go back to Africa. I used to go to the market and play soccer with the kids there, but it is less free and easy now because I have become more popular.'

Though a timely first goal had preserved Chelsea's unbeaten European record, Desailly admitted that fluency had yet to return to his football. A sore Achilles tendon was one problem, the sheer relentless pace of the English game another. Adjusting to life after the World Cup was an added complication, quite apart from the culture shock of being left alone in restaurants and finding a fox at the bottom of his garden. And he turned thirty in September. 'I'm cool now, not looking for an image any more. If I had stayed at Milan I think maybe I would not have had the will to be at the top any more, but coming to Chelsea means I have to find another level, find new personalities and new responsibilities. This is good for me and I am really enjoying myself. Don't ask me if the football is better or worse than in Italy. It's just different. In Italy, even if it is a big game, the two teams will look at each other for a time. Here it's straight away: kick the ball, you run, you jump, you fight from beginning to the end. It's really very surprising, but I will get used to it. I still have thirty per cent to go to be at the top of my game. The team too can grow.'

All the Italians – plus two from Spurs – gathered again at the new Venetian resturant Canaletto's for a night out for the Business Club Italia. During a short interview, Vialli said: 'I would never advise Italian players between twenty and twenty-five to come to play in England. Instead I would tell them to achieve their peak in Italy, and only go abroad once they have had their fill. That is what I did at the age of thirty-two after winning everything with Juventus.' His comments were totally misinterpreted. His words came across as a damning indictment on the Premiership, with the Chelsea boss warning Europe's top stars not to come to England until they are past it. In reality, Vialli was praising the Premiership and merely advising leading internationals about the sort of success he had experienced when he moved to Chelsea two and a half years ago. A jokey remark from Luca about his future also captured the headlines: 'Would I return home to coach Juve? Let's see whether the Juventus president, Giovanni Agnelli, puts in that phone call to me.' But Bates knew precisely the context in which Luca had made his remarks; he had gone on to say: 'Seriously I hope to stay as long as possible at Chelsea. Being a player-manager is very pleasant here. Coaching in Italy can become a source of regret because of all the responsibilities, tensions and pressures. But you can never say never in this life.'

Lambourde and Flo, together with their partners, were spotted in a more down-to-earth establishment: the Pizza Express in the Fulham Road, a quarter of a mile from the Bridge. They'd been to see *Buddy* together. 'It was really good,' enthused Lambourde. Flo had a house in Ascot which he shared with his girlfriend. 'It's a very nice area. I always seem to have visitors from Norway over to watch football. They love it.' Flo's room-mate was de Goey. 'We need to stick together because we need longer beds and longer rooms.'

Duberry was now a family man, as he explained: 'I'm a dad now, so I've matured a bit. I go home and relax a lot more. I still spend a couple of hours going out with the chaps after training, but then I go home to the little girl and my girlfriend. I must mention them because she always moans about me not doing so. My girlfriend's Sarah and my little girl's Kayci.'

Ahead of Sunday's game, Leeds were in disarray, with Graham quitting, moves to lure O'Neill from Leicester failing, and O'Leary stalling on whether to join Graham at Spurs.

France finally pulled out of the controversial Confederations Cup due to be played in Mexico in January. The World Cup winners were to represent Europe in the eight-nation tournament. It was especially good news for Chelsea and Arsenal.

SATURDAY, 24 OCTOBER

In the *News of the World* the next morning Zola criticised Vialli's rotation system. Although the interview had been vetted by Jon Smith, with full headline approval, no one informed Gianfranco's representative that there would also be a back-page headline. Not good timing after the get-tough warnings following the Laudrup episode.

Zola was upset after being substituted against Charlton. He was quoted as saying: 'I just walked away. I could not speak to Vialli. It's not the first time, either. I have played well in other games and it has still happened. The rotation system makes it difficult for me to find the rhythm to get my form back. You lose your place, your position, and I struggled with it. We have to sort this out. Casiraghi is doing well, Laudrup is doing well, I'm doing well and the team is doing well. Tore Andre Flo is another very good player. But we will find out if the team has true character the moment things start to go wrong for us. When the team is doing well I can't tell Vialli anything. If the rotation is good for the team then I accept it, but obviously it is normal to be disappointed when substituted.'

Old boy Danny Granville explained why he couldn't hang around to wait for his chance at the Bridge. 'I didn't want to be a squad player at Chelsea, I wanted to be a regular. But their argument was that we can't guarantee Gianfranco Zola first-team football, so we can hardly do that for you. If there is a £5m player who is an England international and a £300,000 player, it doesn't take a scientist to work out who they are going to pick. I thought about this all the time I was there and I decided I couldn't do much more than I did at Chelsea.'

SUNDAY, 25 OCTOBER

Leeds United 0   Chelsea 0

Vialli launched a bitter broadside at the performance of referee Mike Reed after he set a Premiership record for cautions at Elland Road. The Birmingham official dished out a crazy thirteen yellow cards – eight of them to Chelsea players – including a double for Leboeuf. Vialli chased Reed down the tunnel at half-time and went into his dressing room, demanding an explanation for his actions and accusing him of ruining all the hard work he had put in to prepare for the trip to Yorkshire. 'Sometimes it is impossible not to complain about referees,' he said later. 'We worked our socks off during the week and then the referee is making mistakes like that all through the match. I complained to him about the number of yellow cards he handed out. Not just about ours, but about the ones he gave to Leeds as well.' The game was played in driving rain and gale force conditions, and Vialli said, 'Sometimes referees have to understand the problems for the players. The pitch was heavy, the weather was bad and it's a high-tempo game with some clumsy challenges going in. They don't understand that players are not trying to hurt each other.'

But Leboeuf was in trouble with Vialli for his second-half dismissal. The Frenchman had been carded in the first half for throwing up his hands in fake celebration as Reed awarded a foul against him, and was later dismissed for a crude late tackle from behind on Harry Kewell. Vialli had little sympathy with his defender. 'Leboeuf deserved his yellow card for dissent, and the tackle on Kewell was definitely worth a booking. I think the referee got his decisions right on both occasions.'

David O'Leary was equally disgusted with the performance of the financial manager from Birmingham, but Reed said: 'What David O'Leary said was not insulting, it was humorous and, more importantly, my match controller was delighted with the way I handled the game.'

Here's the tale of yellow woe:

29 mins: Zola booked for pulling back Kewell (undeserved);
30 mins: Di Matteo booked for a trip on Hopkin (undeserved);
32 mins: Leboeuf booked for mocking the referee (undeserved);
34 mins: de Goey booked for a foul on Hasselbaink outside the area (deserved);
38 mins: Wise booked for a foul on Hopkin (undeserved);
39 mins: Bowyer booked for a foul on Zola (deserved);
42 mins: Molenaar booked for a foul on Laudrup (undeserved);
43 mins: Duberry booked for pulling Hasselbaink's shirt (deserved);
61 mins: Leboeuf booked for a late tackle on Kewell (deserved);
65 mins: Babayaro booked for a sliding challenge on Hasselbaink (undeserved);
74 mins: Hasselbaink booked for a foul on Wise (undeserved);
85 mins: Wijnhard booked for elbowing Desailly off the ball (deserved);
90 mins: Radebe booked for a challenge on Laudrup, despite clearly taking the ball (undeserved).

Reed also awarded Leeds a dubious-looking penalty on the stroke of half-time for Duberry's challenge on Hasselbaink, but the spot-kick was saved by his Dutch compatriot de Goey. The goalkeeping hero felt, at least, that this dispelled the myth about a lack of championship quality in defence. 'It riles the players to see all the criticism about our defence because anyone who watched this game will see we can play well at the back. We showed the same against Liverpool earlier in the season. We were very solid and Leeds did not make that many chances despite having the extra man. I thought we played very well, but we are slightly disappointed because we came for three points and, even after the sending-off, we still could have won the match.' Vialli endorsed that view: 'I am delighted with the players because Chelsea have trouble coming to Leeds and getting anything, but we have ended that and they deserve credit.'

United had not won since Graham left for Spurs a month earlier, and Hasselbaink's third penalty failure in succession cost them dearly – they were now seven matches without a win. Leeds were themselves indebted to their goalkeeper, rookie Paul Robinson, for producing three outstanding saves. Victory for Chelsea would have taken them into third place in the table, four points behind leaders Aston Villa, who visited Stamford Bridge next, but Robinson refused to be overcome by the occasion – apart from a dodgy moment in the seventh minute when Wise's swinging corner swerved over his head and had to be headed off the line at the far post by former Chelsea defender Danny Granville. After that the Wetherby-born teenager settled down with the help of a flying save to keep out Laudrup in the thirty-third minute, and he followed that up with two more outstanding stops to beat away a long-range shot from Zola and a Casiraghi header from the six-yard line.

Unfortunately, Zola had to be sacrificed once Leboeuf was dismissed, as Vialli explained: 'Rixy and I started thinking about a change. We had three strikers on, which was a little bit of a luxury when we were a man short. When we called out to the linesman for the substitution, even before we told him he shouted: "Okay, just tell me who is coming on for Gianfranco!" I joke. Truly it is a pity when sometimes our strikers deserve to stay on the pitch for ninety minutes because they work really hard, and then we have others so frustrated on the bench who deserve to be playing. But they have to stick with that, and to be honest, apart from a few articles a long time ago, I think everyone is pulling the same way. Despite what you sometimes read in the newspapers, there is a great atmosphere in the dressing room and a great team spirit.'

The match was an important landmark for Di Matteo – his hundredth game for Chelsea.

MONDAY, 26 OCTOBER

Bates ridiculed the ever-diminishing value of the League Cup, but wanted to retain it, all right. 'What's the League Cup called this year? I think they should call it the Worthington Pint. Or the Worthington Glass. Or the Worthington Mug! But I think our fans want us to keep it. Just as when we won the FA Cup they didn't want us to be knocked out in the third round by Manchester United.' The chairman certainly didn't want Vialli to field a reserve team on Wednesday to put the holders in jeopardy. But Arsenal and Manchester United, with designs on bigger prizes, dispatched reserve sides, just as they did a year ago. Then sponsored by Coca-Cola, the competition was dubbed the Joka-Cola Cup.

Luca promised the fans that his team would not downgrade the competition, the first he won as a manager, but he was clearly going to rotate full circle. 'We must continue to think about the number of matches we have played recently, and those to come in the future. I might give some players a rest and some of the unfortunate ones who have been on the bench too often despite their ability could get a chance in the team. I wish them good luck because I know it won't be easy. We are taking everything very seriously this season. We respect every competition we play in, and we have respect for the supporters who pay good money and travel to see us play.'

TUESDAY, 27 OCTOBER

Luca stopped the training session and sent all his players off. Flo was shocked. 'He told us to just get back in the changing rooms and go home and rest for tomorrow because we were playing so bad. We didn't play for very long, but the score was 7–7. I don't think he was very satisfied with the way we defended!' Lambourde said: 'Luca was a bit fed up with us. We all had to talk about it afterwards.'

For the next day's game the stakes couldn't have been higher: Chelsea unbeaten since the opening day of the season, Villa unbeaten since April. Villa boss John Gregory had added spice to the contest by making a point of rebuking the foreign invasion and buying British (Villa had more British players than any other club). And Prime Minister Tony Blair backed Gregory's buy-British policy. Blair and Wenger met in Downing Street to launch the year's Royal British Legion Poppy Appeal and, not surprisingly, football was at the top of the agenda. 'There was quite an animated discussion between them about the fact that the team at the top of the Premiership contains no overseas players,' said Charles Lewis of the RBL. 'Both Mr Blair and Arsene Wenger agreed it was good for English football.'

Villa's England Under-21 international midfielder Lee Hendrie, destined for the national team, underlined the fascinating contest: 'There couldn't be a bigger contrast between the two sides. Chelsea are the ultimate example of continental football in Britain. But that won't stop us going there with nothing less than the thought of victory on our minds.'

Paul Hughes was in talks with Second Division Wrexham for a month's loan in a bid to kickstart his faltering career. Hughes, twenty-three, was a regular member of Gullit's squad last season making twenty-three appearances, but had been frozen out since Vialli took over and had had trials with Norwich in pre-season with a view to a permanent move to Carrow Road. Wrexham manager Brian Flynn wanted to complete the deal in time for Hughes to make his debut against Millwall on Saturday.

Desailly was facing a court battle over a love child. Single mum Helene Mendy accused the defender of fathering her eight-year-old daughter after reading that he was considering adopting an African baby. Helene, twenty-nine, from Senegal, insisted: 'I saw red and thought, You've already got one, Marcel.' Jobless Helene, who lives near Toulon, claimed she gave birth to Aida after a one-night stand with Desailly in 1989. The father of three, now settled in Surrey with wife Virginie and their three kids, knew Helene but denied fathering Aida. He was refusing her lawyer's demand that he submit to DNA tests. The lawyer had persuaded a judge to look into the matter and make a ruling in December. Desailly's own lawyer said: 'She has only come up with this because he's rich and famous.'

The club's war with the local council over plans for the new stand turned into a battle of the celebs. Local resident Susan Hampshire lobbied against the development, but Lord Attenborough told the public inquiry how plans to redevelop the Bridge would prevent future generations of supporters from being priced out of watching their team. The lifelong Chelsea supporter and life vice-president insisted: 'In my view it would be tragic if the club was denied the opportunity of creating further seating to foster inclusive initiatives which bring into the football family those who, through various forms of disadvantage, would otherwise be excluded. I support the provision of additional entertainment rooms in the West Stand. These are an essential element of the income-generating capability of Chelsea. Their construction will ensure that high-quality Premier League football continues to be played at Stamford Bridge and that the present facilities and subsidies continue to be available to the community.'

The planning inquiry had been set up after Bates became frustrated at the failure of Hammersmith and Fulham Council to grant planning permission for his redevelopment plans. The council was concerned that any future plans to expand the ground and open new entertainment facilities would cause extra disruption to an already congested area.

WEDNESDAY, 28 OCTOBER

Chelsea 4   Aston Villa 1

Vialli's glorious hat-trick – the first Chelsea hat-trick in this competition since Gordon Durie against Reading eleven years ago – was tainted by Wise's fifth sending-off in the past five years. Vialli reacted angrily after the Wise dismissal, engaging in a touchline bust-up with referee Graham Barber after responding to a comment from Villa physio Jimmy Walker, the debate holding up play while Villa lined up to take a free-kick. Vialli stood close to the dug-outs, and Barber marched over to show him the yellow card. He stood toe-to-toe with the ref and twice put his right hand on the referee's chest to emphasise a point. A couple of minutes later Vialli was substituted, and when the final whistle sounded he turned straight down the tunnel with no attempt at the usual after-match pleasantries.

The clash with Barber, in the light of the Di Canio affair, was not serious enough to merit a mention in the referee's report, but Rix admitted his boss was close to breaking point: 'Luca thought straight away that Dennis would miss key games. He's an emotional man, Luca, always living on the edge. Someone on the Villa bench said something like "Get back on the pitch" to him in a nice way, but he didn't hear them and went over to speak to them. There was no animosity. The way he played tonight was magnificent.' Rix made no excuses for the Wise red card, for a two-footed lunge on Darren Byfield. 'It was a bad tackle, he deserved to go. You make split-second decisions, and he made the wrong one there.'

If that wasn't enough, Petrescu had been substituted a few minutes earlier and had kicked a chair and the ground in disgust, throwing down his tracksuit top as he headed for an early shower. Young debutant John Terry came on, but Petrescu failed to shake hands with the kid. He reflected on that moment some time later: 'I regret it just for the fans and the young kid. I was waiting a long time just to play one game and I thought it was a good performance and I didn't deserve to be substituted. Straight away after the game I did say sorry to the kid because it was his first game.'

It was a memorable moment for Terry nonetheless, even though he was only on the pitch for five minutes at centre-half: 'I touched the ball three times. I took a free-kick, there was a clearance, I sliced into the crowd and I had another little touch.'

It should have been a night of undiluted glory for Vialli and his Chelsea reserves, who had exceeded one of the longest undefeated club runs in football, Villa's defiance stretching back to 25 April. In a contest billed as the Battle of Britain against the Rest of the World, Part One, this was a comprehensive victory for Vialli's multi-national team.

Both the holders and the Premiership leaders made numerous changes, eight of them in the Vialli line-up. The player-coach selected himself alongside Flo, with Zola as the only established star on the bench to unleash in case of emergency. The Chelsea reserves produced the best result of the season, and one or two performances – notably Lambourde's and Poyet's – would test Vialli's resolve to keep the rotation system going. But the outstanding performance belonged to Vialli himself. After Mark Draper opened the scoring for Villa in the tenth minute with a free-kick – inevitably after a Wise foul – that clipped off the head of Poyet to find the top corner, Vialli staged a wonderful comeback virtually on his own. Goal number one came after thirty-two minutes with Lambourde winning two vital tackles, powering forward and timing his pass to perfection to allow Vialli to stroke the ball into the corner through the keeper's legs. Goal number two came in the sixty-seventh minute from a delightful Poyet through-ball. Vialli's first touch was memorable; he turned sharply and shot into the corner. Goal number three for Vialli was the best, with exquisite passes from Wise and Poyet. Vialli's shot found the corner. But before he completed his hat-trick, the contest was already over: Ian Taylor had been shown a yellow card for a foul on Flo, and from the Wise free-kick Flo had headed superbly from the far post into the corner. Villa fans' only redress was to chant 'Top of the League'.

Wise recognised the quality of Vialli's contribution: 'Luca was magnificent, and he wasn't the only one. Tore caused them problems all evening.' As for his dismissal, he said: 'I'm still kicking myself. I am disappointed with myself at the way I got sent off. I seem to be one of those players who get the red card every time. But it wasn't a great tackle and I'm not proud of it.'

Vialli left it to Rix to deal with the media, and everyone seemed to be unable to answer the question about Laudrup, after Danish TV had put out the story that the Dane had agreed to sign for Chelsea's Cup Winners Cup opponents FC Copenhagen.

Rix said: 'Talks with Copenhagen? Not that I know of . . . Unconfirmed reports? I'm hardly going to respond to unconfirmed reports! Give me a ring if you hear anything.'

Williams pointed out that Laudrup had been training in the morning, but no one knew for sure whether he had turned up at the Bridge for the game. Bates strolled out of the press room insisting he knew nothing about it.

A few days later Luca spoke about the incident. 'It was a pity that with five minutes to go Wisey got sent off for a bad tackle. It was a pity that the incident stole all the headlines in the newspapers the next day from the great victory. I think my argument with the referee was made a bit bigger than it was really. When Dennis got sent off I just walked to our bench to speak to Graham. We needed to talk, we were a man short. I did not know I was not allowed to do this as a player-manager. So the referee booked me and told me I had broken the rules. So I got angry.' He did not have a bust-up with anyone on the Villa bench: 'They said something polite to me. I said something polite back. I had a very polite exchange of views with their bench and I wasn't arguing at all. That's why when the referee booked me for going off the pitch I nearly lost my cool. I thought that as manager

I should have the right to get as close as possible to my bench and speak to Rixy. Anyway, it is a lesson learnt.'

On the positive side, Luca savoured his hat-trick, and analysed the art of goal-scoring. 'Shooting early is how it should be done. But it also depends on the run you make, on the way your team-mates pass the ball to you, and the way you control the ball with your first touch. Everything must be well synchronised. With the first goal, I was lucky. I didn't know where the goalkeeper was, I just wanted to hit it quickly. My main concern was to keep the ball low, down and on target. The second goal was in my opinion the best; the pass and action were very good. My first touch was okay. I turned my body and managed to make the defender turn, and then I just tried to hit the target as quickly as possible. With the third goal there was good movement. When Gus got the ball I knew I had to make movement, so I went inside and then outside, and then it was two against one, I had found the space. The pass was perfect and I hit the ball at the near post. Sometimes goalkeeeepers think you will go to the far post and anticipate that, and with a low, quick shot you can catch them out.

'The one I missed from Jody's pass, obviously that was a bad bounce.'

The fourth-round draw brought gasps: Liverpool were pitted against Spurs, Newcastle got Blackburn, and Chelsea were up against the Premier League champions, Arsenal.

THURSDAY, 29 OCTOBER

A subdued mood with the news of Laudrup's imminent departure, but not for talkaholic Gus. He spotted moody Dan in the canteen on his way to lunch. Poyet leapt back and joked: 'Hey, Dan! Don't kick me!'

In the morning, Copenhagen denied media reports Laudrup was to join them. Trading in FC Copenhagen shares was suspended briefly on the Copenhagen Stock Exchange as the shares soared 14 per cent. Copenhagen's general manager Flemming Ostergaard had 'a super secret meeting' with Hutchinson in London where an agreement was reached on Laudrup's departure, but the move was not yet official, the TV2 Channel said. Laudrup wanted to return to Denmark mainly because his two children didn't feel comfortable in London. Ostergaard confirmed that representatives of the two clubs had met, but he said the meeting was to discuss preparations for the cup tie in Copenhagen. Unidentified Danish sources suggested Laudrup was offered a three-year playing contract, plus a further seven years as general manager of the club.

Speculation that a deal was on continued as Chelsea called a news conference at the Bridge. At 4.02 p.m. Hutchinson and Laudrup entered the packed press room.

Laudrup confirmed that he couldn't wait to return to Denmark. 'I must admit, in my heart I have decided to go back home. It is down to myself, my personal life, and I am going to go back to my home country, to my roots. I've had a couple of meetings to discuss the situation and I want to make it clear it has absolutely nothing to do with the very famous rotation situation at this club.'

In an amazing half hour of typical football double-speak, Laudrup tried to justify how he has trampled on the dreams of the supporters. Laudrup had been unsettled for *seven* weeks, despite signing one of the most lucrative contracts in English football. Indeed, he had had his doubts from day one. 'Even before I joined Chelsea I was a little confused. There comes a period in your life and sporting career when you question your appetite for the game, and in my case I think it is due to being ten years abroad. I have reached the stage where I would like to go back. It is very difficult for me to say when I will go. After the return leg of the Cup Winners Cup the two clubs will meet again and there will be a decision then. It is too early to say whether it will be weeks or months. I have a three-year contract and it is down to Chelsea to decide when and where they will agree, it is not for me to say it will be now or in a month's time.'

Hutchinson conceded the club was upset by Laudrup's decision. 'We are gutted that such a top-class player may well go back to Denmark. He has three options: he stays here and plays for Chelsea, and that is our preferred one; he retires, which would be a waste of a talent at twenty-nine; or he goes to play in Denmark at the right time, and we will put that together to help him. It is something we are exploring, but we are not prepared to do anything until after the Cup Winners Cup tie.'

Laudrup had been discussing a way out for weeks, and had rejected all Chelsea's compromise solutions, such as allowing him to commute regularly from Denmark. Chelsea wanted strings attached – what Hutchinson called 'stringent safeguards' – to any deal with Copenhagen, a clause that ensured he could not be sold on without a percentage going to Chelsea, and that he could only play in Denmark. In addition Chelsea demanded as much as £1.5m – the amount of wages, signing-on fees and bonuses they had already paid the player. Laudrup earned more in a week than the average Chelsea fan earned years, but the player supposed to give the club a championship shine was on his way.

Laudrup added: 'It also has nothing to do with my family. They are quite settled in London. I feel like this now and that's the decision. At the end of the day the decision has to be in your heart. You might say why sign a three-year contract. But when I signed it I had an opportunity to go to various clubs including Copenhagen, but I felt at that time there was a challenge to go to the English Premiership, and that I could help my new club.' What did Laudrup have to say about the fans, especially those who'd invested their money in a Chelsea shirt with Laudrup's name on the back? 'Yes, it is normal for people to be very disillusioned, sad, and angry or whatever. I must admit my feelings are that it must be difficult for people to understand that I have to do this for myself.'

Vialli didn't attend the extraordinary events at the Bridge, and Hutchinson stressed that the subject of Laudrup's selection would be off the agenda for the player-coach the following day at Harlington. But as Chelsea continued to pay his exorbitant salary, they wanted to utilise his talents, and the player expressed the surprise view that he had been playing virtually all the time while discussing the way out anyway, so a couple more games wouldn't matter. But they would matter. Now the fans knew what had been lurking behind the scenes, he was hardly likely to be the most popular player at the Bridge. Laudrup said about his possible selection: 'I'm not the one to ask, and whether I think I will or not I will keep to myself. But I am a Chelsea player and will remain so until another deal is struck.' He added that he would like to leave with a goal, at least, after what amounted to a poor return for his massive pay cheque. He refused to be branded a failure or a mercenary, with four clubs now under his belt at the age of twenty-nine.

'The Chelsea squad,' he continued, 'is one of the most talented group of players in the Premiership and they can go on and win the Premiership. I believe in that. The players are magnificent. The squad has a brilliant bunch of players, one of the most exciting in Europe. I have spoken with Vialli, of course – he's the boss – but I haven't spoken to the players about it, but it is a personal matter and I am sure the players will feel like I do that it is down to myself. I don't think there will be any blame from the other players about my decision.'

So does a contract mean anything? Laudrup said: 'When you enter a contract you intend to see it out, but you have got to learn in life that it is not always a reality, it is sometimes not easy to stay as long as you might like. If you are not entirely happy then money is of no importance whatsoever. I am not thinking of money. A lot of players wouldn't give up the contract I've signed – it's not a bad one, I can tell you. People can say what they like, but what is money worth if you are not happy as a private person?'

This unsavoury episode wouldn't put Chelsea off buying the big-name foreign stars, Hutchinson confirmed: 'We are constantly reminded about this. We have bought quite a few foreigners and we've had no problems whatsoever. This is a unique situation involving a rather unique man, who has pinpointed the areas for his decision. It saddens us as we worked very hard to put the deal together. We had to move very quickly, and we worked non-stop to try to make Brian and his family as happy as possible in London. I believed, and still believe, that we brought here one of the top players in the world. If we lose him tomorrow, in two weeks or two months or at the end of the season, it will leave us with a gap in our squad, and he is not the kind of player you can go out and replace overnight. I don't think that should mean we should scrap our foreigners policy. We shall sign players from anywhere in the world if they can improve the squad.'

Hutchinson is an expert in PR. He almost had people crying in sympathy with the poor hard-done-by boy from Denmark who wanted to go home to make himself, his wife and family happy. So far there had been no mention of the pots of gold on offer in Copenhagen. But within twenty-four hours it emerged that Laudrup would earn a fortune back home in a deal that included a £500,000-a-year basic salary, a percentage of the gate at the 41,000-capacity National Stadium over a certain level, a share option scheme and a percentage of the sales from Laudrup replica shirts. He would also be allowed to play for as long as he wanted before becoming a director with a ten-year contract. Just to ensure he knew the money situation, his father Finn was made marketing director.

FC Copenhagen expected Laudrup to sign at eleven a.m. next Friday, but Hutchinson said: 'Until we sign a deal with Copenhagen, he won't be going anywhere. We expect him to be back in training in London on Friday.' However, privately Chelsea would not be surprised if Laudrup and FC Copenhagen had already done a deal.

FRIDAY, 30 OCTOBER

Tony Blair dropped in on Chelsea's training session along with his Minister for Sport, Tony Banks, and a group of young French footballers who were part of a programme encouraging sporting links. Vialli presented the Newcastle-supporting PM with a Chelsea number ten shirt with BLAIR on the back. Vialli said: 'You can be right wing or left wing, but for me Tony Blair is doing a great job in defence of the realm! He is honest and straight. Coming from Italy, you must understand how lucky this country is. He is doing a good job.'

After the PM's proposal to relax the quarantine laws, Leboeuf asked the Premier: 'When can I bring my pet dog over here from France?' Leboeuf added: 'The event got me thinking, and I have to say there is a worrying trend. My concern is that it is too easy for young people to see footballers now as celebrities rather than sportsmen. Instead of dreaming of becoming a professional because of the love of the game, there is a danger that their ambition is based purely on money, status and the chance to be in *Hello!* magazine. I am sure that Michael Owen is the best striker in England now because he thought only of being a brilliant player. He was not concerned with all the trappings. His dedication meant that he has come through, even though English clubs do not seem to put the same importance on football academies as we do in France. I just hope that young people continue to see football as a sport and not a business because, as Brian Laudrup has explained, you cannot be happy unless you are content in your game.'

Despite Hutchinson's warning, Vialli did not duck questions about Laudrup's place in the team. In fact he was ready to let Laudrup run the gauntlet of the Chelsea fans, pledging that he would only be withdrawn from the firing line for footballing reasons. 'Brian is available for selection like everyone else while he is still here with us. If he does go, then I will respect his decision because it's a personal one and has nothing to do with football or with Chelsea. Brian has assured me that, as long as he is going to be here, he will do his best. We will just have to see what happens.'

Laudrup was included in Vialli's twenty-man squad for the next match.

Hutchinson insisted the saga could have a few more twists. 'We certainly haven't ruled out Brian coming back to Stamford Bridge in six or twelve months' time when he has got his head straight. I don't think Brian knows himself what he wants. His head is in turmoil. He signed pre-contracts with us in February and his transfer was completed in Copenhagen on 6 June. It's fair to say that, even then, he was already in a confused state because Glasgow Rangers were making ludicrous compensation claims, Ajax were threatening to sue him and he felt he was dragged unfairly into Ruud Gullit's departure from the club. Then he was worried that a lot of Denmark's hopes at the World Cup rested on his shoulders. So we have not given up hope of talking him into changing his mind, not least because he has promised to give 101 per cent to the cause for as long as he is at Chelsea. We will insist on a clause in the contract saying that if he leaves Danish football, his playing registration will automatically revert to Chelsea.'

Leboeuf said: 'I just feel sad and disappointed that he might be leaving because he is a great player and a good person. I would never tell him "Don't leave" or "You are right to go", but maybe some of the other players will try and talk him round. People have an idea that, to a man, all professional footballers care about is how much they are earning. Brian is not the first player to sacrifice a lot of wages – Christophe Dugarry moving from Barcelona to Marseilles springs to mind. If Chelsea supporters are upset, I think they just have to realise that there is nothing the club can do other than agree to let him go. If he was being sold to Real Madrid or Barcelona, their anger would be justified, but moving back home shows that he is genuine about being homesick. Of course football is important, but occasionally there is more to life.'

SATURDAY, 31 OCTOBER

Vialli criticised referee Alan Wilkie's decision to call off the match with Aston Villa an hour before kick-off. 'It is very strange when a referee calls off a match an hour before kick-off. He should have waited longer and allowed us time to sort out the pitch. Everyone here was gutted, we really felt we would have beaten Aston Villa. We thought that the pitch was playable, and also we all felt sympathy for all the fans who turned up, some after a long journey.'

John Gregory praised Wilkie's 'common sense' decision. The referee himself explained that he took an early 'courageous decision' because of the standing water on the pitch, the forecast for further rain and his fears that players could sustain a serious injury in the conditions. It was a close call, especially as the rain had virtually stopped by 3.45 p.m., yet questions had to be asked about the lack of a protective cover and the way in which water dropped on to the pitch from the top of the stands.

Laudrup had been included in the starting line-up in a three-pronged strike force with Zola and Casiraghi. Bates supported his coach, fed up hearing about his highly paid players moaning. Living in his penthouse suite at Chelsea Village, no one was more committed than Bates. 'I have no interest in reading what individual players may or may not feel about their ambitions at Stamford Bridge. I have read all the players' contracts and in none of them does it mention guaranteed first-team football. It simply says that in return for making themselves available for selection, they will be paid hundreds of thousands of pounds per week. Chelsea are honouring their side of the bargain – we expect every player to honour their side.' Bates refused to comment on Laudrup's embarrassing request for a move but, no doubt, was happy to offload the club's highest wage-earner if he didn't want to serve the Blues. 'What comes first at Chelsea is winning matches; what comes second are the players' personal aspirations. We need a large squad. Look at most successful Italian teams in Serie A. They all have large squads, which means that some top players don't play. When you get suspensions and injuries you need a big squad.'

Poyet agreed with Bates that the team must adhere to Vialli's rotation system, whether they like it or not. 'I want to play in every game but I understand what Gianluca wants and he can only pick eleven players for every game. But you can't leave a great player like Gianfranco Zola on the bench for three or four games – you must pick him some time. It is very difficult for us and for Luca, but we understand his situation.'

Wise apologised for his reckless Worthington Cup tackle in the programme; the only person he has failed to apologise to is Byfield, the player who was the target of the dreadful two-footed lunge. 'I'm sorry. I apologise to you fans, to the players, to Luca, to everyone at Chelsea. I said a few weeks ago that I'll never get sent off again and now, not surprisingly, I'm being hammered. I meant what I said. It's a horrible feeling, and after the pre-season game I was determined it wouldn't happen again. I don't know what happened: the ball ran loose, I was on the ground, I saw it and went for it. To me, it was as simple as that. I asked several people afterwards if they thought it was that bad a tackle, 'cause all I'd done was give it my all. I've got to admit, most people said it was.'

Wise's team-mates suggested he should be in charge of the Ryder Cup team – because he's so used to being a non-playing captain.

November...
November...
November

*Bye to Brian ... Gigi crippled for the season
... so much for Luca's Famous Five
forwards?*

SUNDAY, I NOVEMBER

Luca took his players training in the afternoon because of the postponed game.

Zola was targeted by the media as the next potential Laudrup because he had often made it clear he would like to finish off his career in Sardinia. Zola said: 'I can understand the frustration felt by Brian Laudrup – it can be frustrating when you are not playing regularly in the side. I think people should respect his decision and I hope everything works out for him now.' But Zola was staying. He signed a two-year contract extension last February, tying him to Stamford Bridge until 2002, when he will be thirty-six. 'If at any stage it becomes clear that Chelsea don't want him any more, Zola can come here,' said Cagliari President Massimo Cellino. 'The door is open and there remains a possibility that it will happen. I'm not sure what Gianfranco is getting paid right now but he knows that what I can pay, I will. I know Zola well, and his intermediaries too. They have only to pick up a phone.'

Flo was advised by Norwegian club manager Nils Eggen to leave Chelsea for the sake of his international career.

MONDAY, 2 NOVEMBER

Leboeuf appeared on BBC TV's *On Side*. He feared Michael Owen was playing too many games and could suffer a breakdown similar to the one Ronaldo endured before the World Cup final, and added: 'To be honest, I am getting a bit tired of reading and hearing that the only reason I won a World Cup winners' medal was because the Brazil striker was ill. Of course, Ronaldo was not at his best, but as far as I am concerned, it had nothing to do with conspiracy theories, Nike's involvement or any political pressures. He was simply exhausted, as any young man would be playing up to seventy games in a season, and all of them under intense scrutiny. I don't think many people could cope with that.'

TUESDAY, 3 NOVEMBER

Barcelona and Juventus angered Chelsea by trying to hijack Laudrup, but the player insisted he will only quit for a return to his native country.

Vialli was deciding whether to indulge in the ultimate act of brinkmanship by asking Laudrup to help knock his prospective employers out of Europe. Laudrup said: 'At the moment, the plan is for me to leave Copenhagen after the match on Thursday night and fly back to London with the rest of the Chelsea team. And from there I will prepare with the squad for our game at West Ham – unless I am told to do otherwise. Until my situation becomes clearer, I must continue my daily life around London. But everyone at the club can count on me giving a hundred per cent to the cause until I switch clubs. I'm still a Chelsea player and, at the moment, I have no idea how long that will last. When I explained my situation to the other players at training last Friday, I was very happy that they all seemed to understand and backed my decision. The Chelsea management have also been fantastic. They recognise I have been open and honest with them, and it only shows there is still room for some humanity in professional football.'

Of Danish coach Johansson's olive branch, Laudrup added: 'I have agreed to speak with him on Thursday and I will be interested to hear what he has to say. It's too early to give a definitive answer, but as things stand right now I still don't think I will play international football again. So much has been happening to me over the past few months that it will be difficult to get my head round that as well.'

WEDNESDAY, 4 NOVEMBER

Bates wanted to retain the Cup Winners Cup in the competition's final year before it is merged with the UEFA Cup in the shake-up of European competitions. 'We want to be the last club to defend the trophy and win it back, and, hopefully, if UEFA are really nice to us, we will keep it for ever if we do that.'

Laudrup checked in only one piece of baggage at Gatwick airport instead of hiring a removal van, so Chelsea had withheld their blessing for a rapid transfer. The Danish star was travelling on a return ticket like everyone else in the holders' party. Hutchinson said: 'Any suggestion that Brian will be signing for Copenhagen on Friday is well wide of the mark. We've had no contact with them since last week, and if he leaves, it will be at Chelsea's convenience.'

Laudrup was ready to play against the Danes. 'If I can get a good result for Chelsea I'll be happy. I have a contract with Chelsea and as long as they pay my wages I am ready to do my best for them and remain a hundred per cent professional. I don't feel awkward about playing against Copenhagen. I'm too long in the tooth to be afraid of playing in games like this and I don't feel under any pressure. Of course I can't promise I will play brilliantly, but if I don't I will not be blaming it on my personal situation. I am twenty-nine years old now and I've been around long enough to cope with these circumstances, even if they are a bit unusual.'

Amid the peanuts and bar stools of a Copenhagen hotel lobby bar, Laudrup held court, pledging to help knock his prospective employers out of Europe. Speaking only in his mother tongue, he confirmed he would fly back to London with the

Chelsea squad after the match regardless of whether the Blues were in or out of Europe. That has caused jitters on the Scandinavian stock markets, because Copenhagen were planning to unveil Laudrup as their superstar signing at a news conference just hours later.

Vialli had insisted Laudrup stay for at least three more games. He said: 'This is probably the most important match of our season so far – and the start of a decisive week for the club. We want to stay in Europe here, stay in touch with the Premiership leaders at West Ham on Sunday and keep hold of the League Cup at Arsenal next Wednesday. After those three games, we will know where we stand, what we can achieve and where our season is heading. I believe I'm going to have everyone around for the next three games, and that includes Brian Laudrup. I realise that playing him against Copenhagen could work for or against us and that these things cut both ways. Brian might show everyone in his native country what a great player he still is, or the emotion of the occasion might affect him – but who knows? One thing is for sure: Brian is old enough, professional enough and experienced enough to give his best for us, or at least smart enough to come and tell me if he wasn't feeling up to it.'

Morris was Vialli's only injury casualty for a match in which Chelsea had to score to stand any chance of reaching the last eight of the Cup Winners Cup for the third time in four years.

Liverpool described as 'garbage' claims that Chelsea were interested in McManaman, whose contract expired at the end of the season. Hutchinson said: 'We've not made any approach to Liverpool, but I believe he is a Bosman free.' With Laudrup going, it made sense to be kept informed on McManaman.

THURSDAY, 5 NOVEMBER

FC Copenhagen 0   Chelsea 1 (agg. 1–2)

Surely it was fate. Boos and abuse greeted Brian Laudrup, but he scored his first and last goal for the club to take Chelsea through to the quarter-finals.

Bates waded into a section of the travelling fans, who unfurled an offensive banner telling the Dane to 'Fuck off home'. Bates, who left his seat in the directors' box to remonstrate with the dissenters at half-time, raged afterwards: 'I thought the banner was in very bad taste. These people are just the scum that made their way over here and they have nothing to do with our official party of supporters. We got the banner taken down, which is the most important thing, and it shouldn't detract from us reaching another major quarter-final. Brian promised to give his best for as long as he wore the Chelsea shirt, and he's been as good as his word. After all, he scored the winner – and he could have put it wide, couldn't he? These morons displayed a foul banner for all the world to see on TV. We have spent years rebuilding Chelsea's reputation in Europe and at home. Free speech is a fundamental principle of this country's unwritten constitution, but you can express it without the crudest of epithets in full view of the world.'

Wise supported his chairman. 'We did not hear the fans booing him in Copenhagen and I hope they will not do that to him again because, if he is leaving, at least he has given us something to remember him by. He is not here for the money. It took a lot of guts for him to come clean with the club about his situation. A lot of people would not have been strong enough to follow their hearts instead of their wallets. Brian has admitted he may have made a mistake signing for Chelsea when he could have kept quiet and kept picking up his wages. For that, I hope our fans will give him a good reception whenever he goes. I had a funny feeling that Brian would score the winning goal or do something special to get us through. Now, thanks to him, we can put Europe to one side until March and concentrate on the Premiership.'

In Frank Leboeuf's excellent *Times* column the next day, the French defender added: 'Football dressing rooms are merciless places when there is the chance of a good joke at someone's expense, but not a word was said in jest to Brian Laudrup on Thursday night ... I certainly don't condemn him for wanting to leave Chelsea, unlike those supporters who put an offensive banner up in Copenhagen. They must have felt pretty stupid when he scored, just as the FC Copenhagen supporters who booed him should feel daft when he signs for them. Brian was very quiet before the game and he must have had plenty on his mind.'

The club could also be in trouble with UEFA after fans let off an orange smoke bomb as Laudrup was substituted midway through the second half, a merciful end to his ordeal.

FC Copenhagen set a deadline of three p.m. on Sunday to complete negotiations for Laudrup's homecoming. General manager Flemming Ostergaard said: 'I will be flying over to London to discuss the move with Chelsea's managing director Colin Hutchinson, over the weekend. I have a feeling that Brian will be a Copenhagen player by Monday. Even though he scored the goal that knocked us out tonight you could tell the fans here love him.' Vialli was less forthcoming about Laudrup's future, saying cryptically: 'I know what's going to happen to Brian, but I'm not telling you yet.'

Vialli's gamble in challenging Laudrup to put professional pride ahead of personal sentiment was vindicated, but the passage into the last eight was as uncomfortable as the arctic wind. The underdogs were on £5000-a-man bonuses to pull off the greatest ever upset in Scandinavia, and on a heavy pitch the Blues had to resort to the English virtues of spirit ahead of continental sophistication. They could have made life easier for themselves, but Casiraghi – one goal in 890 minutes – and substitute Flo spurned clear-cut chances in the last ten minutes. Casiraghi was lucky to escape with just a yellow card for an unnecessary bout of mud-wrestling with Goldbaek in the dying minutes, while Vialli engaged hapless French referee Claude Colombo in animated conversation on the final whistle. He had to be ushered away from the confrontation by Rix, and the boss's agitation served to underline how grateful Chelsea were to survive.

Chelsea had made a bright enough start, Stensgaard's reflexes proving equal to Casiraghi's full-blooded header and Le Saux beating the turf in frustration after a dreadful miss after twenty-two minutes. Bursting into the box to meet Di Matteo's perceptive pass, the England full-back miscued hopelessly into the side netting.

De Goey was required to make a few important saves in the space of a minute. The Dutchman had his doubters, but his only real scare came seventeen minutes after the restart when Rytter's shot was blocked on the line by Babayaro and sub Todi Jonsson scooped a simple chance over the bar from the rebound. The crucial incision came after thirty-one minutes when Le Saux, the best player on the pitch, crossed from the left without breaking stride and Casiraghi's near-post header cannoned off the woodwork. Laudrup, lurking in the six-yard box, nodded the rebound beyond former Liverpool goalkeeper Michael Stensgaard. It didn't silence his most vocal critics at the other end of the half-empty stadium, but it did at least stem the waves of abuse raining down for a while.

Vialli said: 'Football is a funny game because Brian hadn't scored in his ten previous games for us. I knew he was having a difficult time because of everything that's been going on over the past few days. But he has been outstanding in the past few games and has looked sharp in training, and I never thought it was a gamble to play him here.' Not that Vialli let Laudrup hang around to join his team-mates milking the applause on the final whistle – he was withdrawn midway through the second half.

Laudrup admitted after the match: 'It wasn't easy for me to play. I tried not to think too much about all the aspects of the tie and blot them out of my mind. I just ran out there and did my best for Chelsea. I tried to work as hard as I could, and I scored my first goal for the club and I'm delighted. Before the game I told our assistant manager Graham Rix that I would score with a diving header, and he promised to give me five pounds if I did. We never shook hands on the deal, so I'm not sure if he will pay up. We were under a lot of pressure before the game but I think I showed a lot of commitment and took my chance. In the end, we were a bit lucky, but we could have scored more goals with the chances we had.'

On the plane journey home, the plan was hatched to sign Copenhagen's most awkward opponent, Bjarne Goldbaek. Hutchinson explained: 'Luca, Graham and I chatted about him. They'd liked what they saw and asked me to have a look at the situation. I spoke to their president about it on the Friday after we had concluded the Laudrup agreement. We thrashed out the basis of a deal, and I did some checking on his background with Jakob Kjeldbjerg, who became most helpful to Chelsea and the player. I talked to Bjarne at length on the Friday night, then on the Monday he came over to meet Luca and Graham. He was very impressed with our set-up at Harlington and what they had to say.'

Goldbaek also had an insight into when the Laudrup deal was first starting to be hatched. He said the Copenhagen players were less shocked than the media. 'We had already speculated a little bit because we had seen in the hotel when we played the first leg that his manager was here and they were sitting with our president. We were talking about it but we couldn't really believe it because he was earning so much money. But it wasn't a big surprise.'

FRIDAY, 6 NOVEMBER

Gigi was accused of plunging his teeth into the leg of defender Mikkel Mio Nielsen. The Dane said: 'I have four teeth marks in my leg. He did not break the skin, but it is red and blue. I spoke to the doctor about it afterwards, but because there was no blood I didn't need a tetanus injection. I was really surprised when he bit me. We had our battles over the two games, and yes, there were some elbows out there, but that is part of the game. But you never spit at another player and certainly never bite them. I've never been bitten before, and I was rather surprised when it happened. I only thought that kind of thing happened in boxing!'

The incident had occurred late in the tie when the centre-forward was pulled down but still managed an overhead kick. As the pair scrapped on the floor, TV cameras captured Casiraghi back-heading Nielsen in the unmentionables. Nielsen also divulged the banter between the two: 'I said to him, "It's not normal to bite." He said something to me in Italian which I didn't understand.' The Copenhagen players gave Casiraghi the nickname 'Tyson', but Nielsen planned no formal complaint. In fact he still admired the Italian international. 'The marks are a souvenir of our two games, but it was a great experience to play against a player of his stature. There are certainly no hard feelings. I have not discussed the matter with the manager or with the club, and I have no intention of making a fuss about it.'

Luca laughed, and declined to make any public comment.

At last an end to the farcical situation surrounding Laudrup. Hutchinson, who spent most of the morning on the phone to Copenhagen, explained: 'Sad though we are that Brian is going, we felt that the matter should be brought to a conclusion to let us get on with life, to take all the publicity and speculation away and to let the rest of the team – those that really want to play for Chelsea – get on with winning matches. It's an ongoing circus, and I do think it's time to get back to normality. I decided that we should get the deal done now to allow Brian to be registered with Copenhagen so they could have the benefit of him for three matches before the winter close-down. All parties have now signed the agreement and Brian's registration with Chelsea was cancelled at the FA this afternoon. He will be registered today for FC Copenhagen.'

No financial details were released, although Hutchinson did confirm that the 'compensation fee' paid by FC Copenhagen 'beats by a mile' the existing Danish transfer record for an incoming player of £300,000 (for Claus Thomsen). The statement to the Copenhagen Stock Exchange also gave no details of the transfer sum or the contract, but the day Laudrup ceases to play for FC Copenhagen his registration will revert to Chelsea, and should they sell him on outside his own country then a fee of around £5m would be payable to the west London club. Hutchinson ensured the club had fully covered its costs.

Within hours of submitting to the demands of the unsettled Dane, Bates was calling on the PFA's Gordon Taylor to take action against players who want to renege on their contracts. 'Gordon is a very strong man when it comes to protecting his players' interests and condemning everybody in sight when anything goes wrong,' said Bates. 'It is about time now that he came out and initiated the introduction of new standards. That would do his standing in the game a great deal of good; at the moment he is basically regarded as an old-style "Arthur Scargill" union man. It would be an important statement from him if he demonstrated that the PFA are heading for the twenty-first century by taking a lead.'

Bates is a firm adherent to the call for either a transfer window or a shifting of the transfer deadline to apply to players and managers equally, except in emergency situations. 'In most parts of Europe they have a transfer opportunity window, and I would be in favour of either that or moving the transfer deadline from the third week of March to the third week of November. That would stop the business we have just gone through.' Bates also believes there should be a similar cut-off on transfers in the summer, some time in mid-July. 'You get clubs who won't sign a player until the last minute before a season starts to save on wages through the summer. I think that is penny-wise, pound-foolish. We try and sign new players at the end of a season even though that means we pay their wages for what is a dead three months. We signed Frank Leboeuf before the 1996 European Championships, and then got Marcel Desailly before the 1998 World Cup. What would they have cost us if we had waited until after those events to go after them?'

Unbeaten in thirteen League and Cup games, Luca was without the suspended Leboeuf and Duberry for the Hammers match. Wise was still struggling with the knee injury sustained at Blackburn six weeks ago, but was expected to play before his enforced sabbatical.

Vialli allegedly faced a lawsuit after claims that he described Zdenek Zeman as a 'terrorist trying to destabilise football'. Zeman had instructed his lawyer to start legal action over the alleged remarks.

On a lighter note, in the gym, during the team meeting, Gigi fell off the bench. Lambourde recalled: 'We just heard a big bang and he was on the floor. We all laughed!'

SUNDAY, 8 NOVEMBER

West Ham 1   Chelsea 1

Casiraghi's first season with Chelsea was over after a horrifying injury. In the private ambulance on the way to Charing Cross Hospital, accompanied by his agent Fabio Parisi, he said: 'It was a cross from Zola. I was going for the ball and preparing to slam it with my left foot when I collided with the keeper. People were talking to me but I could not hear a thing. I couldn't move my toes. I looked at Graeme Le Saux; his face was bright red and he appeared to be crying because he could see how much pain I was in. So I knew it must be bad. Dennis Wise and Neil Ruddock were looking down, saying something, and I was trying to read their lips. But I couldn't hear a thing because everyone was yelling and running around in panic. All I could think of was the pain I was in. I tried to focus on things around me but everything was a complete blur.

'I should have been playing with a rabbit's foot in my shorts, I have had such bad luck here in England. I've never believed in such things, I've never been superstitious, but after what's happened I am beginning to wonder if all this scientific approach is the right way. I am completely devastated by what has happened. But I have to try to be positive and hope things are not as bad as they could be.' But although initial X-rays ruled out any bone damage, it was serious. He suffered the additional complication of a lack of movement in his foot, but Vialli said: 'That might just be because of a blood clot. Fortunately there are no broken bones. He's been so unlucky so far it didn't surprise me that he got injured.'

Zola was so shocked when he saw the damage that he sank to his knees in shock and yelled: 'No! Oh, no!' There was a ridiculous delay providing treatment on the pitch and finding the right stretcher as the Italian star writhed in agony. There was such deep concern that Le Saux snatched the stretcher from an overweight and slow medic to race to Casiraghi's aid. When the Italian star was finally carried off four minutes later, Wise threw away the second stretcher in disgust at the time it took to assist the stricken star. 'I was bitterly disappointed with the people here because they did not seem to react quickly enough. It seemed like ten minutes before Pierluigi could get the treatment he needed. Our physio kept asking for straps to hold his knees together. But all they kept doing was bringing on different stretchers. He was in an awful mess.' Ruddock said: 'It was not nice to see. His face was contorted with pain.' West Ham doctor John Lawrence had attended to Casiraghi on the pitch. He said: 'He was in an awful lot of pain. We all knew something serious had happened as soon as he went down.'

Vialli was satisfied with a point that left Chelsea back in fifth place with games in hand, but he conceded: 'This must be a good lesson for us if we don't start in the right way. We might have got a point, but in the future we might get nothing. Yes it was one of our best away performances, but we had to chase the game for the first twenty minutes after they scored early on. We did play some nice football though, and I'm very pleased with some of the boys who are usually on the bench who played: Lambourde, Petrescu, Gustavo and Nicholls.' Nicholls had come on as a second-half substitute for Zola, and there would be further opportunities for one of the few English players in Vialli's squad. Terry also came on as substitute for the second time, and it was a proud moment again for him. Certainly Flo wouldn't be spending much time on the bench in the days to come either. He would have to do better than he did at Upton Park though. Chelsea dominated the second half and peppered the West Ham goal, missing far too many chances, although Flo wasn't guilty of all of them.

West Ham had gone a goal ahead in the fourth minute, when Berkovic was fouled by Babayaro, who had played a stray pass in the first place and was anxious to make amends as he backtracked. Berkovic rolled the free-kick into the path of Ruddock, and the giant centre-half curled his shot from outside the area into the corner beyond de Goey. Vialli made his first substitution for the start of the second half, bringing on Petrescu for the ineffective Di Matteo to switch Poyet into a central midfield position. When Wright was hauled back by Desailly the crowd howled for a free-kick, but referee Graham Barber waved play on – it would have meant a red card as he was the last man in defence. Flo was overelaborate manoeuvring into a shooting position before the interval, and when he was successful, turning sharply in the second half, the shot was saved by Hislop.

With fifteen minutes left, Wise swung in a corner and Nicholls was one of several players to get a touch in a mad scramble which culminated in Babayaro's far-post header crossing the line. Flo then turned Ruddock, but his left-foot shot was saved superbly down low by Hislop. Wright had a header saved by de Goey at the other end, and then it was Chelsea's turn to threaten again, but Hislop was alert enough to save from Poyet. With Chelsea looking the more likely winners, West Ham fought back and Berkovic struck the inside of the post with a couple of minutes left. Berkovic was only eight yards out, and his angled drive beat de Goey, but the inside of the post came to Chelsea's rescue and the effort of it all caused Berkovic to limp away with cramp.

Redknapp, with one eye on his own team's comparative lack of resources, had little sympathy with his opposite number's striker 'crisis': 'Chelsea have such a strong squad they could put out two teams, whereas we are often down to the bare minimum. We were short of bodies today, but when you look at their bench they had the likes of Petrescu and Flo ready to come on. I don't know how the injury to Casiraghi happened, but I hope he's okay. But they have four world-class strikers – and the manager is world-class in my opinion.'

MONDAY, 9 NOVEMBER

At 4.30 a.m. Lambourde was at the side of his girlfriend Carolle Biffe to witness the birth of his son Melvyn. Luca said: 'This is what happens when you are too passionate. It must be the air in London!'

Laudrup said his farewells at the training ground, and Goldbaek arrived. The thirty-year-old Dane was available for the tie at Arsenal after signing a three-and-a-half-year deal, and cost £330,000. He was intent on leaving the country after playing for just over two years there following nine years in the Bundesliga. 'I hope I will be able to score some more goals at Stamford Bridge, but this time in a Chelsea shirt. It's up to me to show I'm good enough. I was missing the feeling of playing in front of crowds of up to forty thousand, and I'm looking forward to doing that again in England. It was okay to live in Denmark, it was very nice to play there again, but sometimes there are only two or three thousand people in the crowd. It was important for me to hear from Mr Vialli that he thought I had the qualities to play in the team. He said that there are no guarantees, but he said that if I could bring some of the qualities that he had seen in the two games Copenhagen played against Chelsea then he could use me. That was what gave me the sign to come to Chelsea.'

Mikkel Forssell, still only seventeen but one of the most exciting talents in Finnish football, was available on a Bosman transfer from HJK Helsinki after signing a pre-contract in the summer. His appearance in the Champions League, in a 2–2 draw at Benfica, ruled him out of the Cup Winners Cup for Chelsea. Despite press reports to the contrary, the teenager had not been recruited to replace Laudrup.

After training the players visited Gigi in hospital. It was an emotional time. Ken and Suzannah Bates also paid a visit. Even Gazza turned up. Casiraghi's former Lazio team-mate had been treated in the same Princess Grace Hospital. Gazza's secret visit was mentioned on Chelsea's TV station Blue Tomorrow on Cable 17. Leboeuf said: 'He's okay but he has a long way to recover. Gustavo explained to me how hard he had to work to come back and how bad he found it to watch his team-mates play.'

Gigi hid the true extent of his pain and suffering from everyone, as he feared his career was over. 'It has been hard, but when things like this happen there are many people who are willing to give you support and affection. I have never felt abandoned because so many people were around wishing me well and covering me in love and friendship. Paul Gascoigne came to see me. I must admit, everything was still a bit foggy because it was the week of the accident. I honestly don't remember what he said to me, but it made me happy because I didn't expect him to come and see me. It meant a lot because he, too, had a terrible injury. He probably saw a little of himself in me. What I do remember well, and will never forget, is what happened when he pulled off the sheets and took a look at my knee. He made an awful face and turned away in disgust. It was hilarious, and I could not stop laughing. Gazza truly has a good heart. He has so many emotions swirling inside him. Sure, he made mistakes, but he is a real person and a genuine friend. All my team-mates have become very close, especially Zola. He is like a crutch to me. It goes beyond the hospital visits and the phone calls. The others have been a big help too – Vialli, Petrescu, Di Matteo and Poyet. Even a guy like Albert Ferrer, who has just come to England and hardly knows me, was there for me at every turn.

'On the day itself I was calm. It was the next day that I was terrible – that's when they told me I had a serious injury. That day I was sure my career was over. But the doctors looked at me after surgery and guaranteed I would play again. I want to believe that, but I know it's up to me and how badly I want to come back. I truly believe I can do it, and hope to be back for next season.'

Petrescu was determined not to be forced out. Vialli was ready to offload him but changed his mind and wanted the Romanian as an integral part of his squad. Speculation continued, with Gullit monitoring his situation. Petrescu said: 'I do not want to move on at all. I want to play more often and that is frustrating, but I don't want to leave the club. The only success I've had is with Chelsea. I am very happy with my team-mates and with the manager. My family have also settled in London very well and I am ready to apply for residency papers in England so that I do not have to apply for a work permit. I am so settled here that it will have to be a great offer to take me away from Stamford Bridge. Some clubs have been in for me recently, but they are not the ones I would like to go to anyway. If I do move on, it will have to be to a greater club than Chelsea, and there are not many of those.'

Desailly and Flo figured alongside Laudrup and five players from Arsenal in the shortlisted nominations for European Footballer of the Year. In all, ten Premiership-based players figured in the list – the highest tally for years. Zola also received a nomination, but finished narrowly outside the top fifty.

TUESDAY, 10 NOVEMBER

Vialli spent a harrowing evening at the hospital as Casiraghi had a four-hour operation. Surgeons repaired some of the damage to his knee, the outside lateral ligaments. It would be four to six weeks before a second, more major operation. Russian keeper Dmitri Kharine had had a similar knee problem and was out for nine months. Williams said: 'The important thing was to stabilise and repair the lateral ligament, which was the initial problem. He needs to see an expert, probably in Venice, when there will be a reassessment of the damage to the cruciate ligament. The priority is to ensure that the man can live a normal life rather than rush back to play football. This is not going to be a short one.'

Before the operation at the Princess Grace clinic, Luca was optimistic: 'Gigi is a very strong lad. This is not the first time that he has got injured so I think he knows what he has to face and he can cope with that. I'm sure he's going to get over it very soon, sooner than expected, and will wear a Chelsea shirt very soon. At the moment he's a bit down of course, but he's really looking forward to this operation so he can think about the day when he will be able to play football again.'

Despite being linked with Nigerian international Nwankwo Kanu, Vialli dismissed the prospect of immediately signing a big-name replacement. 'After a while we may do something, we may go back into the market and sign somebody else, maybe on loan or something like that. But I'm sure we are capable of doing well without Gigi and Brian.'

Ironically, Zola also had trouble with a slight knee injury. Suddenly Luca's attacking options were being restricted virtually by the day. After being relentlessly criticised for leaving out Flo there was absolutely no excuse for leaving him on the bench against Arsenal now – there was no one else!

WEDNESDAY, 11 NOVEMBER

Arsenal 0   Chelsea 5

Arsenal's biggest home defeat in seventy-three years! Chelsea's biggest-ever win against the Gunners! The first time Chelsea have scored five times against the north London giants in 140 games!

But not even two more goals by the player-coach to add to his hat-trick in the last round consoled a traumatised Vialli. He declined to talk about Chelsea's biggest win of the season because he was so upset about the devastating injury to Gigi. Instead, Vialli sent Williams into the packed media room at Highbury. 'Luca has been with Pierluigi today and is still feeling too upset to speak. He's tired and drained both physically and emotionally after the match. Pierluigi had an operation today, and Luca came away from seeing him knowing exactly how he feels. Luca wants to dedicate this result to him.'

Luca sipped champagne with his players in the dressing room before his first game in charge against Arsenal in this competition, and it was a sparkling experience. This might have been a contest between reserve teams, but there could be few more satisfying feelings than to hammer Arsenal on their own ground in front of a 37,562 crowd. Before the game Vialli joked that he didn't think he was 'good enough' to score another hat-trick, but he came damn close; if it hadn't been for a stray pass from Flo right at the end, he would have. Even so, five in fifteen days had lifted him to joint top scorer as Chelsea stretched their unbeaten run to seventeen games. Vialli's career total with Chelsea stood at a formidable thirty-five in fifty-four starts, making him the most prolific striker on his own books.

The start of Chelsea's domination came with a controversial decision by referee David Elleray. Vialli began the move in the thirty-fourth minute, heading into Poyet's path as he ran clear on goal before being brought down from behind by a Grimandi tackle. The French defender might have touched the ball first, but it was impossible to have executed such a tackle without bringing down Poyet. The Harrow referee blew for the penalty. Curiously, if Grimandi was guilty it should have been an automatic red card, but instead he received the lesser punishment of a yellow. Leboeuf kept his cool to despatch the penalty with the usual force into the corner, giving Manninger no chance.

Arsenal had plenty of chances before that goal, and after it, but it was not to be. Vialli took over in the second half, grabbing the second in the forty-ninth minute. A pass from debutant Goldbaek cut out Grimandi; Vialli flicked it past an embarrassed Manninger and simply strolled it into the empty net. Shortly after a lacklustre Bergkamp departed, Flo burst clear and cleverly waited at the by-line before cutting his pass back for the onrushing Poyet to finish off. Vialli expertly collected his second from a Poyet pass in the seventy-fourth minute with an angled shot into the corner, and six minutes later Poyet scored goal number five from a Petrescu pass.

Wenger later described the penalty which started the avalanche of goals as 'ridiculous', but his objection fell on deaf ears so far as Chelsea were concerned. Leboeuf, captain in the absence of Dennis Wise, was full of praise for Vialli's contribution. 'He was like a twenty-five-year-old. He's got loads of confidence and that gives us a psychological boost.' Leboeuf was not fazed by the row over his penalty, or the devaluation of the margin of victory because of the strength of the Arsenal team. 'We don't care. We have beaten Arsenal and we're in the next round, that's all that matters. If it was not a penalty than I apologise to Arsenal, but Luca should have scored anyway.'

Goldbaek enjoyed a successful debut. 'This is a dream move for me. I was so, so, so tired after the game I almost didn't know where I was. In the days before, I didn't sleep or eat well because I was in so many minds whether to come to Chelsea as I would have been a free transfer in the summer and I had a good choice of clubs to go to. Also I had my wife and young son to consider. But it is not often in your career that you get such an offer from such a club, especially when you are thirty. Brian Laudrup actually rang me last Sunday and told me Chelsea was a great club. He had nothing bad to say about it. And to win at Arsenal like that was memorable – and the pitch, I couldn't believe it. It was smooth like the green on a golf course. I hope all the pitches are like that in the Premiership. It was wonderful. I shall remember it for a very long time because everything was nice: the stadium, the pitch and the score.'

In the fifth-round draw Wimbledon were pulled out of the bag as Chelsea's next opponents. The club was installed as 5–2 favourites by William Hill, with Manchester United at 11–2.

THURSDAY, 12 NOVEMBER

Bates left a message on the answerphone. Well, it was more a little ditty he had cheerfully invented to the tune of the Dean Martin hit 'That's Amore': 'When the ball hits the back of the Highbury net, that's Vialli!' When he finally got through he said: 'Beating Arsenal was nice, a score which will be remembered long after the team selection is forgotten. However, hang on a minute. Before the game the press was making much of Arsenal's weak young team, but they still fielded at least four internationals. For our part Chelsea made seven changes from the team that started against West Ham, and for one reason or another left eight full inter-nationals out. As one generous Arsenal fan said in their boardroom, "We have a team of stars, Chelsea have a squad of stars", and as injuries, suspensions and international calls take their toll we are going to need our big squad. Gianluca justifies his rotation system with results.'

Leboeuf filmed the first of a new series of *They Think It's All Over.* Presenter Nick

Hancock introduced him as the star from Marseilles, 'the nearest thing to a local boy at Chelsea'.

Le Saux and Morris returned to full training.

FRIDAY, 13 NOVEMBER

A fax arrived at national newspaper offices late Thursday afternoon with the names of the squad of eighteen. 'Luca wishes for the squad to have some privacy this week and would be grateful if you could respect his wishes,' it read. Luca even gave the club's official telephone hotline a cold shoulder. But in his programme notes Vialli finally spoke about Gigi's operation. 'A few really nice things have happened lately, but unfortunately something else also took place. You know what I am talking about. Gigi got injured, as usual courageously challenging in the box, trying very hard to tap in a cross from Gianfranco despite the goalkeeper and defender challenging too. It's a pity because Gigi has played really well and is going to be a loss for the team. It's a pity for him also. It's always sad to see a player forced to stay away from the pitch for a long time. And it's a pity for you supporters. I don't believe you appreciated enough Gigi's first spell at the club, and I think you will now realise what we miss. He was desperate to make a good impression. Maybe that's why he was challenging all the balls and that's why he got injured. Let's wish him altogether good luck.'

Luca was also full of praise for the play in two derby matches. He felt that, apart from the first twenty minutes at West Ham, the team produced its best football so far. 'Another nice thing was to see two young professionals come on, Neil Clement making his third appearance and Luca Percassi his debut. Our young professionals are growing up, growing well and with the right attitude.'

Now for a third London derby. Luca added: 'I know we haven't got a good record against Wimbledon at home. We must work really hard if we want to change the story because as usual they're going to make our lives really difficult.' Chelsea added Morris to their squad for a match which would finally provide Flo with his first Premiership start of the season. 'I have now been here for fifteen months but I always felt that my time would come, and now, maybe, it has. But I'm still not sure. It would be nice if the manager did not go straight into the transfer market at this time.' Flo has a gift for goals and didn't believe the tactics had to alter when he played. 'I think I'm good in the air, but my favourite is when I'm running towards the goal and the ball is played to my feet. Anyway, at Chelsea we try to mix some things up so that the other team cannot be sure about us.'

Leboeuf took over the captain's page in the programme. He was firmly focused on the title. 'Everybody knows we have two games less than the others. If we can win today, if we keep carrying on as we do at the moment, then I believe we can win the championship. But everybody has to be behind us and then this season really can be the Chelsea season.'

SATURDAY, 14 NOVEMBER

Chelsea 3   Wimbledon 0

Vialli couldn't mask his delight; this was close to a perfect performance. 'I always felt we would create chances today. I feel we are one of the best teams in the

Premiership. All we need is that added luck that helps you win the title. All we have to do is pull in the same direction, and that is happening. The squad is very professional.' But still he was cautious: 'As soon as you get happy, you get humbled.'

Wimbledon had rarely been beaten this easily by anyone, not that the scoreline suitably reflected Chelsea's dominance. By the sixty-sixth minute Wimbledon fans were screaming at Kinnear to do something to stop the slaughter.

Flo's powerful right-wing run and Zola's conclusive finish in the thirty-second minute saw the little Italian sprinting towards the bench to hold aloft the number ten shirt for their absent friend, Gigi. Zola's joy was unconfined, but not just because it was his first goal in seven weeks. 'Before the game I asked my team-mates whoever scores the first goal to run to the bench and lift Casiraghi's shirt. We know he's very down and we wanted him to know we are close to him all the time.' Gigi had phoned Franco on the morning of the match to wish him well. Zola said: 'That was something that gave me drive. I was sure I was going to play a good game, although I wasn't sure I was going to score. But I'm really proud to have scored. It was one of the most emotional moments of my career.'

Awarded his first Premiership start of the season, Flo did everything but score. He glided time and again through a usually rock-solid Wimbledon defence, Zola superb beside him. The outcome was one of the most enjoyable performances of the season, despite the key absentees (in addition to Gigi, Ferrer had recovered from a minor pelvic knock and had trained, but it wasn't enough to be selected after a one p.m. test before the kick-off, and Goldbaek, who had picked up a minor knee injury on his Arsenal debut, wasn't risked from the start). Vialli hinted that with a partnership of Flo and Zola at his disposal he might soon be able to dispense with the 'player' bit in his player-manager title. 'At my age it takes time to recover both mentally and physically, and when I have players like Gianfranco Zola, who is so committed, and Tore Andre Flo, so young and powerful, it doesn't worry me if I don't play again. Flo is an exceptional young man with an exceptional talent. He will finish his career here. He has everything a manager needs. I want him to be a legend at Stamford Bridge. He is going that way. From now on you will see a lot more of him in the team.'

Poyet was also influential in the match, darting from deep positions. 'I thought he was excellent, and he has an exceptional record for a midfield player,' said Wimbledon defender Chris Perry. In his final season with Real Zaragoza he had scored fourteen goals from midfield – nine with his head. Poyet, thirty-one the next day, said: 'I so enjoyed today. It was wonderful to be involved in so much that was happening. I like playing in this position, just behind the strikers.' Poyet was also convinced about the club's drive for the title. 'I think now we can win the League. I need to win the League. I never won it before in Spain or France. The Chelsea players think about it all the time. I don't see any reason why we can't win it.'

Petrescu added the third goal. He had a point to prove. 'I care for this club, I want to stay here. I like living in London and see no reason to leave. Chelsea were the club that offered me my first success and I want to finish my career here.' The Romanian was openly worried about his future, but after playing his part in two goals and scoring he was much happier.

Vialli was winning his battle to keep his large squad as happy as possible, but it was taking its toll. He said: 'I am gradually getting used to it, but it is a difficult job, a real challenge, but mentally enjoyable. But the spirit of the club means so much more than the individual. When people speak of their unhappiness they now do it behind closed doors. That is how it should be. It's hard if you think everything is easy. There is always something waiting to kick you in football.' The combined role of player-manager was making it even tougher. 'I really don't want to play any more if I can help it. Mentally and physically it is so hard for me to feel up to it. I now need so long between games to recover fully, and that is down to my age and other duties.'

Both sets of players had been left with freezing water when the dressing-room boiler packed in. The hard men from south London might put up with the Hackney Marshes treatment, but surely not the the highly pampered west London superstars.

Leboeuf emerged with only a towel around his waist shouting, 'Come on, come on, we've sold Laudrup, surely we can pay the water bill!' Old boiler Bates would surely have heard that one!

SUNDAY, 15 NOVEMBER

The *Sunday Mirror* front-page splash story reported that Rix had been charged with having sex with an under-age girl. Police also accused him of three offences of indecently assaulting the fifteen-year-old. Rix, forty-one, was alleged to have committed the offences at the team's hotel – the Novotel in Hammersmith – the night before Chelsea's Premiership defeat against Manchester United last season. He was scheduled to appear in court in west London three days before Christmas. The girl, who had been interviewed by child protection officers, is now sixteen. The newspaper reported that detectives planned to question Poyet and two other players about whether they saw anything at the hotel, although there was no suggestion that Poyet or any other players were involved. They were questioned about whether they saw Rix and the girl at the hotel. Police were also taking evidence from Rix's friends and family. Rix was on unconditional bail. A Scotland Yard spokeswoman confirmed: 'Graham Rix, aged forty-one, a football coach, is bailed to appear at west London magistrates court on 22 December. He is charged with one count of unlawful sexual intercourse with a girl under the age of sixteen on or before 27 February 1998. He is also charged with three counts of indecently assaulting a girl on or about 8 January 1998, between 8 and 30 January 1998, and on 27 February 1998.' The maximum sentence for unlawful sex with a girl aged under sixteen is two years' jail.

The investigation into Rix's alleged liaison with the girl, who cannot be named, began last August after her father made complaints to police. Rix has been married to wife Gill for nineteen years. They have four children: Jenny (seventeen), Robert (fourteen), Gemma (ten) and Gavin (seven). The paper reported that last year their marriage had hit the rocks over allegations he had an affair. Gill and the children were still living in the family home – an £800,000 house in Harpenden, Herts.

MONDAY, 16 NOVEMBER

Flo indicated he would sign a new contract for the next five years. 'They want me to stay at the club and it is true that we have begun talking about that,' he said. 'We have discussed a new contract but I haven't agreed anything with them yet. I have three and a half years left on my present deal and the club want to extend it to five at the moment. It is difficult for me, though, and I will have to think about it very carefully. But I enjoy playing for Chelsea and I would like to stay in London.'

He was also sure he would forge a partnership with Zola, the archetypal Little and Large. 'I think we can play together if we work hard at it. Gianluca Vialli hasn't played us together because he feels we are similar players, even though we look very different. It is true, because we both like to come out of the box to get the ball. It is very important that one of us stays in the box all the time to get involved in the battles for the ball in the air. I am the tallest man, so it's natural that I am the one to do that. I am happy to do it, and I think Gianfranco and I can form a very good partnership.'

TUESDAY, 17 NOVEMBER

Double training. Morning and afternoon.

WEDNESDAY, 18 NOVEMBER

Neil Clement joined Reading on a two-month loan with a view to a £300,000 move. Clement, twenty, born in Reading and the son of former England international Dave, was unable to earn a regular place. The left-sided defender, capped by England at Under-18 level, made just one League appearance after signing professional terms at the start of the previous season. He came up through the apprentice ranks with Morris and Nicholls and featured in Channel Four's *Cutting Edge* documentary on life behind the scenes at Stamford Bridge. Morris and Nicholls played prominent roles in Vialli's plans, but Clement had made only one appearance, as a substitute in the Cup win against Arsenal.

David Lee and Paul Hughes returned from a loan spell at Bristol City that lasted just one training session. Lined up by previous manager John Ward, new boss Benny Lennartsson said: 'They are not the type I want.'

THURSDAY, 19 NOVEMBER

Luca considered how the club's transformation into genuine title challengers had happened. 'Chelsea have always had difficult times against teams weaker on paper, so we have started in a different way this season and we are a bit more consistent. Sometimes you might think, I'm better than them, so you are not in the right frame of mind and that's the worst way to approach a game like that. You need to go out there and work your socks off, and sometimes, when you are considered a superstar, you don't fancy that kind of game and you will lose. I think my players know what they have to do if they want to win those sorts of games. I am very happy with them. Whatever team we play against, whether it's Real Madrid or Wimbledon, they will do their best. A manager's job is to buy the right players and make them fit and in good form, but mainly it's about spirit: the way you make them approach the game, the motivation you give them. Mentally is where you can change a team.'

Vialli was in no rush to buy another striker. He would splash out if necessary, even though he could not compete in the transfer market with the likes of Manchester United, Arsenal and Liverpool. 'At the moment we want to see if we can go on like we are, but we may sit down and decide we want to strengthen our squad. We don't have a lot of money – not enough to waste – but if we need some we will find it.' Arsenal had moved for Milan's Nigerian international Nwankwo Kanu. Vialli admitted: 'He is a great player. We haven't tried to sign him yet, but Gigi's injury means we might have to alter our thoughts. I am happy so far with Zola and Flo. I don't want to touch them because I see the pair running riot this season from now on. I can also play to cover them.'

Zola concurred with Vialli's thoughts on Chelsea's transformation. 'I've never felt fitter, more competitive and determined to do well. My life here at Chelsea is so happy. I feel Chelsea and I have only just started here. Some teams collapse going towards winter. We will get better. That is down to Luca. We used to beat Spurs 6–0, Sheffield Wednesday 4–1, and then lose to a smaller club. We no longer act so arrogantly. Our game is more complete. Luca has given us that. I think Chelsea are quite capable of winning many things. I am not surprised how well we have done. We have not underestimated ourselves. We have players who went to the World Cup and who are now mentally fit again. The important thing is the way you achieve success. Many teams want to be successful but they don't know how to do it. The path we have chosen is the right one. We are mentally and physically strong every time we go into a game. Under Luca we have become tougher. He has worked us hard, ensured we never leave anything to chance. He is tough on us, but we realise you have to work if you want success.

'Juventus in Italy built their success on playing games for ninety-six minutes. We are doing the same. Look at the figures and see how many games we have won or saved in the dying minutes. Personally I feel just as fit after ninety minutes as when I started. We have a passion and commitment here that is different. You can be the best player in the world, but you also have to show it in games other than the top ones. The next two months you will notice that. When the pitches get softer we will be just as fit as in August. We will get even better results.'

Desailly spent an hour in the Megastore signing mementos for the fans, while Williams checked on media reports that Flo had been injured after equalising for Norway in their 1–1 draw in Egypt. Gwyn called Tore and spoke to his girlfriend, Randy. Flo phoned back after the game to say he was fine.

Vialli was concentrating on the match at Filbert Street. He said: 'Leicester is important to us and I hope we can show how we've improved. I have a team here that can adapt to every situation. I'd like to think we can match teams that play football or play tough, those who go for the second ball or for the long ball. I'd like to think I've got into the chaps about how to switch into different moods for different games. Leicester is a better team than the one you see on paper. I admire them immensely, and in particular their manager. But it's been a good working week for us. Apart from Flo and Le Saux I've had a full squad with me, and hopefully we can continue to play the way we have been.'

Flo arrived back from Egypt in the afternoon and reported fit. Vialli said: 'I don't know where that story came from, but he is fit and I am delighted to have yet another full squad available. Leicester on Saturday will be vital to us, as is every game. We no longer treat teams like them any different to the way we treat Manchester United, Arsenal or Liverpool.'

FRIDAY, 20 NOVEMBER

Lunchtime training, afternoon departure to Leicester.

Kevin Keegan wanted to follow Vialli's lead with a rotational system to make the best use of his strike power at Craven Cottage. The Fulham boss had spent almost £11m reinforcing his squad, and had ten forwards! Keegan said: 'I don't want to be compared with Chelsea, but I can see us playing different strikers in different situations depending on the game. You can never have enough strikers because they win you matches, which get you the points for promotion.'

Old pals Duberry and Sinclair got together for a chat. Duberry said: 'We were in the same hotel. We had a little talk in the bar. Not drinking of course – we don't do that, we're good pros. Just talking about what life's like at Leicester. He's very happy.'

SATURDAY, 21 NOVEMBER

Leicester City 2   Chelsea 4

Luca looked serious in his *Match of the Day* interview.

'Do you know the other results?'

'No,' responded Vialli.

When informed that the three top clubs had lost, Luca clenched his fist and punched the air, shouting, 'Yes!' Instantly he returned to the serious pose and said: 'There is still a long and winding road.'

Now eighteen games unbeaten and within range of the top. This match was tremendous, entertaining and gripping, and Vialli was proud of the result. He said: 'For ninety-five minutes we had to play out of our skin. It was one of the most difficult of the season. English football is so difficult because you need to change the way you play depending on the opposition. Sometimes you can play nice football, attractive football. But sometimes you have just to compete and work really hard and fight. In some games we can show our skills, in others we have to fight for everything. Today we had to fight very hard against a team who never gave up.'

Previous Chelsea teams would not have survived such a sustained bombardment, but de Goey and Leboeuf were heroic. De Goey's fabulous saves from Graham Fenton and old boy Frank Sinclair, and Leboeuf's acrobatic goal-line clearance from City's emergency striker Matt Elliott, were the crucial moments. De Goey was Man of the Match, and Martin O'Neill thought he was 'magnificent'. Vialli added: 'Apart from the first months of last season he has always been outstanding. He is doing his job very well and I'm very happy with him.'

Roberto Di Matteo had to have stitches just above the right eye after an elbow from Matt Elliott. The Italian said: 'It was only two stitches. I've had worse experiences, it was not that bad. Because of the white shirt it looked quite horrible, but it wasn't that bad. Basically I went for a header, felt an elbow in my head, I fell down. I didn't realise there was a cut until Frank Leboeuf looked at me in a funny way. After that I was quite scared.' Physio Mike Banks recalled: 'Although the wound bled quite a lot it was only a small one, requiring a couple of stitches at half-time.' He was to develop a black eye, but it would take a few days to see whether or not there would be a tiny scar.

For all their good fortune, Chelsea were clinical when it mattered. Zola arrested half an hour of defending, bundling Goldbaek's cross over the line. Then Poyet's reflexes were sharpest when Desailly's header rebounded off the bar.

Bridge reject Muzzy Izzet poached an instant reply. Then Zola's sublime free-kick rattled a post and Flo potted the rebound to make it 3–1. The travelling fans taunted their hosts, 'You might as well go home.' Good job they didn't. Steve Guppy reduced the deficit again with half an hour to go, and only Zola's second goal in the fifth minute of stoppage time lifted the siege. There was even enough spice left for a spot of churlish posturing involving Elliott, Babayaro and Walsh on the final whistle.

Zola, whose skill and movement were terrific throughout, said: 'This result will give us even greater belief in ourselves because Leicester are strong and this is never an easy place to come and play. We had to struggle, we had to fight and we needed a bit of luck – but this was a performance with all the right ingredients.'

But O'Neill was inconsolable at finishing empty-handed. 'We have pulverised a team studded with world-class players and we did not get our just rewards. I thought we were absolutely fantastic and we blitzed them. We kept conceding the daftest goals imaginable, but we never gave up. Chelsea were entitled to beat us 12–0 with the team they put out, and we are totally distressed in the dressing room. The first time Chelsea put the ball into our box, they scored. Then we went round feeling sorry for ourselves for the next five minutes and, all of a sudden, we were 2–0 down to another daft goal. If you had gone to the toilet when it was goalless, and come back to find us two down, you would not have believed it. People at this football club are lucky: if they live to be a hundred years old they will never see the players put so much effort into a performance as that.'

Sinclair, deprived of a penalty by Desailly's shove at the height of the siege, warned: 'Catch Chelsea in that mood and you are going to struggle against them, no matter how good you are. They are going to be up there at the end of the season. Whoever finishes above Chelsea is going to win the Premiership. We've played all the top four now and each time we rose to the occasion against Villa, Manchester United, Arsenal and now Chelsea. But Chelsea are the only ones to have beaten us, and they have been as good as any of the others.'

Hooliganism still festered in English football. Later, on the BBC's *Six-O-Six* programme, a supporter spoke of a seven-year-old boy so terrified by gangs of Chelsea supporters rampaging through the narrow streets around Filbert Street that he was probably lost to the game. 'When we got home the lad took off his cap and scarf and said that he didn't want to go any more,' the caller said. A Chelsea supporter himself, and big in the government's football Task Force, *Six-O-Six* presenter David Mellor responded to this information with appropriate gravity. Pointing out that Chelsea have done a great deal to isolate the worst elements in their following, he nevertheless agreed that further action may have to be taken. Throughout the match pleas had been made over the Tannoy system to rival groups divided in one corner of the stadium by a thick wedge of police officers.

After the game Zola celebrated with a night out at Wembley at a Lionel Ritchie concert. 'Afterwards Gustavo, his wife and my wife, we went to have something to eat. Very good,' recalled Zola.

SUNDAY, 22 NOVEMBER

The *Mail on Sunday* European Super League table based on domestic and European results showed Chelsea top, ahead of Manchester United, Bayern Munich, Kaiserslautern and Real Madrid.

The sequence of Premiership results at the top of the table revamped the title betting. Chelsea – the only one of the four title favourites to avoid defeat, let alone pick up three points – were down to as short as 9–4 (from 5–1). Vialli's side, second favourites with some firms, were five points behind Aston Villa with a game in hand. Arsenal, whose lack of strength in depth was cruelly exposed against Wimbledon, were out to 3–1 from 5–2, while United could be backed at 6–4.

MONDAY, 23 NOVEMBER

Extra training in the afternoon. There was no let-up, despite the number of exhausting and demanding games. Leboeuf described the session as 'very physical'.

Tickets for the Wimbledon tie were sold out, and 1100 more were sent over from the south London club.

TUESDAY, 24 NOVEMBER

Another tough session. 'Very hard, and we didn't even touch a ball,' observed Leboeuf. 'We work much harder these days.'

WEDNESDAY, 25 NOVEMBER

No day off. Morning training was hard again with the ball, and ended with more running. Leboeuf said: 'We trained in a short area so you had to run very hard and keep going, and after we did some more runs. We are physically well prepared. So against Leicester, when it came to the last ten minutes and they tried to press us, we were better than them.'

Arsenal were knocked out of the Champions League, losing at Wembley to Lens, and suddenly Luca's rotation system was being praised! Martin Keown said: 'The problem is that the Arsenal first eleven basically picks itself, and it's the side that did so well at the end of last season. Manchester United and Chelsea can spin their players around and still have good people in most positions. But it's hard for our lads to just come in, step up to another level and perform and do better than the players they have replaced.'

THURSDAY, 26 NOVEMBER

Training ended with a long game of tennis-football.

Desailly spent an hour in the Guildford store ringing up purchases for the fans. Wise does the same at the Bridge Megastore.

There was an eventful AGM in the Galleria attended by 300. 'It lasted three minutes,' said Bates. The only excitement was that security had to be called to throw out a real old Chelsea pensioner! Bates said: 'He must have been eighty but he went kicking and screaming. When he was thrown out on to the Fulham Road he swung a punch at the security guy, catching him full on the chin, and snatched his pass. The police were called and he was arrested. It was the same cantankerous old fella who turned up last year to cause trouble.'

The Rock launched his own brand of sports clothing at the Guildford Megastore. As he walked out of the shop, past the multitude of branded merchandise including a Rover MGF sports car, Desailly signed autographs and provided his own shopping list: Premier League, then Champions League. 'We're going to win things here,' he told the fans. 'And winning is beautiful, yes?'

FRIDAY, 27 NOVEMBER

Vialli was advised to look at Arsenal as an example of supreme consistency. They had, after all, won the Double using as few players as possible. 'Last season that seemed to be the best way to manage a squad,' Luca said. 'We were criticised because we had a bigger squad, but now that we are getting better results it seems that our policy is better than theirs. It just goes to show that in football you are never right. Whatever you do in this game can turn out very right or very wrong. It is too early yet to say which method is best, but results dictate our way of thinking and we have not been beaten since the opening day.'

One reason for their new-found confidence was the blossoming relationship between Flo and Zola; with that pair at the helm Chelsea had scored twelve goals in their last three games. Vialli admitted: 'It's been a bit of a surprise for me as I thought both Gianfranco and Tore needed to play off a strong striker. But they are a great combination as they're very clever, not selfish, and I'm very happy with their partnership.'

The Rock featured in the programme for the next day's match as the most fair defender in the Premiership. He said: 'It was the same with Milan, I only get booked once or twice a year. It's a good statistic for me. Sometimes I must be careful. When I've just made a foul I have to be careful for five minutes after. But that's all. You have to be intelligent.' Whether in defence or midfield, he had avoided a booking so far this season. 'I don't do many tackles, that helps me a lot. I use pace to get possession, to get the ball away, rather than the tackle.'

SATURDAY, 28 NOVEMBER

Chelsea I   Sheffield Wednesday I

Of course, it was inevitable: in the sixty-eighth minute Desailly collected his first yellow card.

Luca was featured on *Match of the Day*, intensifying interest in his championship chances. Gary Lineker expressed the view that Vialli's rotation system had been 'vindicated', although Mark Lawrenson pointed out that the side 'picks itself' with the loss of two key players in attack. Luca admitted he was still a novice in management terms: 'Yes, it is harder, definitely harder at the moment as a beginner. I couldn't handle the pressure very well, but I am getting used to this job. The way

I am I take things too seriously. I am very critical with myself and the players. But I am enjoying myself a bit more.' He also cleared up any confusion about his future: 'I have two and a half years to go before my contract expires. I hope to still be here in two and a half years' time, which will mean things have gone well.' Could he see himself staying for five years? 'No. To be fair, no. Alex Ferguson has stayed, but he is an exception. The really top managers in the world, sometimes they have got to make a change; it helps find new motivation, new spirit, and it is nice to know new people.' There was a fascinating insight into his management style when it was pointed out that he doesn't appear to be a ranter and raver in the dressing room. 'When I get really angry I can't speak English fluently. I try to say things but they don't come out!'

In his programme notes, Luca insisted that Sheffield Wednesday must not be underestimated, especially after they had beaten Manchester United the previous week. 'As usual we need to perform at our best if we want to continue the good run,' he said, but the match was an anti-climax. The fluency of his TV interview was not matched by his team's performance, which was well short of his relentless quest for perfection. Yet it was still history in the making: this result equalled the club's finest run of undefeated games. The previous nineteen were completed starting on 14 January 1984, in Division Two.

A rare headed goal from Zola in the twenty-seventh minute should have been the start of something big, but Pavel Srnicek in the Wednesday goal produced five outstanding saves and Andy Booth plundered an equaliser in the sixty-seventh minute. Despite all Chelsea's chances, the much-improved Wednesday wasted a chance to win themselves when Booth shot wide, and Desailly survived a penalty appeal. Much was made of this 'handball' which wasn't a penalty, but little attention was drawn to the fact that Poyet had been hauled back by Danny Sonner. Gus said: 'For me, it was a penalty. I tried to play the ball with my head and the defender of Sheffield tried to take my shirt and not play the ball. You never know if it's too hard or a little bit of a pull for the referee to give the penalty. Definitely, I couldn't play the ball because he held on.'

Goldbaek said: 'We sat in the locker room and talked about what we did right and what we did wrong, and we were not satisifed, but I think we didn't play that bad, and we didn't lose the game.' Vialli conceded: 'At least we kept our good run, but the players are a bit disappointed. We lost a great opportunity to improve our position on the table. But there is no way we can win all our games; the competition is so tight, and opponents know how to create problems. So one point is good.' But here was underachievement when a win would have elevated them to second in the table instead of West Ham. For those predicting Chelsea would be top by Christmas, this was a setback.

Flo had got his wish as first-choice striker but failed to make much impression. The fans' favourite admitted: 'It was just not right today, it didn't feel right. I don't know why. I thought to myself it would be okay after all when we scored, but it just didn't happen. I've only had four games. I don't feel any kind of pressure about that.' Nevertheless, Vialli again considered the question of buying a striker. 'I think there is no hurry. At the moment I want to keep on going back to the same squad. But if something comes out that suits us, we could make an effort and sign the right player. I am fully confident in Franco and Tore, so I would not want a top-class player, but maybe one cut out to do what I would want, and that might be to sit on the bench often or most of the time. It is not easy to find the right player, but we shall keep looking.'

SUNDAY, 29 NOVEMBER

Leboeuf had made his 100th appearance, but his four-match term as skipper was over. Wise was back. Frank was delighted that his stint writing in the club pro-gramme was over – at least until Wise's next ban! 'I'm fed up doing this column,' he said. 'I'm having to find too many words with my column in *The Times* as well.'

Luca certainly planned to recall Dennis. 'He is part of our side – everybody is, whether they are on the bench or have a place in the stand. Dennis is our captain. There is no problem; he will come back into the team and do a job.'

Diego Maradona and his wife Claudia were among the crowd at the Rome derby, a thrilling 3–3 draw, and he spoke in defence of Luca and against Zeman. 'Zeman has made inaccurate comments about Vialli and players such as Ferrara without having any proof whatsoever.'

Former Chelsea keeper Dave Beasant was grateful for being able to split his training between London and the Midlands. 'It's great of Luca Vialli to allow me to train with the Chelsea boys. I get on famously with them and it also means I don't have to face long journeys from home every day of the week, and that helps me enormously. When I was at Southampton I used to make the 170-mile journey every day, and I don't think it did me any good in the long term because I used to get very drained towards the end of the week.'

MONDAY, 30 NOVEMBER

In training Vialli rested Flo and Zola, playing himself alone up front.

David Lee, at Stamford Bridge for ten years, in his testimonial season and the club's longest-serving player, was looking to leave Chelsea, claiming the club was obsessed with foreign stars. 'The club bent over backwards to keep Brian Laudrup, who had been there only five minutes. I've been there all my career, but they just don't seem bothered. They appear more interested in foreign signings than those who have been here for years. I've been treated very poorly. It is not a question of me having a moan because I can't get into the team. The manager has made it pretty clear I am not in his first-team plans and I have no problem with that. It is the way the club has treated me which has annoyed me. It's my testimonial season, but no one is worried. They said a game would be organised at the start of the season. With Pierluigi Casiraghi, Marcel Desailly and Albert Ferrer signing, I would have got a good crowd. But the game never materialised and I've heard nothing since. They suddenly stopped talking about it. The club is not interested in what I do.'

Lee, twenty-nine, enjoyed his best season as a sweeper under Glenn Hoddle. He signed a new three-year deal in the summer of 1996, before the arrival of Gullit. He broke a leg against Tottenham three days after the death of Matthew Harding, and has played second fiddle to Leboeuf ever since.

He added: 'The club has given me a free transfer and I just hope I can get a move as soon as possible. But they don't seem to have made it known that I am available, and a lot of clubs seem to think I am injury-prone. I'm not. I broke my leg and was out for eleven months. Yet I have not missed a day's training since and, even before the accident, have only ever been off for six days. I know I will never play in the first team again, so I just turn up for the reserves and try to help the youngsters along.'

There would be a final morning training session at the Bridge before the evening kick-off in the Cup.

December...
December...
December

Out of the Worthington Cup ... but
top of the Premiership for the
first time

TUESDAY, I DECEMBER

Wimbledon 2   Chelsea I

The club record nineteen-game unbeaten run came to a depressing end. Since toasting his players with champagne before their second-leg blitz of Arsenal in the previous season's semi-final, this competition had brought Vialli enviable success. In all forms of knockout football, his previous fourteen ties in charge had yielded only one defeat – and even that reverse, in Europe against Vicenza, was overturned spectacularly at Stamford Bridge.

Vialli rested Le Saux, Desailly, Di Matteo, Zola, Flo, Ferrer and de Goey from his preferred Premiership line-up. The boss started alone up front in an unusual formation. 'The reason I played five in midfield with only myself up front was that I just wanted to outnumber them in the middle of the park where Wimbledon win all the knock downs,' Vialli explained. 'I wanted to play football rather than hit the long ball like Wimbledon. But they outwitted us. I wanted to win that battle because they are very good at picking up those pieces. I think perhaps it confused the players a little bit, and I have to admit I made a tactical mistake, because in the second half when we had our normal system we created a few chances. I will stick with the normal one in future. The players did their best for me, but there are simply no excuses. Wimbledon thoroughly deserved to go through.'

The holders were knocked out on a pitch strewn with divots. Robbie Earle headed Wimbledon in front from a routine set-piece. Too busy admiring the flight path of Neal Ardley's free-kick after twenty-one minutes to notice Earle's late arrival in the box, Kharine allowed the Jamaican World Cup midfielder's header to arrow past him. The Dons were hell-bent on revenge for their FA Cup semi-final drubbing twenty months earlier, and only when Flo emerged after the break was Chelsea's appetite for a scrap restored. Leboeuf's grapple with Gayle gave Man of the Match Hughes the chance to put the tie beyond them from the spot with sixteen minutes left. Even then, Vialli had enough time to poach his sixth goal in three League

Cup ties with four minutes left, and trigger a frantic siege at the Sainsbury's End. But Wimbledon held out and marched into their third semi-final in two years. Ladbroke's immediately installed Wimbledon as the new 5–2 favourites.

Leboeuf could not recall his first rough and tumble with the Crazy Gang with much affection as it had left him nursing a golfball-sized bump on his head. He wouldn't remember this one fondly, either. Earle said: 'I think we had a bit more physical presence with the likes of Marcus Gayle and Carl Leaburn up front, and that is a threat to teams. We wanted to do ourselves justice against Chelsea. They seem to have had it a little bit easy against us. We've never quite felt that we've given them a good enough test. We said before the game we're going to get tight, we're going to make it difficult, and if they're too good for us then we'll hold our hands up. We got amongst them and were good enough to win.'

It was a bitterly disappointing night for Poyet in particular. He was supposed to be playing wide on the left of the advanced midfield four. He explained: 'We missed a good opportunity to go to Wembley. I want to play at Wembley having not done so in the final last year when I was injured. I've played there only one time, the Charity Shield in my first game.' Wise, who played the holding role in a 4–1–4–1 formation, echoed Poyet's disappointment: 'We just couldn't do it. We were focused. We've been focused all season. We knew that we had to get through these Worthington Cup games. But it is a fact that now we can concentrate on the League. There is a lot of focus on that here, and it is one of our ambitions.'

Vialli instantly looked forward too. 'Now we must start all over again. It's a test for myself and the rest of the team. We now have to see how we cope with a defeat and roll our sleeves up like we did after we lost at Coventry on the opening day of the season. I hope we can show we are strong enough to cope with the defeat. My players are absolutely gutted in the dressing room, but it might be useful for everybody because it puts us down to earth and now we have to start again with even more desire than before. Now we must show how strong we are mentally.'

WEDNESDAY, 2 DECEMBER
Training.

Frank and Betty Leboeuf went to dinner with the Prime Minister at Number Ten. Both the PM and his press secretary, Alistair Campbell, speak French.

Frank also appeared on television as a guest on *They Think It's All Over* showing his sense of humour dealing with sharp-witted comedians like Rory McGrath. He answered every waspish one-liner from McGrath with an untouchable put-down: 'I don't care – I won the World Cup.'

Luca's right-hand man Gwyn Williams celebrated nineteen years at the club. Vialli said: 'He needs fresh legs! He does a terrific job for the club, looking after us all in any way. If I were chairman I'd make sure he stays for another fifteen years. He is the one, I promise you, who could write a very interesting book about the last two decades at Chelsea. I really believe it. We need to read it, Gwyn!'

Vialli took stock. He was hard to please. 'I'm not delighted with the way things are going this season, but I am happy. I'll only be delighted at the end of the season if we've done something, or at least know that we've done our best. We went through three months without defeat, but sloppiness is always just around the corner. If you lose concentration you can lose everything. I would hate that.'

THURSDAY, 3 DECEMBER

Gigi went home from hospital for a few days, and then on to spend Christmas with his family in Italy. His team-mates were playing a key role in his recovery. He said: 'I have been moved by my friends at Chelsea. There is far more squad togetherness over here than in Italy. Albert Ferrer, Dan Petrescu and Jody Morris all brought me cakes that their wives had made for me. Gianfranco Zola gave me a bottle of champagne with the message "To the greatest strike partner I have ever played alongside". Roberto Di Matteo, Gianluca Vialli and the others have all brought me things as well. Our masseuse, Terry, gave me an England shirt that all the players had signed. And a little girl brought me a Chelsea teddy bear with its right leg wrapped in bandages! All these things have touched me a great deal.

'When I arrived at the hospital the doctors thought I had been knocked down by a car,' he continued. They had chosen a specialist to perform the operation who was more used to treating the huge fractures suffered by American footballers. 'I had the flu, which made things more difficult, and then I picked up an infection as well. I couldn't understand anything for days, not even when people spoke Italian to me. Now things are far better. I have tried walking around with the aid of crutches for the first time, and my confidence is back.' Casiraghi was determined to play again and repay Vialli.

Zola and Ferrer took their turn for a signing session at the Megastore.

Over 1000 turned out for the Chelsea Village carol service, and to watch Dennis Wise turn on the Christmas lights.

FRIDAY, 4 DECEMBER

Leboeuf's *Times* column provided an insight into Luca's management style. 'A football team inevitably reflects its manager and – the defeat in the Worthington Cup aside – that is the case at Chelsea this season, where Gianluca Vialli is attempting to cast us in his thorough, determined and, most importantly, perfectionist image. Our boss is relentless in his demands. It has been interesting to watch how Luca has settled into the job and established his own style of management, which is very different from that of Ruud Gullit. I suppose it is a question of philosophies. They are hard to sum up, but if Ruud's was that you must enjoy your football, Luca's is that you must deserve it. Different players react to different methods, but I am sure it has made us tougher this season, which is shown by our run of nineteen unbeaten matches. Part of the motivation is trying to make sure that Luca is not in a bad mood after a game because he is so intense about our performances, as though he takes it personally. He feels responsible for everything we do, so it is not surprising that he gets tired or upset after games.'

Vialli was sure Chelsea would never suffer from the same internal power struggles which undermined Everton. Their chairman, Peter Johnson, stepped down after a row with manager Walter Smith over the sale of Duncan Ferguson to Newcastle to help clear the club's overdraft, of which the manager was only informed at the last minute. Vialli accepted that chairmen such as Bates remained in overall control of finances and set budgets, and at Chelsea Hutchinson is in overall charge of transfers and negotiations. However, no deal is done without first receiving the go-ahead from Vialli; the boss would not accept any attempts to undermine his own control over decisions which directly affect his squad.

He said: 'We are always talking about things, but player-wise I'm in charge. I decide what squad I need and then Colin Hutchinson does his best to sign the players I need or to keep the players I need. Of course, we're quite flexible, but we try to do our best to improve the team rather than sell players because we need money. At the moment, Chelsea want to sign players, not sell them. Fortunately we haven't got a problem with money. We have to stay within our budget, of course, but we make our moves before the beginning of the season so we don't need to make any changes during the season. I'm very lucky as a manager that this is the reality at Chelsea. I don't know the reality at Everton, but what happened there won't happen at Chelsea.'

Wise scanned the team sheets for tomorrow's game intently looking for the most important name of all – the identity of the referee. He had returned to Premiership action following his second suspension of the season, vowing not to change the uncompromising style which has earned him an unenviable disciplinary record. He declined to repeat his foolhardy pre-season vow about never getting sent off again, but the realisation that Gary Willard was the referee at Everton would affect his actions on the pitch. 'Sometimes you get booked because of who you are because a referee wants to make a point. Silly bookings like that are just annoying. Some referees you can talk to, some you can't. There are different mentalities. Some you joke with, some you don't. Some you can say certain things to, some will book you. I used to like Roger Milford, but Graham Poll is one of the referees now who's very sensible and he'll have a go back at you, he's a good fella. He speaks to you, and it's nice. He's on the same level. He'll swear at you; you'll say something to him and he'll tell you to shut your mouth. Referees have been put under a lot of pressure this year because of certain rules they've been told they have to stick by. Some of them do stick by them all the way down the line, but some of them use a bit of common sense and know when not to book a player, when it's an accident or it's mistimed.' Willard was in a halfway category after booking twenty-two players in five Premiership games this season, but not having sent anyone off – yet.

Vialli wanted his captain to control his aggression, and was full of praise for English referees, more 'relaxed and understanding' than their Italian counterparts. 'Dennis knows he needs to improve and probably can't go on like that for the rest of his career,' Luca explained. 'But the more you talk about something, the worse it gets – so I won't be talking about it.'

Duberry was adamant Chelsea would recover from their Worthington Cup exit with a serious title challenge. 'Everyone is always knocking Chelsea, and it was the same after the Wimbledon game. But we will bounce back at Goodison. We're used to people putting us down. Either we're being paid too much money, or there is no fighting spirit in the camp, or the foreign players aren't committed or aren't happy. But we believe in ourselves. The team spirit at the club is incredible. There is a great mixture of young players and experienced players and foreign players and English ones. We all play for each other and believe in each other. Now we have to look at the positive things and get back to making a challenge for the championship.'

Vialli made the inevitable changes for the match: Zola and Flo returning up front, and Desailly at the back.

Newton had finally recovered from a foot injury.

SATURDAY, 5 DECEMBER

Everton 0   Chelsea 0

A daft performance from Wise. In his first game back after a four-match ban for a two-footed lunge on Villa midfield player Darren Byfield in the final minute of a Worthington Cup game, he got sent off again. He was booked after just three minutes for tripping Danny Cadamarteri, then clattered into sweeper Marco Materazzi nine minutes before the break. Referee Gary Willard, playing the advantage rule, allowed play to continue for fully a minute before going back to the Materazzi incident and brandishing a second yellow card at Wise. When he was given his marching orders, Wise appeared baffled until Willard jogged his memory: 'The second caution was for unsporting behaviour, namely a late and dangerous challenge.'

He was muttering afterwards about the injustice of it all, and even seemed to suggest that Chelsea might appeal if the sentence was too harsh. But after being sent off twice this season, his challenges did not live up to his surname. They weren't particularly malicious – even Everton boss Walter Smith said Wise was 'unfortunate' – but they were stupid. Why go scything into challenges in harmless positions when you are already identified as a persistent offender?

Vialli had no plans to fine his player, feeling that he had been harshly treated by Willard, and also refused to condemn him, preferring to say that no one should talk about the incident. 'I think in the first half the referee did not perform to his best, probably. But we have got no further comments to make. The less we speak about Dennis, the better for everybody – for us, for Chelsea, for the English game, for referees.' Asked if he had spoken to Wise, Vialli issued only a terse 'No comment.'

But the little midfielder was heavily criticised on David Mellor's phone-in after the game by Chelsea fans, some of whom claimed that Wise didn't deserve to have the captain's armband.

Down to ten men, Chelsea displayed a resolve that had been missing in the past – a testimony to Vialli's preparation of the side. Even before Wise's dismissal they were up against it, yet they calmly held Everton and then carved out enough chances to have strolled to victory. 'We are showing more and more resilience,' Luca enthused, 'and I think that is very important. It is something we are working on, because we know that it must be there if we are going to win the title. After this performance, I would say yes, we are on course for the title.'

It was only the profligacy of Flo that denied an impressive victory. Once in the first half and twice in the second, he found himself in shooting positions within the penalty area. On the first occasion he shot over, then he shot wide, and then stung the fingers of keeper Thomas Myhre, although it would be harsh to point the finger at him because he actually had rather a good match, wayward shooting aside.

Vialli was annoyed with the injury to Gustavo Poyet, who was carried off in the first half with a knee problem. 'It doesn't look as bad as first thought, but we will have to wait to see later how he is. He was fouled, but the referee didn't blow. I was frustrated because one of my players had been hurt. I thought everyone but the referee saw it as a foul. We will take him back to London and investigate the injury properly on Sunday, but it doesn't seem too bad.' Poyet was referred to a specialist; there was some concern he might have sustained ligament damage.

SUNDAY, 6 DECEMBER
In the draw for the third round of the FA Cup, Chelsea were away to Brentford or Oldham.

MONDAY, 7 DECEMBER
Wise missed training with a heavy cold but escaped any internal retribution for his third dismissal of the season. The three-match ban was deemed punishment enough. Among the games missed would be Spurs and Manchester United. An FA spokesman confirmed: 'Being sent off for two yellow cards, as Wise was at Everton, carries a regulation one-match ban. But two more were added because of his previous red cards this season.'

Andrew Wrench, from the Chelsea Independent Supporters' Association, said: 'At the moment the loss of Poyet would be far more damaging than losing Wise again. When he is on song, Dennis makes us tick in midfield, but he was atrocious while he was on the pitch on Saturday and some of the fans were not at all happy with him.'

Wise knew he would have a problem winning back his place after missing so many games through suspension. 'What I do know is that I've got no more right to a first choice place after well over 300 games than I've had at any stage of my Chelsea career, and we've got several world-class midfielders around at the moment all vying for a place.'

Casiraghi felt Wise was a 'marked man'. He said, 'I saw the game at Everton and didn't agree with the referee's decision. The first foul wasn't that bad – just a normal physical English challenge. I think Dennis is now a marked man for referees. He's a hard player and it's a characteristic of his game. I don't think he should change that.'

Casiraghi underwent a four-hour exploratory operation at London's Princess Grace, needing further specialist surgery in Vienna on the nerves in his leg. After a short stay in hospital he returned to his home town, Monza, for rehabilitation. Fortunately, there was no damage to his cruciate ligaments, something which could have threatened his career. 'The knee is a little bit better now. There were some problems with the swelling in the first week, but I'm happy with what's been done. The rehabilitation's started already and I'm getting some movement in my knee and walking on crutches. Hopefully, I'll be able to bend it more in the next two to three weeks. It's a very long way ahead for me to get back to full fitness and I know I'll have to work very hard. I won't play again this season, and the doctors haven't given me a date for return. The important thing is getting rest at the moment. In the meantime, I'll be cheering the boys on from the sidelines more than ever.'

TUESDAY, 8 DECEMBER

Luca apologised to season-ticket holders and members for the cancellation of their dinner-dance because of fixture congestion caused by the Villa match being washed out and then rearranged. He said: 'As you can imagine, with two matches to recover this month, we have a very busy calendar, so that decision had to be taken. We'll try to make it up to those people who had bought tickets by winning as many games as possible. I think if we do that between now and the New Year you won't mind too much.'

Vialli laughed off Italian TV speculation that he would be the next coach of Sampdoria, the Genoese club where he became the world's most expensive footballer. 'I always thought I was going to be the next coach of Juventus,' he said.

Juve's interest in bringing Di Matteo home was ill timed. With Poyet injured and Wise red-carded again, Vialli couldn't afford any more disruption to his midfield.

Chelsea had rejected a £5m bid for Di Matteo from Serie A leaders Fiorentina in the summer, and gave AC Milan, Parma and Di Matteo's former club Lazio no encouragement when they made enquiries about the £4.9m signing. But Juve were in the mood for serious personnel changes, and coach Marcello Lippi decided Di Matteo was the answer. Juve had taken encouragement from Di Matteo's admission earlier in the year that 'if the chance came to return to Italy I certainly wouldn't turn it down. It depends on Chelsea.' But the twenty-eight-year-old Italian always said he was happy at Stamford Bridge with three and a half years to run on his contract.

Petrescu, along with Duberry dismissing mischievous pre-match talk of a Rest of the World v. England clash, knew Chelsea were in for a real battle against Villa, who had drawn with Manchester United on Saturday. 'Aston Villa are a very good team. It was easy for us against them in the Worthington Cup when we beat them 4–1 but that was not their real team, and this time it will be tough. But I'm sure if we show the character we showed at Everton we will prove we are better than them and we will beat them.'

Wise also felt Chelsea would win. 'I laugh when I keep hearing people say that us Englishmen have the advantage when it comes to hard pitches, cold nights and horrible conditions. The blokes here have got a fantastic spirit, will never lie down and die, and are some of the strongest and hardest people I've played with. Many of the lads live in central London now, we all get on, and there's a general feeling that we're going in the right direction.'

Vialli, however, was cautious, and praised Villa in his programme notes. Leboeuf joined Arsenal's Tony Adams to promote an auction of Christmas trees at the National History Museum on behalf of Save the Children, although Frank couldn't stay too long as he had to prepare for the big game.

WEDNESDAY, 9 DECEMBER
Chelsea 2   Aston Villa 1

Vialli hailed super-sub Flo as the 'lethal weapon' as he helped his club swagger into third place with a dramatic ninety-fourth-minute winner. Vialli said of match winner Flo, who made his thirty-fifth appearance as a Chelsea sub: 'I've been delighted with his performances all season. He has been effective when he starts from the kick-off but, when he comes on from the bench, sometimes he is even more effective. He has a special ability to turn a match and create new problems for the opposition. It's great to have such a nice lad, and a talented player, in your squad at times like this.' Flo enjoyed the euphoria in Chelsea's dressing room. 'The mood was unbelievable. It was certainly one of the best feelings I have known since I came to England. It was like a cup-tie.'

Prior to the match, Villa's first away League defeat since John Gregory's accession to the managerial throne nine months earlier, Vialli axed his skipper for the first time. It was a commendable response to his captain's inexcusable lack of discipline. But his decision to leave Flo on the bench was altogether more surprising. Vialli, scorer of a hat-trick against Villa in the Worthington Cup six weeks earlier, picked himself again. No wonder he reserved a special post-match tribute for his Norwegian saviour.

But Flo's latest exile in the dugout appeared irrelevant when Zola curled an exquisite twenty-yard free-kick past Michael Oakes for his eighth goal of the season after twenty-nine minutes. Chelsea's gloating fans had only ninety seconds to celebrate before England midfield starlet Lee Hendrie crowned a brilliant counter-attack with a nifty sidestep past Ferrer and a crisp finish from twelve yards. As Southgate marshalled Villa's brave resistance in the face of Chelsea's second-half siege, Leboeuf and Le Saux hit the woodwork. Finally, Di Matteo's right-wing corner was flicked on by Vialli, and Flo barged in to deliver the knockout blow from point-blank range, leaving Villa's leadership at the mercy of Chelsea and Manchester United. As 34,000 richly entertained fans left the ground many harboured the same ambition as the Spice Girls: to be number one at Christmas.

Vialli said: 'December was always going to be a vital month for us and we will have a better idea of what we can achieve after we have played Manchester United either side of Christmas. But I think we are ready for the challenge ahead because we have prepared so hard. We will be up for it. We are meeting everyone's expectations and, although we know we have a great chance of being successful, it will be important to keep our feet on the ground. The higher we go, the more other teams will want to beat us – and the standard is getting better all the time.'

For the second match running, John Gregory ducked the after-match conference and sent coach Steve Harrison to put a brave face on a demoralising night. Harrison said: 'We will lick our wounds tonight, but Chelsea have to play Manchester United twice later this month and we can enjoy watching them knocking each other off the trail. You expect to come under pressure at places like Stamford Bridge and that performance was nothing for us to be ashamed of.'

This was surely a good enough performance to restore Flo to the front line at Derby; if not, he would again seek the counsel of his Norwegian national coach, Nils Johan Semb. When Flo collected his award as Norwegian Footballer of the

Year in Oslo, Semb inferred that his star striker would walk into any other club side in Europe, saying his prodigy was unfortunate to play 'at the wrong club in the wrong country'.

THURSDAY, 10 DECEMBER

Vialli's proposed signing of Juan Antonio Pizzi from River Plate fell through. The Argentinian club wanted £2m for just a loan. Vialli said: 'I think he is an excellent player, but I don't want to throw Chelsea's money away unnecessarily.'

There was a hidden clause in the deal with River Plate: Pizzi's former club Barcelona, where he was a team-mate of Ferrer, were due £1.5m if Pizzi ever set foot in Europe permanently or on loan. Vialli was upset, but knew the terms were too much for an ageing striker who would only have been a stopgap. Shame old Mark Hughes wasn't still around. Mark was stuck at the bottom of the Premiership with the Saints, playing in an unfamiliar deep midfield role when Chelsea needed a forward. He had not scored and had already served two one-match suspensions.

Wise was as reckless as ever as he launched a crazy two-footed lunge at a team-mate at the training ground. Pictures of his X-rated challenge annoyed Vialli, who was losing patience with his wayward captain. Vialli had axed him from the midweek win over Villa as a warning to mend his ways, but he continued his no-holds-barred approach in training.

Alan Hudson was on the mend a year and nine operations after a horrendous car accident left him in a coma and clinging to life. Still disenchanted with the club and its chairman, he had the utmost respect for Vialli. He said: 'Ten years ago, our game was on its knees. The only reason Chelsea are selling out every week is because of the foreigners. It's the same with the others. Arsenal won two trophies last season, but apart from the influence early on of Ian Wright, their success was mainly down to Dennis Bergkamp and Mark Overmars. Look at Spurs today. You would pay to watch David Ginola any time. The rest, with one or two exceptions, are pretty ordinary. The Southamptons and Blackburns, I wouldn't watch them for all the tea in China.'

FRIDAY, 11 DECEMBER

Chelsea had not been at the head of England's top flight since November 1989, but if results went their way, starting with a defeat of Derby, they would be on top.

'If on Sunday night we are top of the Premiership, I will be the happiest man in the world,' Vialli said. 'We have not been up there yet so I cannot really say how we would cope. It would be very interesting to see how anybody copes in that situation. But I look around at my squad and all I see are players who are used to being the best and used to winning.'

Pressure sharpens the mind and separates men from boys, argued Desailly. 'How people handle pressure is important, and in my mind how that is done is what separates the great players from the mediocre players. I would be a lot more comfortable at the top of the Premiership and I think it would give us a lift.'

In his *Saturday Racing Post* column, Redknapp went for Chelsea as the team to challenge Manchester United. He wrote: 'Gianluca Vialli's side face a tough few days with trips to Derby and Old Trafford coming up, but that 11–4 against them taking the title may well look very big come Wednesday night. They are strong in all areas and have a remarkable squad. To have substitutes of the calibre of Tore Andre Flo and Gustavo Poyet is extraordinary, and Eddie Newton, who I rate quite highly, might not even make the bench! They are entitled to be second favourites and will be up there throughout the season.'

Ten years ago Tony Dorigo was about the most exotic name on the Chelsea team-sheet, an Australian with an Italian surname. Since his departure the entire scene has changed. As he prepared to line up against his old club, he said: 'Obviously I would love to have played in a side like that, but it came ten years too late for me. It really is good to see them doing so well. They definitely have enough quality to win the championship this year and I will be delighted for them if they do.' But respected journalist Bryan Butler wrote in the *Telegraph*: 'Chelsea's unbeaten run in the Premiership now stretches to fourteen games but they still haven't convinced a lot of professional cynics in the north that they are made of the stuff of champions.' Alan Hansen, in his *Express* column, believed the clubs that invested big were getting their reward, and that Desailly was the key to the title. 'There have always been risks when it comes to signing foreign players, but buy the best central defender in the world and your chances of getting it right increase considerably. Then put that player in a team which last season did everything well except defend and you might just be in with a shout of challenging for the big prize. Stamford Bridge is buzzing at the moment. I was there recently and everything about the place impressed me: Chelsea Village, the fact that you cannot get a ticket for love nor money and, of course, the football.'

SATURDAY, 12 DECEMBER

Derby County 2   Chelsea 2

Chelsea were denied top spot for the first time in nine years by a scrappy last-minute goal. Vialli said: 'I'm a little disappointed that we missed going top, but there is no hurry. We have got a little bit of a taste of it in our mouth – and the Premier League doesn't finish tomorrow. These things happen in football. We have got to forget those final minutes when we conceded that late goal and remember that we did so well in the rest of the game.'

Derby boss Jim Smith joined the growing band of Chelsea admirers, although he had a word of caution: 'After losing just one game all season Chelsea have obviously got to be serious title contenders. But Chelsea haven't won enough games away from home to really stamp their authority at the top. We always felt if we could get balls into their box we might get something against them.'

Vialli's team had been the victims of a touch of kidology from Smith, who had pinned up a *Times* article on their dressing-room wall suggesting it would be a walkover for Chelsea. This was interpreted by the media as Chelsea arrogance as Vialli made six changes from the midweek victory over Villa against an unfash-ionable side sent on to the Pride Park pitch with instructions to bring Chelsea down a peg or two. In reality, Vialli had constantly talked about 'keeping your feet on the ground' and actually said Derby would be tougher than anyone expected.

Luca rested the injured Desailly and didn't even find a space for himself on the bench, and the changes appeared to disrupt Chelsea's normal fluent passing pattern, although there was certainly plenty of excitement. Former Blue Tony Dorigo denied Chelsea an early goal when he made a spectacular goal-line clearance from Lambourde. Vialli woke up his sleepy team during the interval, and Chelsea finally got into gear when Petrescu came on for the ineffective Goldbaek. Two goals within four amazing minutes turned the game upside down. The industrious Morris – one of four English players paraded in the line-up – played the ever-dangerous Flo in for a simple chip over goalkeeper Mart Poom on fifty-three minutes to cancel out County's lead from a twenty-fifth-minute Horacio Carbonari free-kick deflected wide of de Goey by Lambourde. Poyet grabbed the second with a curler from outside the box.

Wily veteran Smith made the first triple substitution of his lengthy career to change the pattern. One replacement, Kevin Harper, swung in the injury-time left-wing centre which caught Chelsea napping. When Paulo Wanchope stuck out a long leg to knock the ball back from beyond the far post, number two substitute Dean Sturridge squeezed it inches inside the other upright past Leboeuf and de Goey. It was a moment to savour for Smith, who had outfoxed shaven-headed rival Vialli in this 'Battle of the Bald Eagles'.

Vialli confessed: 'Derby's late change of tactics made it difficult for us to adjust at such a late stage. We were a bit unlucky. It was our own fault to lose these two points. We were not clinical enough; we should have killed off Derby before the end. But I cannot say we will win every week. That is impossible. We have plenty of time this season to make up for what happened today in the last couple of minutes.'

Morris became the first Englishman to raise his voice in protest at the danger of being forgotten behind the imports. Morris, now nineteen, came in for his first Premiership game of the season and never once looked out of place. Vialli made him his Man of the Match. 'I do despair I will never get a regular place,' he said. 'It's bound to play on your mind. It's on my mind I might have to move to achieve it. Every player, no matter how old, how young, wants to play, wants to play from the start in as many games as possible. So of course it gets to you.' Vialli was well aware of trying to keep his English youngsters happy. 'Only yesterday he said he hasn't forgotten about me and I am as important to the squad as anyone else. He said I'm still young, even though I've heard that for the last three years, but I'll keep working on my game and learn off the quality players we have here. But I don't expect to play against Manchester United, and when your name isn't pulled out you do go "Aaarrgh!" and feel gutted.'

Granville had got fed up and moved on. Hughes was on loan to Norwich. Lee couldn't get near the team. Nicholls was still waiting his chance. Vialli tried to ease the pain for his youngsters. 'Jody was very good. It was nice to see an English player do well. In any other side he would be in their first team. It's lucky for me, but unlucky for him I have so many good players.'

SUNDAY, 13 DECEMBER

Villa's title odds were cut from 10–1 to 6–1 joint third favourites after coming back from two goals down against Arsenal to win 3–2. Manchester United were 10–11 favourites, with Chelsea at 5–2 and Arsenal at 6–1.

Speculation, speculation and more speculation. The *News of the World* reported that Vialli was in £13m talks for Juninho. The *People* linked Flo with Lazio and Juventus, reporting that a European agent was trying to broker a deal after he resisted an offer of a new £45,000-a-week contract at the Bridge (Hutchinson reacted quickly to that one: 'Flo has three and a half years left on his contract – there's no way we will let him go'). The *Star* nominated Rangers outcast Marco Negri as a target – but relationships between the Bridge and Ibrox were hardly convivial after the threats of legal action over Laudrup's move! The *Mail's* choice was thirty-two-year-old Argentinian World Cup striker Abel Balbo, third choice with Parma and willing to go on loan. A long-term target was £10m-rated Enrico Chiesa of Parma.

In fact, Luca was lining up his *seventh* Italian: centre-forward Filippo Maniero of Venezia, who was half owned by AC Milan who leased him out. AC Milan gave permission for the loan deal until the end of the season, at a cost of around £700,000. The episode highlighted Vialli's sense of urgency for a stand-by for Flo. Maniero, twenty-six, with experience at Padova, Sampdoria, Verona and Parma, was a good target. He said: 'I know Chelsea want me and I have talked with Luca who confirmed he is interested in signing me on loan. But he also told me that the matter rests between the clubs and I am aware that Venezia are telling Chelsea they want to keep me. This is such a big chance for me that I will do everything in my power to make it happen. I want to play for Vialli, I want to move to London and I absolutely want to leave Venezia. Perhaps part of the problem is that I am owned by both Milan and Venezia, but my agents tell me that AC Milan have no difficulty with me going on loan to Chelsea, so it is only Venezia who can stand in the way.'

The deal fell through.

MONDAY, 14 DECEMBER

Ferrer had become a key defender, a consistent performer of the highest quality. 'I found it very difficult at first because the pace of the game in England is much faster than anything else I've experienced, but I think I have come to terms with it now and I'm enjoying my football here. I would have only ever left Barcelona to join a club as big as Chelsea. But I was left with no choice but to leave Barcelona as the coach made it clear that I did not figure in his team plans for the new season. When the opportunity came to join Chelsea, I did not hesitate.

Mark Lawrenson, in his *Mirror* column, admitted: 'Earlier this season I remember saying that Chelsea would not figure in the title race because Gianluca Vialli kept changing his front line. [But now the Flo/Zola] partnership could bring the title to Stamford Bridge for the first time in forty-four years. The more the pair play together, the better they will become, and that is bad news for all their rivals. At the back Chelsea are no longer the soft touch they once were, and in Marcel Desailly and Albert Ferrer they have two of the most consistent performers in the country. The Spaniard does not make headlines or pick up any of the glory, but he could prove as important a signing for Vialli as Denis Irwin was all those years ago at Old Trafford. Ferrer is dependable and rarely puts a foot wrong. You don't play for a club such as Barcelona for as long as he did without being a good player.'

Mikael Forssell officially became a Chelsea player, five months after signing for the club. He arrived at the club with his sister, an international midfielder herself. HJK Helsinki were knocked out of the Champions League, Forssell playing seven games in the qualifiers and the league campaign to gain vital experience. He came on as a substitute three times in the Champions League, for twenty-five minutes at Benfica and for ten minutes against PSV Eindhoven and Kaiserslautern. 'I trained a lot on technique,' said the young Finn. 'Ball control is my real strength. Pace? I'm not that fast, but I'm not slow either. I'm good with my head. I like to score goals a lot.'

It wasn't long before Mikael made an impact. Wise said: 'I'll tell you who's going to be a star 'cause we've got him, and that's Mikael Forssell. I've trained with some seventeen-year-olds in my time, but none like him. I reckon he'll play in the first team before the end of the season.' Goldbaek had helped Forssell to settle in. The Dane said: 'I'm staying sometimes alone and sometimes with Mikael Forssell. We can speak together in some Swedish. He went to Swedish school.'

TUESDAY, 15 DECEMBER

The day before the big match, Alex Ferguson paid tribute to Luca. 'Vialli has done very well. His approach has brought consistency to Chelsea and I rate them very highly. They have been a team of entertainment in the past but now they are up at the top of the League and you have to respect what Vialli has done in achieving that. He thinks along the same lines as I do about the squad system. He tends to employ the Italian mentality in picking his teams and using his players. It's very difficult to predict what team he's going to play at any time. Obviously I could probably pick seven or eight of them most weeks. But Vialli often rotates his strikers. You never know which two he's going to use. Everyone is going to get a turn, though. And that's why they have got this consistency. If you want to challenge for everything in a big season then these are the only methods you can use. You can't rely on the same players all the time. Chelsea are in Europe, heavily involved in the championship, and there's the FA Cup still to come. You can't go for that lot with just one team.'

Chelsea hadn't lost at Old Trafford in five seasons, but neither manager believed the championship would be shaped by the next two results against each other. Vialli said: 'Win, lose or draw tomorrow, the outcome will not change anything. It's still a long, hard season ahead of us. It is not this match alone that matters. But we shall do our best.' Ferguson agreed: 'It's going to be a belter of a game. But it's just a coincidence with the fixture list that these two games are so close together. It's not going to turn into a Christmas knockout. The championship goes on a lot longer than that.'

Poyet's continued presence was the key to the team's success. After he picked up a cruciate knee ligament injury last season, the London side lost nine games without his driving, goalscoring aggression in midfield and fell out of League contention. Gullit was the first to admit he had left a gem behind at Stamford Bridge: 'Gustavo is like a Keane, a Batty or an Ince – a player who thinks about the team, not himself. He has good technique, he plays with passion and has an attacking attitude.' Poyet's previous two meetings with Manchester United had produced fireworks – particularly his encounters with Roy Keane. Their first clash came in Poyet's Chelsea debut at the 1997 Charity Shield at Wembley, when the Irishman left him with studmarks on his chest following a high challenge. He had clearly not forgotten the welcome Keane had given him when the sides met again two months later at Old Trafford as the two players were at each other's throats for the entire game as Chelsea fought to a 2–2 draw.

All thoughts of revenge were put out of his mind now, though. 'I think about my injury last year when things were very bad for me. I like to play all the time, and when I don't play, I'm not happy. I love the aggression of the English game and now I am really enjoying myself on the pitch because we are winning. I enjoy the position I play in now because I can arrive in the box alone, without any marking. When you play as a striker, you have a man on you all the time.' Under the rotation system the Uruguayan missed fewer games than most. Despite scoring at Derby, he was surprised to find himself on the bench at Old Trafford. 'Sometimes Luca plays me because he thinks it's right for such a game and sometimes he thinks it's good for the team if I don't. It's hard for me to understand because I think about me, the player. But I have to accept it, and I do.'

Ferguson also had his surprises: Beckham and Giggs were on the bench. Poyet added: 'Before the games you normally have a meeting and you talk about Manchester United and how to shut out Beckham and Ryan Giggs. So it was a big surprise when we saw the team – especially Beckham. I think he may be the best crosser in the world. I've never seen a man who can cross the ball like him.'

Still, Chelsea faced the ultimate test of their resurgence. The fourth-placed Blues would defend their fifteen-game unbeaten League record without suspended Leboeuf (five yellow cards), while Desailly had a knee injury, which is why Vialli had rested him at Derby. Superstitious Luca was horrified to learn just how successful Chelsea had been on their trips to United since 1966, losing just two of their League games there in the intervening thirty-two years. Chelsea's proud record registers ten victories and eleven draws in those twenty-three encounters, including two wins and three draws in the five games since their last defeat – a 3–0 setback in April 1993.

Titles are never won in December, but if Chelsea emerged from their two impending games against United with their growing reputation untarnished, they would earn the right to be taken seriously.

Jakob Kjeldbjerg acknowledged the side's debt to Dennis Wise, even though his suspect temperament could undermine Vialli's first attempt as a manager to take points at Old Trafford. 'If one name sums up the reason that the club hasn't lost at United for five seasons, then it is Dennis Wise. The first time I experienced it was in 1993–94 when Wisey took us all aside to tell us that we had to believe in ourselves because we were good enough to play on the biggest footballing stage. I was sceptical and thought about how you could get destroyed at Old Trafford, but rose to the occasion. Dennis is the key, there is no doubt about it, and the best fun will be him up against Keane – whoever wins that midfield battle wins the match. But Dennis's strength is also his weakness. His need to win and hatred of losing means that in the heat of the moment he will always be a risk, no matter how careful the manager has told him to be. The crucial thing for Chelsea is not to let United push them back into the penalty box for the first twenty minutes.'

According to Ray Wilkins, the 1999 Premiership champions were on show. The former Manchester United and Chelsea midfielder was sure one of his old clubs would lift the crown. 'It's a massive game, a monstrous game, but it's not a title decider. It's too early to say that. It will give a good benchmark to see who might be going to nick it at the finish. I don't know who it will be.'

Naturally all the top pundits were out in force for this one. Trevor Brooking, for instance, in his *Evening Standard* column, suggested Chelsea could only afford one defeat in their next four games. 'For me, Manchester United and Chelsea are the two best passing teams in the Premiership, with a guile and movement capable of unlocking any defence. It is no coincidence that they are also the only two British clubs, out of a dozen starters, who have managed to progress in Europe beyond Christmas.'

Former Chelsea and United boss Dave Sexton, who had four wins and three draws from his seven trips to Old Trafford with the Blues, felt that playing in the Theatre of Dreams suited Chelsea's style. 'Traditionally Old Trafford has always been a good hunting ground for Chelsea. I don't know for definite why that is, but I think it could be down to the fact that Chelsea have always had a good attack. You will always have a good chance away from home if you have got good forwards – and Chelsea have had that over the years. Also, everyone raises their game for matches at Old Trafford because it's a bit like going to Wembley. They've got a wonderful stage to perform on, and that inspires players to really do well. I think Chelsea, despite all their ups and downs, have always had the type of players who relish the opportunity of playing on a great stage. Despite their great record at Old Trafford, though, it will still be very daunting for them going there.'

WEDNESDAY, 16 DECEMBER

Manchester United 1   Chelsea 1

On the morning of the match Chelsea were drawn against yet another Norwegian side – Valerenga, coached by former Norwegian national coach Egil Olsen – in the quarter-finals of the Cup Winners Cup. Olsen's side were currently seventh in their First Division. They were surprise quarter-finalists, having beaten fancied outsiders Besiktas of Turkey 4–3 on aggregate in the previous round. Chelsea had fond memories of Scandinavia, but were less keen for a repeat of their last trip to Norway when they faced Tromso in sub-zero temperatures on a snow-covered pitch. The Blues had lost 3–2 that night, before cruising home 7–1 at Stamford Bridge. Nevertheless, Vialli was pleased to have avoided Lazio.

Later that night, Vialli proudly announced his side's title pedigree after another superb Zola goal. 'We are playing against the best team in England, and we have shown we are good enough to win the title. We had to make changes, and it underlines why I have to have twenty-two great players at our football club. I have used up all the words I can think of to describe Gianfranco. He has been outstanding all season. Franco's goal was outstanding because he has such skill. I hope he goes on doing that for a long time. He is thirty-two, but we know what he can do with the ball. What I want is for him to do a lot more when the opposition has the ball. We are a humble team, but we are definitely contenders for the championship.'

Still breathless after his inspirational Man of the Match display, Zola insisted that his fine start to the season, with nine goals, was down to a fresh outlook on life at Stamford Bridge. 'I am more devoted to Chelsea than I was when I won the player of the year, and I think I am playing better. This is the most goals I've ever scored at the start of a season, and I believe I am more involved in the team, and more effective in doing work for the team. We are playing well, and we are consistent. We had a very hard match against Manchester United, but we came through it well. Maybe my form is less spectacular than when I first came to Chelsea, but I am able to score important goals for us. I was pleased to get that goal because we really didn't deserve to lose the match. We played really well at times and had United under a lot of pressure, so we deserved our equaliser.'

Even Ferguson was forced to pay tribute to Zola's genius, despite the lost chance to go above Villa at the top of the table on goal difference. 'Sometimes you have to hold your hands up and admit you were second best. I think my players found Chelsea a bit too lively. The problem is that we have played so many tough games over the last few weeks, but we have come through it and we are still in contention.' But the United manager was still fuming over a decision which could have swung the match United's way, when Lambourde – already booked in the tenth minute for a late tackle on Cole – was lucky to escape punishment as he appeared to drag down Yorke. 'The same referee sent off Nicky Butt at Arsenal when he was supposed to be the last man – even though he wasn't. He should have been sent off, and the most frustrating thing is that the referee shows no consistency. If you knew what he would do from game to game, then at least you could accept it.'

Wise picked up his fifth booking of the season to extend a three-match ban for being sent off at Everton to four. Wise sinned in the thirty-first minute when he took away Scholes's legs; the incident was compounded by Petrescu, who was also shown yellow for bitterly complaining about the judgement. Wise moaned: 'The number of Chelsea bookings was a disappointment. But referees are under a lot of pressure these days and he called the game the way he saw it.' And Le Saux instantly became public enemy number one to the United faithful for a scrap with Nicky Butt, who had backed into the defender on the touchline and caught him with a forearm. Then, three minutes after the break, substitute Poyet further incensed United followers when he collapsed under a challenge from Wes Brown, who earned a booking for his troubles. Poyet rolled in apparent agony until a stretcher was shown, whereupon he suddenly sprang to his feet. Tempers boiled even more in the thirty-seventh minute when Cole got in a challenge on Le Saux, who became the fall guy again, and this time only the stretcher eased his pain. On the stroke of half-time he could take no more punishment and he was replaced by Poyet.

Le Saux limped wearily down the touchline and had his back to the action as United took the lead three minutes into first-half injury time. Scholes picked out Blomqvist and his inviting cross fell to the feet of Butt, who unleashed a drive which smacked into Cole's boot, but the United number nine reacted instantly to crash the loose ball into the bottom corner.

Then came Lambourde's flirtation with a sending-off which had so infuriated Ferguson, but Scholes's subsequent brilliant ball to Blomqvist nearly appeased him. The Swedish winger brought it under control, only to volley wide when he should have scored. It was a costly miss, as Chelsea levelled in the eighty-third minute. Poyet played a neat one-two with Zola and the little Sardinian cleverly clipped the ball over Schmeichel to send the Chelsea travellers wild. They would have been even more ecstatic in the final seconds if Babayaro's thirty-yard sizzler hadn't glanced the outside of the post.

George Best, who was at Old Trafford for the game, felt the champions would come from the current top three. 'I said at the start of the season that I felt Arsenal would be the team to beat. I've changed my mind, because they don't have anything up front. People keep thinking Aston Villa will fade away, but I don't think they will, while Leeds are coming through as dark horses. For me, though, it's between Chelsea, Aston Villa and United.' No prizes for guessing which team Best was tipping for the title, though. 'I never back against the Reds.'

THURSDAY, 17 DECEMBER

Luca maintained the 'bonding' exercise that is the karaoke canteen Christmas lunch. Each of the players, including the youth team and the managerial staff, took his turn to sing. Luca said: 'All our new boys had to give a solo performance. Marcel sang the French national anthem, and the English players responded and drowned him out with "God Save the Queen". The Scottish baldie, Jim Duffy, said he didn't know either song. Albert sang "La Bamba" and everyone joined in. Bjarne sang "Rudolph the Red-Nosed Reindeer" in Danish and dedicated it to a member of his national team. Our new boy, Mikael Forssell, sang a Finnish folk song, and Luca Percassi and Sam Dalla Bona sang a song that all us Italians could join in with. It was very, very funny and everyone was great.' But Gianfranco wasn't impressed. 'I think Antonio Pintus's singing was absolutely disgraceful. "Ciao bella, ciao bella, ciao, ciao, ciao." I was embarrassed to be Italian at that.'

Luca endorsed his close friend David Platt to president Enrico Mantovani for the job as Sampdoria manager. 'David Platt is a good man. He will have a great deal of incentive to do well because Sampdoria has remained in his heart.' Platt said: 'I'm not too proud to ring anyone up to ask for assistance, and my first call will be to Gianluca. He knows exactly the position I am in, having taken over at Chelsea, and he has certainly done a terrific job there. So I will ask him what he did on his first day, then his second, then his third, and so on. There is no reason why I shouldn't ask a friend for help, particularly one who knows this club and area the same as I do.'

However, Luca criticised the Italian Football Federation for blocking the former England captain from taking the title 'coach' at the Luigi Ferraris stadium because of his lack of credentials. Vialli himself would be unable to manage a top-level club in Italy because he too did not possess the UEFA coaching badge necessary to take on such a post. Luca felt that having seen the rule bent in the past to accommodate others, the Italian Football Federation had gone out of its way to make an example out of Platt. 'My opinion on the matter is quite simple. If you are the chairman and you put your own money into a club and team, you should have the right to make your own decisions. If you want somebody to be the coach of your team, then they should be allowed. If I wanted to appoint somebody unqualified to help at Chelsea, I should be able to do that. I agree with the statement once made by the former Milan and Italy manager Arrigo Sacchi: you don't have to have been a horse to be a good jockey.'

FRIDAY, 18 DECEMBER

Vialli warned his team not to give Ginola an inch as the Frenchman held the key to everything Tottenham did in attack. Luca also praised George Graham for turning Spurs into the team nobody wanted to play. 'I think Tottenham are the best team in England at making the opposition look poor. No team ever looks at their best against them. They will make it very hard for us to play classic football. I am also expecting a lot of problems from Ginola.'

Graham, in turn, was won over by Vialli. He tipped Chelsea to win the title – although he admitted he could never be comfortable using his rotation system. 'It's working for them, but I don't know if I could do it quite as often as he does. If I did, I would probably do it more in bursts. I think it could sometimes affect a player when he has done well or scored a winning goal and is then dropped for the next match. You can't, however, argue with what Chelsea have achieved so far.'

Stamford Bridge legend Peter Osgood nominated Zola as one of the greatest players in the club's history. 'There is no doubt about it, he is one of the great Chelsea players. He had a stunning first season but was disappointing last year. He was injured and also, I think, homesick for Italy, which showed in his games. But he got on with things, got his act together and showed he's a first-class player. He loves to get forward, is a hard worker and has great vision. He also takes players on, which few people can do. He makes goals out of nothing, which marks him out as a special player. The nearest player to him I can think of is Jimmy Greaves. He can beat two or three players and has such superb control, the ball seems to stick to his feet. He makes things so hard for defenders that often they have no option but to bring him down. He forces them to make mistakes.'

Osgood was convinced Chelsea would qualify for the Champions League, if not win the Premiership. 'I was sure, at the start of the season, they would end in the top three. Now I think they will finish in the top two. They have played most of the big clubs and showed at Old Trafford they were as good as Manchester United. I've always said I wanted to see a more settled side. Now that Vialli's hand has been forced by the sale of Brian Laudrup and the injury to Pierluigi Casiraghi, we are seeing Zola establish an effective partnership with Tore Andre Flo.'

Former team-mate Steve Clarke, now Gullit's number two at Newcastle, agreed with Osgood, comparing the Italian to the likes of Osgood himself, Alan Hudson and 1955 title-winning skipper Roy Bentley. 'He is definitely one of the best players I've worked with and must rank alongside the club's greatest. His special quality is that he has the great skill and ability to turn and win a game on his own. I wouldn't say Chelsea will win the title just because of Zola. But he definitely helps make them one of the outstanding contenders. The great thing about him is that, even though he's such a good player, he always wants to improve and work on his game. He's a tremendous talent and his sheer dedication is amazing.'

Vialli turned down a request from Morris to go out on loan. He was growing frustrated at his lack of first-team chances. He did not ask to leave, but said: 'I just want to play more games.'

SATURDAY, 19 DECEMBER

Chelsea 2   Tottenham Hotspur 0

Luca took Chelsea to the top for the first time since the old First Division days in 1989 when Bobby Campbell was boss. Manchester United's surprise 3–2 home defeat against Middlesbrough combined with this win to take Chelsea to the summit of the Premiership. 'It's nice to be top, much better than being bottom, even if it might only be for twenty-four hours,' Luca said. 'The players are very pleased, very happy, and it might give us a lot of confidence.'

For this game, Vialli played himself with Flo on the bench, and made the calculated decision to bring off Zola. It worked, but when Zola departed for Flo, the decision was greeted with boos. He explained why he opted not to go on full assault with three strikers when Spurs were reduced to ten men after the sending-off of Chris Armstrong on the hour: 'I don't think by putting more strikers on the pitch it means better play or more chances created, especially against opponents with one man less. You then go forward with too many players. Three strikers is probably wrong, as they then play with extra defenders and you cannot find any space. Both Franco and Tore have played a lot of matches recently, and after Wednesday's demanding game we came back at four in the morning. Tore was ready to come on and Franco was to do a job without thinking of lasting the full ninety minutes. Everything was planned before the game.'

Poyet broke the deadlock in the eighty-first minute with his tenth goal of the season to make him a contender for Footballer of the Year, potentially following Zola to the award if he continued to score at this rate. Flo missed one good chance before scoring in the ninetieth minute with a far-post header, picked out by the outstanding Petrescu who chased a seemingly lost cause to keep in play another long-ranger from Leboeuf, finally delivering the perfect cross. Vialli missed a couple himself, and said: 'I could have done better, especially in front of goal. When I know I'm not having one of my best games, I work hard.'

Graham was very upset at Armstrong's dismissal. Spurs were seething because Leboeuf had dashed thirty yards to make his feelings known to Tring referee Graham Poll. When Poll brandished a second yellow card at Armstrong, followed by the red, Spurs went mad. Ferdinand hacked the ball away, and Vialli became involved in some push-and-shove with Allan Nielsen. The most significant alter-cation was instigated by Graham, who appeared to instruct Ginola to have a word with Leboeuf about his involvement; Ginola gave Leboeuf an earful after a finger-jabbing row on the pitch which continued later in the tunnel. Ferdinand, booked for flying off the handle as tempers frayed, admitted: 'That's the most frustrated I've felt on the pitch for a while.'

As Leboeuf chatted with Ginola's family after the match, the half-dressed Spurs winger appeared at the visitors' dressing-room door to continue the lecture. The pair used to knock around St Tropez as teenagers, but Leboeuf repeatedly refused to discuss his part as an agent provocateur, while Ginola would only say cryptically: 'I told him he is still my friend – after all, it is the season of goodwill. Merry Christmas, Frank.' But Ferdinand raged: 'As the manager said, it's not a nice thing to see players get a fellow professional sent off unless it's a really serious foul or bad challenge. What Chris did was nothing more than a bit of a trip, and the mayhem afterwards didn't help him at all. We all know who we're talking about here and I don't want to say too much because the last time I felt like this it cost me two thousand pounds, for speaking out after our Cup tie at Barnsley last season. But I saw a Chelsea player running to get involved, then there was all the mayhem, and next thing you know Chris Armstrong is gone.'

Chelsea, of course, went on to make their numerical advantage count by scoring twice in the last ten minutes, and Graham could not hide his distaste for Leboeuf's antics. He spluttered: 'If the referee has made his mind up about two bookable offences, that's fine. What we don't need is opposition players running thirty yards to remonstrate with the referee.' Graham had confronted Leboeuf in the tunnel as the players left the field. Leboeuf said: 'George was there when I came off and it was obvious that he was trying to insult me. But I couldn't understand what he was saying because of his Scottish accent, and I went straight to the dressing room.'

Despite all the scare-mongering in the past few months about discontent among those involved in Vialli's squad rotation, there was a team spirit that was tangible on and off the pitch. Hard work and application mixed with extravagant talent makes this Chelsea team perhaps the greatest in the club's history – no longer the swinging sixties; no longer clinging to memories. In Osgood's day it would be spectacular entertainment at the Bridge, and ten or more pints in the nearest King's Road bar by way of celebration; now it's a glass or two of champagne at a trendy new resturant and an upmarket meal. A new regime, with a more sophisticated Continental approach. Little point in embracing a new Italian fitness regime and wrecking it all on the booze.

Poyet – who just about epitomised the New Chelsea: resilient, determined, gifted and effective – explained the new philosophy that overcame a George Graham team that made Spurs a much tougher proposition than had been usual: 'We are able to handle the physical side a lot better now. Chelsea sides in the past, and certainly last season, would have been pushed over by Tottenham. Vialli says every week that we have to compete to be successful. We have to be physical as well as play good football.' Vialli had no doubts about Poyet's value. 'He is one of the most clever players I have ever played with in all of my career.' That's some accolade. Vialli continued: 'He scores goals, lots of goals, works very hard for the team, and he has an unbelievable attitude, always positive. He's the type a manager always like to have. It was unfortunate for him that he missed six months of last season. Probably people have only really started talking about Poyet this season because he has regular football. He can do everything, and his running is always very clever, positive, direct and decisive – a complete midfield player.'

Vialli also sensed there was never going to be a better chance to land the title. 'It's important to get into a great position, but it's more important to keep that position. But now everybody will think Chelsea are one of the best teams in England, and will try everything to beat us. Our lives will be more difficult in future. But I think we are able to cope with that, with our experienced players in the side. I'm quite curious to see how they will react to being top of the table.'

After the game, Zola dashed off for Heathrow for a flight to Rome and a visit to cheer up Casiraghi, who had had another operation to repair a nerve running down the shin. He might have been substituted late on, but he couldn't restrain himself when Poyet scored. 'I started running towards Gustavo and just jumped on him, celebrating. The referee came close and I just brushed his cheek and he looked at me in a strange way as if to say, "What are you doing?" I was out of my head. We went first and we had that satisfaction. It was a good taste in our mouth, and next year I hope we have a taste for that even more.'

Franco missed the opening of Roberto's new restaurant Friends in Hollywood Road, just off the Fulham Road, attended by Poyet, Wise, Petrescu, Desailly, Leboeuf, Le Saux, Lambourde, Babayaro, Newton and Hughes. Luca wasn't there, but his big pal Attilio Lombardo from Crystal Palace was, together with Nicola Berti from Spurs. Di Matteo had been linked with a move back to Lazio, rumours fuelled by the news that he had sold his Italian restaurant La Perla and was ready to move home in a bid to win back his place in the Italian national side. 'I did sell the restaurant, but this means nothing. It is difficult to say why I did it, it's just that I am moving in new ways.' The new way was just half a mile down the Fulham Road to this new restaurant venture.

His aspirations in this direction attracted a touch of banter from his chairman, who had five restaurants of his own within the Chelsea Village complex, including one upmarket Italian. Di Matteo added: 'I used to get lots of jokes all the time from Ken Bates about our restaurants. I think his are quite nice as well. I have been there twice and it's been good.'

He had a simple way of dealing with the rumour-mongers: 'You know what I do? I don't read the newspapers so I don't even know what they write, but these stories are not annoying at all. I am happy at Chelsea. Stories that I am going back to Italy are not true. But it is nice to know that some of the teams in Italy are looking at me because it means they still think I am a good player. Of course sometimes I get homesick, that's just normal. But I am quite happy over here. Colin Hutchinson is the man to ask about transfers, but I have the last say. Without my agreement, I think any move can't happen.'

Whereas last season Roberto hit ten goals, including one in the Coca-Cola Cup final against Middlesbrough, this season he had yet to get off the mark. 'I had a difficult start to the season after the first two or three games. I think I have played at quite a high standard and a high consistency. I now feel on the top of my form and I feel very good. I have not scored, but I am also playing sometimes a bit more defensively than the last two seasons. When we have played with three midfield players, you have to hold your position and have less chance to go forward, and when we've had four midfield players, we've had some injuries and suspensions and I've played the defensive part. I think Gustavo Poyet and Zola are getting all my goals. As long as the team does all right it doesn't bother me if I score or not.'

With all the praise for the players' fitness levels, Luca was stung by criticism of his own fitness by *Match of the Day* pundit Alan Hansen, who highlighted one tussle involving England defender Sol Campbell, when the Spurs captain overtook the thirty-four-year-old Italian in a short sprint. Hansen likened Vialli's movement to 'running in quicksand'.

SUNDAY, 20 DECEMBER

Arsenal overwhelmed Leeds 3–1 at Highbury and emerged as 9–2 third favourites for the title behind joint favourites Chelsea and Manchester United at 7–4.

MONDAY, 21 DECEMBER

The last time Chelsea topped the League, in November 1989, the team comprised: Dave Beasant (now keeps goal for Forest at the age of thirty-nine); Steve Clarke (now on the management team at Newcastle); Tony Dorigo (now with Derby); Graham Roberts (player-boss of Slough); Ken Monkou (still playing at Southampton); David Lee (ironically his Chelsea contract was cancelled by mutual consent the day before the Spurs game, and he joined Bristol Rovers after fifteen years at the Bridge); Peter Nicholas (Crystal Palace youth team coach); John Bumstead (left for Charlton where injury wrecked his career; now a London cabbie); Kerry Dixon (now a Luton publican playing for Borehamwood); Kevin Wilson (Northampton Town assistant manager); and Alan Dickens (also a London cabbie, after spells with Colchester and Brentford). Few took their challenge seriously, and the doubters were quickly justified as Chelsea took two points from the next five games, conceding sixteen goals in the process.

This time round, Chelsea were knocked off the top spot when Villa won 1–0 at Charlton. But the old Blues Boys were out in force, predicting their team could even become the new Liverpool of Europe should they win the title. Dixon said: 'I see Chelsea as the title-winners for sure. There is no reason why they cannot go on and dominate Europe. The potential of the team is that good. Manchester United and maybe Arsenal are their only rivals. But I saw Chelsea play United a couple of weeks ago and Chelsea were by far the better side. It is now a very different place to when I was there, both on and off the pitch. But I wouldn't want to see the old Stamford Bridge again.' Bumstead added: 'We had a great team, but our squad was never big enough. Vialli's is, and it is crammed with talent. I'm sure they'll go all the way. We were just happy to be top because we were tipped for relegation that season.' In charge of that Chelsea side nine years ago was Bobby Campbell. He said: 'I built a side out of experience and youth. We had good players and a great spirit. Considering what was going on at the club around that time it was a great achievement. The club was under siege from people on the outside wanting to turn Stamford Bridge into a housing estate. Chairman Ken Bates held firm, and without him there would be no Chelsea today. He can take credit for what is happening now. The one regret I have is that, after finishing fifth that season, we were unable to play in Europe because of the UEFA ban. That would have been a marvellous experience. They're doing well in Europe now, but they can go on to win the League.'

Halfway through the season, Mark Lawrenson's verdict was that Manchester United were still the team to beat, but Chelsea 'have plenty on the bench, as well as a first eleven that is a joy to behold when on form. Add to that a great team spirit, players who would be comfortable in any team in Europe and a decent manager who has their respect, and I can see them pushing United all the way. But I still back the Red Devils.'

Casiraghi left hospital in Vienna to return 'home'. He had undergone a fifth operation, performed by Dr Hanno Millesi, the world-renowned Austrian specialist. Dr Millesi was delighted at Gigi's powers of recovery after the delicate nerve-grafting operation. 'Pierluigi is making notable progress. It is not out of the question for him to be back at home in time for Christmas.' A return to the Casiraghi family home near Monza would give the former international a huge morale boost ahead of his rehabilitation in the new year.

TUESDAY, 22 DECEMBER

Trevor Brooking tipped Chelsea for the title, and Spurs and Liverpool to lift the cups. In the *Evening Standard*, he wrote: 'Des Lynam forced me to make a prediction on *Match of the Day* about who would win the Premiership title, and I went for Chelsea. It's forty-four years since they won the championship so they hardly have to worry about too much anxiety caused by the expectancy of their supporters. They are certainly the form team, and they have variety and ability in their squad and great depth. Success will be down to maintaining this season's consistency and beating the lesser teams. However, that has often been Chelsea's Achilles' heel. I take Arsenal and Manchester United to be the main challengers, with perhaps Arsene Wenger's side offering yet another Premiership surge.'

Hoddle returned to Chelsea, but couldn't stop Vialli's coaching staff crashing 7–2 to the youth team! The England coach was a star guest for the annual management v. YTS match. Not even his silky skills could save the day. 'It was awful,' moaned Rix. 'We were beaten by a side who were quicker, fitter, stronger and technically more able. It was a humiliating experience. The fact that we've been top of the League means nothing now – not when you've just lost to the YTS boys! Glenn came in to help and did his best, but he's put on a few kilos and he couldn't save us. Mind you, that boy Vialli could have a future if he keeps plugging away!' Vialli had flown back from Rome, where he had been on holiday, to play in the traditional 'grudge' match. He was tightly marked by John Terry. After the game Luca presented a magnum of champagne to Eddie Niedzwiecki whose heroics in goal kept the score down.

Poyet was released for a friendly in San Sebastian where the Basques took on Uruguay, although they held back Ferrer and Babayaro from the Catalunya v. Nigeria game. Chelsea hoped the gesture would help in trying to keep him when Uruguay played Chile in mid-February. While on international duty Poyet gave a controversial interview to the newspaper *Marca*, in which he said he much preferred the style under Vialli to the flamboyant tactics favoured by Gullit, who brought him to the Bridge. 'Ruud Gullit and Gianluca Vialli are very different types of manager. Gullit set great store by playing attractive football, whereas with Vialli we play more in the Italian manner. I have got on well with both ways. But now I am playing as an attacking midfielder, which is where I feel most at home. Gullit talks about playing "sexy football", but I would much prefer to win the championship. I want to win the League with Chelsea, even if we don't do it playing in a spectacular style.'

Morris celebrated his twentieth birthday by joining Duberry in treating the rest of the Chelsea lads to dinner in the New Year – their combined 'fine' for being late for training. Morris joked: 'We'll probably take them to a Kentucky Fried Chicken.'

A little different from a few years ago, when he was involved in a nightclub incident that left him with a badly swollen face and bit of a reputation. At 5ft 5in, he is the smallest player at Stamford Bridge (Zola and Wise are both an inch taller). Wise, twelve years his senior, had taken a close interest in the development of the lad who used to clean his boots. It was alleged that Wise once became so frustrated at the way Morris was failing to achieve that he got the youngster by the collar in the dressing room and told him to change or forget about a career in football. Morris admitted: 'I didn't always handle things as I might have. I was young and didn't behave as a professional off the pitch. I was perhaps socialising too much and not doing enough in training. I was even dropped from training with the first team, and that was when Dennis got hold of me. He is not the kind of person to give you a cuddle. Instead he puts a bunch of fives under your nose. He tells you as it is and what he thinks. It's the reason, I suppose, he is the captain of the team. He used to give me twenty quid every time he scored a goal but, more than anything, he gave me the belief in myself that I had lacked.

'I went to the manager and asked him why I couldn't go on loan and get the first-team football I so badly needed. I asked if I could go out on loan even though I don't want to leave here. We talked, and the advice he gave me has helped me come to terms with the situation. I have to accept I am now just another player, not a promising youngster who has time on his side. Now when I get in, I feel I have to stand out and perhaps achieve more than other players do. All I know is that I came out of that meeting with the boss on a high. He had told me the things I had wanted to hear, and now I want to make my way here, despite the competition for places that comes from quality players. I don't want to get to twenty-two without a bit of experience and a few games under my belt.'

Vialli understood his problems. 'Even though I am thirty-four, I remember what it was like to be twenty. I know he can be a very, very good player, because not only is he technically sound but tactically, too. The fact that he is in the first-team squad with one of the best clubs in England speaks for itself. Of course, he is not at his best yet – who is at twenty? He needs to be stronger, faster, fitter, and also to take in the experience he can pick up from watching great players around him. I understand him and know his frustrations, but I also know he has great ability and, for me, that is everything.'

WEDNESDAY, 23 DECEMBER

Duberry warned Chelsea's title rivals that they have the fittest squad in the Premiership, ready to go the distance. 'My fitness has improved and I feel great now. When the ninety minutes is up, I can still keep on going. I don't go to sleep during the game any more, which is what used to happen to me. Even with two games a week, I still feel good. I think the whole team is much fittter this season and that is down to Antonio [Pintus]. I feel about forty per cent fitter than last year and I have just got more running in me. Our fitness will help us over the winter months when hopefully other teams start to tire, because we really want to improve on what we did last year.'

THURSDAY, 24 DECEMBER

Vialli was still searching for the right recipe for success. 'As a player I thought the manager was like a cook: he's got the ingredients, and if they are good ingredients you can cook a good cake. If they are bad ingredients, you get a bad cake. If something is missing, the cake is going to be a bad one. I am trying to make a good cake, but sometimes you make a little mistake and the cake doesn't come out the way you wanted it to. We've got a few meals to go to get the right recipe, but by the end of the season I hope we've got a nice cake with icing on the top.

'I never pat myself on the back. I actually think better when I am having a bad time, because when I am having a good time, I am afraid of a bad time around the corner. At the moment Aston Villa are three points ahead despite some saying Chelsea are the best side. It is nice to stay in the shade for a while, but then you can hide for too long. This is a time in the season when you can't do that.

'We have coped well with the loss of Laudrup and Pierluigi Casiraghi. Gianfranco Zola is playing some of the best football of his entire career, and Flo is proving to be a true superstar. I think he is a very unusual player who is tremendously gifted on the ball. His speed of execution is astounding. Although I remain that bald old guy sitting on the end of the bench who occasionally enjoys sticking them in the net, the presence of Zola and Flo on the pitch makes me feel safe.'

FRIDAY, 25 DECEMBER

Le Saux was granted compassionate leave after his wife Mariane gave birth to a baby daughter. Luca said: 'He had stayed for about twenty hours beside her and was very tired. I think they went to hospital about one o'clock in the morning and she gave birth at five or six o'clock in the evening. He was certainly too exhausted to play. But now he is a father we expect him to fly!' Graeme was also treated for three separate injuries after the game at Old Trafford, and it was a week before he could train properly. Physio Mike Banks said: 'Graeme still wasn't one hundred per cent fit, so in view of everything it seemed too demanding to push him through ninety more minutes of Premiership football at Southampton.'

Young Mikael Forssell enjoyed Christmas lunch at Tore's home. With father Brent spending a lot of time at his consultancy in Berlin, Colin Hutchinson suggested the boy's mother came over to look after him. Colin said: 'The family had Christmas planned in Finland, but Mikael said he would prefer to stay here. So Tore took him under his wing for Christmas Day.' Tore's girlfriend Randy was in Norway, but his mum was over to cook the lunch – traditional Norwegian fare of lamb ribs in a sauce.

SATURDAY, 26 DECEMBER

Southampton 0   Chelsea 2

Mikael's Christmas treat was to join the first-team squad on Boxing Day, and he sat on the bench for the first time. Strangely, Forssell, Goldbaek and Flo seemed to be able to converse despite their three different languages.

A sobering thought for this time of year: the team occupying top spot on Boxing Day rarely wins the title. Only three of the last thirteen champions led at the halfway stage. When Chelsea won the last time, in 1955, they were fifth behind Sunderland, Wolves, Charlton and Portsmouth the day after Christmas.

New Saints signing Patrick Colleter's crippling challenge on Poyet in this game was a defining moment in the entire season. The anxiety with which Poyet's team-mates viewed the knee problem clearly indicated that they knew it even then. Petrescu feared Poyet had suffered another career-threatening injury. It wasn't that bad, but it was bad enough. Petrescu said: 'I hope the injury is not serious because Gustavo is so important for us. Every time he plays, he gives us something different. It's not just his goalscoring; he's so good on the ball. It did not look good when he went down and I was very worried about him because he is my best friend. He was out for a long time last season with a knee injury and we really missed him. I was very worried that it might be happening again.'

The half-time announcer at The Dell poked fun at Chelsea's foreign legion. After displaying a schoolboy grasp of several languages, he announced: 'The last time I was at a game like this it was England versus the Rest of the World.' Ironically, it was a display of true British grit that saw Chelsea through. Before each game, as his players feast on their pasta and olive oil, Vialli plucks a word from his phrasebook and asks them to apply it on the pitch. The word on Vialli's blackboard at the pre-match team meeting today was 'personality'. The boss wanted his players to express themselves, impose their dynamism on vulnerable opposition. They did just that, regained the Premiership lead, but lost Poyet.

There was unanimous disbelief in the dressing room that Colleter had not been red-carded. The Frenchman later apologised for the tackle: 'I am sorry if my challenge has caused an injury, but there was no malicious intent on my part. Yes, my tackle was hard, and yes, it was a little late. But the ball was there to be won and Poyet was off balance. I do not agree with those who say I deserved to be sent off. It was my first game in English football and I was still adjusting to the pace of the game. I hope Chelsea understand that.'

Poyet was able to walk on to the Chelsea team bus and report for treatment the next day before seeing a specialist to discover the full extent of the injury. Vialli knew it was not a repeat of the cruciate ligament injury he had suffered within weeks of joining Chelsea from Real Zaragoza, but it was the same right knee. Rix remained tight-lipped about the challenge which saw Poyet stretchered off in the seventy-first minute: 'Gus got a tweak and won't play against United. It's a blow, but we have to stand up and be counted. Challenge? That's part of football, and I don't know how bad it is yet. We are in the hands of the medical staff. It's disappointing, and if he is out we are going to miss him because he's on fire at the moment. We are not going to moan about injuries. If anything, this will spur us on.'

At least Chelsea won the match. In a monsoon, Morris and substitute Terry managed to levy a degree of influence. Rix revealed: 'John Terry, a seventeen-year-old boy rubbing shoulders with World Cup winners, didn't look out of place. He accepted responsibility and pushed people around. And Jody Morris is only twenty, but he did great competing against big Carlton Palmer. He even beat him in the air once, but when he gets the ball down Jody is a progressive lad.' The Saints' frenzied first-half onslaught was repelled, and Flo's twenty-third goal in thirty-four starts, expertly and delightfully conceived by Zola, arrived against the run of play. A Le Tissier corner was cleared, and Zola raced a good forty yards before clipping a delightful cross over Palmer for Flo to calmly volley his eighth goal of the season. When keeper Jones spilled Petrescu's cross three minutes after the restart, the ill-fated Poyet lapped up the rebound.

Back from his cruise around the Far East and Australia, Bates was just in time to celebrate Chelsea's repossession of the Premiership's number one spot. 'It's where you finish in May that counts,' chimed the chairman before disappearing towards the Ted Bates lounge.

MONDAY, 28 DECEMBER

Luca voiced the controversial view that the whole of England preferred Villa's Union Jack XI to win the title rather than his collection of expensive foreigners. Almost singlehandedly he had changed the public perception of the 'mercenary' Italian stars; now he had to convince Little England that Chelsea would be worthy English champions.

Asked whether he is liked in England, he replied with remarkable frankness: 'They are very nationalistic and they struggle to admit when somebody brings something good into their island. I believe I have made them change their views of Italians. We are not pampered stars, we can fight; we've come over here to live, and come over to work hard, not steal the money. We can work very hard, not just play tricks.'

John Gregory was most amused to hear Luca's views. He responded: 'You're lucky, Luca, because most foreign players in this country don't give a toss about their clubs or English football. Mind you, if Luca is worried that people are swinging behind Villa because we are all English, he could easily let me have Zola or Desailly. I am not some kind of football Alf Garnett. But I do appreciate that English players are never afraid of a hard day's work.'

And neither was Luca about to return home, despite a campaign among the Juventus fans for him to return as coach. Outgoing Marcello Lippi recommended his appointment; instead Juve lined up Parma coach and former Italian number two Carlo Ancelotti. Vialli had a job to complete at the Bridge. Equally, he wasn't ready for a move back to Italy, where the stress is far greater than he already experiences taking charge of the Blues in the Premiership. 'Rationally, I'd say I'm not ready,' Luca said, 'particularly because we are not talking about Cremonese or Reggiana, but of Juventus and Sampdoria. The day when the Agnellis of this world should decide to call me, I'd probably shit myself! But I would probably decide on my instincts, as I did with Chelsea eight months ago.'

He still couldn't quite get to grips with the idiosyncrasies of being both player and boss. When he is on the field, he said, 'some of the games go over the top because they pass the ball to me too much because I'm also the manager, while somebody else doesn't give me the ball at all because they don't want to be seen as a creep. Not everything is perfect but we've reached a good point. I accept there remain barriers. There is a lot of respect, but also we are on easy terms. There are times for jokes and times for criticism. During a pre-season tournament, for instance, I had a very serious quarrel with Di Matteo to the point of telling him to fuck off. At the end of the day I told him that because I was playing it was okay, but if I'd been on the bench I would have taken it differently.'

Chelsea's title credentials were about to undergo their second serious examination by Manchester United. The stage was set for the return of Desailly, who had missed four games with a knee injury, including the draw at Old Trafford. With Wise suspended and Poyet out, the timing of Desailly's return could hardly have been better. It was a measure of the strength of the squad that just when they looked to have a crisis in central midfield, they could recall Di Matteo, who missed the trip to The Dell through suspension. The performances of Duberry and Morris had also impressed the management team. Rix said: 'Doobs has been outstanding over the last four or five games, while Jody has also shown just what he can do. He's realised that he has a chance to make a name for himself and is working hard on and off the pitch. He's got to keep it up, keep his feet on the ground and he's got a great chance.' Le Saux was also back in contention.

Vialli knew that while Chelsea's record at Old Trafford was second to none, their record against United at Stamford Bridge was poor. So victory would be a big psychological advantage. Rix had already indicated that Vialli's watchword for tomorrow would be 'calmness'.

Bates summoned half a dozen leading soccer writers to a drink in the Bridge Bar, followed by lunch at the adjacent Kings Brasserie. Over pink champagne – Chelsea Village Pouilly Fumé, his favourite – the chairman held a war council as he announced his candidacy to become FA chairman. After all, had he not predicted three years ago that Chelsea would become the Manchester United of the south? The Godfather of the Bridge believed he could also revolutionise the FA.

Ever since the resignation of Graham Kelly over the controversy of a loan to the Welsh FA, it had become obvious that there was a scramble for power under way. Bates only desired a short-term appointment, a caretaker role to give a younger man like David Sheepshanks a little more time before he took charge. But heaven help the FA lame ducks if Bates was voted into office.

Bates said: 'I can confirm that I was approached unofficially to see if I would stand. I made it clear I wasn't interested in the position. Under pressure, I was asked if I was prepared to be an interim chairman to see through the kind of changes that are clearly required. I should point out that I have never made any secret that I have no ambition within the FA for the trappings of power or aggrandisement that go with the position of chairman. I do not think that at the present time there is any clear candidate. I am worried about the people throwing their hat into the ring because they are either doing it for the wrong reasons or, however well-meaning, they are not equipped for the job. I did say somewhat reluctantly that if there was real pressure I would consider being chairman for eighteen months to two years to try and push through the radical changes. Maybe because I have no long-term ambition in the FA other than to see it modernise and be successful, there are people who consider that I would be the appropriate person to be approached to enable the FA to have the time to go forward in the long term.'

Fans made representations to Bates not to abandon Chelsea; Bates insisted that Chelsea, and indeed his partner Suzannah Dwyer, come first in his life. But his indignation of an organisation where little to nothing can be achieved in the advancement of the game has no bounds. He went on: 'There are so many rules and regulations. I've yet to understand the difference between their rules and their regulations. Don't ask me, I'm still puzzled! When each council member votes he can do so on behalf of a whole variety of affiliated organisations. One man can have 453 votes. It's just a joke. At Chelsea, we would have a committee meeting and the minutes would be circulated within seven days; at the FA there are four council meetings a year and the committees report seven days beforehand. In some cases the minutes from committee meetings can reach you ninety days late. I commented on this a year ago and was assured there would be an improvement, but there hasn't been.'

But the focal point remained the title challenge. In his programme notes Luca flirted with danger. 'Now then, I have a feeling that Chelsea supporters might not like this, but I'm going to write it anyway. I think Manchester United are the best team in England and have been for the last six or seven years. All they're missing is a big win in Europe. We all know they are desperate to win the Champions League. I believe this season they have a great chance to do just that. And we all support them here because the more they concentrate on the Champions League the less they might care about the Premier League. The more we support them, the better chance we have.'

TUESDAY, 29 DECEMBER

Chelsea 0   Manchester United 0

Luca took as much satisfaction out of this result as he could. 'We had chances to win it in the first half, but unfortunately we missed them, and in the second half United gained the upper hand. We looked a bit tired, but a point is better than nothing and we have kept our unbeaten League run going.' Poyet was badly missed, but Vialli added: 'He shouldn't be out for too long. We are talking weeks, not months.'

United were saved by the profligate finishing of Flo and two crucial saves by Schmeichel either side of the interval when Zola was clean through, but rarely has Schmeichel's goal been peppered with so many shots and chances and come out unscathed. Only Cole seemed capable of responding to the catalogue of chances created by Chelsea. Ferguson was the more relieved of the two managers. 'We allowed Zola too much room and we nearly paid for it in terms of chances created and his movement off the ball.' Not often has Ferguson been so grateful to escape from Stamford Bridge with a precious point.

For a match that was billed as a defining moment in this very open championship race, potentially the match of the season, between two sides whose philosophies placed the priority on attack, it seemed almost destined that this classic encounter should end fruitless. But sterile it never was, Zola illuminating the contest with some amazing juggling skills bordering on the cheeky, and certainly as good as anything that drove him to the coveted prize of Footballer of the Year two years ago. Making a comeback, Beckham and Giggs were muted by a more resilient Chelsea team than those on parade in recent seasons.

It began from the very first minute with Di Matteo, returning to the team, cleverly controlling a mishit clearance from Leboeuf, gliding past Butt and threading through the pass for Zola to shoot on the run from just outside the box, but just over.

Di Matteo and Zola were again at the hub of a move that set Petrescu free on the right, his cross juggled at the near post by Flo before he directed a five-yard volley wide. Then Babayaro supplied Zola with the ball at his feet and space to run at Stam. Zola turned the Dutch defender inside out, deceiving him when he shaped to shoot, leaving him stranded; the shot was saved by Schmeichel and somehow Flo missed from six yards. Vialli leapt off the bench, grasping his bald head in disbelief.

Cole responded by drawing Leboeuf out of position and completing his run by rounding de Goey, but his angled shot was saved by Duberry on the line, the rebound caught by the grateful keeper.

Schmeichel read Zola's specialist free-kick, and midway through the first half Zola produced a sharp turn and pass and Flo nudged past Schmeichel agonisingly wide of the open goal with the keeper outside the box. Di Matteo was booked for a foul on Keane, and from Beckham's free-kick a glancing header from Butt found de Goey well placed. Flo was again off target, though in mitigation he was stretching to reach the ball before Schmeichel, and five minutes before the interval Keane senselessly squandered possession and Zola had his chance, but Schmeichel was again quickly out to smother at his feet.

Ferguson brought on Sheringham for Scholes on the hour, and shortly afterwards Leboeuf was booked for a foul on Cole when he dived into a reckless tackle. Vialli brought on Desailly in place of Morris after seventy-three minutes.

Leboeuf was caught rampaging forward and snapping at Beckham's heels as the England star crashed to the ground. He received a lecture from referee Mike Riley when a less lenient referee would have raised the red card. Again Keane gave the ball away in a dangerous position, and when Petrescu found Zola his attempt to place the ball through the keeper's legs deflected the shot around the post. Vialli threw on Goldbaek for Le Saux with a couple of minutes remaining, just seconds after Giggs's twenty-five-yarder found de Goey right behind it (although a routine stop, the ball almost crept between his legs as he pushed it into the ground), but the game finished goalless.

Leboeuf confessed he was lucky not to be sent off as Ferguson accused referees of being biased towards home teams. 'I think I deserved a red card. I touched his foot then grabbed him from behind as he was through, so for that I apologise, but it wasn't intentional. I was pleased that I was not sent off because I did not mean

The Nigerian, the Frenchman, the Spaniard, the Uruguayan, the Englishman the Norwegian . . . the United Nations of Chelsea.

In seasons past, Luca had hit a few against Coventry. But this year he started the season on the bench.

He helped put England out of the World Cup, but 'Super Dan' remains a favourite at the Bridge.

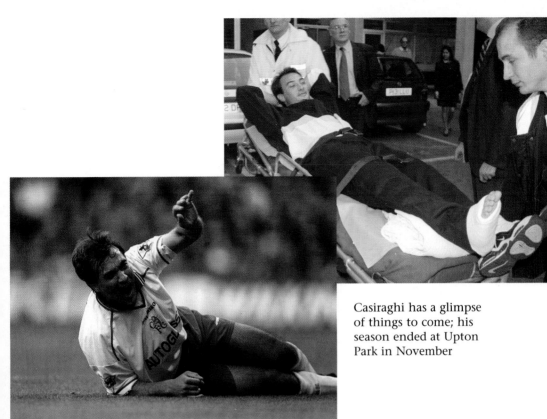

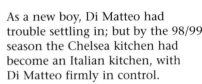

Casiraghi has a glimpse of things to come; his season ended at Upton Park in November

As a new boy, Di Matteo had trouble settling in; but by the 98/99 season the Chelsea kitchen had become an Italian kitchen, with Di Matteo firmly in control.

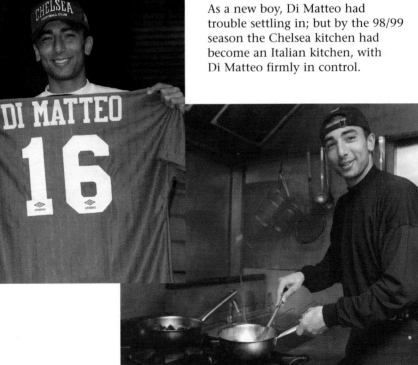

De Goey's superior goal keeping at Elland Road helped dispel the myth of a shaky Chelsea defence in this 0–0 draw with Leeds.

Opposite Fans heap praise on the golden forehead of Gustavo Poyet after he scores in Chelsea's 2–1 win over Charlton.

Another piece of history: a rare header from Zola in a 1–1 draw with Sheffield Wednesday.

Luca celebrates having
strolled the ball into the
Arsenal net in Chelsea's
historic 5–0 victory.

The men who make the
man: in the past two sea-
sons, scenes like this one
have been frequent
thanks to Di Matteo's and
Wise's superior control of
the midfield.

Whether missing goals or games, Dennis
Wise had a frustrating 98/99 season.

Another successful cup appearance by
Vialli, scoring against Oldham Athletic
in a 2–0 win.

Jody Morris' tenacity ensures that he's still a first team selection despite
Chelsea's foreign legion.

Thanks to 'the Rock',
Valerenga find little comfort
at the Bridge in the Cup
Winners Cup quarter-final.
Integrating Desailly's world
class defending into the
Chelsea side was one of
Vialli's more welcome
puzzles this season.

to make a foul.' Vialli agreed: 'Frank should have gone. I don't think that he meant it, but it was a foul and because of that it should have been a second yellow card. I was almost sure the referee was going to book him again, but we got away with it.' Ferguson was ushered back to the dugout by fourth official Gary Willard when Leboeuf was reprieved. Riley, however, insisted he was right not to send off Leboeuf. 'I did not believe the contact by the Chelsea player warranted any further action. I considered the free-kick was sufficient.' When the final whistle blew, Leboeuf chased Beckham up the tunnel to apologise, and the two players shook hands.

January...
January...

January

*Chelsea start 1999 as championship
favourites, two points behind leaders
Aston Villa*

FRIDAY, 1 JANUARY
As the open championship race moved into the New Year just four points separated
the top four teams. The former Prime Minister was tipping his team for the title.
John Major said: 'Chelsea could well win the title this year. They seem to have
stopped leaking goals. It doesn't bother me how many foreigners we have at the
club now. It hasn't really changed that much; the side has always been very
cosmopolitan – it used to be full of Scotsmen.' Major has been a fan since 1955,
the last time Chelsea won the championship. His favourite player is Flo. 'Flo shows
great pace and remarkable co-ordination and balance, like a ballet dancer. He seems
to make things happen and is marvellous to watch. People like Roberto Di Matteo
and Gianfranco Zola can hit the ball so well.'

Despite the end-of-the-year draw with Manchester United, Chelsea began the
New Year 6–4 favourites with William Hill to win the Premiership title, with United
at 7–4, Arsenal at 7–2 and Aston Villa at 13–2. Luca's New Year message for the
fans was: 'I wish you all a very Happy New Year, both in your life away from
Chelsea and in your support for us. I hope it will be very special.'

Tommy Docherty, always good for a laugh, was convinced his old club wouldn't
win the title as the foreigners wouldn't be able to stand the English winter. 'The
excess of foreign players may count against them,' he said. Watch out for that
snow, Flo! Manchester United and Villa had more of a chance as they were
'made of predominantly British players'. Di Matteo scoffed at all this gloves-in-
winter nonsense: 'We have winter in Italy too, you know! It can get cold there
as well.'

But title talk was no secret inside the Bridge dressing room. Leboeuf said: 'Since
I was at Chelsea I never mentioned we could win the League. When I came two
years ago I said I thought we could win the Cup because I believed we had the
team to do it. Last year I didn't mention the League, but said we could win the
Cup Winners Cup. Now I say we can win the League. I hope my wishes will be
realised.' He recalled the time he first walked into Chelsea. 'I remember seeing a

picture of all the unforgettable players of Chelsea. I always said that one day I want to be a player in that picture. It's what I try to do. I hope soon I will be a part of it.'

Life was also good off the field for the Frenchman: a mansion near Richmond Park and a lavish social diary. 'Everything in London is like I expected. I was sure I would settle down easily and find my friends, enjoy life here. I never wondered if something would disturb me, and everything has been okay. Of course the culture is different, but it is my job to make the effort as when you come into a country it's your part to meet the people. It's not the people who must meet you.'

Chairman Ken Bates had his message too. 'Well, we were top for forty-eight hours and I must say I enjoyed the experience. No nosebleeds, just a warm glow. I think the players enjoyed it too. Given them a taste for it, and perhaps it will encourage them to strive even harder. Looking forward to 1999, we can expect to see the upper tiers of the West Stand starting to give us a 41,300 capacity stadium with the best facilities in the country, and our younger players continuing to progress. Yes, media, we do have a first-class youth development programme. We can also expect the completion of the Court Hotel and the Stamford Bridge entrance, and a start on the sports and leisure complex. Chelsea are now a force to be reckoned with, and 1999 will be the year when we sit down and formulate our strategic plan for the next century.

'To Pierlugi Casiraghi, may 1999 repay you for a lousy 1998. To all supporters everywhere a fantastic New Year, and to all Manchester United supporters, may you enjoy being runners-up for the second year running, and here's hoping we meet you in the final of the European Super League in 2000.'

Casiraghi was given the all-clear to begin his rehabilitation after operations in London and Vienna. He said: 'It will be mind-numbingly boring, but results will encourage me.' He wanted to cheer on Chelsea for the title. 'If they go into the last month two points off the top, that's okay. That's when everything will be decided.'

First assignment of the New Year was the first FA Cup meeting with Oldham. Manager Andy Ritchie banned video footage featuring Vialli's side in their recent 1–1 draw against Manchester United at Old Trafford, a performance which left the Second Division strugglers spellbound. 'All the lads saw that match on television and came in the next day saying Chelsea were awesome,' Ritchie explained as he prepared for the Boundary Park sell-out. 'I've got it on video, but to be honest it would be better if I didn't let them see it again. I think if we look at them too much we'll frighten ourselves to death.

'It goes without saying we are hoping it will be as cold as possible. If it's below freezing and a bit icy, don't worry about us, but it will be interesting to see how they fancy it. We will nick their gloves and turn off the heating in the changing rooms to give them a nice surprise, and see how they react.'

Striker John McGinlay was also hoping for a bracing winter's day. 'This is not the most inviting place for visiting teams. It will be freezing cold with a swirling wind and the Chelsea boys will be decked out in their gloves in their little dressing room. Hopefully they won't fancy it one bit. They will be used to plush surroundings, and if they come here with the wrong attitude they will get a shock because it can be a bit grim to say the least.'

Wise was back after yet another ban. 'I watched on television when Oldham beat Brentford on penalties, and I wanted Brentford to win because we've got Oldham and we've got to win. Performance isn't important in the Cup, it's the result. We've got to be very careful. Never mind that they're struggling in the League, it'll be very hard. By the way, John Sheridan's penalty was one of the worst I've seen in my life. He nearly broke his foot!'

Vialli was without suspended Petrescu, and Poyet and Lambourde (injured) for the match, as Luca protected his proud record of just one defeat in fifteen Cup ties as a manager. The boss was expecting a gale-force challenge from Oldham. 'This isn't going to be a difficult match just because of the wind. Oldham have been giant-killers in the past and we must be prepared for anything. Sure, if the wind is gusting, we will try and keep the ball on the ground and play our football. But if Oldham don't allow us to do that, we will have to adapt our style.'

Without money to spend – he had already exhausted the transfer budget agreed for the season with Bates and Hutchinson – Luca lowered his sights to signing a striker on loan. Vialli admitted: 'At the moment I can't say we won't be bringing in somebody else, but I can't say we will. Obviously it has to be right for the club.' Paradoxically, in the climate of scrupulous accounting at Stamford Bridge, and in the wake of Real Madrid's offer of £5.72m a year – or £110,000 a week – to his one-time target Steve McManaman, Vialli reaffirmed his determination to pay the going rate for top-class performers. 'This is the way of the world, and I'm happy for those players who can take advantage of post-Bosman regulations. We took advantage of a similar situation when we brought Laudrup to Chelsea: we spent nothing on the transfer so we had a lot of money in hand for his wages. It is a question of simple economics: if you don't spend anything on transfer fees, you can afford to pay more in wages. The overall cost of the package doesn't change. That's why I'm not surprised if Real are offering McManaman a hundred thousand a week.'

SATURDAY, 2 JANUARY
Oldham Athletic 0   Chelsea 2

John Kettley is a weatherman ... and he should concentrate on predicting high winds and thundery showers, because his first stab at today's weather was an abject failure. Making an appearance on *Football Focus*, hosted by Gary Lineker, he joined in a playful blast directed at the foreign legion. It proved to be as damp as his prediction that the north-westerlies blowing down the Pennines would put the wind up Vialli's team of gloved softies. The worst weather was, in fact, down south.

Ritchie couldn't stop wittering on about how Chelsea couldn't be called southern softies any more because they hadn't got any southerners in their team (So what about Wise, Duberry, Le Saux, Morris and Terry? In among those Cockney accents Leboeuf sounds like Prince Charles). Ritchie also banged on about how the fierce weather up north would put the wind up the Blues. But they breezed through those insults.

The biting wind and driving rain did duly whip in from the Pennines. The only element Oldham could not provide was a team to challenge Chelsea after Vialli's first goal. What a beauty it was. Revelling in the inhospitable conditions and a typical duel with Oldham's committed defence, he dispossessed Stuart Thom thirty yards out, took two strides forward then buried the ball in the bottom left-hand corner. It was Vialli's first sniff at goal, and illustrated perfectly the difference in class between the teams. Oldham, all grit and graft, enjoyed glimpses of goal, but none so clear-cut as those fashioned by Chelsea. Mark Allott hit a post as the first half came to a close, and two further attempts were blocked in a mêlée which left de Goey needing treatment. In the second half, Goldbaek supplied the low cross from the right for his boss to sidefoot into the roof of the net for the second.

Sadly, the major talking point of the match was not the marvellous contribution of Vialli but a hot dog that almost ko'd John Durkin. A fan managed to pick out the back of the referee's head from row ten of the Rochdale Road end. They laughed as the mustard and ketchup trickled down Durkin's neck, but he thought it was blood as bottles and coins were also being thrown. The flashpoint had been the Oldham players surrounding Durkin with menace after he had failed to spot a handball by Babayaro in the build-up to a Wise 'goal'. Durkin was on his way back to the centre circle when the hot dog struck.

'He's lucky it weren't a pie, that would have killed him,' joked Richie. It was a joke Durkin was able to share once he had reached the safety of the Wiltshire countryside. 'Everybody laughs, I know,' he said. 'Ref gets hit by hot dog is a funny story. Even I can laugh at that. Who knows, I might even get sponsorship from Burger King now. But there is a serious side, too. Coins and a bottle of Coke were also thrown. I'm thankful it was the hot dog and not the bottle that hit me. Who knows what might have happened then.'

Everyone in the stadium believed Durkin and the linesman had given a goal. There was a four-minute delay while the referee spoke to police officers. Durkin eventually disallowed the goal, booked Babayaro, and an Oldham supporter was led from the crowd by police. Before being escorted to his car after the match by an Oldham steward, the referee confirmed that he would include the incident in his report – and that would mean an FA probe.

The hot dog struck at the same time as the buzzer linking him to the linesman went off. 'To be fair, I thought the goal was okay,' added Durkin. 'I'm just relieved the linesman spotted it. I was unsighted, but it was clear from the reactions of players that something had happened and I was on my way to the linesman when I was hit. The whole thing would have been cleared up a lot earlier had I not been dealing with the police to sort the situation out. I feel sorry for the club. Oldham are now facing sanctions from the FA once it has received my report.'

John Terry was handed his full debut for this match. Wise said: 'He's going to be a good player. He'll stick his foot in, his head in; he's strong and he's good on the ball. He's got the right frame of mind as well. He's a nice lad.'

So, progress in the Cup – but at a high cost. Flo came off the bench, only to limp off soon afterwards. He was taken to hospital when the squad returned to London where an X-ray showed no bone damage. But Flo was badly hurt.

SUNDAY, 3 JANUARY

Bates and Suzannah attended a disjointed fourth-round draw with forty teams going into the hat because of replays and holders Arsenal travelling to Preston the next day. Chelsea, number fifteen out of the hat, were drawn away to debt-ridden Oxford United to provide a welcome cash windfall for the First Division strugglers.

Vialli's men were immediately made 11–2 favourites by bookies William Hill, who also fancied Manchester United to beat Liverpool after installing them as 7–1 third favourites behind 13–2 shots Aston Villa, who were at home to Southampton or Fulham. Chelsea proposed a switch to the Bridge, but Oxford declined. Bates said: 'In view of their financial problems we did suggest that the game be switched here, but Oxford decided to keep faith with their fans and stay at the Manor Ground. They increased their admission prices by fifty per cent.'

MONDAY, 4 JANUARY

Flo's injured right foot was put in plaster and he was on crutches. After seeing a specialist in London he immediately left for Oslo for consultation with the Norway national team's orthopaedic surgeon and senior consultant, Dr Trygve Kase, sure to be missing for at least a month. Flo said: 'Obviously people are saying I will be out a long time but I do not see it that way. I can stand on the foot, but still have to use the crutches to help ease the pressure. I can't understand what is wrong.'

Poyet, the Premiership's top scorer from midfield with eleven goals, also saw a specialist on an injured knee and needed an exploratory operation. He was expected to be out for six weeks. Assistant manager Gwyn Williams said: 'He'll need a scope to check the damage or to remove any floating matter. Gus will probably go into hospital next week. The good news is it's nothing to do with the injury that kept him out for a long spell last season.' Williams added: 'Tore had an X-ray after Saturday's match and nothing was broken, but he was still in considerable pain. What now? A thirty-four-year-old player-manager will have to play a lot more!'

TUESDAY, 5 JANUARY

Lucky Luca felt his season was jinxed. The season had hit crisis point with the operation on Flo's ankle and Poyet's knee. Vialli's Famous Five forwards were down to two: Zola and the boss himself. Vialli's plan to pick himself only for Cup ties was under review because he simply didn't have anyone left but himself.

Flo's second specialist report carried the worst possible news: cartilage damage in the ankle joint. Trygve Kase performed the delicate operation. Flo would not be allowed to resume full training for a minimum of six weeks, and it was 'dangerous' to rush him back. Kase said: 'We removed small and pretty large bits of cartilage which were smashed off the bone, and the ligament is off the bone too. The ligament can be treated by rehabilitation, but the cartilage damage is not very common – it is serious without being extremely serious. Tore must not do anything which could rotate the ankle for six weeks, then it will be important to see how it will take force when he puts weight on it in a football situation. In my experience it is important to move smoothly and slowly back to full-out match situations after an injury like this.'

Flo would miss at least four Premiership matches. Chelsea insisted the full extent of Flo's injury would not be known until he returned to the club. Flo said: 'I'll be out for a while but I don't look too darkly on it. If this had come at the same time last year it would have been worse, because it would have hit my preparation for the World Cup. This will work out all right. I'll have to take my time and get well again.'

Williams said: 'He could be out for anything from two to five weeks. We will know more when he returns to the club on Saturday.'

Vialli's need to recruit another striker on loan was now urgent. Norwegian striker John Carew, who ironically plays for Cup Winners Cup quarter-final opponents Valerenga, was a target. Carew had returned from Italy where he had rejected a move to Perugia, but his transfer evaluation was £3.5m. Vialli tried to persuade the club that money was urgently needed to keep the team on track for potentially their greatest season in their history.

WEDNESDAY, 6 JANUARY

Juventus fans continued their campaign to lure Vialli back to the Stadio Delle Alpi to replace coach Marcello Lippi when his contract ran out in the summer. They unfurled a giant banner during Juve's 1–1 draw at AC Milan bearing the message: LIPPI IN OUR HEARTS, BUT VIALLI FOR COACH.

De Goey felt Chelsea's miserly defence would be enough to win the team the title. The Dutch international goalkeeper had kept four clean sheets in a row – a far cry from the days when Chelsea were said to have a soft underbelly. De Goey's defence had completed fourteen shut-outs already this season – just four short of their total throughout the entire 1997–98 campaign. And while Chelsea had conceded sixty-four goals in all competitions the previous season, this time they had only let in twenty so far – and just seven at Stamford Bridge. The days of Gullit's sexy football with a dodgy defence were in the past. Arsenal were the only side conceding fewer Premiership goals, but their embarrassing 5–0 defeat in the Worthington Cup meant they had let in more in total. De Goey said: 'It isn't just down to me. The defence is very strong and very important. They block a lot for me on the edge of the box and they do it well. I don't have to face many shots.'

THURSDAY, 7 JANUARY

Newton considered rejecting a new contract for talks with Gullit at Newcastle. Newton, twenty-seven, who scored one of the goals in Chelsea's 1997 FA Cup final victory over Middlesbrough, was a free agent at the end of the season. Gullit was in touch, and the pair planned to meet up in the next week to discuss a move. Newton said: 'I enjoy it at Chelsea but I do want first-team football. I have achieved a lot in my career so far and I want to carry on winning trophies. Whether that will be with Chelsea or with another club, I don't know at the minute.' Newton had played just once this season, but was only just back in training following an Achilles problem after being injured in a tackle with Tottenham's John Scales in a reserve match last October. Chelsea wanted £1.5m for him if he moved immediately. Derby, Leicester and Sheffield Wednesday were also interested, and Italian side Bologna asked for talks after being sent videos of him in action by his agent.

Neil Clement also wanted to leave in search of regular first-team football.

Clement, on loan at Second Division Reading, was a free agent in the summer and had also become frustrated at his lack of first-team opportunities, having appeared only twice as a substitute this season. 'It's been very hard to get into the Chelsea team. I went on loan to get some experience and I don't want to sit in the reserves any more. I've been at Chelsea since I was sixteen and worked under Hoddle, Gullit and Vialli. I've seen some great players, but I think I'll be leaving.' Clement was hopeful of completing a £300,000 move after impressing Reading manager Tommy Burns during his two-month loan.

Babayaro was held by police for an alleged sex assault on a woman. Allegedly, Baba abused the woman with another man the day after he helped Chelsea to the 2–0 win against Oldham. The twenty-one-year-old woman reported the alleged assault to police in Hounslow, Middlesex. Babayaro and the other man were arrested in the afternoon. Police confirmed he was being held over at Fulham police station, opposite the Stamford Bridge ground, for an alleged indecent assault at a house in Chiswick, West London. Williams said: 'I'm making no comment until I receive some more information from official sources.' It was the second unsavoury case to affect the club, after Rix denied unlawful sex with a fifteen-year-old girl and three counts of indecent assault.

FRIDAY, 8 JANUARY

The last time Bates shook hands with Gullit, it was to hand him his P45. When they met up again at St James's Park the next day, the hand that sacked Gullit would be extended again. Surely it was bound to be the most acrimonious reunion of all time.

The circumstances of the Gullit departure would have done justice to a John Le Carré plot. In fact, there were so many twists of the knife even Le Carré would have rejected it as far-fetched. Yet Bates insisted there would be no animosity when they met up again. 'It is not in my nature,' retorted the Chelsea chairman. Bates had not spoken to Gullit since the day he was sacked. 'I've not spoken to him, but then again why should I have done? We move in vastly different circles and our paths haven't crossed. We left on good terms personally. We shook hands. I said that we should stay friends because we live in the same world of football and you never know one day that our paths might cross again. Now our paths will cross again, and I will shake hands with him again if I see him. I will be in the directors' box, and if he comes into the directors' lounge I will be more than happy to speak with him and shake his hand.'

Bates anticipated a classic encounter rather than worrying about dented egos and events of the past. 'In view of Ruud Gullit's reputation for wanting to play good football, and given Chelsea's reputation for exciting football, it should be a magnificent game. I cannot understand why this match is not live on Sky so millions can enjoy it rather than just those lucky forty thousand Geordies.'

After a week of taking the FA to task, and declaring his candidacy as chairman to put the whole game to rights, everyone expected Bates not to hold back about the reunion with the dreadlocked genius he kicked out. But Bates knew everyone expected it, and he opted to do exactly the opposite. He was diplomacy itself. 'As far as Ruud Gullit at Newcastle is concerned I have nothing to say on the matter, except that he is obviously at a club in a transitional stage of the season and it will take time for him to get it right. Ruud Gullit won us the FA Cup in his first season, the first time in twenty-six years. The only reason he left us is that we couldn't afford him.' Surely there had been more to it than that? 'Not at all,' insisted Bates.

Gullit's contract had been due to expire in the summer of 1998, and when it finally came to negotiations over a new one, Chelsea claimed his demands were far too high. It was disclosed that Gullit had asked for his salary 'netto' – that is, free of tax. Bates always insisted his £2m a year demands were the reason for his abrupt exit.

Gullit's version, in his book *Ruud Gullit: My Autobiography*, told a vastly different story. He said in it: 'Everybody knows it wasn't about money. It's pretty transparent that that was the big stick with which they hoped to beat me, and it failed. Because it didn't work they had to come up with another reason.' One of those 'reasons' emerged when Bates accused Gullit of being a 'playboy boss' more interested in 'pizza adverts' and selling Ruud Wear, his personalised fashion line. The accusation that he was not dedicated and committed to his work on the training ground ensured that first Aston Villa and then Spurs ignored him. Little wonder that when Gullit resurfaced at Newcastle he was bitterly upset when he was attacked as a 'semi-detached' manager by a fan at the recent AGM because he returns to Estelle and his baby Joelle after each game. One can imagine a smirk of satisfaction from Bates when that story hit the headlines. Naturally enough that was an issue Bates chose not to comment upon.

Gullit had many friends at the Bridge, but it is hard to believe that he counted Bates among them. Gullit recalled that final meeting with Bates most vividly in his autobiography. 'They had planned everything behind my back. I was bitterly disappointed about what had happened to me and I wanted Ken Bates to tell me why. I never got an answer; I know I never shall. I was in shock. I am totally amazed at the way I have been treated by the club I have given so much to. I had gone to the meeting in search of answers and I wasn't going to get them. Finally I turned round to Bates and told him, "Don't worry, I am very confident about myself and everything will come straight again for me one day. Maybe we shall meet each other again. When that happens, don't forget me." I then left with a final few words: "Give my regards to Suzannah." As I got up to go he took a letter out of his pocket and handed it to me. I went outside the hotel and got into my car, where I read the letter. I was sacked, and I was not even allowed access to the training ground.'

Deep inside Gullit there remains a deep affection for his 'lovely boys' at the Bridge. Equally there is a residue of anger, hurt and, yes, even a feeling of humili- ation over the way he was booted out of the club. Even when the memories of his acrimonious departure were still fresh in Gullit's mind, he said: 'I'm not angry with Luca, I am not angry with any of the players, but I am angry and extremely disappointed with some of those people I had around me. I would also say what comes around goes around. It's been a good lesson in life for me. I have suffered a lot of grief, experienced a lot of anger and said many things, but I have never singled out anybody because I still say I experienced a lot of good times and a lot of good things at Chelsea and I owe so much to many people at the club, although

I would also say there are quite a few people at Chelsea who owe a lot to me.' Gullit had not named names, but it was clear he was referring to Graham Rix and Gwyn Williams. Rix had suggested that Gullit had lost the plot, and that he once caught him hitting himself over the head with his own notes at half-time (vehemently denied by Ruud), while Williams was one of his golfing partners who he felt let him down when he discovered that Brian Laudrup was having talks with Franco Zola and Vialli the day before his dismissal.

The constant recycling of Bates's original insults about him being a part-time manager-cum-playboy fashion model did not ruffle those famous dreadlocks. He expected them. 'I am not in this game for revenge,' Ruud said. 'I'm not trying to get back at anybody. I know I was accused of being distracted by my other activities, but the proof of how hard I work is there to be seen in my golf game. During the interval of "resting" between Chelsea and Newcastle I was hitting the ball great, but now I'm playing rubbish. I hardly ever get to the course and my handicap has shot up.'

The scene was set for press conferences separated by the length of the country: Luca at Harlington close to Heathrow airport, Ruud at Chester-le-Street, near Durham. The relationship between the two was best summed up by the Italian: 'Probably people will say that he wants his own back and I want my revenge. I hope you believe me when I say that we are trying to treat this as a normal game – to get three points and fly back home. I will be different with Ruud there. It is only a year since he left and people have good memories about him as he did well for the club. But when the whistle goes everything else is forgotten. I do not see why he should be more motivated than usual. We weren't the best of friends, but there was friendship and there was a professional rapport. And our professional rapport, despite us having different ideas, was always honest and correct. Sometimes I didn't understand his ideas, but I always tried to respect them. I don't think I ever apologised to him for things I said, and he didn't to me. But then, I don't think a manager needs to apologise unless he's sure he has made a mistake. I was thirty-two and wanted to play football and had plenty of enthusiasm. I found myself sitting on the bench, and that affects your confidence. You feel you want to play for someone else. I put up with the situation when I could have left. I think I put up with the treatment, even if I say so myself, very well. I decided to stay and fight, fight for my life, and now I am talking to you as manager. It was worth it.'

Behind Durham's Chester-le-Street cricket ground, a larger than usual media contingent was assembled as Ruud held court. 'I'm very calm at this moment,' he said, 'but I'm very excited also because I will be seeing my players again.' Yes – 'my' players. There was no longer any doubt: Gullit still thought of Chelsea as his team, the vast majority of their side as his players. In addition, he felt had left Vialli with a championship team on a plate. 'I think Gianluca has to go for the title this season – there's no hiding from it any more. But it's easy for him. He has the players there, the right system and the rotation system as well. Everyone learned from what I did there, so I did my job very well. My methods are still in practice. I was going for it last season and I had the team in second place when I was sacked. I didn't talk about going for the championship, but that was my plan. Now it's a possibility that Vialli can do it. The players who are there were successful for me, and they have gone on to achieve more since I left. They are my players. I put the team together and that makes me very proud.' Gullit was also prepared to shake hands with the man who axed him. 'He has said that he will shake my hand when he sees me and, yes, I will do it. You can't keep thinking about the past, and I've forgotten about it now. The most important thing is that you get on with life. A lot of bad things have happened to me in the past, but you have to forget about them and just get on with things.'

Vialli sportingly and openly conceded the Dutchman had left him with a fine squad, and that it was Gullit alone who had convinced him to join Chelsea from Juventus. 'I don't think I would have joined Chelsea but for Ruudi. He knew me and was one of the managers who trusted me. That's why he called me and asked me to join Chelsea. I also think he did very well here. He improved the team and the club and brought in a lot of new continental ideas. And he won the FA Cup. People talk about whether it's my team or his, but we should look at it in a different way. Glenn Hoddle started the revolution by bringing Ruudi in, and he, in turn, continued it. He brought players like Leboeuf, Di Matteo, Zola, Babayaro and Poyet to the club. All I had to do was improve on that. I took over and added what I thought was right. Then, again, it was easier for me to improve things because so many good players had been brought to the club.'

In Genoa, the Luca–Ruud confrontation was the subject of conversation at their old club Sampdoria. David Platt played with both, and has remained a close friend of Luca's. The new Sampdoria boss said: 'Luca's grateful for what Ruud left him. He accepts that he wouldn't be anywhere near where he is if it hadn't been for Ruud. Sure, Luca has gone in there and changed one or two things around, but things were already moving at Chelsea under Ruud. Luca took that view and felt there was no point in tampering with too much. But he's added to it too, not just with the players, but with his personality. I know his personality well – we've been on holiday together for the past four years – and he's such a nice guy, a diamond. Luca's also prepared to hold his hands up if he's made a mistake. Players respect that. Ruud detached himself and created a bit of friction. He's a different personality to Luca.'

SATURDAY, 9 JANUARY
Newcastle United 0   Chelsea 1

Wild scenes of jubilation greeted Chelsea's first League win at St James's Park in twenty games dating back thirteen years. Their twentieth unbeaten Premiership match of the season took them back to the top of the table as Villa drew at Boro and Arsenal and Liverpool had a goalless draw.

After suffering his third successive League defeat, Gullit conceded: 'It was an emotional day for me. I was very quiet, very relaxed about it. It was good to see each other again, talk with the players; it was good to see them again "live" and good to see that what I left is in such good shape. If you look at a game like this, the difference is that one team has the quality throughout to decide a situation that is tight. Chelsea have that. I'm very happy with our performance, but I'd rather have the result. We played some good stuff, especially in the first half, but I thought Chelsea defended very well.'

Gullit's attacking 3–4–3 formation, with Shearer the spearhead in a diamond formation up front, worked impressively at the start, which encouraged the crowd, but once Petrescu scored the opener, the title contenders took command. Gullit observed: 'We were very adventurous, and did very well. We are struggling a little bit with pace so I had to find something else to enable us to play in their half. We created so many chances in the first half, but got nothing.' Gullit was pleased with Dietmar Hamann's first-half display, but it was difficult for anyone to shine once Chelsea took a grip after the interval.

De Goey was outstanding with a double save in the opening couple of minutes, first from a thirty-yarder from Hamann and then the follow-up from Speed, and Leboeuf absorbed a full-blooded shot from Glass on the line. But de Goey reserved his best save for a wicked twenty-five-yarder from Speed with the merest of touches on to the bar, and in the second half turned away a Hamann twenty-five-yarder. His only blunder was to drop the ball at Shearer's feet, and then lunge at the loose ball. Domi enjoyed an outstanding debut, but after the early assault Chelsea's opening goal after thirty-nine minutes put paid to Gullit's hopes. A left-wing cross from Wise, Vialli made a crucial challenge with Hughes at the near post, and the ball dropped invitingly to the unmarked Petrescu, whose close-range shot flew through Given.

Gullit said: 'We were caught ball-watching. Dennis Wise was left all on his own, and that was the biggest disappointment for me. After that it was always going to be difficult for us without Duncan Ferguson. The way they sit back and defend very well as a whole team, this game would have suited him; he could have made an impact by keeping the ball up there. We didn't have quality enough outside to get past people; we did it a couple of times, but not enough, and then only down the left side.'

Twice Di Matteo, and then Wise, had wonderful chances: Di Matteo was thwarted by the keeper on both occasions, while Wise scuffed the ground for a tame finish. Chelsea controlled the second half with the aura of champions. Rix offered a handshake on the final whistle, duly accepted by Gullit, but Vialli – who had defied the advancing years to produce a performance full of energy and commitment, with that wonderful technique in front of goal and in the build-up; right at the end he had turned typically in the box, his angled shot going just wide – was in the middle of his players celebrating in one corner of the ground with the massed ranks of the Chelsea fans.

There was never going to be any warm sincerity floating around St James's Park. Too much had gone on for any of that. As for either Gullit or Bates seeking out the other to shake hands, that was never going to happen. It was naive to think it would. It was just a touch of pre-match diplomacy on their part. Neither was there any real intent for Vialli or Gullit to pass any pleasantries to each other. They have a professional admiration for each other, nothing more.

In fact there was some bad feeling in the air off the pitch. Vialli accused Gullit of trying to be 'smart' for mischievously putting extra pressure on him to deliver the title. Vialli was not amused when Gullit said: 'There is no escape for them.

They have to go for the title, they have to win, and it's a fair chance that they will. But yes, they have to win it with the quality they have got, there is no hiding from that. I see it as a natural progression because anything else would be taking them backwards.' Vialli ran out of time waiting for Gullit to deliver his after-match verdict as the Chelsea team had a plane to catch, but when he conducted his after-match press conference via a mobile on the team bus, and when he was informed about Gullit's comments, he retorted: 'Of course we don't have to win the title. If he's trying to be smart we will not fall for that. It is just our duty to do the best that we can.'

When asked if he had seen the bald-headed one, the dreadlocked one said: 'Yes, I've just seen him for ninety minutes! Why would I have seen him? When he's playing he is busy focusing on the game.' Had he seen Ken Bates? 'I haven't seen him, no. I don't know, very strange questions.' By this stage of the interview Vialli had already left with his team. Just as well, because Gullit went on to reiterate his belief that Chelsea was still his team. Vialli was naturally a touch riled by Gullit's preoccupation with being responsible for this outstanding Chelsea team. Vialli began, 'I don't really want to speak too much about whether or not this is my team or Ruud's team ...' and then proceeded to do just that.

Vialli was in no doubt that he had refined Gullit's version of Chelsea from a flamboyant, total-football Dutch philosophy to a more organised, balanced and defensive Italian style; less adventurous, fewer goals, more consistent and just the finishing touch to winning a title. Vialli gave Gullit due credit for getting the whole thing going, but resented not being given sufficient credit for taking it on a stage further. 'This was not Ruud Gullit's Chelsea or Gianluca Vialli's Chelsea. This was just Chelsea versus Newcastle. Ruud did a great job at the club, and then he left. I tried to continue where he left off by doing things my way. But things do not happen at a club just because of one man. It's also about the supporters, the club and the players. I inherited a very good team, but then I had to feel the pressure because I knew I had to produce with that team. Sometimes when you get a very good team it is easy to take over because you do not have to aim so high. I had a good team, and in some ways that makes it difficult to do the job.'

Vialli then turned his thoughts to the game and his club's aspirations. 'Looking at the way they played today I'm confident they're up to it. I'm always happy when we get three points; I'm happy for ourselves, I'm happy for the supporters. People tried to make something extra out of this match with Newcastle, but we played our match without any particular feeling. I thought we played very well apart from the first twenty minutes.'

Dennis Wise had played well – on the left wing. 'Yeah, it drives me mad, I thought those days had gone. Baba was suspended and Luca thought I was the only one who could play that side. I prefer the middle, but sometimes you have to do things you don't want to do. But it was nice to be back and involved! I hope I won't be suspended again, but one more yellow and I'll have another one-game ban.' Of the goal he created, he said: 'Yes, it was a good ball. The idea is to get them into the six-yard box, and we caught them napping a little bit and Dan slotted it home. They put us under the cosh for the first twenty minutes; apart from that, that was it. I should have scored myself, but the divot went further than the shot.'

Shearer thought Chelsea would go very close in the title race. 'We didn't deserve to be one down at half-time, but you don't always get what you deserve. We were delighted with the way we played in the first half, but it is a sign of a good side to go in at half-time ahead despite not deserving it, then to hold on to a lead. We knew when we had them under the cosh we had to take our chances. Teams up at the top fighting for the title don't give you many chances. As far as I'm concerned there is no doubt about it: Chelsea will go to the wire for the title. Their defensive record speaks for itself. You don't get to the top by conceding goals. In the second half we just didn't look like equalising, to be fair.'

On *Match of the Day*, Vialli was nominated the player of the day and the manager of the day. It was pointed out that his team had gone a record twenty games without defeat. Vialli stroked the top of his bald head, looking worried. 'Don't say that,' he begged, 'because it will bring bad luck.' *Match of the Day* was wrong about the record – Chelsea were still seven games short of their best-ever League run, set in the 1988–89 season – but the twenty-game sequence was currently the best in Europe, ahead of AIK Stockholm on nineteen and both Belgrade sides, Obilic and Partizan, on eighteen.

MONDAY, 11 JANUARY
Training was in the afternoon to provide an extra rest period after the long haul back from Newcastle.

Poyet returned to the training ground after an operation in Belgium to clean out his knee. He would be in a brace for ten days before resuming rehabilitation. Newspaper speculation suggested he would be out for three months, based on comments by Dr Marc Martens, the surgeon who saved the career of Gullit, but physio Mike Banks felt Poyet would be playing within eight weeks, and Flo even sooner. 'Gus is very well. Obviously his knee is still a bit swollen, but I'm very pleased with him. He will be running hard after seven weeks and then we'll discuss it with the surgeon from there. But he could be training with the first team straight after that and playing very quickly. As far as Tore is concerned he thinks he can play already, but we have to be a bit careful with him over the next few weeks. Hopefully it won't be as long as people think, though. He's walking at full speed already, without limping. We'll start running with him on the treadmill next week and keep him fit so that as soon as he can start twisting and turning he will be ready for the team.'

Flo had had arthroscopic surgery to remove a couple of fragments from his ankle. Banks explained how the injury occurred. 'While shooting his foot followed through the tackle and it seems that the blow blocked his foot. Although he wasn't in any discomfort when he wasn't bearing weight, any attempt to bear weight did cause pain. We tried to move the fragment into a less intrusive part of the joint which would have enabled him to carry on without pain, but unfortunately this couldn't be done.' Flo's operation in the Ostfold Hospital in Moss, an hour's drive outside Oslo, created a storm of protest about the player jumping the six months to a year waiting list. Complaints flowed on TV, radio and the newspapers, but Flo countered: 'I paid for the operation out of my own pocket.' Dr Kase confirmed that no one had had to wait longer for an operation because of the situation.

Flo halted talks over an extension to his current three-and-a-half-year contract. Chelsea wanted to extend it by eighteen months, but Flo saw no reason to rush things and was happy with the present deal.

TUESDAY, 12 JANUARY

Euro opponents Valerenga had a goalkeeping crisis. Tore Krogstad was out with a back injury and they were desperately trying to find a replacement to register in time for the quarter-final. Froda Grodas declined to return to his native Norway and remained in Germany. General manager Jon Nordbrekken commented: 'We are working under high pressure. It's either a short-term loan or we'll buy a new keeper.'

Managing director Anders Krystad once lived in Fulham and supported Chelsea! His five-year-old daughter once asked who he'd support if Chelsea played Valerenga. 'I answered that this would never happen and that the question was as stupid as to ask whether the moon was made of cheese. How wrong can a man get?'

PSV Eindhoven's striker Gilles De Bilde was the latest name linked to a move. Vialli hoped to sign the Belgian on loan for the rest of the season with an option to buy him in the summer. The £3.5m-rated striker declared his eagerness to join Chelsea, but Eindhoven insisted they would only consider selling him, and wouldn't let him go out on loan. 'Chelsea's offer certainly interests me,' said De Bilde, twenty-seven. 'I am eager to play for them.' PSV general manager Frank Arnesen declared: 'We have told De Bilde we are willing to sell him, but we are not interested in loaning him out. A Swiss club has already made a similar approach for him, and we told them the same story.' De Bilde was PSV's joint top scorer last season with thirteen goals in twenty-one games, helping them to the Dutch title in 1997. Williams confirmed: 'We were approached by an agent and offered Gilles on loan. We were keen. Then we were told five million. The deal is a non-starter at that amount of money.'

In another bid, Chelsea failed to land £4.8m Barcelona striker Oscar Garcia, who was recommended to Vialli by Ferrer. Garcia said: 'That the leaders in England are interested in me is a source of pride. But it would make me more proud to know that Barcelona value me.' Barcelona refused to loan him for three months because they wanted to loan him out for two and a half years! Hutchinson revealed: 'A move is highly unlikely. It turned into a complex arrangement that had no chance of coming off. It's a non-starter unless Barcelona come back to us.'

Meanwhile, ill-informed weekend reports that Chelsea wanted to take Les Ferdinand on loan until the end of the season to solve their injury crisis hit a snag even before the striker's knee injury at Sheffield Wednesday. The problem was that Premiership clubs are not allowed to loan each other players! 'It's a rule I recommended,' said Bates.

WEDNESDAY, 13 JANUARY

Newton made a comeback after three months out with a broken bone in his foot. He had made one appearance for the Blues all season. He was back in training for a week and started the game against Watford at Northwood FC.

Lambourde, who missed the match at Newcastle with a groin injury, was also pencilled in. He was waiting to see what Chelsea offered him before making any decisions about his future.

During Scotland's three-week winter break Craig Burley dropped into the gym to work on an injured groin, and Japan's Toshinide Salto, a centre-half with Shimizu S-Pluse, trained with the team. He went to the World Cup without getting off the bench, but marked Ronaldo in a pre-tournament game. Although Japan lost 3–2, Ronaldo failed to score.

THURSDAY, 14 JANUARY

There was praise for Luca's squad system from Villa's John Gregory. 'It is no good trying to fight Manchester United, Arsenal and Chelsea with our present squad. Our rivals possess squads absolutely packed with top players, some of them world-class individuals. My target must be to build a similar work force numbering at least twenty leading performers. There are so many games, such demands, that you really can't have too large a squad in the modern era.'

FRIDAY, 15 JANUARY

The best unbeaten run in Europe. That was enough to make the superstitious Vialli groan, quickly touch the wooden table with both hands, and smilingly gasp: 'Oh my God!' He would rather talk about any subject than the unbeaten run.

De Goey had not been beaten in almost 500 minutes' play, and a sixth shut-out would mark the club's best defensive run for almost eighty-eight years. Vialli declared: 'Ed de Goey is playing really well and this is another secret of our consistency. When the goalkeeper is outstanding, it's easy to keep a clean sheet. He's very confident, experienced, determined and he wants to be successful. He's a bit crazy like all goalkeepers – in a nice way – but he can handle the pressure and is physically fit. It takes a while to settle in a new environment and he was probably criticised too much, but since then he's been outstanding almost all of the time.' De Goey insisted Vialli was the main catalyst in altering the emphasis on attack which ultimately handicapped the club under Gullit. 'We can concentrate now for ninety-five minutes and that's an improvement on what it was, which is especially important for defenders as one mistake can lead to a goal.'

Vialli insisted he would not join in the ludicrous spending spree that had gripped the Premiership. Having seen Wimbledon splash out an incredible £7.5m on John Hartson, Vialli would not be pressurised into buying just for the sake of it. 'I am not going to criticise the price paid for John Hartson. We did not make any enquiries about him, but he can be the difference between winning and losing a game. We may be rich, but we are not stupid. I signed four first-class players during the summer for £12m, while £8m worth of talent left the club, but some clubs signed individual players for £12m. I have money to spend on the right player, but we are not going to throw it away.'

Luca picked up yet another colloquialism and used it in his programme notes for Coventry's visit. 'They've got nothing to lose again. We are the team everybody says is going to win the League, so I expect Coventry to play a very good match and try to upset the apple cart.' Luca praised his players for their attitude over the holiday period. 'It's been a very good start to the year. This is down to the players.

Christmas is a difficult time when you want to stay with your family and you want to enjoy an extra glass of red wine and an extra piece of turkey. But we must make sacrifices. The players behaved very professionally, for which I'm very thankful, and in the most difficult part of the season they got their reward. We have been consistent throughout Christmas and the New Year, and in the FA Cup and Premiership we got good results. That's why we're back at the top of the table.'

Gordon Strachan was demanding extra protection for Darren Huckerby from another rough ride against Vialli's men. Strachan was worried that Huckerby would be kicked out of the game. 'When we went to Chelsea last time, he got kicked from one end of the pitch to the other. It is at times like this that the referees should use every law available to remedy the situation.'

SATURDAY, 16 JANUARY
Chelsea 2   Coventry City 1

As he headed for Tenerife with his players to recharge batteries, Vialli uttered a battle cry of Churchillian proportions. 'If we try this hard then the only way people will get past us is to walk over our dead bodies. We will be doing this right until the end of the season – fighting.' The Dunkirk spirit in the most international line-up in the Premiership.

True grit and sweat kept Chelsea at the summit of the Premiership rather than any fancy footwork from their cast of stars. From their worst performance of the season came victory over the only side to beat them so far in the League. Perhaps the foreign legion don't like the summer sun in England and prefer the bitter cold? Goals in the fourth minute of extra time at the end of each half rescued Chelsea from a match of disjointed ineptitude. Vialli confessed: 'Yes, we were a little lucky as we were not at our best, and Coventry did really well. But we showed great spirit and it shows our attitude to winning in that we struck in the last minute of the first half and the last minute of the second half. To me it doesn't matter that we play our best or not, it's whether we can still win. It was not an easy match, but it doesn't matter if it's Manchester United or Coventry, they are all very difficult and they will become even more difficult from now on until the end of the season.'

Luca and his players condemned the Bridge pitch, as overnight rain had wrecked the surface. Vialli felt the poor state of the pitch contributed to a terrible performance. 'The pitch at Stamford Bridge is in a terrible condition. Our game is a passing game so it makes it twice as hard for us to play at home with such a pitch. We like to run with the ball, dribble, and it's difficult to achieve a level of accuracy.' Leboeuf said: 'The pitch had a big part to play. We've got the worst grass in the Premiership and it needs improving.' Bates pointed out that the pitch was covered for most of the week, and the lack of air to the surface caused the excessive dampness. Ferguson had complained about the state of the Old Trafford pitch a year ago, and the club spent a great deal of money to repair it. Chelsea planned a similar repair job in the summer, and stressed to worried supporters that they had no agreement with London Irish to play rugby on the pitch after their experience with American football.

Di Matteo added: 'Stamford Bridge is like a potato patch. It is something that comes with winter. The ground is really heavy and irregular.' But Di Matteo had finally scored his first goal of the season. 'I can't remember the last time I scored – I'm sure it was in the Cup. Whatever, it doesn't matter who scores as long as we go on to win games like these.' Leboeuf cracked a wonderful twenty-yarder for a morale-boosting equaliser after Huckerby – alone in attack – had scored the opener after just eight minutes after a glorious looped pass by McAllister cleared Lambourde and Leboeuf, then Di Matteo struck his goal with impeccable timing. Vialli had missed a sitter early on, miscuing in front of goal, and then from his second chance he struck a close-range half-volley that Magnus Hedman pushed aside. Shorn of any world-class substitutes, there were no alternative attacking options apart from the unused Nicholls. Vialli confessed: 'I was a little bit too deliberate in front of goal. I made mistakes. I should have scored twice.'

Huckerby's strike denied de Goey his shut-out record; considering Coventry came to the Bridge with only five away goals in the Premiership all season, it was some feat by the striker. But before the first half was out Leboeuf came to the rescue. 'It was one of the best goals I've ever scored. My goals against Leicester might be better, but this one was more important.' Leboeuf had had a torrid time against Huckerby, and advised Hoddle to pick him for England. The Frenchman said: 'Huckerby was very good, one of the toughest I've faced this season. He has the talent and power to be in the England team. Owen might be a bit quicker, but Huckerby has the extra power, and Huckerby is a bit more clever as a player than Owen. Maybe we will see both of them together.'

Le Saux had a philosophical view of the dreadful level of performance. He argued: 'It was very tight. They came and did a very good job with a formation of a midfield five, then went and scored a goal very early that could have cost us quite dearly. The way we played was not the classic Chelsea we have become used to, but we did carry on trying and battling away. Thankfully Frank scored an excellent goal right on half-time – he couldn't have timed it better. In the second half we had a lot more possession, penned them in at times, but it was difficult for us. Robbie chose the right time to score his first goal. It was our first shot on target in the second half. It was a hard, hard game, but if we look on the positive side as we always do, and I will do, we played poorly and won – that's a good sign.'

Of course it wouldn't be Chelsea without more than a touch of controversy. Boateng's injury and failed penalty appeal was the catalyst for a bench brawl. Boateng was left needing de Goey to give him impromptu treatment for cramp after he was tackled by Lambourde. Manager Gordon Strachan took charge of the ball after it was kicked out of play, and that sparked a free-for-all between the personnel on both benches. When Strachan got hold of the ball, physio Terry Byrne grabbed it back, but kit man Aaron Lincoln was singled out by the referee, shown the yellow card, and pointed out to the police. Leboeuf was quickly on the scene. He observed: 'It was a pity that all those things happened on the bench. Our man just wanted to get the ball from Strachan to play quickly because they kept wasting time and it was getting a bit annoying. The fracas was stupid. On the pitch we were all laughing among ourselves. It was just one of those silly things. It was the first time I've seen a kit man sent off. Luckily, his role is in the dressing room, so we won't have to worry about him being suspended!'

Boateng was shown the yellow card after the final whistle for prolonging the row with the referee, Jeff Winter. Boateng said: 'It was definitely a penalty when Lambourde tripped me. Referees have to look at themselves and be honest. He wasn't even concentrating when we were attacking, only when Chelsea had the ball. You see, we don't count as a small club, but the way we played we deserved some credit, but then the ref comes along. I was lying on the ground when it all happened. I just saw Gordon went mad. The whole crowd saw it, everybody saw that it was a penalty, except one man in the whole stadium. I asked him near the end how long left, and he said one minute, and that was even before my penalty appeal, and we end up with another five or ten minutes.'

Strachan was facing a disrepute charge, but insisted: 'I'm not evil, I've not committed a crime. I've got nothing to apologise for. I tried to get the attention of the referee. I felt the lad was injured. If that's a crime ...' When Strachan was ordered out of the dugout by the referee for persistently stepping outside the designated coaching confines, he headed back to the dressing room extremely reluctantly, and missed Chelsea's winner. He said: 'I heard the roar, but I had gone back to the dressing room and had a cup of tea. I didn't want to sit in the directors' box because you cannot affect anything from there.' Coventry complained bitterly about the amount of stoppage time at the end of the game.

Chelsea's unbeaten League run was now only four behind Nottingham Forest's record for the Premiership of twenty-five set over two seasons in 1995 (in the old First Division, Forest were actually unbeaten for forty-two consecutive matches: the last twenty-six of 1977–78 and the first sixteen of 1978–79).

SUNDAY, 17 JANUARY
Gregory was unfazed by Chelsea and Manchester United climbing above Villa. He called for a convincing home win against Everton, saying: 'Why should we start getting any hang-ups? We haven't done too much wrong so far and there's no reason to start worrying now. I've already been asked how I feel about being third in the table. Well, I'm delighted to be in such an elevated position after twenty-one games. It was always going to hot up by this stage, but we are in there rubbing shoulders with the very best.'

MONDAY, 18 JANUARY
There was little sympathy from Bates for his superstar moaners. 'Manchester United have a crap pitch but they've won five championships in six years on it. All right, it's not as good as it should be, but we have to get on with it, and it's the same for both sides.' So far there was definitely no deal with London Irish. 'They came to see us some time ago, and we told them the cost of opening up the ground, and we haven't heard from them since.' Bates also tempered the hype about being top. 'Everybody is talking about Chelsea as possible champions, but we are not. We have to work hard for every point and that is what the team is doing, working hard and showing tremendous team spirit and character in adversity. Yes, it's marvellous being top, but it doesn't mean a bloody thing. We want to be top in four months' time. We've got forty-three points, so at least that means we can't be relegated this year.'

Chelsea were again linked to a transfer move, this time for Faustino Asprilla, but the tentative enquiries fizzled out. Zola had remained a close friend since their Parma days together. With Hutchinson on holiday in Dubai, transfers were on hold.

Hughes's loan period at Stockport was extended for a further month.

TUESDAY, 19 JANUARY

Ferrer nominated himself as 'Mug of the Month' for getting injured in Tenerife. 'I was just running on the track training and I felt something in my calf. This was a hot-weather holiday and I got injured.' His room-mate was Gus. 'Maybe I can talk with him and he helps me a lot. For me it's still sometimes quite difficult to understand when you speak, but I am improving. I have a good relationship with Baba, he's a really quiet man. Sometimes games can be good, can be bad, and sometimes everything can be different, but Baba is always really quiet, doing his job, never angry, never excited.' The Spaniard had settled well in Chelsea Harbour with his wife, Genny. 'It is a very nice area, really quiet, but King's Road is five minutes' walking. We're really happy there.'

John Terry won a round of golf with Le Saux and Goldbaek, and observed: 'Graeme's quite good, but Bjarne's just mad. He screams at his ball all the time. He'd hit his shot and then almost before it landed he'd jump quickly in his buggy and drive off. We could hear him in the distance still screaming like mad.' Kharine said: 'We saw Motherwell and we saw Spenny. It was nice to see him, I hadn't seen him for a long time. It's two years since he left. He's still a small Scottish bloke, still funny. I had a lot of good nights out in Tenerife. Chappie [Albert Ferrer], me, Graeme Le Saux, Robbie, Dan Petrescu, Gus, we've been out every night. Chappie showed us a good fish restaurant. He was great company.'

Poyet was out of the brace and had full extension of the knee, as Mike Banks explained: 'That means it straightens and locks properly. Over the next few weeks we have to restore his thigh muscles to normality, get him to regain full movement of his knee and then progress to sprinting work. Once he's achieved all this we should get the go-ahead for him to resume full training.'

Reading manager Tommy Burns needed £500,000 to sign unsettled defender Neil Clement. Clement had had his loan spell extended into a third month at the start of the week. Burns hoped to negotiate a £300,000 deal, but Chelsea wanted substantially more. Clement said: 'I'm delighted to be here for another month and I'm hoping something can be sorted out in the next month to keep me here permanently. I've got another three or four games to go here but the lads have been great and I've really enjoyed my time here. I don't want to go back to Chelsea and sit in the reserves, so hopefully something will happen within the month.'

WEDNESDAY, 20 JANUARY

Marcel and Frank were on international duty in Marseilles with Petit, Vieira and Anelka. In the build-up to the friendly with Morocco, Desailly suggested he might need a new challenge should Chelsea win the title, a stint in a country where he has never played before, such as Spain. 'If we win the title with Chelsea at the end of the season I could spring a surprise. If I am a champion of the English League, I could very well head for Spain or France after that. But if I do come back one day to France, it will be during the run-up to the 2002 World Cup, while I'm still totally committed, and not afterwards. I would find it challenging to help a big club in trouble, like ailing Paris St Germain.'

He felt strongly that France's World Cup defence in 2002 would signal the end of his career, and he would like to add the 2000 European Championships to the one his country so spectacularly won in 1984 under the great Michel Platini. 'My career is totally planned in relation to the World Cup of 2002. It is an enormous motivation, although there is Euro 2000 first. Our generation of 1967, 1968 and 1969 will carry on right into Euro 2000. After that, our World Cup future is down entirely to us.'

Lambourde became a target of Monaco. They would pay up to £3m and offered him regular football.

THURSDAY, 21 JANUARY

Di Matteo hinted that he, too, could quit Stamford Bridge. 'Many Italian clubs have made enquiries about me but I have always refused. I'm happy at Chelsea and I feel I have found the right balance here. However, if we win something important this season and the right offer comes along, I'd have to consider it carefully.' But Di Matteo suggested the prospect of going home was a long way off. 'It's true that I said if I was going to leave Chelsea I could never play for anyone else in this country, it would only be to return to Italy,' he explained, 'but that's a long way off in the future. This is my third season at Chelsea and we're only really just becoming a great team. We've worked so hard to get where we are and yet I feel we haven't reached the highest peaks yet. The Italian media love to run stories about Italian players coming home. So every time I go back to Italy for whatever reason, they always assume I'm coming home for good. But I want the fans to know that I really feel a part of things here. Chelsea are a club that gets into your heart – you can't help but give everything that you have.'

Bates upset Oxford fans who wrote to him about their debt-ridden club with a reply they claimed was flippant and insensitive. Bates was approached by supporters' group FOUL (Fighting for Oxford United's Life) to see if he would give Chelsea's expected £40,000 gate receipts to Oxford, who are £13m in debt. Bates declined in a reply typed on official Chelsea notepaper, with a handwritten post-script about Oxford's plight saying: 'This is the second time this has happened – Maxwell saved you last time!' Mark Mallinson, who approached Bates as marketing officer for FOUL, said: 'It's worrying that he could be the new FA chairman – it clearly shows he doesn't care for anyone outside the Premiership. His comments about Maxwell are a gross over-simplification from someone who clearly doesn't understand life outside of Premiership. Some of our problems are because of the Maxwell era. His letter is incredibly patronising. Chelsea will get around £40,000 from gate receipts which is nothing to them, but it could be life or death for Oxford. Yes, Oxford's problems are partly down to mismanagement, but it's much more than that, which is why so many lower clubs are having such desperate financial problems.'

Bates offered sympathy to Oxford in his written reply to Mallinson's home in the university town. But Chelsea would not consider donating any gate receipts.

He wrote: 'While yours is an interesting proposal I am afraid that Chelsea Football Club cannot accede to your request. I very much regret that Oxford Utd find themselves in the predicament that they are in, but this situation has arisen due to mismanagement of the club. If the people of Oxford want a Football League club then it is up to them to refinance the club and take control of their own destiny. There are sufficient large institutions, from universities and colleges (who are extremely well endowed) to many financial and industrial operations, and it is in that direction to which you should be devoting your energies.'

FRIDAY, 22 JANUARY

Luca and the squad returned from Tenerife.

Di Matteo discovered he was headline news. 'It was just an article in an Italian magazine. I merely said that at the end of the season I'll be twenty-nine, a very important age in the career of any player, and will have to consider any further steps. I have one more major move to make. But it all depends on what happens at the end of the season, then I will look at my options.' Certainly he enjoyed a week of sunshine. 'We had a fantastic time in Tenerife, a lot of fun, a lot of training. The weather was marvellous, but as soon as we come back here it is raining and cold.'

Flo had been left behind and was making good progress. 'I'm fine – cycling only, but next week I hope to start running as well. I'm bored with all the cycling. They said I could start normal training six weeks after the operation, but I hope it will be sooner, but they keep saying I must be patient. I watched the Coventry game, very exciting; a little bit lucky, but I was very glad to see that final goal go in.'

SATURDAY, 23 JANUARY

Luca was taking the FA Cup as seriously as the League, and to prove it he would be playing at the Manor Ground with a full-strength team – at least, as full as he could muster. Vialli said: 'We are still looking for a new player, we are keeping our eyes open, but we are looking for the right sort of player, one with a good mentality.'

That ruled out Asprilla and Di Canio – as well as Stan Collymore! 'It is not easy because all the best strikers are settled and we are not going to spend silly money on somebody who is not top notch. In any case, Tore Andre Flo is getting much better and news from our physio is that he could be fit sooner than expected.'

Of Forssell, still seventeen, Vialli said: 'He's young, strong, powerful and a great talent. He's already played in the Champions League with Helsinki so he's already got top-level experience. I know I can count on him, but at the moment I'm happy with myself and Franco. Of course Forssell and Mark Nicholls are ready, but it's important with the youngsters that we give them the right start in order not to dampen their spirits.'

Ferrer was banned, Lambourde injured, and Babayaro, back from Saturday's international in Nigeria, was on the bench.

Vialli dismissed the notion that he put the title before everything else – even the FA Cup. 'No, it is not a distraction, particularly at this stage, but we are fortunate that we are only playing once a week and that the team has a full week to prepare in training. There is no point not taking this match seriously. Despite being foreigners we know how important the FA Cup is in England and we haven't made any decision which trophies we are going for at this moment. All the matches are important. All the competitions still have a long way to go.'

Oxford's assistant manager Mark Harrison felt, like Oldham's Andy Ritchie had, that the crumbling stadium and shabby changing rooms would unsettle Chelsea's millionaires. He said: 'There's more pressure on Chelsea to win the game. I've been with clubs when we've played non-League teams, and there is that fear factor. The lads are right up for it. It is a great night for the lads to pit themselves against world-class players. The game is at the Manor Ground, and there will be a partisan crowd in. You never know – we might just upset them.'

MONDAY, 25 JANUARY
Oxford United 1   Chelsea 1

The paupers had put Chelsea out of business until their favourite referee Mike Reed hauled them back from an FA Cup exit with another controversial penalty decision. Tony Banks MP spluttered: 'If someone had landed from Mars they would have thought Chelsea were the First Division team and Oxford were in the Premiership.' Leboeuf converted his fifteenth successive spot-kick and left the field in clench-fisted triumph as Reed was hurried down the tunnel by three burly policemen protecting him from all the furore. Two years ago, as Chelsea were heading out of the FA Cup at Stamford Bridge, Reed awarded a penalty against Leicester's Spencer Pryor when video evidence of the incident proved that Erland Johnsen hadn't been touched. Reed had handed Chelsea a passport to the quarter-finals in that fifth-round replay, and he did it again tonight, pointing to the penalty spot in the ninety-second minute as Manor Road was about to erupt in celebration of the biggest Cup upset of the season.

Oxford are one of the poorest clubs in the country, their players at times waiting patiently for their salaries, but a team that cost £1.3m to assemble deserved to put out the £36m collection of superstars topping the Premiership. Reed, with seventy-four yellow and four red cards already this season, only booked one player, when the giant substitute Kevin Francis oafishly crashed straight into Leboeuf early in the second half. Not long after that Leboeuf went to ground in a challenge with Paul Tait, who trampled on his right knee leaving him writhing in agony as Oxford countered and set up a second goal that would have put Chelsea out of the competition. But from Paul Powell's cross Francis tore into the area and stood unmarked on the penalty spot as the ball bounced off his shins and Jamie Cooke sliced the rebound hopelessly wide. After treatment Leboeuf limped off and exchanged violent gestures with Shotton, who had to be restrained from lunging into a full-scale fight.

Dean Windass had opened the scoring after fifty-two minutes with a near-post header from Cook's corner, and Vialli decided to have a quiet word with the referee over a number of decisions he felt had gone against his team. Soon after that a succession of famous names were hauled off – Babayaro and Goldbaek on for Desailly and Petrescu, and Nicholls on for Zola – mainly because the Chelsea players seemed to be still relaxing as they strolled through a first half littered with sloppy passes. Leboeuf had gone close in the first half with a shot which rebounded off the outside of the post, but with Desailly looking jaded and Wise on the periphery of the action on the left, the Premiership leaders looked well below par.

It was halfway through the four minutes of overtime when the cumbersome Francis, who had been sent on to terrorise a defence susceptible to crosses from both flanks, ended up defending a corner at which he lunged into Vialli from behind as the player-manager held the ball at his feet. Francis took both ball and Vialli's legs, the referee blew his whistle, and Leboeuf saved Chelsea's bacon.

Leboeuf admitted: 'We didn't deserve to draw and we played very badly. We were in Tenerife last week and maybe our minds were still on holiday. Oxford played better than us so we are lucky. We were also lucky against Coventry when we got a late goal to win 2–1, and we have to play better – we all know that. But then again, maybe this luck is a sign that we are going to win something at the end of the season.'

A relieved Vialli admitted: 'I thought straight away that it was a penalty. Those sorts of incidents don't only happen to Chelsea – they go on every week. It was a clumsy challenge from the Oxford player – he caught my left foot. Even though I had my back to goal and don't think I could have shot, it was a foul. But we are very relieved still to be in the FA Cup. We played very poorly and I thought we were out. It was not the real Chelsea for the second game in a row, but this must be a lesson for us. We must get back to our usual kind of performances.'

Francis and most of the 9059 crowd packed into Oxford's Lego-set of a ground begged to differ with Vialli's views. The lanky striker said: 'I came in from the side and took the ball, which went out for a throw-in. If I had made contact with Vialli, it would have been him that would have gone out for the throw-in. There was only one person in the ground who thought it was a penalty. Unfortunately, he was the one whose opinion mattered. It was a bad decision, but we can't do anything about it now. It leaves a bitter taste, but if we play with the same attitude in the replay, then we still have a chance.'

TUESDAY, 26 JANUARY

Luca's injured foot was X-rayed, but it was only severely bruised.

The FA issued mass charges for the bench brawl. The FA's new compliance officer, Graham Bean, pinpointed the offenders: three from Coventry (striker Noel Whelan, who was sitting on the bench as he was suspended for the game, goalkeeping coach Jim Blyth and Strachan); and three from Chelsea (kit man Aaron Lincoln, unused substitute Nicholls and physio Terry Byrne).

Oxford did not ask the FA to replace referee Mike Reed for the FA Cup fourth-round replay, nor did they make an official complaint despite disquiet that the official insisted he was right to award a late penalty after reviewing TV replays. Oxford managing director Keith Cox confirmed: 'We have not and will not be making an official complaint or requesting a change of referee for the replay. Our view is that it would be counter-productive and that if clubs are allowed to pick referees for matches, then we are all on a slippery slope. Referees do make mistakes as they are only human. What does concern and disappoint me personally, however, is the reported comments from Mr Reed after the match that he had seen the incident again on television and was one hundred per cent sure he had been correct. Now I don't know if he was quoted correctly, but if he was then it is extremely surprising that he does not agree with the rest of the country, who know it wasn't a penalty.'

WEDNESDAY, 27 JANUARY

Lucky Luca didn't have his watch stolen when thieves broke into Chelsea's training ground. Around £20,000 in watches, jewellery and cash were stolen from the dressing rooms. But wise old Luca had worn his watch! Vialli, who has his own dressing room as the Boss of the Bridge, said: 'I always wear my watch when I train – you never know.' Scotland Yard refused to name which players had items stolen. The police said there were four watches stolen worth £15,000, a wrist bracelet worth £1,500 and £500 in cash. Di Matteo was one of the victims; he lost a precious watch that cannot be replaced. He explained: 'It was a gold watch that was presented to me when I won the Swiss championship. It is a sentimental loss. A watch can be replaced, but not this one, it meant a lot to me.' Zola had £200 taken from his wallet.

Bates was coming to terms with the financial loss of the public inquiry into the construction of the rest of the new stand, which he hoped would be built this summer. 'We were promised planning permission in February 1998, so whose fault do you think it is?' Little wonder there was no cash for a new player.

THURSDAY, 28 JANUARY

Vialli dismissed rumours of a player exodus. 'I am looking to bring players in, not lose any. I have been looking at new players but I won't be panicked into a move that I later regret. We have an excellent squad here which continues to win games and I will only buy someone who can improve things. There are a number of strikers I would like, but this is not an easy time of the year to attract the best ones because they are likely to still be in Europe or doing well in their own leagues.'

Less than a week after both Di Matteo and Desailly cast doubts over their long-term futures at the Bridge, Petrescu was in a more positive mood. Vialli almost sold him at the beginning of the season, but he stayed and fought for his place. Super Dan said: 'I was surprised at the start of the season when I read about me being made available for transfer. I don't think you should sell your best players and I like being at Chelsea. I don't want to leave the club and I like living in London. It is better now that I am back in the team, although you don't know if you are going to be in until about an hour before kick-off. I think I am playing well and I want to be in the side. But even if I am left out I don't want to leave Chelsea.'

Zola had also pledged his future to Chelsea. 'I'm certainly not thinking about returning home. All I want to do is to win the championship, and if I do I know I will seal my place in Chelsea's history.'

Vialli had decided to campaign for Premiership clubs to be allowed seven subs. 'I want it to be seven players on the bench, like in Italy and in Europe. These days squads consist of more than twenty players. So, if you have a squad of twenty-four or twenty-five, you have to leave nine players out. If you can have seven on the bench it keeps everyone involved, even if you can only use three. Perhaps you can say that two of them must be under twenty-three, so you can encourage young players. I want to see what the other managers think about it.'

Goldbaek found himself fighting for a regular place. 'When I signed they told me that I could not expect to play every game, and we are top of the League so I cannot argue with the manager. I knew that I was joining a good team so it is up to me to train hard every day and take my chance when it comes to show the manager what I can do. The important thing for me is that everyone at Chelsea has been very positive towards me and I have been comfortable from the first day. All the players and staff are very friendly and there is great spirit here.'

FRIDAY, 29 JANUARY

Luca faced the media, speaking quietly and authoritatively as usual, issuing his response to the fear that he cannot cope with being both a player and a manager. 'Yes, I'm under pressure, but I'm the happiest man in the world. I'm healthy, wealthy and handsome, as you can see. There is a lot of pressure at the moment, and of course I am feeling it. I am only human, and I know that my reputation is on the line every time we play because there are such big expectations for the club this season. I could have done without those two performances, though. They have put extra pressure on me. Being both a player and manager means there's too much on my mind. I enjoy being a manager and also being on the pitch, but I know I can't do it all the time. Before it was easy because I could select from a lot of players, but now I have no choice. I've got to keep going and hope Tore Andre Flo will be back soon.

'I've tried to work out what has gone wrong and can't really fathom it. In the end I've put it down to one of those things. Against Coventry the pitch was poor, but at Oxford it was good and it was our worst performance of the season. At the start of the week I would have thought if Arsenal watched those games they would be more physically and mentally prepared for this game, but the few days in training this week have convinced me we are also up for this game.'

Duberry wanted to use the Highbury platform on Sunday to again try and impress Hoddle. He denied that Desailly's arrival had galvanised him into action. 'Marcel being here didn't make any difference. I made the decision. I looked back at what I'd done and thought I should be further than I am now, and worked at my game. Now I'm happy with where I am.'

The Premiership's most talented individuals – Zola and Bergkamp – were due to clash head-on. Zola said: 'Bergkamp was voted Footballer of the Year and deserved it. He played great last year and scored wonderful goals, and is one of those kind of players I'd pay to watch perform. In Italy we say he's a player that is worth the ticket for admission. But there are a lot of players at the moment in England you'd say that about, and Arsenal have many of them in players like Overmars, Anelka, Vieira and Petit.' Adams is another Zola rates highly. 'I very much admire the way Adams plays. He's always so focused, he always gives his best. It's not so nice if you're playing against him because he makes life very hard, but I respect him for inspiring his side.'

Vialli paid tribute to an Arsenal defence he compared with AC Milan in the late

1980s and early 1990s. Vialli had faced many tough battles himself against Mauro Tassotti, Alessandro Costacurta, Franco Baresi and Paolo Maldini. He said: 'The Arsenal defence is as good as the Milan defence under Arrigo Sacchi and Fabio Capello. They have a great understanding and help each other. If you want to be successful, you have to have a solid defence. This is why Arsenal were so successful last season. They are solid and know they can keep a clean sheet. Then with players like Dennis Bergkamp, Nicolas Anelka and Marc Overmars, they also know they can score and win a lot of matches one- or two-nil.' Vialli told his players to forget all about their 5–0 Cup win and concentrate on the old mean machine. 'We cannot even dream of another five-nil score like last time. This will be a completely different match because Arsenal will have their defence back together.'

Despite all the pressure, perceived or manufactured, there was still time for Le Saux to entertain eight-year-old Andrew Lapthorne – who's confined to a wheel-chair with cerebal palsy in his legs – for lunch at the training ground. Andrew's Christmas wish was fulfilled as he met his heroes.

SATURDAY, 30 JANUARY

Bates revealed he was ecstatic with Luca as his choice of manager. 'The transition was seamless. The first thing he said was: "I want to bring back happiness and harmony to the dressing room." And that speaks for itself. If you look at the way Chelsea play today, even if they perform badly they play for each other. That's something that's been missing in the past. Quite frankly, three or four years ago we would have lost at Oxford. We would have given up. But our lot didn't. Luca consults very closely. He's very close to Rixy and Gwyn Williams and his fitness trainer. He's a team leader rather than a solitary person. So technically we're the champions of Europe, and we're first in the League. Luca's a winner; he's very dedicated and an inspirational leader. We were observing him on Monday night warming up, and he was doing more pre-match exercise than anybody else. He really pushes himself. In fact, Suzannah said to me: "He'd better pack it in soon or he'll be exhausted before they kick off." '

Williams added: 'He's a perfectionist. He wants everybody organised and on the ball. He's different from Ruudi, who I got on with as well, but it's like having different wives. You've got to understand what they want and what they don't want. Ruudi never used to train that much, and there was a day off with him. With Luca, there are virtually no weekdays off.'

The *Sunday Mirror* headlined that Shearer would be on his way to the Bridge in a summer move, possibly by offering Flo in part-exchange. That didn't go down too well at the Bridge! It wasn't even deemed worthy of a response! Nor did the Sunday paper story that Desailly had an escape clause in his contract allowing him to leave for £5m to a foreign club. It provoked a quick and angry response. Hutchinson said: 'Total garbage. There is no transfer clause in his contract. Chelsea and Marcel entered into a four-year contract that expires in June 2002. He is happy at Chelsea. We are happy with him. End of story.'

SUNDAY, 31 JANUARY

Arsenal 1   Chelsea 0

The trademark greeny-grey V-neck jumper was on show again at the post-match press conference, but for the end of Chelsea's glorious unbeaten run Luca had shed the loosened tie from the always unbuttoned button-down white shirt. He moaned: 'We had a few chances, but unfortunately we didn't look very sharp when we were close to goal. That's why they managed to clear the box a few times. Dan Petrescu felt he was pushed when Bergkamp scored the winner, but they were in control of the game at the time and I think they would have gone on to score first anyway.' Luca was asked whether he would now shave, as the backroom staff had vowed to grow goaties until they lost in the League. Williams stood in the press room with a noticeable growth, but Eddie Niedzwiecki had to shave because he was not making much progress.

Chelsea surrendered the top spot to Manchester United, 1–0 winners at Charlton, and appeared to be running out of steam fast, hustled out of their stride by the Gunners with their seventh win in their last eight games. The overall conclusion of an enthralling title eliminator was that Arsenal were not going to give up their championship laurels lightly, although Chelsea fought hard after the interval. Vialli reckoned they were the best defence in English football, and there were precious few occasions when captain Tony Adams and co. looked like being breached.

It had looked far too easy for Arsenal as they dominated the first half, Leboeuf booked as early as the second minute for a handball offence. When Babayaro fouled Dixon, Petit's free-kick searched out Adams at the far post in a well-rehearsed move, but his header was blocked by Duberry. Bergkamp sidestepped a defender to launch a shot from the edge of the box, but keeper de Goey was right behind it. Next, Bergkamp set up Overmars, who again cut inside from the flank, but his shot was touched round the post.

The breakthrough arrived after thirty-two minutes, almost inevitably from a long-range pass from Petit. Chelsea protested vehemently that Overmars had backed into Petrescu, leading with his arm, the ball bouncing off the Romanian's face into the path of Bergkamp. Leboeuf disputed the fact that no foul was given, but Bergkamp finished in style, curling his shot into the corner wide of de Goey. Wise reacted with a foul on Bergkamp within yards of the referee, who shook his head and waved play on. But when play stopped Keown confronted Wise. A few minutes later Bergkamp pushed over Duberry, who eventually had to be stretchered off in some distress. Desailly complained bitterly to Bergkamp, but the petty squabbling never boiled over.

Duberry was replaced by Goldbaek, and as play went into overtime at the end of the first half a dangerous right-wing cross from the Dane was Chelsea's only real attacking move of the entire opening stage.

Chelsea vastly improved after the restart, although a glorious pass from Parlour almost presented Bergkamp with a second goal but for the intervention of the keeper and Petrescu. Early in the second half Di Matteo cracked a shot from just outside the box that was tipped over by Seaman, making his return after a seven-game absence to replace Manninger. Chelsea's best spell was at this stage in the second half. Vialli beat the offside trap and would have set up a certain goal with a pass intended for Zola, but Petit made the vital interception. Goldbaek was booked for a foul on Anelka, who was eventually substituted, and then Keown was the last of the bookings, following through with a tackle behind on Vialli.

Both camps sent on their new young strikers, Forssell replacing Zola and Diawara coming on for Overmars. Wise said: 'It was lovely to see Mikael come on and be involved. I asked him how he found it and he said, "Very quick." Welcome to the Premiership, son. I'm sure he'll learn quickly and be fine. He showed good touches in the fifteen minutes he was on.'

But Arsenal won the match and moved to within a point of Chelsea, who did not take defeat very kindly. Leboeuf waited until the referee had left the field before making his views clearly heard as he departed down the tunnel.

February ...

February ...

February

February ...
February ...
February

Luca's crisis team meeting ...
seventeen-year-old Mikael's two-goal
debut

MONDAY, I FEBRUARY

Luca conducted an hour-long inquest into the reasons behind Chelsea's faltering season. The perfectionist was alarmed by a series of poor performances, culminating in the 1–0 defeat at Arsenal which knocked the Blues off the Premiership's number one spot. He summoned his squad to the gymnasium at the Harlington training base to spell out a few home truths.

He had admitted that being both manager and player was a strain, and that injured strikers Tore Andre Flo and Gigi Casiraghi were being missed. Vialli had been part of a player-power movement almost a year ago when Chelsea went through similar panic. Together with Zola and Wise, they had held a meeting without Gullit following similar hiccups. He cancelled training and demanded everyone air their views. 'I learned a lot of things, some I didn't realise. The meeting was very fruitful. I called it before it was too late. We needed to put our fingers back on the pulse again. It's no good people blaming each other. We're all in it together. I wanted to learn everything, from tactics to training, and we thrashed out a foundation to go forward. People in England might think this is unusual at a football club, but in Italy managers always have meetings with players. It's important not just to be physically right, but mentally also. I've thought long and hard about what is going on, but at the moment can't find the answer. I could go out today and buy a striker but it might not be the right decision in the long run.'

Wise said: 'The biggest disappointment about Arsenal was that we didn't play very well in the first half. We went through why we felt we had started off very slowly. But in the second half we deserved to get something out of the game. Obviously Arsenal defended well – shock! – but by not playing well in the first half we gave them the chance to take the lead and then defend like that. It would and should have been a different game if we'd played all ninety minutes like we played the second forty-five.'

Babayaro admitted: 'We spent a lot of time talking about where we went wrong and how we could have approached the game better at Arsenal. We discussed many things, including the tactics used in the first half against Arsenal. We accepted they weren't good. But the message now is to be calm and cool. We had to wait until the last minute at Oxford, but we're still in the Cup and we could still sail through.'

There were no self-doubts in the boardroom. 'We're still seventeen points better off than last season,' Bates said with pride. 'When we appointed Luca there were an awful lot of scoffers here and abroad. But today, if you'll forgive the appropriate saying, even the ranks of Tuscany could scarce forbear to cheer.'

Vialli was also set to axe himself from the replay with Oxford and hand Forssell his full debut. 'He was one of the positive points for us at Arsenal. He is a young player, determined and very hungry to get involved, and now we know he can cope with first-team football. He adds another string to our bow. He has no fears and I think he has shown he can play for us. We have choices again now. I enjoy playing and I'm not ready to hang up my boots yet, but there is a lot on my mind.'

TUESDAY, 2 FEBRUARY

Was there no end to Luca's grasp of the cliché? The programme notes overflowed with them. 'Hats off' to Oxford for the way they nearly 'upset the apple cart' and 'gave us a hard time'. He added: 'This is what the FA Cup is all about. Spirit. Determination. Teams from the lower divisions getting great headlines. Fairy-tale stories about giant-killing. This competition has such a great tradition, that's why it's so magical and special.' 'We got away with murder', he wrote, and called for his team to 'get right back on track'. He went on: 'We know that we are not at our best at the moment. Looking at our recent results and performances we know we can do much better. But there's no way in England you can perform at your best for nine months in a row. We're not robots, we are human beings. It's quite normal to have at least one bad run during the season and I'm pleased that despite that we're still in a great position, second in the table and still in contention in both the FA Cup and Cup Winners Cup.'

Oxford were boosted by a wealthy hotelier lining himself up as the club's prospective new owner.

WEDNESDAY, 3 FEBRUARY

Chelsea 4   Oxford United 2

Wise's season of discontent reached crisis point as he was sent off for a record fourth time. He was booked two minutes before half-time for a handball and then a complaint to the linesman; he got his marching orders after seventy-five minutes when he blocked Dean Windass's shot with his hand and conceded a penalty from which Windass scored the last goal of the game. Head bowed, Wise made a slow walk back to the dressing room, ripping his shirt over his head as he went down the tunnel almost in tears. Vialli refused to condemn his Stamford Bridge skipper for possessing the worst disciplinary record in the Premiership. 'Dennis is unique. I've have never known or met anyone like him, either here or in Italy. I will defend him for ever. I will be lenient when it comes to fining him. He is my kind of man.

Dennis feels frustrated about it. His first handball wasn't intentional, and the second pure instinct. We will fight it.'

The sending-off of Wise overshadowed the sensational debut of Mikael Forssell, but irrespective of the injustice they had felt at the Manor Ground, Oxford came to the Bridge to prove that the First Division side's gutsy display wasn't just a one-off. They took the lead after just five minutes from a Cook corner that struck first Di Matteo, then Gilchrist, and finally Desailly before beating de Goey at the near post. As if in an effort to compensate for his injury-time penalty decision at the Manor Ground, referee Reed allowed goalkeeper Elliott Jackson to stay on the field after a ninth-minute incident in which he sent Morris, racing on to a Petrescu pass, flying. It could easily have been a red card, but it was only a yellow.

A poor back-pass by Robinson gave Babayaro a twelfth-minute chance to equalise, but his shot was smothered by the keeper. A minute later Leboeuf won possession on the edge of his own box, and raced into Oxford's half to deliver a perfect pass to Zola, who took it in his imperious stride. Wise covered the ground to receive Zola's pass inside the box and shot wide of the keeper for his first goal in eleven months, some comfort in view of his later transgressions. Suddenly the supporters had their first glimpse of Forssell as a goal-scoring force as he rounded the keeper but was driven too wide after collecting Zola's pass.

Chelsea's first goal was a delight, but their second was magnificent. After a cutting one-two between Zola and Wise, from the angle of the penalty area Zola celebrated his 100th game for Chelsea with a glorious lob over the keeper going in over the far post.

Forssell took the game by storm at the start of the second half. After just a minute his precision angled drive found the top far corner, and six minutes later he whacked one from outside the box giving the keeper no chance. In between he had had a goal disallowed after collecting Leboeuf's long ball and shrugging off a defender. Much taller than Owen but not quite as fast – but then again, who is? – Forssell proved himself a natural born goalscorer.

When Oxford threw on their giant striker Kevin Francis, Leboeuf was wisely removed from the action. The Frenchman waved to the baying Oxford fans but exchanged a warm handshake and hug with Shotton. Forssell was substituted after minutes for another youngster, Nicholls, and was afforded the standing ovation he thoroughly deserved.

Vialli explained why he left himself out. 'I dropped myself because I was tired. Now after Mikael's performance I can never see myself playing again. We are talking here of an exceptional talent, a player for the future. He is mature beyond his years. He is another string to our bow and it means I can rest myself more often. We got our confidence back tonight and we can hopefully see the same Chelsea until the end of the season.'

Forssell joined the list of Chelsea all-time greats who scored on their debut: Jimmy Greaves got one, Peter Osgood and Kerry Dixon two, Seamus O'Connell scored a hat-trick in 1954, and George Hilsdon in 1906 bagged five. The fresh-faced Finn said: 'I thought I blew it, that it was my fault that we were behind because I was through in the first half and blew it. I thought, what do I do now? Then when Baba gave me the ball back I thought I would give it a shot. I will always remember these goals and I will get the video just to refresh my mind. I liked to play in attack with Zola; it's so easy as he always gives you good passes. It's a dream come true to play for Chelsea and I am learning every day from players like Flo, Vialli and Zola. It was good to play with no pressure, but now Graham Rix has told me I have to score two goals in every game!'

The youngster had been surprised by the whole organisation of the club. 'It is very impressive, the way the players took me in. I had some pressure when I came here as I didn't know anyone, and now it's easy.' He roomed with Goldbaek. 'He's very good but in the morning we get woken up and he keeps on sleeping. He never gets up straight away. I have to shout at him.' He lived in west London with his mum. 'She does the cooking and the cleaning so I can concentrate on football. She cooks mostly Italian, that's my favourite, and Mexican. Tacos, I love them – they're the best food ever.'

Wise's sending-off carried a four-match ban: one for the two yellow cards and three as part of the totting-up procedures from his previous sendings-off. That took his total so far to fourteen games suspended. If he was shown the red card again for violent conduct it would be a seven-match ban. His last game before the next enforced rest would be the FA Cup fifth-round tie at Sheffield Wednesday.

Petrescu was upset that his captain's sending-off might hamper the quest for the title. The Romanian said the rest of the team (apart from Vialli) felt let down. 'I could not believe Dennis did it. Even if the ball was going in it didn't really matter as we were already 4–1 up with fifteen minutes to go. All the lads were disappointed afterwards even though we had won the game. We need more people on the pitch because with Gustavo Poyet and Tore Andre Flo missing through injury, we are short already. But now Dennis will be out for a long time again. He has already missed a lot of games this season and he really should not have handled the ball. There was no need – it was unbelievable.'

Wise was in apologetic mood – again.

THURSDAY, 4 FEBRUARY

There were still genuine fears that Casiraghi would not make it back, though no one had told him. After a hundred days he was still recovering in a specialist isokinetic clinic in Bologna which had successfully treated Baggio and Signori, as well as skiing champion Alberto Tomba. 'I will stay in Bologna until the end of the summer,' Gigi said. 'I will wait for whatever I have to wait for, but I will be back. It is pointless to ask when I will be able to run again; all I need to know is that I will because no doctor has told me the opposite. So there are no forecasts. They took the plaster off two weeks ago and I've started to work on bending the knee; progress is minimal but the worst is over.'

As well as ruptured knee ligaments, he had damaged the nerve controlling his foot which required an implant of a nerve grown elsewhere in his body. He had to make football history to play again. 'A full recovery depends on three main factors: fifty per cent on the operations, twenty-five per cent on the rehabilitation and the last twenty-five per cent on my will. The operations went perfectly, I am in good hands and, as far as my will is concerned, that is one hundred per cent. The signs are good and it is a relief. There are no records of a similar injury in football, but the best news I had was when the specialist told me although I was badly injured, I would be able to play again.'

He spent six hours a day at the rehab clinic in Bologna. 'I'm still on crutches and move around slowly. Going upstairs is painful, and I still have to be careful of certain movements. I make my targets all the time. The first was to walk, then to go home from hospital, then to walk with crutches, then without them. It is a small step at a time until I can play for Chelsea again. The ultimate target is to score my next goal. I know I'll be back because I have promised myself. In the last three months I've cried a lot with pain and frustration. Now there is only determination.'

He was touched by the visits he had received from team-mates. 'Gianfranco Zola came to visit me in Vienna and he even missed training to see me in hospital in London. And my other team-mates, as well as my Italian colleagues, have been brilliant. I have found friends close to me I didn't know I had. We are in daily contact and, thanks to satellite, I can watch all Chelsea's games. I hope they finish at the top because I have never played in the Champions League and that's where I want to restart. Shaka Hislop also came to see me. There are no hard feelings.'

He will never forget the incident. 'I've seen many times the accident on video slow-motion. My verdict is that it was just bad luck. In my career I've had similar clashes more than a thousand times, but this time I've paid for them all. The match was going okay when Zola put me through. I tried to meet the ball, and so did Hislop. It was not a great clash and I think he felt some responsibility, but that was not the case. It was just bad luck. Everything happened in a fraction of a second. I knew immediately something major had occurred. Then it became a hazy memory: the stretcher that did not arrive, the team-mates running round asking for one, the silence of the crowd, the expressions on all the faces. I thought I'd lost my ligaments, then I feared I had broken my calf bone, too. It was then like a film on fast forward, the race to Charing Cross Hospital. In the ambulance I just hoped they'd reveal less damage than I feared. I couldn't be moved, so they decided to operate at the Princess Grace Hospital. The operation went well. I woke up some days later and Paul, one of the male nurses, told me that under the effect of the anaesthetic I shouted an avalanche of dirty words in Italian to him to the point where he got a dictionary and translated them. Of course, I told him I was sorry.'

Luca added three new names to the Cup Winners Cup squad for the second part of the tournament. A maximum of twenty-five was permitted and Forssell and Gold-baek were cup-tied, so Goldbaek's number seven shirt went to Luca Percassi, the available number fifteen to Sam Dalla Bona, and number twenty to Danny Slatter.

FRIDAY, 5 FEBRUARY

Vialli pushed himself through a long, punishing training session, suggesting once again that he was thinking of a return.

Although Luca was continuing to defend his captain, Wise received an anony-mous letter at his home address signed 'a season-ticket holder'. The letter stated: 'You are a very able footballer and your recent career has been a glorious success. Having watched Chelsea for eighteen years, this achievement has been fantastic for fans old and new. Do you not think, however, that you might be remembered as being mouthy, incredibly rash and the captain who missed forty-plus games through suspension? Can you justify your wages when you cannot take the field week after week? Please win the League.' Wise didn't object to being criticised for his sendings-off, but wanted his home life kept apart from his profession.

SATURDAY, 6 FEBRUARY
Chelsea 1   Southampton 0

Boring, boring Chelsea. Arsenal in disguise? Vialli didn't care. 'We are winning although we are playing badly, which is what Arsenal have done when they had a very shaky spell before they started to produce their present sort of performances. So I'm confident that we can go on getting the right results. Of course we were awful, but I can't see any reason to panic, and I didn't come into the press room because it was only right and proper that Graham Rix gets his chance.' Rix said: 'Luca always lets me do the press conference when it's a crap game!'

Rix began: 'How many matches in the last three months last season did Arsenal win by a goal to nil? I'd hardly call Chelsea boring, but yes, today they were boring. But it's not easy to play at the same level of fluency and confidence day after day. When it's not happening you have to have enough about you to get a one-nil and say "See you later". You can hear the fans groaning when we're not really flowing, but you have to give credit to the opposition.'

Vialli had trained vigorously from eleven a.m. on the morning of the game, and although he looked sprightly enough, he ruled himself out and gave the teenage Finn his Premiership debut. But there were no Forssell fireworks today. David Jones's team did anything but lie down, and in the second half outplayed Chelsea, and there were a couple of torrid moments in the title-chasing team's defence. Rix added: 'I didn't expect too much from Mikael. He was great on Wednesday, and we thought keep him in and let's see how he goes, but really he can still be in the youth team and it's a lot to lead the line in a title-chasing team. I think Flo is the man. You can't sign anybody like him anywhere in the world. We have saved ourselves a few bob and scrapped through in the last few weeks, waiting for Flo. He will be back in contention fairly soon, a week or two weeks. Flo is kicking a ball, albeit not far, we are moving on his exercises and gradually he will join the squad. Poyet is also influential in both boxes, and we miss him, but he will definitely be playing before the end of the season.'

As United hit eight and Arsenal four, Chelsea's goal difference was far behind. Rix said: 'United and Arsenal have not done our goal difference any good, but we keep winning. We must hope they have a mini-slump and lose confidence, and we'll take advantage.'

An early Zola free-kick sealed the points, but Vialli leapt from his touchline seat near the end for an uncharacteristic blast at his players and returned shaking his head. Rix said: 'We're not a one-man band. Frank Leboeuf has been excellent today and has been for the last few months, but we need to get the best out of everybody.'

Zola was happy with his goal, but insisted the players were still unhappy with the bumpy surface. 'At the moment our best cannot come out. The pitch is not helping. We're a team that likes to play football, but on such a pitch it's not easy.'

It was suggested to Franco on Channel Chelsea that the solution might be to practise more on the bumpy surface. He laughed. 'It's new to me. Surely nobody trains on the pitch in order not to spoil it!' Rix said: 'The pitch is not great; it's bobbly and the players have lost confidence. They are not as fluent as they can be.'

A high challenge from Desailly caught Hughes on his return to the Bridge, and the former Chelsea favourite was stretchered off. Hughes had received a cut-glass rose bowl before the start, but left the ground on crutches with Jones accusing Desailly of deliberately cutting him down. 'He was "done" and the ref missed it, as did the linesman. Sparky is the type that doesn't go down for nothing. It was a bad tackle and the officials missed it. I saw who it was, all right.' Vialli countered: 'I didn't even know it was Desailly who clashed with Hughes. I'm saddened that their manager is accusing Marcel of deliberately harming Hughes.' Rix went much further: 'We have nothing but respect for Mark Hughes and nothing was premeditated. I can understand his disappointment – Sparky is an influential player – but none of our players goes out to "do" anybody.'

MONDAY, 8 FEBRUARY

As a result of a Zola complaint about the pitch, a meeting took place between Bates and Hutchinson and action was decided upon. After the midweek Blackburn game the club planned to lay a new surface which would be ready in a week. Then, at the end of the season that too would be torn up and the whole pitch reseeded.

Hutchinson said the work should be completed before any potential FA Cup replay against Sheffield Wednesday. 'This has to go ahead whether we draw or not. It would certainly help for the very tight work schedule to get an outright result at Hillsborough. The operation will be similar to what Manchester United did when they replaced the turf on their pitch. We have been unhappy with the pitch for some weeks. The remedy was simple, but not so far as the middle of the season is concerned. At the moment we have a cake of turf on the top which retains water. It doesn't go away and has become very sticky and uneven. We will rip the top ten or so inches off and replace it with deep swabs of turf ferried in from Yorkshire.'

Optimism over an early Flo return disappeared. Flo's spokesman in Norway, Bent Raknas, said: 'The specialist and Chelsea have taken this decision together. They want to be careful and not take any chances.' Flo said: 'It's been real agony having to sit and watch, but the good thing is that the end of the tunnel is getting near and I will be coming back at a crucial stage.'

TUESDAY, 9 FEBRUARY

Leboeuf threatened to quit the club if he did not get a big pay rise. In an interview with a French football magazine ahead of the Wembley friendly with England, he said: 'Chairman Ken Bates likes to say I was the deal of his life. That pleases me and I'm happy at Chelsea, but I don't want to be the club cretin. I signed a very good contract when I came here. I've doubled it since and I hope to quadruple it soon. If the bosses don't make an effort, I may think about leaving. We'll see at the end of the season.'

Leboeuf had joined Chelsea in 1996 and was under contract until 2001. Since then he has had lucrative offers from Liverpool and Lazio, but ideally Leboeuf wanted to stay. He described the Premier League as 'one of the most attractive and best in the world'. 'The soccer here is rich and allows us to live very well. Every ninety-minute match I played in France I had the impression I was playing a whole hour for an income tax inspector and just the remaining half an hour for myself. You can perhaps compare me with one of the many French business bosses who have decided to come here to escape being harassed by the tax people at home. The grounds here are always full. Fans can wear the club colours in the street, and are proud to do so. And I always feel a great thrill when I arrive at the ground and hear the rumble from the huge crowd. I signed for Chelsea mainly to experience those sensations. It's marvellous.'

Leboeuf had new admirers, particularly among women. Not quite in the same league as David Ginola, but he made his debut as a catwalk model in Paris and his appearance on Ian Wright's ITV show sent a frisson of appreciation through female viewers because he sounded exactly like Maurice Chevalier when he sang. He said: 'I love English people. I didn't come just for the money. I found in London a fantastic city, many friends. If I enjoy my life in football, I also enjoy my life in general. We've got only one life and I want to be involved in many cultures, so it was very important to come abroad and see how English people live.' The cameras followed him into a series of expensive boutiques. 'I called my wife and said I would like to spend two hours shopping and forget football for a little bit. The main thing I like is to walk and see decorations and people. That's the most important thing for me. You can find the reality of life. When you're involved in football you don't see what happens in the world. You can see poor people and say my life is good, but it's not the same for everybody. You see also many rich people with Rolls-Royces and you can go in a shop and buy many things without asking the price. I could be considered a rich person but I try to have my heart richer than my wallet. I don't buy many things. I have two nice cars but they are not Ferraris or something like that. I prefer to buy flats, houses – a better investment, I think.'

Football Supporters' Association chairman Alison Pilling said: 'Most fans believe that Premiership players are paid enough. If Frank Leboeuf thinks he is worth more, he needs to think about where that money is coming from.' Ken Bates wanted to be assured that Frank's comments had not been twisted in translation. 'It always seems that scare-mongering about Chelsea stars seems to emanate from alleged comments from foreign magazines. Neither Chelsea nor Ken Bates discusses financial affairs in public. It would be in everyone's interest if the players did the same.' He was reluctant to issue a public rebuke so close to the FA Cup tie; instead, David Mellor, in his *Evening Standard* column, took up the cudgels (sheer coincidence, of course).

Mellor, who has the ear of the chairman, warned of the impending problems of the delayed public hearing into the club's planning application for the completion of the new stand, which he estimated would cost Chelsea £20m. 'The people who will have to make up that shortfall are the fans.' He went on: 'Which is why a lot of them will have choked on their cornflakes to read the thoughts of Frank Leboeuf. He is on £1m a year but wants parity with Desailly, who is rumoured to earn nearer to £2m. Leboeuf has been great for Chelsea, as he so often tells us, but the club have been good for him, too. Before he arrived at the Bridge few, even in France, had heard of him. The adulation he now basks in stems from his time in London. Silly then, to sacrifice all that esteem with crude public threats and tactics better suited to a highwayman.'

The day before Mellor's judgement on Frank went to press, Bates's mood would not have improved by a prominent back-page picture in the *Standard* of Frank leaving San Lorenzo's in Beauchamp Place with none other than Mr Ruud Gullit.

Desailly was also grumbling. 'There's neither the passion nor the pressure here that you find in Italian soccer. I prefer too much rather than too little. You get too much violence in every match too, and that's not my cup of tea. I have to make a big effort all the time to avoid being swallowed up.' Though he had signed a four-year contract, he said: 'I'm honouring it for the moment, but I'll review the situation at the end of the season.'

WEDNESDAY, 10 FEBRUARY

Leboeuf accused England of lacking the bulldog spirit in the Wembley friendly. 'You saw the best performance by a French team since the World Cup. We showed that physically we are very tough and technically and tactically superior. We were very passionate but also took our time to play our football, and to be in the French side which won at Wembley for the first time made me feel very proud. It was very important to play like that away from home and was a massive boost to our confidence. But I was shocked with England in the sense that once they went a goal behind they didn't want to fight any more. I think England were disappointed with not scoring in the first half and felt they didn't deserve to go behind, but you have to keep your spirit. What happened greatly surprised me.'

Leboeuf rejected the idea England have a dearth of talent and believes the young blood at Manchester United and Arsenal and in the current England Under-21 side will provide a team to be feared by the 2002 World Cup. 'England have to find the right mixture and get a good feeling in the squad. They haven't done that yet but many of the players are still young. By the next World Cup I do think England will have one of the best teams in the world. You have many young players who play for the best team in the Premiership – Manchester United – and they would help win the World Cup for you. Arsenal also have many good players who will soon be ready to play for the national team, and the current England Under-21 side showed their talent this week against France. I honestly don't think that to have foreign players in this country gives you less chance of having a good team. But I think some English players should go abroad to get the extra experience. If you look at the four semi-finalists in the World Cup, most of those players were playing abroad. They had extra knowledge, and maybe that is the solution for English players – but then maybe it is not in your culture to do such things.'

Laudrup had yet to play a competitive game for Copenhagen, having joined them as they went into hibernation for the winter, and was now engaged in the pre-season warm-up on the Costa Del Sol. 'I've had the longest holiday in my career, which has been nice,' he said. Copenhagen club president Flemming Ostergaard knew that their timing with the raid on Laudrup had worked out perfectly. 'Casiraghi was injured one week after the deal, and Chelsea would not have wanted to make a deal if that had happened a week earlier. There is no way Brian is going back to Chelsea, and Chelsea know that.'

THURSDAY, 11 FEBRUARY

Carbone criticised Zoff for not selecting Zola and urged the appointment of Vialli as national boss. Carbone, also ignored by Zoff, said: 'It is incredible that Zola is not in the national team. He is a genius, but the coach does not pick him because he is in England. Gianfranco is one of the four best Italian players along with Alessandro del Piero, who is injured, Roberto Mancini, who does not want to play for his country, and Roberto Baggio, who has just been recalled to the national team. By and large, the coach wants to bring more young players through the squad. But there should still be room for an experienced and brilliant footballer like Zola. I just do not understand why there is no place for him.'

Morris, who was keeping Di Matteo on the bench even though Desailly had returned to central defence, said: 'I've played a few games on the spin which makes me feel better, but I know when everybody's available I'll be out.' Ferrer was also back.

Babayaro was charged, along with his friend Colin Egebuige, with indecently assaulting a woman at his house and would appear the following week at Feltham Magistrates Court. Also charged was Chibuzo Obasi.

FRIDAY, 12 FEBRUARY

Luca blew out the candles on a cake to celebrate one year in office with enormous pride. 'It has been a very special year for me. We can say it has been quite successful because we have managed to win three trophies and we are still in a good position in the Premiership table this season. Chelsea are three trophies more important than we were a year ago, and winning those trophies adds prestige to the club and confidence. Important players want to come and join this club, which is why in the past year players such as Marcel Desailly, Pierluigi Casiraghi and Brian Laudrup have signed for Chelsea. We are getting more and more famous around the world. I've helped make this club successful and in future I want to make it even more successful. I've made mistakes, of course, but that is part of the process when you are a beginner. But you learn from them and next time try to do things better. I enjoy being a manager, I like playing football, and this is an important part of my life.'

Zola said: 'I'm very proud of Luca. He has made an excellent job of a difficult one. I know what being a footballer means, it means you just think of yourself and no one else. Luca has had to do two difficult jobs and has done them very well. As a player he's had a successful career so he knows how to treat people. He listens to players and is keen to have meetings with us to sort out any problems. It works. We are more of a unit now, and it does help in matches when things go against you.'

Vialli believed the Cup battle with Sheffield Wednesday would be won if Zola overcame the magic of Carbone. 'Each player has a special flair and when Carbone plays well so does his team. Zola is a better goalscorer, but Carbone has a special touch and it will be an interesting battle.'

On Leboeuf and Desailly, he said: 'I hope things can be sorted out. I work on the continental basis and deal only with coaching. Every other situation is dealt with by the board. Neither player has spoken to me about their situation but I am sure Chelsea will act in a proper mannaer. We can't afford to lose players of their quality.'

SATURDAY, 13 FEBRUARY

Sheffield Wednesday 0   Chelsea 1

Di Matteo unveiled his shocking new blond barnet to wolf-whistles at Hillsborough. Luca joked: 'Bjarne did very well, but it was easy for him to pick out Di Matteo because of that haircut. Ten years ago I bleached my hair like that, and look what happened to me! But seriously, the players are professional and young men will always want to indulge themselves. As far as I care, they can do as they please as long as they play well. I have no problem with Di Matteo's haircut if he keeps scoring important goals.

'It was great to win against opponents who had played so well in the last couple of months with consistency and effectiveness. We went up there and gave a very good performance, showed plenty of personality, controlled the game and had better chances but, as too often happens, we had to wait until seven minutes to go to score. As long as we win matches I don't care if we score in the last minute. But sometimes it would be nice to score earlier in the game and then control the opposition's reaction and play some counter-attack.'

Di Matteo's team-mates took the mickey mercilessly. It takes a brave man to show his face in Yorkshire with Bart Simpson hair and dandy blue boots. Concealing his crop beneath a woolly black ski hat afterwards, Di Matteo said: 'There's no particular reason or superstition behind my haircut. I suppose I just did it to play a joke on myself. Dan Petrescu had a similar one done at the World Cup, so I thought, Why not? Obviously the manager didn't like it very much because he didn't pick me from the start today, and all the lads have been taking the mickey all week. But it's all gone quiet now. Hopefully, I've had the last laugh.'

Zola feigned a downcast expression when asked about Roberto's thatch. 'Oh, please, don't mention it. We have some time before the final to sort it out. He can't meet the Queen with hair like that. We are all horrified in the dressing room. Nothing can prepare you for such a shocking sight. In the context of our season, Roberto's hair is an emergency, but if he keeps scoring important goals like that, we can forgive him everything.'

Chelsea should have been ahead as early as the seventh minute when a superb ball from Morris, who dominated Jonk in the midfield, put Petrescu clear. But with just the exposed Pressman to beat the Romanian fired into the side netting from eight yards. Zola saw a shot of his deflected behind for a corner. Then Babayaro headed straight at Pressman after Leboeuf flicked on a Wise corner. Di Matteo made an immediate impact when he came on by flashing a twenty-yard drive just wide of Pressman's post, and his decisive header came from the first decent cross, delivered by late sub Goldbaek. For eighty-five minutes Chelsea's superior movement and brisk passing lacked the final cutting edge that Poyet and Flo might have supplied. Yet they remained fiendishly difficult to beat: just two defeats in thirty-five games. Leboeuf and Desailly were in total command, and behind them de Goey only had to make one save with his feet, from Alexandersson.

Once Carbone's early fizz had dissipated, Wednesday were bereft of any composure or imagination in the final third. Beaten manager Danny Wilson conceded: 'Di Matteo was possibly the best player on the pitch. I would have been quite happy to see him stay on the bench, but Chelsea have so much quality throughout their side. Vialli has had a lot of injuries to worry about, yet he was still able to field an array of international players like that. No one will want to draw Chelsea, that's for sure.'

SUNDAY, 14 FEBRUARY

The top two sides in the Premiership were to slug it out for a place in the FA Cup semi-finals. Manchester United and Chelsea, who clashed in last season's third round, were due to meet at Old Trafford days after both clubs faced testing European quarter-finals. It was inevitably earmarked as the Sky match, but it was switched to Sunday after both sides gained permission from the Premier League because of their involvement in Europe.

After the draw Arsenal (due to face either Derby or Huddersfield) were installed as 11–4 favourites, with Manchester United at 3–1 and Chelsea at 11–2.

Hutchinson observed: 'There have been claims that the lottery-style machine used this season is not mixing the balls properly. Such a suggestion is hard to prove, but the cynics were given more ammunition when the quarter-final pairings came out: seven versus six, four versus three, and one versus two. Eight versus five, Manchester United and Chelsea, was the only tie to break the sequential-number scenario.'

MONDAY, 15 FEBRUARY

Nicholls knew Vialli was searching for a new forward. 'You do find it frustrating but obviously Luca's looking for a bit of experience, someone he knows can score goals on a regular basis. The likes of myself and Mikael Forssell haven't had a run where we can turn round and say we have scored eight or nine goals in ten or eleven games. I think Luca's looking just to steady the ship and get us back on track scoring goals again. We need strength in depth, and that's what he's looking for.' Sporting the Beckham look didn't help! 'I am getting a bit of stick for it. It's just that my style has changed. I had short hair a couple of seasons ago and I looked about twelve so I've grown it a little longer and had a change of colour, but I don't want to look like him.'

TUESDAY, 16 FEBRUARY

Ahead of next day's game with Blackburn, Luca said he was impressed with their performance in holding Ruud's team at St James's Park in the FA Cup. 'They play good football, are well organised and they fight. This is all down to their new manager who has brought a new, strong attitude to the club. On top of that he has already been awarded Manager of the Month. Brian Kidd has got a lot of potential and I am sure he will bring the club back to its recent good days.'

Luca was also concerned with the pile-up of fixtures. 'We like to play well, but it's not easy because of the fixture schedule. It's nice to see that after a few games in which we didn't perform to our best we are now playing very good football. This is the way we would like to play. But it's not always possible because when you play so many matches in England it is difficult. Sometimes you struggle a little bit to get results. But we hope from now to the end of the season we can keep giving good performances and keep winning games. This is our aim.'

Wise started his latest ban, but Newton, Lambourde, Myers and Nicholls were added to the squad. Morris continued in central midfield after another star performance in Sheffield.

WEDNESDAY, 17 FEBRUARY
Chelsea 1   Blackburn Rovers 1

Luca knew the question was coming. 'It happens in football,' he said, referring to his own dismissal.

Frustrated strikers are prone to lashing out with their studs at niggling defenders who have given them little peace all match, but it was hardly an action befitting the player-manager. Vialli's frustrations boiled over at the end of a match which had presented Chelsea with a cast-iron opportunity to gain ground in the title race. He had a go at Marlon Broomes – both were sent off as a result – but it could be his real target was himself. In six Premiership games he had yet to score. Eight goals in eight Cup games was fine, but Vialli's side were crying out for a taker of half-chances.

Vialli, who had been dismissed against Blackburn last year, tried to get out of trouble by leaving the scene of the tussle and limping off, but referee Uriah Rennie chased after him and showed him the red card as he left the field. Then, when the fourth official indicated just one minute of injury time remained, Vialli, who had stayed on the bench instead of going down the tunnel, leapt to his feet and pointed in mock disgust. After Babayaro brought down Ward, Kidd had to be pulled away from Vialli. Vialli was ordered out of the dugout and down the tunnel by Rennie. Kidd and Vialli had a heated exchange on the touchline, which Kidd tried to play down. When asked what he said to Vialli, Kidd replied: 'My daughter's learning Italian and I wanted a few tips.'

The Chelsea boss questioned the performance of Rennie in a game with two red and seven yellow cards. 'I have to say I'm disappointed with him because you can make mistakes but it's about the attitude as well. I thought the referee was arrogant. He reminded me of my years spent in Italy when you couldn't communicate with the referees. To be fair to the English referees you can always speak to them. They will always speak to you. But this evening it was really so difficult to stay cool and calm.'

Sutton emerged after the match with a damning description of Leboeuf, with whom he had endured ninety minutes of bickering. 'Leboeuf has got a big ego,' he said. 'He was being very critical of the English game and saying what a bad team Blackburn were. He always seemed a perfect gent before.' After Blackburn's late equaliser Sutton made a one-finger gesture to Leboeuf and goalscorer Ward mockingly slapped his head. Vialli distanced himself from Sutton's accusation, but he wasn't happy about Leboeuf's constant media comments. Perhaps it was contrition over his own sending-off that made him unwilling to condemn his central defender. Vialli said: 'There is no room for retribution or vendettas in football.'

The outcome pleased relegation-haunted Rovers far more than title-chasing Chelsea. In the eighth minute a penalty was awarded when Broomes tugged at Vialli's jersey. Leboeuf's kick was pushed against a post by Filan and cleared for a corner – the first penalty missed since he joined Chelsea. A minute before half-time Chelsea broke the deadlock when, following a short corner on the left, Vialli headed the ball back for Morris to score from twenty yards. With the goal at his mercy in the sixty-third minute Di Matteo headed straight at Filan, though Blackburn, with substitute Gillespie making his presence felt, were slowly but surely coming back into the game. With seven minutes remaining Ward's firm header, from Gillespie's cross, secured the visitors a point, and a minute later tempers flared.

Chelsea suffered another early blow when Le Saux hobbled off unable to recover from an earlier tackle by McAteer. Newton came on to make his comeback after a long series of injuries.

Vialli knew he had to recapture his composure to collect maximum points from the trip to struggling Nottingham Forest. 'To go on the pitch with a frustrated attitude would be wrong,' he said. 'We must go out and play the match and try to get three points. Nottingham Forest are not in a very good position in the table and I think they are going to fight. That's the problem in English football. There's never an easy match.'

Luca decided to show his remorse to the fans. 'First of all, I'd like to apologise to everybody for being sent off. I would say that sometimes it is difficult to keep your head, keep your cool. Sometimes you get a bit frustrated because of the referee's decisions. Sometimes because you want to fight for your team you go over the edge and ... blah, blah, blah. You know. But as the player-manager I have to set an example. Do what I say, not what I do.'

THURSDAY, 18 FEBRUARY

Between seven a.m. and noon the Stamford Bridge turf was stripped away. The whole operation was over by midday on Saturday. A giant machine removed the top surface and 400 tons of earth was carted off to be replaced by new green turf. Bates said: 'I understand that Man Utd took thirteen and a half days to complete theirs. Hopefully this will enable the boys to finish the season in style. Come the first of June we rip it up again, but this time it will be sown with seed to enable the new-growth roots to become entwined with the nylon buried under the surface.'

The FA looked into Vialli's verbal attack on the referee, but no action was taken. Referees spokesman Philip Don backed Rennie: 'There's not been any problem with Uriah. The communication is there, especially on match days.' Kidd turned up the heat when he said: 'If there was a problem with my players I would not duck the issue, I would deal with it. But if you look at the incident you can make your own minds up. I didn't see what happened until I got back to the hotel and watched it on TV. But there was nothing vicious in that from Marlon. The club are looking into it. I'm not one who starts moaning and groaning and we're not looking to make excuses, but we are not a dirty team.' Rovers were considering an appeal to save Broomes from a three-game ban.

Casiraghi had yet another op, an arthroscopy to clear any adhesions.

FRIDAY, 19 FEBRUARY

Rix was facing a stretch in prison after pleading guilty to having sex with a fifteen-year-old girl and admitting a second charge of indecent assault. He confirmed he took the teenager to the Novotel in Hammersmith last February on the night before Chelsea's Premiership clash with Manchester United. Judge Timothy Pontius, who released Rix on bail while reports were being prepared – with a condition that he made no contact directly or indirectly with his alleged victim or her family – would sentence at Knightsbridge Crown Court. The charge carries a maximum term of two years. The judge warned: 'The fact that I am about to release you on bail should not for one moment be taken by you that that will be the sentence you will ultimately receive. Because of the gravity of the offences, I must keep all my sentencing options open, and they include, perhaps at the forefront, imprisonment. I want you to be realistic about your position.' Rix, accompanied by his agent Dennis Roach and Chelsea chief executive Colin Hutchinson, sat staring at the floor in the dock throughout the ten-minute hearing.

Rix was described in court as 'a man of good character in the broader sense', but had appeared in court twice before for motoring offences. In July 1985 he had been sacked as Arsenal skipper after being convicted for drink-driving. He was fined again by west London magistrates last month for failing to stop for a pedestrian on a crossing and failing to produce his licence. After eighteen years of marriage to his wife Gill, Rix left the £800,000 family home in Harpenden and gave his new address as Queen's Road, Richmond.

The *News of the World* were preparing their exposé of Rix on the front page. They alleged that he had admitted seducing a fifteen-year-old virgin after plying her with drink and drugs. He allegedly told the schoolgirl's dad how they drank red wine, smoked a cannabis joint together and then had sex without using a condom. Rix was unaware that his amazing confession was being secretly tape-recorded. The girl's dad accused him of being a 'drug-taking paedophile' who should never be allowed near a football club.

SATURDAY, 20 FEBRUARY

Nottingham Forest 1   Chelsea 3

Luca avoided the customary post-match press conference, but he reflected on another key win. 'We had the odds in our favour but this is where it gets even more difficult. It was a good, professional performance, an effective one. I'm not saying we were comfortable, but we certainly did the job very well.'

Vialli expected a fight from the side looking least likely to survive the Premiership cut, and he was not wrong. The chant of 'We want ten' rose from the travelling Chelsea faithful, but it was soon silenced as Forest, constantly urged on by Atkinson's voice on the touchline, countered Chelsea's bright start with a series of raids that stretched the visitors to the limit. Petrescu was run ragged by Rogers; Vialli withdrew him at half-time. He might also have replaced Desailly, who clearly took his foot off the gas. Pierre van Hooijdonk provided a glimpse of hope for the home team just before half-time, but by then Forssell and Goldbaek had helped themselves to a couple of gift offerings.

With the squad depleted by injuries and suspensions, a manager needs luck. Vialli had assembled a side without Wise and Di Matteo – both suspended, the latter for collecting eight yellow cards in domestic competitions – as well as Le Saux, who was injured against Blackburn along with the manager himself. On a City Ground pitch they would have torn up had it been their own, Chelsea had before them a potential minefield, so the nerve-steadier of an early gift goal was precisely what was required. It came courtesy of the Forest captain, Steve Chettle, who failed to cut out a long, wind-assisted clearance by de Goey, which then bounced conveniently for Forssell. The Finn glided around Beasant and put Chelsea ahead with his first Premiership goal. Chelsea extended their lead with another embarrassingly easy goal: Zola's right-wing corner was glanced on by Leboeuf and turned in by Goldbaek. Flo, back on the bench after a six-week absence, made his entrance with just under half an hour to go and, eager to make an impact, tried to make sure with a shot from the edge of the box. Beasant thwarted the Norwegian, but could not hold the ball or prevent Goldbaek from claiming his second goal.

Flo said: 'For me, the whole season so far has been one of frustration. I have missed too many matches. Whether my latest absence proves to be a blessing in disguise, giving me the rest I never had after the World Cup finals, I don't really know. But I do know that my appetite for football is sharper than ever, and I will be training extra hard so my fitness improves a lot.'

Goldbaek was grinning after the game. 'I feel like I've landed in heaven! Wearing the number seven shirt which belonged to Brian, who is truly world-class, is a dream for me. I'm just a worker. All I can do is try my best, so it was a great pleasure to score my first goals for Chelsea.' Leboeuf said: 'I said to Bjarne straight after the game, "I'm delighted to see you can score goals also for Chelsea, not just against us." He was very pleased.'

Beasant was impressed with Forssell. 'He rolled the ball under his foot on the run – I've seen people do that before – but in his next strike he rolled it under the other foot, and I've never seen that. Our defence was turning all over the place.' Leboeuf was delighted with the young Finn. 'Mikael did a very good job up front. Carlton Palmer tried to intimidate him and he was really professional, he didn't say a word back to him, and he was a winner at the end of the day. It was good for him, good for his confidence.' Luca added: 'Mikael confirmed his quality in scoring the opening goal. I hope he doesn't lose this good habit of scoring goals.'

Luca was also delighted by the return of Newton. 'Applause to Eddie Newton. After a long-term injury he's back and he has shown he can be a very useful member of the team.' Newton, however, was still considering his future. 'I am now completely fit and would like to stay at Chelsea. But I am waiting to see what they offer me and I am free to talk to other clubs. If I have to wait until the summer and leave on a free then that's the way it will be. It's up to Chelsea.'

Rix cut a forlorn figure in the dugout. A stern-faced Gwyn Williams insisted: 'There will be no statement concerning Graham's position. If you are seeking any form of official comment on the matter, try chairman Ken Bates.' But neither Bates, Hutchinson or Vialli could be contacted at the City Ground. Rix, surrounded by photographers, had joined Vialli on the bench before kick-off. En route to the visitors' dugout, he was patted on the back by Forest assistant boss Peter Shreeves and received a brief handshake from Atkinson. During the match, Rix emerged from cover on a couple of occasions to shout instructions from the touchline. There were chants of 'paedophile' from both Chelsea and Forest supporters.

SUNDAY, 21 FEBRUARY

Ray Wilkins was on stand-by for Rix when Luca was spotted with old pal David Platt at San Lorenzo's. Luca was well wrapped up in his overcoat.

Rix's lawyers hadn't given up, but they privately feared a two-year jail sentence. Rix's hopes rested with his outstanding QC, Desmond de Silva, who successfully defended Hans Segers in the match-fixing case. Bates wrote: 'Chelsea has been heavily criticised in two newspapers re. the Graham Rix affair for not acting or commenting on the matter. Our stance has been consistent. Until the matter was resolved by the court we had to await the outcome. The father tried to get Chelsea involved but we told him we were a football club, not judge or magistrate, and he should go to the police if his allegations were correct. We will continue to maintain this stance until the final outcome – not when just one side of the story has been told. However, in the interim I would ask just three questions. Firstly, did the father get paid for selling his story to the Screws of the World? Rumour has it that it was over £100,000. Secondly, if the crime was committed in February 1998, why did the father not go to the police until September, some seven months later? Thirdly, is it true that the father and daughter came to the Man Utd match the day after the crime, and where did the tickets come from? I believe there is more to this than meets the eye.'

MONDAY, 22 FEBRUARY

Luca teamed up with Sporty Spice for a charity photo-shoot. Keen photographer Mel C took pictures of Vialli, then tipped him to become the Premiership's new pin-up. She added: 'I like taking pictures. And good lighting and a great photographer could do wonders for Luca!' Vialli said: 'I hope she will do a good job because I need a good photographer to bring out the best in me as a model!'

Half-term at the training ground. Andrea Zola showed off his left-footed shooting power with Franco forced to don goalkeeper's gloves. Then he had to deal with the dribbling skills of Cassius Newton. Finally, the kids shared a plate of spaghetti in the canteen. Outside, a crowd gathered for autographs.

IBM announced sponsorship of the Chelsea website for twelve months. Bates said: 'We have made another significant step forward. It is a growing recognition of our brand name that we are becoming increasingly associated with major international companies.'

TUESDAY, 23 FEBRUARY

Vialli advised his stars that spiralling wage demands would push ticket prices out of control. He said: 'Nobody has to be greedy. We are part of a business and there's a lot of money in the game. Players have a right to ask for a lot. We are the actors in this business. But players have to be aware of the supporters who have to pay for tickets.'

Vialli felt his team had ridden through their sticky patch. 'We've had a bad patch because of injuries and suspensions, but with great luck and determination we've sailed through it. Now I hope the worst is over and that we can take part in the final rush, which will be very demanding with a team that is at its best.'

And not everyone on the bench was discontented. Kevin Hitchcock signed a new one-year contract despite being a permanent sub. 'I enjoy every day and I just want to keep going on and on and on until someone says you can't play any more. It was always fun and it just gets better and better. My contract was up in the summer so I negotiated another one, and probably next February I'll negotiate another. I'm happy to work for Luca. He's very professional and I like playing here under him. He makes me feel wanted, and that's a big part of it. The coaching staff hasn't changed here over the last few years.' He had so far played only six competitive games in the reserves. 'It is a bit frustrating, but I like to train hard, and you still think you are going to play in the first team so I always treat it as if I'm going to play, and if the opportunity comes along I don't think I'll let anybody down. I don't play in the reserves that often because we share it between myself, Dmitri, Rhys Evans and Paul Nicholls, and because there is a backlog of first-team games I'm often involved with them.'

Kevin hadn't yet considered coaching, but had gone into business. 'I've just started a little business in ventilation hygiene with a friend. We clean all the dust in the systems, and we've done a couple of jobs here at Stamford Bridge which has been nice, and it is going really well.' Now the senior player since the departure of Clarke, he added: 'The quality of players now is awesome. We've got quality English players and they are picking up off the foreigners, and their game is just going from strength to strength. You look at Jody Morris this season compared with two years ago. Give him another two and he is going to be a world-class player. He cannot help but learn off these stars.'

Gwyn Williams was spying on Valerenga, returning for the Liverpool game, with Eddie Niedzwiecki taking over. Luca said: 'In Norway everyone follows the Premiership and English football closely, so maybe Valerenga know more about Chelsea than Chelsea do about Valerenga. But we do our homework. Right now they are out of season in Norway, so Gwyn went to Spain to see them play in a pre-season tournament on Monday and Wednesday. He complained a lot about the weather out there but didn't seem to complain so much about the round of golf he had on the Tuesday. He told us what we expected to hear: that they are very well-organised, big and strong, they all know what they are doing, and we must be very focused in all parts of the field. He told us a little more than that, of course. They played again on Friday and Eddie went out to watch them and said they reminded him in some ways of Helsingborgs. They have scored a lot of goals away in Europe this season, so we have to be careful and patient as well as seeking out home advantage.'

Vialli also sent Niedzwiecki to Glasgow to spy on Celtic keeper Stewart Kerr in an Under-21 clash with Dundee. De Goey was Vialli's first choice, but Kharine's contract expired in the summer. It was reported that Kerr had a verbal agreement to join Chelsea in the summer for £1m. Kerr was also assured he would be given a fair crack at Ed de Goey's number one position. The Scottish Under-21 international had turned down a £850,000 move to Leeds because he had little chance of dislodging Nigel Martyn. Kerr was out of favour at Celtic Park under the management of Josef Venglos, who preferred Jonathan Gould. Kerr admitted he saw his future south of the border, saying: 'It's difficult for me to comment at the moment, but I would like to try my hand in England.'

Egil Olsen told Chelsea that he could have made a better job of coaching their team than Vialli or Gullit. From his team's training camp in Spain he criticised the preparation of the Londoners. Said Olsen, who took Norway to the World Cup finals in 1994: 'I believe my philosophy would have made Chelsea better than they are. They possess many good players but their performance varies considerably. It has always been my ambition to coach a team with so many good players. Unfortunately for Valerenga, the most consistent part of the Chelsea team is in defence. But they are too inconsistent and get too little end product with their offensive play for the quality of the players they have. While we feel we can do better than their previous opponents FC Copenhagen and Helsingborgs, I am sure Chelsea will start strong favourites and they have on their bench players worth more than the sum total of my starting eleven.'

Inter Milan offered Taribo West. The Nigerian was involved in an angry dressing-room clash with coach Mircea Lucescu following Inter's 1–0 weekend defeat at Lazio after enraging club chiefs by flinging his shirt at the bench when substituted during a game. The six-foot defender, famed for his trademark green-beaded dreadlocks, had come close to a move to Liverpool last summer.

WEDNESDAY, 24 FEBRUARY

Imperial College own the Harlington training ground, and the students use the facilities on the day that is traditionally the club's day off, as well as at weekends. With the Italian influence, Monday is more likely to be a day off, and now they train on Wednesdays when the canteen doesn't open and they have to be finished by 1.30 p.m. Desailly, Zola and Petrescu were later than everyone else finishing their session and found themselves evicted with all their belongings having been moved from the changing rooms – the students had moved in! It was a touch of a shock for those world-class stars! 'It couldn't happen at Steaua Bucharest!' suggested Dan.

There are often surprises at the training ground. Grove Challengers Under-11s turned up once on Luca's invitation as he responded to a plea for help from one of the boys' mothers. The team couldn't win a game. The kids watched training, collected autographs and met Luca. And it worked. They won a game. Coach Reg Goodchild wrote a thank you letter: 'May I, on behalf of our boys and Grove Challengers, thank Chelsea FC, and Mr Vialli in particular, for the time and trouble taken to encourage young children in the interest of football.'

Poyet returned to training. 'I am running gently. I see the doctor on Monday and hope to be back within three or four weeks.'

THURSDAY, 25 FEBRUARY

Ray Wilkins was lined up for a return to football if Rix was jailed. Out of work after being sacked by Fulham, the former Chelsea skipper was available to answer the call. It would be a huge challenge for Wilkins, following his managerial jobs at QPR and Fulham. He had not received his sacking settlement after leaving Fulham last May, but that would not stop him accepting a Chelsea offer. Wilkins, forty-two, said: 'I'm playing in the Masters League, a competition for former players at London clubs, in May and wanted to get fit. So I contacted Chelsea asking if I could come along to training sessions. They not only said yes but asked me to help out if possible. I'm used to being around footballers and have missed that, so it's great to be doing this. It also gives me the chance to practise my Italian – although I've discovered it's as bad as it always was.'

Vialli's players trained on the relaid surface for the first time barely a week after it had taken root. Ferrer admitted: 'It's not too bad, but maybe I expected a bit more because it's new.' Morris added: 'You could say the seams are showing, but with a bit of rain and a good roll overnight, it should still be a big improvement on the old surface.'

Vialli still refused to answer all questions about Rix.

FRIDAY, 26 FEBRUARY

Luca regarded Liverpool as a 'great club with a great history and great players'. He added: 'We expect a tough and difficult match tomorrow, but we've got very important things to play for. So expect us to play out of our skin and do our best to win the game.'

Morris had become a standard bearer for the Union Jack and the Stamford Bridge youth policy, both of which were presumed obsolete. When he opened the scoring against Blackburn he remarkably became the first English player to score for Chelsea in the Premiership this season. 'That was a red-letter day in my career, a really important game for me,' said the England Under-21 international nicknamed Midget. 'Until then, I had been forced to settle for the odd League Cup tie when the boss wanted to rest a few senior players, and a few cameos as sub in the League. But at Derby, I was in the side on merit and I knew it was now or never. Fortunately my luck was in, I did all right, and I have not really looked back. At a club like Chelsea, if you feel overawed when you rub shoulders with all those big names and you feel out of place, you are going to look out of place on the pitch. You need confidence in your own ability and the personality to express yourself when it matters.

'I've had my bad moments and paid my dues. A couple of years ago I had been training with the first-team squad when I got done for drink-driving, which wasn't clever. When Ruud found out he went mad, and before I knew it I was back in the youth team for a couple of months. When you are young, you can take things for granted too much. I thought I could get away with going out two or three nights a week and, when people tried to pull me up about it, I just thought they were having a nag. But when your close mates, like Michael Duberry and Andy Myers, start warning you about going off the rails, it's time to have a look in the mirror.'

Houllier made some interesting comments ahead of tomorrow's match: 'If I'm honest, then I've always felt since I came here that there was a gap between Chelsea, Arsenal, Manchester United and ourselves. I told the board that before the start of the season. But Chelsea started their revolution four or five years ago under Gullit, and they still haven't won a title yet. What they have done is use the transfer market well to give them a strength in depth that we haven't really got here at Anfield. I know we have got plenty of work to do here, but I hope it won't take four or five years. I just hope I'll be in for a busy summer. My job is to the use the current climate in the transfer market to build a squad you can rotate, and have top-class players on the bench. If you want to build a title-winning side, you have to understand that a top player is a team player. You need players who accept they will not start every game.'

Yet another backing for the rotation system.

Owen was refusing to allow Leboeuf's declaration after France's Wembley victory over England that Anelka is 'a better all-round player' get under his skin. Leboeuf had also said of the England striker: 'The limitation for Owen is that he needs space to be at his most dangerous, because his speed is dependent on him being able to run at defenders with room to spare. I think Nicolas is a little more versatile.'

Owen's response was a neat sidestep: 'I don't really care what people say. I'm just interested in myself, in what I and Liverpool can do. Anelka is a good player, but I'm certainly confident in my ability.'

Babayaro was away with Nigeria on African Nations Cup duty.

SATURDAY, 27 FEBRUARY

Chelsea 2   Liverpool 1

'Charity' was the general consensus, and it brought a wry smile to Luca's face. The many chances his team had not capitalised on were not lost on him, but the three points were all that mattered. But Luca was distressed that his team had allowed themselves to be distracted by two running feuds. 'Something was wrong on the pitch that affected the whole game. For seventy minutes we were out of this world. It is bad for us because we want to play football, not get involved in arguments.'

Le Saux narrowly avoided a red card after World Cup referee Paul Durkin decided to take no action after an off-the-ball incident with Fowler. The feud began when Fowler was booked for a late challenge as Le Saux cleared down the touchline. Le Saux was then booked himself for persisting in his protests that the Liverpool striker was mocking him as he tried to take the free-kick (Fowler stuck out his backside). Le Saux was furious, and took revenge off the ball. Fowler went down clutching his head. Vialli said: 'Certainly something happened. I don't know if Graeme was provoked. Sometimes players give you stick all the time. They were a bit angry with each other, and it went on too long in my opinion. Graeme is okay. After a while he got kicked. He was limping and couldn't carry on playing.' Houllier was very guarded with his comments. 'I know what happened, Robbie told me. I just regret it. Even if I'm not very happy it belongs in the past.'

Desailly was a colossus, despite some bizarre altercations with James; it was suggested that the keeper was less than respectful as the teams came out of the tunnel before kick-off. Liverpool didn't see the funny side when it provoked the Frenchman into one of his most imperious performances. When Desailly left the field he confronted James and there ensued a heated discussion. A steward stepped between the players as they disappeared down the tunnel still engaged in their debate. Desailly refused to be drawn on the incident. 'Nothing happened. I was just concentrating on the game.' Desailly reminded the reporter the interview was being recorded. 'Remember what I'm saying, do you understand? Or I'll kill you!' The *Daily Express* journalist was at pains to observe Marcel's wishes.

Liverpool's undoing began with a Ferrer cross-field pass to Le Saux and a deft ball inside to Zola in the seventh minute. Zola's cross, aimed for Flo – back in the starting line-up – took a deflection, but as Flo challenged at the near post Babb raised his hand to punch the ball away (he later claimed he was pushed in the back). Referee Durkin ordered the penalty and rebuked Babb, but didn't book him. Leboeuf resumed normal service by sending James the wrong way. Luca observed: 'In the dugout, so far away, it isn't easy to see, but we spotted a handball. It is difficult to say if he was pushed or did it on purpose. When the referee says "Penalty", it's a penalty – especially when it's for you, there is nothing to complain about!'

Liverpool's problems mounted when Heggem went off after just ten minutes with a strained groin injury. Houllier abandoned his defensive strategy with five at the back to accommodate McManaman coming off the bench early. When Flo headed down for Zola to twist and shoot just over, it was a warning sign that the new flat back four were in for a torrid period. Desailly's tackle on Fowler on the edge of the box was royal, and later he beat Owen with a combination of strength and speed. Fowler wasted a good chance with a shot over after Leboeuf cut out a Berger cross, then Redknapp threaded through a pass enabling Owen to shoot on the run, but de Goey was behind a weak shot as Leboeuf struggled out of position and limped off to be replaced by Lambourde. Luca said: 'He twisted an ankle, not in a bad way, and I'm pretty confident he will play on Thursday.' Ince lunged at the near post after the corner but hit the side netting, although the travelling fans mistakenly thought he had equalised.

Chelsea's second came from a back-heel by Zola which gave Petrescu the space to cross to the far post where the unmarked Goldbaek volleyed through James's legs to continue his rich vein of form. Luca said: 'Now he knows exactly what we expect when we've got the ball, and when they've got it. He's doing a great job. I hope he keeps playing like that.' Petrescu crashed a close-range volley against the post from a curling Zola cross before the interval, and it was a measure of Chelsea's superiority that Houllier was grateful for half-time.

Flo had a half chance at the start of the second half from a Zola cross, and a superb tackle by Matteo on Petrescu saved Liverpool from going three down. There were a number of other chances for the Blues before a rare lapse by Desailly and a failed Le Saux tackle on Owen brought Liverpool back for a late surge and a nervous end, curtailing chants from the Chelsea fans of 'You're Not Very Good'.

Luca summarised: 'This was a really important result because it was a very difficult game. They're a good team of many big players. I think we did really well at the beginning of the game. We started quickly – that's the power of Chelsea. We had a lot of chances, but if we want to be successful we have to improve, be more clinical when we have opportunities to score. It is impossible with ten chances to score ten times, but we have to improve our percentage otherwise we will suffer a little bit. But in the first seventy-five minutes we were out of this world in my opinion. In the second half we had a few problems because myself and the rest of the defence were sitting too deep, but we're still strong and keep getting results and we really could have won this game by four.'

Despite the final frantic siege in search of an elusive equaliser, Houllier conceded: 'They were better than us, anyway. On the whole I didn't like the football we played. We have lost some kind of fluidity. I was glad that half-time came; I have never suffered so much in a game.'

Aston Villa's challenge for the title all but collapsed in a 4–1 home defeat at the hands of Coventry.

Vialli was delighted with the new pitch. 'It was in good condition and allowed us to pass the ball around. We hope the weather remains fine so the new surface can settle. We need a good pitch. We are determined to leave nothing to chance, and getting the new pitch was important because in the past teams have had the advantage at Stamford Bridge. It was very heavy and made it easier for defenders, so it was ideal for teams just looking for a draw.'

Interviewed by Garth Crooks for *Match of the Day*, by radio reporters and two sections of the written press, there was bound to be a slip of the tongue, particularly when you're addressing the multitude of questions in a foreign tongue. Asked about whether he was trying to follow Clough's example of keeping clean sheets to win the title, Luca responded that it was different now with three points instead of two for a win, and that you had to take more risks to go for the maximum points, referring to the former Forest boss throughout as 'Nigel'.

SUNDAY, 28 FEBRUARY

The television cameras had caught Le Saux punching Fowler to the ground. Durkin said: 'It's a shame I did not see it during the match otherwise I would certainly have sent Graeme Le Saux off. The television pictures are pretty damning.' Durkin said it was up to the FA to decide what action to take against the Chelsea defender.

Television evidence has already been used by the FA to discipline players whose antics were missed by the officials. John Hartson was fined £20,000 and banned for four matches by the FA after a training-ground attack on his then West Ham colleague Eyal Berkovic, which was caught on Sky TV cameras, and Ian Wright was banned after he was seen punching David Howells by *Match of the Day* viewers in the north London derby between Arsenal and Tottenham.

Arsenal's title assault faltered too as they drew 1–1 at Newcastle. Wenger admitted that in the race for the Premiership crown he 'would give a slight advantage to Chelsea'.

March...
March...
March

Manchester United knock Chelsea out of the FA Cup ... four days later home defeat by West Ham ... Chelsea on the slide as Rix is jailed and Wilkins takes over

MONDAY, I MARCH

Ray Wilkins believed that Gianluca Vialli's team would stay the course despite a hectic climax. 'I have read suggestions that Gianluca's fitness regime will backfire on him and that Chelsea won't last the pace, but I have seen absolutely no evidence of that. We all know there are some immensely talented players at the club, but the impressive thing is that they all work their socks off. Gianluca and Graham must take a lot of the credit for that. There is the obvious Italian influence there, not only with the players but also the fitness coach, Antonio Pintus. The players there are all finely tuned and work a lot on power in training. In my humble opinion, far from weakening, they will be going just as strongly at the end of the season.' Wilkins planned to be at the Bridge to watch the tie against Valerenga. 'I know how keen the Chelsea lads are to retain the trophy in its final year, and I wouldn't bet against them doing exactly that.'

Blackburn were considering reporting Chelsea to the FA for allegedly making an illegal approach to Chris Sutton. Sutton claimed he was tapped up by Ken Bates's girlfriend Suzannah with a 'serious' transfer offer after their game at Stamford Bridge. 'She approached me at Stamford Bridge and asked if I wanted to play for Chelsea. I thought it was a joke and I was embarrassed by it. I don't like seeing these stories. It makes me look as though I'm looking to leave Blackburn when nothing could be further from the truth.' Sutton rang Rovers owner Jack Walker to assure him there was no substance in any of the stories. 'I have never said I wanted to leave. I have been here a long time and the club has been good to me so I would like to return that loyalty. We have just moved house and the family is very settled.' Chief executive John Williams said: 'We have not spoken to anyone from Chelsea and we don't expect to. Chris has said all along that he is happy at Blackburn, and these stories are not helpful.'

Newton was relishing the busy schedule after so long out. 'We want to win the

League but we also want to win the two Cups as well. There's no point in being in all three competitions if you aren't trying to do your best in all three. We are a team built to play patient, possession football. But at the same time we've got to look for a win to take to Norway because we can't rely on getting a result in the away leg the way we have in the last two rounds. It will be their first game of the season and that's a help for us because we're well into the routine of our season. I don't know much about Valerenga but we'll be looking at the videos and we'll know what to expect.'

Next assignment: Manchester United in the FA Cup. Newton said: 'I just knew we were going to get them in the draw. I'm sure that a lot of Chelsea fans feel we owe them one by now and I can assure you that the players feel the same way as well. It's up to us to do the business. We've just got to concentrate on playing our own game and not worry about them. We've proved in the past few years that we have the players who can handle the pressure of the big occasion, so there's no reason why we can't win. There will be about nine thousand Chelsea fans there instead of the usual couple of thousand stuck away in the corner, and that's going to make a big difference. It's going to give all our players a great lift to run out in front of that support.'

TUESDAY, 2 MARCH

Vialli was concerned players and fans would intensify attacks on Le Saux as the FA charged him and Fowler for misconduct. Fowler was the first player ever to be charged for making gay insults on a soccer field. Le Saux is highly sensitive to taunts from rival fans about his sexuality and was shocked that Fowler should repeat them. Luca said: 'I'd like to see Graeme and Robbie get together, shake hands and apologise, but I don't think that will happen. They were both wrong to do what they did and now I think it would be fine to see the pair of them get together, admit that they both made a mistake, and then say "Let's forget it".' Vialli took no action against Le Saux, whom he described as 'a very nice guy'. The club would mount a strong defence to save him from a possible four-match ban.

Vialli added: 'Graeme must learn to accept the taunts. If you don't, you end up the loser yourself. It doesn't matter if he or anyone is provoked, if you do something wrong you end up being on the same level of those that have accused you. It happens all the time in Italy, and it's why we can handle these situations better than the English. If Graeme wasn't such a special player he would not be taunted. It's sad, but you have to be able to handle it. You have to be stronger than even you realise you are and keep playing football. I've spoken to him about the situation, but I can't point too much of a heavy finger because I was recently sent off against Blackburn. What I told him is that we are human beings. I said I'm not saying Fowler was wrong and you were right and the supporters shouldn't wind you up, but what I did say is ignore it and be a better player for it.'

The PFA held talks with the FA. Gordon Taylor was appalled. 'It has gone on long enough and it has to stop otherwise the danger is that it will ruin the career of one of the outstanding England internationals. Graeme is a sensitive lad, married with a family, and this kind of attack is unacceptable, and it is fair enough to use the analogy of racial abuse. Both are totally unacceptable and have to be condemned and dealt with. Graeme is entitled to better treatment from fellow professionals. It is impossible to control the chants and taunts from spectators, but we can control our members. We shall stand up and be counted on this issue, just as we have taken a stand against racism in football. We want to have a profession we can be proud of, not one that can descend to the level of the gutter. The gesture made to Le Saux at the free-kick was unacceptable provocation.'

David Mellor of the government's Task Force insisted the two England internationals must not allow the spat to turn into a vicious bust-up every time they meet. 'They should publicly make up. The last time there was a spat between two leading players – Ian Wright and Peter Schmeichel – it was allowed to drag on. This bad blood must be stopped. Sledging must be stopped. Referees have a duty to stamp it out. The ridiculous situation where Fowler was waggling his backside at Le Saux and Le Saux protested and got a yellow card was not what the game is all about. It is important that football recognises this as a turning point – a defining moment. The game has taken great strides forward in not being a male-dominated place where all kinds of chauvinist attitudes persist. We want to get back to family values.

'I was at that game. It was very discreditable, and made all the worse by the referee's inability to see anything that was going on. You wonder sometimes why refs bother to be there when they miss that. I think Fowler waggling his backside at Le Saux was obvious to everyone there except the ref. What he said to Le Saux may be a matter of dispute. We know what Le Saux says and there is no doubt that he has had to put up with a lot of this sort of stuff, which is completely groundless. But that doesn't matter to football fans who want to taunt and jeer. This should be a turning point for football where we say that homophobia, in that extreme form, and sledging on the pitch between professional players who are paid thousands of pounds a week to play the game is unacceptable.'

Gordon Taylor was not impressed that Fowler was reluctant to go ahead with a plan for the two players to meet and clear the air, even though Liverpool chief executive Peter Robinson and Vialli agreed in principle. Taylor's assistant, Brendon Batson, spoke to Robinson, Le Saux and Fowler and was hopeful of a resolution.

WEDNESDAY, 3 MARCH

Vialli insisted there was huge pride in being the holders of the Cup Winners Cup, even though the competition would be scrapped next season to accommodate the new-look Champions League and UEFA Cup format. He added: 'I think it's very good to be playing in Europe again because the last time was in November and it's certainly a great feeling to compete in European games. People kept telling me we should decide which competition we cared about and really go for it. But if we relax in one we might lose all.'

Valerenga manager Egil Olsen has a history of baiting managers (he'd already tried it on Vialli) and winning the psychological war games. He twice got the better of Graham Taylor, then with England, and more recently out-thought former Brazil manager Mario Zagallo, and also John Toshack in the previous round of the competition. Flo said: 'Egil lives for his teams, particularly when he was the Norwegian coach. They are physical and can match anything in that department, so it's up to us to play better football to beat them. They'll have four to five thousand fans cheering them on, and it's a night where we must stay calm and cool. Egil has organised a side where everyone knows his job, and I look forward to seeing him again. I know him well and also respect his views on soccer. Like all his sides, Valerenga are tall, strong and physical, so we have to keep the ball on the ground and play at a high tempo.'

Flo needed more match sharpness. 'The ankle is getting better every day, and although it might take a little while longer for me to find the form I had before I was injured, I'm feeling really great. It is a really big week for us and it has already started well with that win over Liverpool on Saturday. But we have not even started talking yet about Manchester United in the FA Cup quarter-final at Old Trafford on Sunday. We want to concentrate everything on winning this game against Valerenga first.'

Vialli added: 'This game will be entirely different to what we've had previously in this competition. We must be on our toes. We must not lose concentration. I am fully fit and refreshed. I cannot wait for each game. I have done a lot of running recently in training to try to get fit, so it was not like I had a holiday, but I think sometimes the pressures on playing so many games can be more mental than physical. We know that it will be difficult to win all the time, but we will do our best and I am very confident. You always have to work hard for success, but you only have to look at the determination of all the players every time we play to see that we all believe we can win everything. Tomorrow is very important to us all because Europe is the highest stage for a club. The final in Stockholm was one of my best memories in football, and I want to do it again. We know that no team has won the Cup and then successfully defended it, and it is the last time that any club can win it, so we want to be the last. That will be history.'

Chelsea fans remember Erland Johnsen with affection. Signed from Bayern Munich, he spent six seasons at Stamford Bridge, making more than 150 senior appearances before returning to his native Norway in the spring of 1997 to play for Stromsgodset. 'I won't be at Stamford Bridge,' he said, 'but I will be watching the match on TV back in Norway, and I can tell you right now how I expect Valerenga to play. They will sit back at Stamford Bridge, they will have everyone behind the ball and they will soak up the pressure. You see, before Egil Olsen joined them they were in decline. They were at the bottom of their league and going nowhere. Since then Olsen has changed everything and, above all, he has got them organised to such an extent that when we played them in October they beat us five-nil. They will play John Carew up front on his own. He is a useful player; he has pace and he can run well with the ball. I would say, all in all, that they are a decent, hard-working team defensively, but offensively perhaps not so good. The Chelsea fans should not expect an easy game tomorrow.'

Flo had played alongside Carew and gave his team-mates the lowdown. Williams had also watched the striker in a mini-tournament at La Manga in Spain. He said: 'Carew is quality. He is quick, with two good feet.' Vialli added: 'I have watched him and he is a striker who is already good, but one day will become a superstar. He is the first name to mention when we speak of the dangers to us – him and the way Valerenga will organise their game.'

Carew was not overawed at the prospect of playing against Leboeuf and Desailly. 'Leboeuf likes to pull shirts and go in hard on attackers. I'm bigger than him, but I won't react if anything happens. I don't want a red card. We're confident because Chelsea always seem to have a problem in Cup games against teams considered inferior. We are unknown to them, and maybe they will be a little complacent. That may be why they are not as good as Manchester United. In the last round we played Besiktas of Turkey and they paid me some special attention by putting two markers on me. Chelsea might do the same, but I guess they know by now it didn't work for Besiktas – I still scored twice. I always feel I have a chance in the air and I'm sure I'll be able to cause Chelsea a few problems if I get the right service.'

Wise was back. 'I've been hammered, I've been fined, I've had to take all the banter, I've been running and running till it does my head in. All I want to do is play football, all I want to do is win some silverware this season. We want to be the only team ever to win it two years running. We can put Chelsea in the record books for ever more.' Bates said he was looking forward to one of Dennis's 'guest appearances'.

THURSDAY, 4 MARCH

Chelsea 3   Valerenga 0

Luca praised the performance as goals from Babayaro, Zola and Wise was the least Chelsea deserved for their domination. 'I would like us to play like that every game and get a result like that every match. We scored three and created many chances. That's not bad for a team that was supposed to be on the verge of implosion.'

Having beaten Helsingborgs of Sweden 1–0 and been held 1–1 by FC Copenhagen in their previous home ties, this was a high-scoring match by the standards of their Scandinavian odyssey, but it was not entirely satisfactory. Chances were missed, and there were periods when the Norwegians had control. But Chelsea always carried the greater threat. That ensured a victory that made Olsen's claim that he could have done a better job with the Chelsea side than Vialli look foolish, although he said: 'I think Chelsea would have won with me as coach as well.' Olsen did concede his side were outclassed. 'They were too fast for us, too quick with the ball, and we weren't able to prevent them creating chances. I feared that might be the case, and so it turned out. At two-nil down I thought we might have a chance, but the third goal really hurt us. I won't say it's impossible, but it's nearly impossible.'

After ten minutes a nine-pass move, involving Vialli, Wise and Zola in its latter stages, concluded with Zola's pass to Babayaro, rushing up unseen on the left to lash the ball inside the near post from a tight angle. The goal was marked with the trademark somersault. The match could have been settled within the next two minutes as Vialli twice had shots blocked: Hai Ngoc Tran intervened after Mikko Kaven had missed Le Saux's cross, then, from the subsequent corner, Walltin cleared off the line after the unmarked player-manager had been found by Desailly. The Chelsea fans, who turned up in twice the numbers they had for previous matches in this European campaign, had instead to wait until the twenty-sixth minute when Zola, running on to Babayaro's superb pass, held off Tran before scoring. Tom Henning Hovi, with a shot which rasped just past the post, provided a quick response and a reminder that the tie was not over. So did Fredrik Kjolner, whose shot was blocked on the line by Lambourde in first-half injury-time.

Chelsea's response, with an eye on Old Trafford, was to bring on Flo for the second half in place of Zola. Within minutes of the resumption Chelsea should have been three up. Vialli released Di Matteo behind the offside trap, but his shot was far too close to Kaven. Then Petrescu, unchallenged, headed wide from Le Saux's cross. Le Saux, after a one-two with Vialli, almost scored too; so did Di Matteo and Petrescu with twenty-yard shots. Petrescu, frustrated, was booked for dissent, and it looked as if Chelsea would have to settle for the uncertain security of a two-goal lead when, with five minutes left, their movement created a third. Di Matteo played the ball in for Flo whose cushioned pass, off his thigh, fell for Wise, breaking through. As the visitors looked for a linesman's flag Wise coolly celebrated a rare appearance – he is not suspended in Europe – with a goal.

Vialli was pleased but circumspect: 'I can't think about retaining the Cup yet. Valerenga came from three-nil down in Turkey in the last round to go through, so we will have to concentrate in the second leg, and even if we win the tie, we've still probably got to beat two from Lazio, Real Mallorca and Lokomotiv Moscow to win it again. We played very well against Valerenga and gave them little chance to hurt us, but we will see a different side in Norway and we must remain focused. We can put thoughts of the second leg away now and concentrate on Manchester United. It is a very big task for us without four suspended players, but a lot will depend on how both sides react to the European games this week.' Vialli was anxious to avoid Lazio at the next stage after the Italians' 4–0 demolition job on Panionios.

But Di Matteo was already thinking about a final with his old club Lazio, currently top of Serie A. 'I think that hopefully we will play them in the final because I think we are the best two teams in the competition. If it's like that it's going to be a great final. My old team. Yeah, yeah, it would be nice.'

The fans hadn't forgotten Casiraghi. HAPPY BIRTHDAY GIGI read a banner unfurled in the Matthew Harding Lower Tier to recognise his thirtieth.

Man of the Match Dennis Wise, nominated by sponsors Nivea for Men, was unable to collect his award because he was one of the players routinely drug-tested after the tie. Tucked away in an office behind the referee's changing room, he was too exhausted and dehydrated to provide a sample, despite litres of water and even a can of lager. By the time he managed one, everyone had gone home.

In his first *Evening Standard* column, Le Saux gave an insight into how he felt Chelsea would last the course under Vialli. 'Luca leads by example. He demands a lot of himself and, by definition, the rest of us as well. Everyone just loves playing for this club now. With success within reach on three fronts, where else would we want to go? Luca encourages that extra competitive edge in training, and I must say that, despite a busy World Cup summer, physically this is the best I've felt. Someone else who should take a lot of credit for that is our fitness coach Antonio Pintus. There have been suggestions in the media that the training is taking too much out of us, and I know that really upset him. He took it as a reflection on himself. It's not been easy for Antonio to leave his family in Italy and come to work in a strange country, but he's a really genuine character and I can't speak too highly of him. He has us trying things in training we would never have dreamt of before he came. In spite of everything, though, I am sure there are plenty of people expecting us to blow up as the season reaches its peak. Our opponents on Sunday are the benchmark as far as consistency is concerned over the years, whether you like it or not, and we are all striving to reach that standard.'

Ken Bates waded in with his own views on the Anfield incident involving Fowler and Le Saux, and was also critical of Owen and James. 'Michael Owen may be angel-faced, but angel he isn't. David James's childish behaviour was unnecessary, but Robbie Fowler's behaviour quite frankly was disgusting.' Bates said he was mystified as to why Houllier had allowed such goings-on at Liverpool to go unchecked.

Paul Ince responded immediately in his *News of the World* column: 'Ken Bates should keep his opinions to himself. Everyone knows what a loud mouth Bates has but, luckily for him, he has a great manager and player in Gianluca Vialli. Without him, Bates wouldn't have a chance of achieving anything, and he should try to keep his own house in order instead of sticking his oar in other people's business. Chelsea have made it their business to make Robbie look like the villain. If anyone should be condemned for what has happened it should be Graeme Le Saux. For Bates to say that about Robbie Fowler is simply a blinkered attitude. He should know some of the things his players get up to. Everyone has been trying to jump on this gay bandwagon to slaughter Robbie when the real issue is what Le Saux did. All week Robbie has been attacked and this is why I couldn't stay silent any longer. Someone has to speak out and defend Liverpool's corner. What Bates said about Michael Owen is complete rubbish. The nation loves Mike. He is a great player and always plays to win.'

FRIDAY, 5 MARCH

As both sides were chasing trophies on three fronts, permission was granted to Chelsea (at their request) and Manchester United to play an FA Cup replay, if required, three days after the original tie. Ordinarily, a replay would have been played on 17 March, but both clubs return from European quarter-finals that week. They could not play the following week because most of their players were on international duty, and the European semi-final first legs were the week after that. FA spokesman Steve Double said: 'There has always been provision to play the following week in exceptional circumstances, but the chances of returning to that in every situation are unlikely.'

Ferguson voiced his admiration for Gullit's Bridge revolution, and applauded Vialli's success in carrying on from where Gullit left off to establish Chelsea as a front-runner for major trophies along with United and Arsenal. 'Chelsea have been the best side we have played against this season. They are having a great season and the manager has done a fantastic job. It's an art blending all his players, but you also have to pick the right ones, too. Ruud Gullit did a fantastic job bringing in Vialli, Gianfranco Zola, Gustavo Poyet and Tore Andre Flo. Vialli, though, has added his own style to it with Marcel Desailly and Albert Ferrer. It's his own vision of the game, and there looks to be a good team spirit, too. You need to mix a lot of things to get a team playing to the level they have been reaching. That's why you have to give Gullit his place in all this. He started it. But I have been impressed with Vialli. He's done exceptionally well and has successfully carried on the Chelsea revolution.'

Ferguson was one of the first to congratulate David Beckham with a mobile phone call after the birth of his first son, Brooklyn – best wishes followed by a timely reminder he was expected back in training for final preparations for the showpiece tie with Chelsea.

De Goey would march out to confront the demons of his worst hour as a goalkeeper, United's 5–3 win at Stamford Bridge. Schmeichel rated de Goey the best keeper in the Premiership this season. De Goey said: 'It's only fourteen months ago that United were five up and cruising against us. Yes, that was one of the worst hours of my career. Fortunately I haven't conceded five too often either at Chelsea or with Feyenoord before that, but we will see on Sunday how much we've closed the gap on United over the last year. Already this season we have drawn twice with them in the Premiership, and both times we made them work hard for their point. We've come a long way down the track as a side since losing that Cup tie last year, and United know we can deal with them better now.'

Zola, scorer of the Blues' equaliser in the 1–1 draw between the teams before Christmas, and due to partner Flo up front at Old Trafford, said: 'Games between Chelsea and United seem to be getting bigger and bigger, and both teams want it badly this time. Andy Cole and Dwight Yorke proved against Inter why they deserve to be recognised as two of the best strikers in Europe. They have struck up a fantastic partnership and you can understand why United are keen to channel so much possession towards them. It's a big game and I like to play well in big games. Of course I try to play my best all the time. but there's certain games where it's easy to get the right boost. When Chelsea play Manchester United, even if it's only a friendly, it's always a very important game.'

Ferguson selfishly wanted Chelsea to continue in Europe. 'It wouldn't do to have Chelsea concentrating on the League race while we take on Europe and the FA Cup as well! Certainly we will be doing our best to end their FA Cup interest, though Chelsea will no doubt have other ideas about that. It will certainly not be an easy task because there is not a lot to choose between the teams, a fact borne out by the two draws in the Premiership this season.'

Le Saux tried to end the running feud with Fowler by issuing a public and private apology. Fowler responded by claiming he had been made a 'scapegoat', and that his infamous crude gesture was 'misinterpreted'. Le Saux backed down first by sending a letter to Fowler admitting he had acted badly. Fowler then made a conciliatory reply, but his carefully worded statement offered 'regret', but no apology.

Le Saux said: 'I recognise that the use of elbows can be dangerous and I should not have reacted in the way I did. People in all walks of life occasionally face provocation, and deal with it. I realise I have to deal with it in a more mature manner. I accept that I will face punishment from the FA, and I recognise now that I was lucky not to have been sent off for the way I reacted.'

Fowler responded more guardedly through his solicitor, Kevin Dooley. 'The incident during last Saturday's match at Chelsea in which I was elbowed on the back of the head by Graeme Le Saux was highly regrettable. Graeme may have misinterpreted my actions, which were not intended to cause any offence, and it is unfortunate that attempts have been made since the game by others to make me the scapegoat for what took place. I would like to think that this is the end of the matter and I look forward to the opportunity of playing alongside Graeme in future England matches.' Dooley added: 'This has been a very unfortunate incident which could have tarnished the reputation of the game. We hope that with the expressions of regret by both players this is the end of it.'

The apology was suggested by Gordon Taylor, who had been surprised by Fowler's reluctance to comply. Taylor said: 'I spoke personally to Robbie and I advised him to follow suit and also offer a letter of apology. Our message is quite clear; we would have been disappointed with anything less.' PFA deputy chief executive Brendon Batson added: 'We have been talking to all parties for several days, and we are pleased that Graeme Le Saux saw fit to offer an apology. It has been a delicate discussion and sometimes tortuous, but we have been attempting to broker a situation that meets with the approval of both parties. In the end it was up to two individuals to settle their differences in an adult way. Le Saux's letter was the first step.'

Le Saux had been ready to release his apology for more than forty-eight hours, but held back because of Fowler's insistence he would not say sorry. Both players were approached by a number of people eager to set up what has been described as a 'stunt' to bring the two together, but they declined as it would have looked insincere.

Le Saux's side decided that they would wait no longer for Fowler to agree to the joint apology, and issued their own despatches without him.

Le Saux is the most targeted player in the Chelsea team this season because opponents know they can wind him up. He has been the culprit eleven times in incidents which have provoked either a booking or a sending-off for an opponent. The Chelsea full-back alone accounts for just over ten per cent of the total incidents of this kind involving Chelsea players. Opponents know that Le Saux will eventually react; more fool him, then, for rising to the bait.

Whether he likes it or not, Le Saux is the living embodiment of the twisted set of values which permeate the modern game. Here is a brief guide to what is and is not permitted: winding up opponents is acceptable; diving, or falling over to get an opponent sent off is not acceptable; rushing over to the referee to raise a phantom card to get an opponent booked or sent off is seen as a foreign trick imported to the Premiership, and therefore unacceptable; an over-the-top leg-breaker is acceptable – after all, it is a man's game and very British; and deliberate handball to score a goal is acceptable if the player is on your side, but totally unacceptable if it's done by a foreigner (particularly an Argentinian). Players believe it's quite in order to taunt an opponent about his sexuality, but it's totally unacceptable and crosses the line which divides acceptable gamesmanship and bad taste.

Fowler might have thought he was the victim of a witch-hunt by southern softies frightened of a jibe or two about the possibility of being a poofter. He perceives football as the last bastion of macho male homophobia; in fact, it is the last refuge of the half-witted mickey-taker. Life can become intolerable if you are not one of the boys. It might be hard for Fowler to comprehend, but his vile remarks were not amusing. He and Liverpool should be thoroughly embarrassed by the whole afffair. Houllier is deluded to think it merely a southern media conspiracy.

SATURDAY, 6 MARCH

Bates had been fascinated by the questioning of his manager after the Valerenga match, and reported the exchange in his programme notes.

Q: Luca, you must be feeling tired, will you play yourself on Sunday?
A: I will be on the bench.
Q: So you will be a substitute?
A: No, I'm suspended.
Q: Leboeuf was injured, will he play on Sunday?
A: No, he's suspended.
Q: You must be pleased to have Dennis back.
A: No, he's suspended.
Q: Babayaro was outstanding today.
A: Yes, but he's suspended.

   David Baddiel also featured in the programme. Unable to attend the tie because of the sixtieth birthday celebrations of his mother, Sarah, the *Fantasy Football* star said: 'It couldn't have been worse-timed, and there is no way I can say I am going to Manchester for the day because it is a big family party.' He planned to slip away to the pub to watch on TV. 'I don't know what it is like to win the title as it has never happened in my lifetime. Our only championship was in 1955 when we won with the least number of points ever, and I think Chelsea fans treat the 1970 FA Cup triumph as a more historic event. It has usually been a case of watching Chelsea play out the second half of the season, so I feel I am at least getting full value for my season ticket. There are some who criticise the amount of foreign players here, but a team of Italians, Frenchmen and the like fits into the Chelsea tradition because we have always been a flair side.'

SUNDAY, 7 MARCH

Manchester United 0   Chelsea 0
Ferguson lined them all up for this one: Solskjaer, Scholes, Beckham, Blomqvist, Sheringham, Yorke and Cole, but still Manchester United couldn't score in one of the bravest FA Cup contests ever mounted by Chelsea. For fully forty minutes Vialli's team were down to ten men, but stubbornly refused to cave in. Who was the joker who accused the foreign stars of coming on a Bosman holiday? Vialli's league of nations filled Old Trafford with spirit, commitment and old-fashioned British never-say-die.

   Having succumbed to Ferguson's side three times in the last five years in the FA Cup, this was always going to be an uphill struggle, and so it transpired as early as the fourth minute when Keane brought a flying save from de Goey. The Irish midfielder was first into the book after just ten minutes for showing dissent over a throw-in decision following a fifty-fifty challenge with Morris. Then a clever chip from Beckham gave Scholes a chance, but as he stretched his shot squirmed wide with de Goey unhappy about the lunge. Desailly was cautioned for holding back Solskjaer, but the Frenchman turned in a wonderful display and was unfortunate to be edged out of Man of the Match by his goalkeeper.

The first booking for Di Matteo came after twenty-five minutes after a challenge on Beckham, a borderline case and hardly the most vicious of tackles.

Chelsea mustered their first and only shot on target after thirty-seven minutes: Goldbaek's pass across goal searched out Morris whose attempted curler failed to outfox Schmeichel. One of Beckham's specialist right-wing crosses gained just a touch from Gary Neville a minute later, striking the foot of the far post. Then a Blomqvist cross found Scholes unmarked at the far post, but his shot was wide. Just before injury time in the first half Di Matteo's lunge into Scholes inevitably saw him walking back to the dressing room just ahead of his team-mates.

With Wise and Leboeuf suspended, Petrescu wore the skipper's armband, but he failed to show for the start of the second half; Newton substituted and took on the mantle of captain. Naturally enough, with their numerical advantage United piled on the chances: Beckham scooped a shot over the bar, Blomqvist shot just wide, Keane's effort hit the side netting, and de Goey produced a fine save from Scholes. On the hour Vialli replaced the tiring Flo with Forssell, and after seventy-two minutes Ferguson lost patience and threw on Yorke for Phil Neville. De Goey saved his best moment for the seventy-sixth minute, turning over a Scholes close-range effort. Understandably, Chelsea surrendered much of their attacking play with Desailly marshalling their defence superbly. A Zola free-kick was Chelsea's only relief, but then he was withdrawn in favour of another defender, Andy Myers. With less than ten minutes left, on came Cole and Sheringham for Solskjaer and Blomqvist. Scholes mistimed a tackle on Goldbaek and got his marching orders too.

Ferguson and Vialli cursed the replay that would clog up their title run-ins. Ferguson suggested that the extra game gave Arsenal a massive advantage in the Premiership, the Gunners' semi-final spot already booked after they beat Derby twenty-four hours earlier. He clearly wasn't happy at Durkin's display: two red cards and seven yellows. 'Referees do put themselves under pressure by booking immediately for innocuous challenges. They leave themselves no leeway. Di Matteo was booked for a kick at Keane off the ball, but his later challenge didn't merit a sending-off. Then Durkin redresses the balance by sending off Scholes for an equally innocuous challenge – but that's about the state of refereeing at the moment, and this referee is probably the best in the country. You would have thought he would have used his experience more today. Now his test will come in the replay.' Vialli held back. 'I don't like to talk about referees.'

Vialli was pleased with the performance, but not the dreaded replay which postponed the Premiership trip to Middlesbrough. 'The winner today is Arsenal. Now is a very decisive moment in the season. The less games you have to play the better. These games take a lot out of you. Although it is a big pleasure to be playing Manchester United in the quarter-finals of the FA Cup and we will give it everything in the replay, it is another very tough game which tests the squad.

'I thought both teams were afraid of each other for thirty minutes when it wasn't a good game. After the sending-off, Manchester United could have won the game. It wasn't our best performance in terms of passing and movement, but in spirit and determination we did very well. Our defenders were great. Marcel Desailly was superb.'

At least Vialli left Manchester confident of recalling a squad free of suspension and injury.

Inevitably, Le Saux was targeted by the United fans (in response, the Chelsea supporters aimed their taunts at Beckham: 'Who's the father of your kid?'), and Vialli praised Le Saux's self-control. But this did nothing to mask Chelsea's mounting disciplinary problems. Di Matteo was the seventh player to receive his marching orders this season, and he got a one-match ban, although he did not receive an additional suspension for reaching eleven bookings. Seven red cards put them on a par with Arsenal.

Minutes after the two managers spoke, the draw for the semi-finals paired the winners of the tie with the Cup holders, Arsenal. Newcastle, who lost to Arsenal in last season's final, beat Everton 4–1 in their quarter-final and would meet the winners of the postponed Barnsley–Tottenham Hotspur tie. The possibility of a repeat of the 1998 FA Cup final was kept alive. The door was also left ajar for the possibility of Gullit facing his former club.

Casiraghi conceded he would not be fit for the start of next season. 'I work six hours a day in the rehabilitation centre – every morning and every afternoon. The doctors haven't told me when they think I will play again, but it will not be until November or December. It's very hard, but I'm being positive.' Gigi was in the country to commentate for an Italian TV station taking the game live. He went to the hotel where the team stayed on Saturday night. 'It was a lovely surprise for some of the chaps because only a few knew about him being here,' said physio Mike Banks. 'He looks a heck of a lot better than when I saw him last. He is moving well, but he's still using crutches because he so recently had the arthroscopy. He's in much better spirits too, probably because the knee has begun to move so well and he's starting to feel real improvement. He's still got a lot of hard work to do, but things are starting to fall into place for him.'

MONDAY, 8 MARCH

Ferguson cranked up the pressure on Durkin, claiming the replay would be a huge test for the FIFA official. Durkin knew all eyes would be on him at the Bridge and he refused to add further fuel to the controversy by becoming involved in a war of words. He was adamant, though, that he had been right to give Scholes and Di Matteo their marching orders.

The FA decided that if the semi-final was between the two London sides, then Wembley would stage the game on Monday evening, 12 April. It was possible that Chelsea would be involved in Cup Winners Cup action on the preceding Thursday, and Wembley was unavailable on Sunday the eleventh due to the Wales v. England Five Nations match. The semi would be switched to Sunday lunchtime at Villa Park if Manchester United won.

Bates met a group of football writers in Fishnets for lunch and a briefing on next season's ticket prices, discussing a wide range of issues in the process. On Vialli he said: 'I have been delighted with what we have achieved so far in terms of the football and the results achieved. We have lost just three times in forty-one matches. He will be concentrating on coaching, we shall retain his playing registration, and if he wants to pick himself, he can. As for going to Italy, forget that one – he isn't qualified to manage there.'

During the meal, Bates called for players serving suspension to be docked wages and restrictions on players' ability to cash in on playing for England, revealed the money at stake for winning or losing the League, and announced more price increases, up nine per cent across the board in order to maintain Chelsea's lofty position at the top of the Premiership. He told the fans: 'You only get what you pay for. The biggest sponsors of football are still the supporters. And they will continue to be the main sponsors. Our supporters will say that if we give them great football they don't mind paying. The question is a simple one: do you want to stay in the Premiership, or do you want to win it?'

That is certainly the case at the Bridge, where the financial boost promised by the hotels, flats and restaurants is still to take effect. Until the club becomes self-sufficient in other areas besides football, such as Manchester United's massive marketing and commercial operation, then entrance money will still pay for new players' fees and salaries. Bates has surpassed the wage bills even at Old Trafford to bring the glory days back to the Bridge.

With record season-ticket sales every year since the Hoddle days, the current record of 18,000 was sure to be beaten again, with around 20,000 sold, bringing in £13m. But with the local council delaying the new stand the capacity was only 34,500. Bates added: 'Arsenal need seventy thousand, and once they have it Aston Villa and Chelsea will have the smallest capacity of the big clubs. I don't apologise for being the most expensive club in the country because we have to compete, and it cannot be a level playing field if the likes of Manchester United and Newcastle have far bigger capacities.' Bates stressed that season tickets also included all domestic cup ties as well as discounts in the club shop, and other advantages. He argued: 'It is a comprehensive package that has suited our supporters for the last fifteen years.' He maintains a balance by not issuing all available seats to season-ticket holders. 'For those who are really poor we were on TV nineteen times last season, and it will be about the same this time. You can also see the games on the big screen in the Shed Bar for a tenner.'

Malcolm Carle, chairman of the club's north-west regional supporters' association, said: 'Nine per cent does sound a bit high, but I think supporters would accept it as the money is being ploughed back into the club. It's still not as bad as having to pay twenty-nine pounds to watch Chelsea at Tottenham.'

Indiscipline had been on the agenda all season, with Chelsea's stars suffering as much as anyone, and Bates wanted to rewrite contracts so that banned players would not be paid. 'In what other walk of life would you get paid if you were suspended? It's time the FA hit players with punitive punishments, and clubs should not pay players when they are suspended. If they play for England under suspension they should not get any appearance money or their cut of all the commercial deals.'

Certainly Bates would have saved a lot of money on Dennis Wise alone! But the PFA dismissed Bates's idea as 'impractical'. Brendon Batson declared: 'A player is competing for his club and it is a physical contact sport. If he ends up having his wages docked as a result of a slightly mistimed tackle, that may make him think twice about making such a tackle again, and I'm sure his manager might have something to say about that. As things stand, players can already be fined by their clubs, and if there is serious foul play then they can be charged by the FA, which could lead to a further fine. A suspended player also loses out on any win bonuses, which can prove very costly.'

One way in which clubs could act is to increase the pay-as-you-play element in contracts, a move normally used to reward younger players who fulfil their potential, but this is also hardly practical – not to mention divisive – in a world in which squad rotation is employed.

TUESDAY, 9 MARCH

Vialli declared his faith in Flo as he strove to rediscover his scoring touch ahead of the replay. The boss was fully aware of the huge boost a goal would provide for Flo as he continued his comeback. He had not scored since 26 December at Southampton. Luca said: 'Obviously Tore's not at his best yet as he's been out for several weeks, but he's very close to being at his best in my opinion. Every match he improves his performance a little bit. Obviously he needs to play games to find his form, and I'll be waiting for him as he's going to be a key player until the end of the season.'

Chelsea had not defeated United at Stamford Bridge since 11 September 1993, and had only beaten United in the FA Cup just once in their entire history – a 2–0 victory back in 1950 in the sixth round – but 'when the task is difficult,' said Vialli, 'you have to look to your inner strength and try to pull out everything you've got inside. I hope you believe me when I say it's not up to me – it's up to the players. They go on the pitch, they play the game, they make the tactics. Yes, you can give them tips or something, but then it's up to them. Obviously these types of matches take a lot out of you, but it must be done. We have to be up for it, play better, try everything to go through and make sure that the effort which we produced in the second half at Old Trafford does not go to waste.'

Stam had returned from suspension and Ferguson was also able to call upon Ryan Giggs, who had recovered from a broken nose and black eye. However, any advantage gained from the availability of Stam and Giggs was cancelled out by the return of Babayaro, Leboeuf, Wise and Duberry (although Petrescu was away on international duty, and a painful kick in the calf at Old Trafford had ruled Ferrer out). But Ferguson took heart from United's fine record at Stamford Bridge. 'We should have won the game at Old Trafford, and we all know that, but we're going to a ground where we have a terrific record. Somebody pointed out that we've only lost three times there in the last twenty-five years or something, which is a heck of a record.'

Ferguson felt an historic European, Premiership and FA Cup Treble bid was an impossible dream. 'I don't think the Treble is a realistic target. I think it's more a romantic one. I do think, though, that anyone in this position should go for it, but you know, deep down, that you are not going to do it. It needs almost a miracle to pull off the Treble. To lift the FA Cup we need to win three games. To win the European Cup we must at least draw in Milan next week and win the next three. In the League we have only ten matches left. So you have to go at it.'

WEDNESDAY, 10 MARCH
Chelsea 0   Manchester United 2

Ferguson strode into Luca's office after the match, with coach Steve McLaren not far behind. Over a bottle of wine and a can or two with Luca, Gwyn and Colin, they discussed a wide range of football-related subjects. Vialli took as much comfort from defeat as he could: 'Manchester United and Arsenal meet in the semi-finals now, and we must hope they get tired a little; when they will be playing, we will be resting.' The race for the title was now really on.

Two-goal Yorke – whom Ferguson described as 'absolutely magnificent' – was the match winner. Vialli conceded: 'At the moment I would have to agree that Yorke has been one of the most decisive players in European football this season – but there's still enough time for one of my players to prove even more influential, and I can't fault my team tonight because we gave it our best shot, although we were not clinical enough. When you play Manchester United you have to be perfect. We started off on the wrong foot when we conceded a sloppy goal. We controlled the game for most of the match and created chances, but unfortunately sometimes the more you try the less you look like you're going to score. When the second goal went in I realised it wasn't going to be our night.'

Chelsea went into this game genuinely feeling that they had a chance to end United's run of success over them in this competition, but Beckham's free-kick caused panic in the defence after just three minutes, Leboeuf heading the ball up in the air and tumbling over in the process. Cole won the ball in the air unchallenged in front of Flo, and Leboeuf couldn't recover in time to block Yorke's first-time shot on the turn, which flew past de Goey into the corner. Beckham joined Yorke to celebrate the goal, rock-a-bye-baby Bebeto style, which provoked an angry reaction and some missile-throwing from the crowd. Yorke said: 'The celebration was for Brooklyn, the latest addition to the United team.' Chelsea faced an anxious wait to find out whether they would be censored by the FA for the incident, but Durkin did not report it.

Chelsea hit back hard with their brand of possession football, but after they had sorted out their defensive problems they still could not resolve their current lack of punch up front. Morris thumped a shot straight at Schmeichel, the Danish goalkeeper punching out for the first of a series of outstanding saves, and Desailly initiated another move during which Morris turned past his marker on the edge of the box, but his shot was again saved. When Zola took on Di Matteo's pass to leave him with a run on goal, Schmeichel raced out to block superbly with his outstretched right leg, even though the linesman missed the offside.

Beckham produced a magnificent pass soon after the interval, giving Gary Neville the freedom of the wing, but his cross-shot deflected into the side netting. In the fifty-fifth minute, after a measured move involving Di Matteo, Babayaro crossed to the far post where Wise lurked unmarked. His effort, which was going in, was deflected wide of the post by Flo. A few minutes later Yorke crowned an outstanding individual performance with an exquisite chip over the advancing de Goey to seal Chelsea's fate. Latching on to Cole's tackle on Desailly, Yorke chipped from twenty yards out with the outside of his right boot.

After Yorke's decisive second, Ferguson brought on Phil Neville to shore up the defence, while Vialli juggled his attacking options with Morris and Flo coming off for Goldbaek and Forssell. The seventeen-year-old was presented immediately with a great chance by Zola, but he tried to dribble round Schmeichel and screwed his shot wide. Ferguson took off Yorke with seven minutes left, bringing on Solskjaer, and when the Norwegian was brought down by Desailly, Beckham's wickedly curling free-kick was acrobatically pushed over by a flying de Goey save. In the four minutes of overtime Schmeichel made another save from Le Saux.

Leboeuf and Beckham were in conciliatory mood, and when Wise became entangled with the latter in an innocuous fifty-fifty challenge, the pair shook hands and embraced. Wise was once described by Ferguson as a player who could start a fight in an empty room, but for a change his behaviour in this match was little short of exemplary. 'It's good to play tough and be competitive but always try and play within the rules,' said Vialli.

Zola hailed Yorke as one of the greatest strikers he had ever played against. 'He's great. I would put him in the greatest category. He's doing very well this season and has completed his game. Above all, he is in complete symphony with his team – that's a point which makes him very effective. I'm really impressed at the way he is playing at the moment. Apart from the goals, he is playing very well as he holds the ball at the right moment and allows the team to get up. He is very effective for his team.' Di Matteo added: 'He's certainly one of the top strikers I've seen, and I've seen some good strikers in my time. He's in great shape and is making the difference at the moment for Manchester United. Give him half a chance and he scores, even when they're not playing well – and that's vital.'

So, United still on course, but Chelsea's ambitions of completing their own Treble were wiped away. The key for Chelsea was to show resilience by immediately bouncing back, and with Duberry close to match fitness and Poyet also close to a welcome return, things were looking good.

Leboeuf had picked up a thigh muscle injury, which had prevented him from starting the second half, but that didn't stop him painting the town red. He was snapped outside his favourite Italian restaurant, San Lorenzo's, with supermodel Elle Macpherson. Frank was not amused to see the picture, in which he had his hand up as if he didn't want to be seen with the supermodel. In fact his wife, Betty, and Elle's boyfriend were also in the picture, but were cut out.

THURSDAY, 11 MARCH

Fowler finally ended his feud with Le Saux by thanking him for his apology and issuing one of his own, delivering a letter to Stamford Bridge. Le Saux's advisers scrutinised the contents of Fowler's apology before greeting it with their seal of approval. Fowler – under legal advice – was again careful not to admit he had done anything wrong, and once again used the term 'misinterpreted' in the letter, having made the same claim in his statement. The letter read, in full: 'I am in receipt of your without-prejudice letter about what occurred on Saturday, 27 February at Stamford Bridge. I am sorry if you misinterpreted my actions during the game, which were not meant to cause any offence to yourself or anyone else. Hopefully this unhappy incident can now be brought to an end. I am sure you share my hope that when we play together again, either on opposite sides or on international duty, people have no reason to judge us other than on our footballing abilities.' The letter hardly went far enough, and Fowler made it clear he was determined to defend himself. He would take video evidence to the inquiry, documenting the moments when he was elbowed on three occasions by his opponent.

As for Le Saux, he blamed it all on the famous curse of *Hello!* magazine. Together with his Argentinian wife Mariane and baby Georgina, the Le Sauxs were extensively pictured in the glossy magazine with a spooky reputation for focusing on personalities whose relationships then collapse. He said: 'We had the spread done before the Oxford FA Cup tie, then I got involved with Robbie. So maybe that's why everything has happened.'

The FA wanted to deal with this case once and for all before Keegan met up with his first England squad, but that was proving tricky. Le Saux said: 'I don't know if Lancaster Gate will attempt to ask us to get together or anything like that before the England squad meets up. Personally I have no problem with the situation, or with him. I have never had anything but a good relationship with him in the past. We are professionals. These things happen. Not everybody gets along with each other, but you still have to go out and play a game.'

Vialli said: 'It has now gone far enough. I think the FA will lecture both of them and perhaps fine them. But we certainly don't want any more suspensions hanging over our heads at such an important part of the season.'

Paul Hughes begged Chelsea to lower his transfer fee and allow him to leave. Hughes, who had been at Chelsea since the age of ten, had finally come to the conclusion he would have to go. The twenty-two-year-old midfielder spent two months on loan at Stockport, and was expected to return there after recovering from a hamstring injury, but Chelsea told the First Division club they had to pay £750,000 if they wanted the player back. Hughes said: 'Stockport are just a small club and even two hundred thousand is a big signing for them. I just hope Chelsea can be sensible about the fee, or clubs will be put off. I have spoken to Gianluca Vialli about it and I just hope he can help.'

FRIDAY, 12 MARCH

Luca announced that he had abandoned his mobile phone, and that for the past few weeks his assistant Virginia had been taking all his calls and organising his personal diary. 'The fact that mobiles can damage your brain, I've decided I can do without them,' he informed the Italian media. He also explained that far too many people had obtained his number.

Vialli would not set a points total for the title. 'It is impossible to say how many points we'll need to be champions, because there are three teams involved and both United and Arsenal seem to win every week. Those two are the favourites at the moment. I just hope they get side-tracked by the European Cup and FA Cup and leave the title to us! We cannot drop any more silly points. It is so important we qualify for the Champions League.'

Desailly was grumbling again. He blamed 'excessive aggression' for becoming disillusioned with the Premiership. He said: 'I was right to choose Chelsea from the point of view of playing ambition, and London is a cosmopolitan city that suits me perfectly. But the other side of the coin is the atmosphere surrounding English matches. There is a style of play favoured in England that I have no control over. I will sit down and take stock at the end of the season. I won't just give in to a whim because the set-up and the people at Chelsea are marvellous, but my agent is drawing up plans for next season for me, and the truth is I had an unforgettable time with Marseille. I like the club and the city. Going back would mean a major drop in salary, but I can live with that. The money is no longer the most important thing in my life.'

No wonder. Desailly was the top earner at the Bridge on £40,000-plus a week, having signed a four-year contract. Unlike Laudrup, hired as a Bosman free, the club also paid a substantial fee for the Frenchman, but didn't want to cash in at any price. Hutchinson explained: 'He is not for sale. Marseille have not contacted us and in all the discussions I've had with Marcel he said he is very happy here. If he had a problem I would have expected him to sit down and discuss it with us by now, but whenever I see him, and it's quite often, he has always said he is quite happy. In any case, he will have three years left on his contract and we are not prepared to sell him as he figures very much in our plans.' But Desailly's agent, Pape Diouf, said: 'Two big Italian clubs are keen on Marcel, but it is Marseille who are in a financial position to grant him his wish to return to France.' So far the evidence for this has only come from articles in France.

There was deep confusion among the fans. Outwardly Desailly seemed happy at the club. In fact he was featured in the weekend's club programme talking contentedly about his home life in Kingston Hill with his kids. He also seemed to be enjoying his football, notably the win over Liverpool, and he socialised with the players – Lambourde, Ferrer and Poyet were mentioned. His ideal night out involved 'a nice restaurant, or a show or concert, and to come back home and kiss the children goodnight'. No hint of any discontent there.

Chelsea were in the market to buy more stars, not sell their best players. A tenuous link was made with Italian star Filippo Inzaghi. Juve valued Inzaghi at £20m and Roma were willing to pay that plus increase his current wages of £1.2m tax-free to £2.2m. John Toshack, back at Real Madrid, also wanted him. The figures were out of Chelsea's price range, and in any case he was not one of the players on Vialli's wanted list. A more realistic target was Roma's out-of-favour striker Marco Delvecchio. The club, however, were determined to give Casiraghi every chance to recover. Hutchinson said: 'We are giving him every encouragement to play football again with Chelsea as soon as possible. No one is writing him off.'

West Ham boss Harry Redknapp, an admirer of Chelsea, said in anticipation of tomorrow's meeting at the Bridge: 'You look at Manchester United, Arsenal and Chelsea and you can't see a weakness there at all. I've been thinking of a way to try and play against Chelsea all week, and it's not easy, believe me. The gulf between that trio and the rest is widening all the time. How do you compete with them? The answer is, with great difficulty. How do we play against Chelsea tomorrow? Do we go defensive and take it on the chin? That's not my nature. I like my teams to have a go at the opposition. You can't be too cavalier, though, otherwise the certainty is you will get mullered. We'll try to be solid, but we will also try and pose them problems. It's certainly possible to beat Chelsea or any other of the top teams on a given day, and we have to be positive.'

West Ham signing Paolo Di Canio, a good pal of Vialli's, was going to miss out. 'I'm disappointed about not playing. I don't know whether I'll even be there. My groin is a problem. I would rather miss one than the next ten.' West Ham were also missing Ian Wright, out for another fortnight after his cartilage operation. That's part of the reason why Redknapp, like Vialli, appointed an Italian fitness coach, who would begin work next season.

Luca was again circumspect in his programme notes. He explained: 'I hope you can forgive me, but we'd rather talk on the pitch than in the programme, so expect a good performance.' In one of his briefest ever pieces, Luca was apologetic for losing in the Cup: 'They were better than us at finishing. They created very few chances but scored two. I think we had something like seventeen attempts on goal and unfortunately we couldn't score. Far from me is the idea of blaming anybody. I think you have to judge a successful team in the way it takes victory and defeat. In my opinion they must be treated the same way. Keep your feet firmly on the ground when you're successful, and your chin up when you fail. I think that in our team there are many experienced players who can easily cope with all the situations. As far as I'm concerned it shouldn't be a problem to react in the right way.'

Zola was the first player to be a studio guest on Chelsea's cable TV programme *Blue Tomorrow*, followed by Di Matteo, who had been put on stand-by for the Italian squad, and Morris. Di Matteo made it clear that he wouldn't be sharing a room with his compatriot Zola on any more away trips. 'He snores too much. I used to share a room with him but I had to throw him out. Now I sleep much better.' Zola threatened to follow Di Matteo and Petrescu and get a golden rinse. 'I made a promise to a friend that I would turn my hair yellow if we win the League.'

SATURDAY, 13 MARCH

Chelsea 0   West Ham 1

The world looked like being spared a straw-blond Gianfranco Zola.

Vialli shouldered the blame for the virtual collapse of Chelsea's season inside four days. The shine disappeared from the most famous bald head in football as he insisted it was his decision, and his alone, not to bring in the much-needed new striker. After three successive blanks Vialli pointed the finger only at himself. He was ready for the flak, he didn't mind; he expected it. 'It was my call, and if you think it was a mistake then you can criticise me, not the club, because there was money available. I didn't want to touch the squad I had because there is a great spirit, and we were still getting results. It was my call because the club asked me and I said I was happy with the squad I had. If it was a mistake, then it was my mistake. Four days ago we were still well. We still had Zola, Flo, Forssell and myself, although I am suspended and not available. There were enough players, and that's why I didn't want new faces.'

This admission left just as many questions unanswered. Vialli did want a new striker, otherwise why negotiate for Oscar, only to drop out when Barcelona asked a ludicrous amount for a loan? Vialli also wanted Filippo Maniero on loan, but the move fell through. He had scored freely in Serie A ever since.

Vialli didn't fear the sack. Neither did he expect it. Bates had no intention of considering such an option, yet in the aftermath of such a crushing defeat, Vialli was asked about the demands made by his chairman. 'I've got no pressure from the chairman,' he insisted. 'We get on very well with each other. I try to do my best, and he does his best. If results are not good enough he can do whatever he wants, for what he believes is for the sake of the team. I don't want to think about that now. What I really want to do is get the team into a good position. In my managerial career I want to do my best. If that is not good enough, there is nothing I can do.'

Third place and qualification for the extended Champions League was now the minimum acceptable requirement, but Vialli urgently had to revive morale and sort out the lack of conviction, otherwise third spot would go to a resurgent Leeds, just two points behind. That magical third spot was no longer guaranteed. 'This is a bad moment for us, but all matches are so tight, even against relegation sides. I had a conversation with the players after the match. We speak every time after a game. Yes, they were disappointed, but I expect a great reaction from the players and myself.'

On the other side of the fence, Redknapp was delighted with the result. Whether or not Harry was serious about his wife insisting on the team's tactics as they lay awake the night before the game discussing them, the plan 'had worked a treat'. Sinclair almost got a first-half goal during a period of total Chelsea possession, beating the offside, but a dipping shot cleared the bar. There were sufficient chances for the home side. Di Matteo bundled Lampard off the ball but saw his angled drive pushed over, then Flo headed down Babayaro's cross and Zola's first-time sideways shot rebounded off Ferdinand – one of the rare occasions when Chelsea were direct rather than stringing together a dozen passes that fizzled out in the midst of a heavily populated Hammers defence. Ferdinand also cleared off the line when a Babayaro shot was struck into the ground but still beat Hislop. Just before the interval the Hammers were unhappy when Foe's goal was disallowed for pushing.

The Eastenders showed more ambition in the second half, and it was rewarded in the seventy-fifth minute when Foe's header was saved by de Goey but Kitson turned it in, the ball clearly crossing the line. Before that a Goldbaek shot had been deflected by Ruddock, but still Hislop saved, and Flo had been over-elaborate with a couple of chances. As Alan Hansen later pointed out, Chelsea 'passed the ball to death' but lacked a cutting edge; even when Forssell came on he headed just wide from a Flo cross.

So much went wrong. The fans were shocked that Desailly as well as Le Saux were substituted on the hour, Duberry and Petrescu coming on. Vialli explained that Desailly, who had made one incredible saving tackle on Sinclair, was feeling ill as well as suffering from a hamstring twinge. He added: 'It was a stage of the game that was becoming more open and defenders had to cover more spaces.'

Three defeats all season, now two in a row. Vialli's first full season as a manager was in danger of being completely derailed unless he could rescue it in the final ten League games, and in Europe. He emphatically wrote off the title: 'Now it is a two-horse race, Manchester United and Arsenal. We shall do our best to finish in the best possible position, and try to win all the games to the end of the season.' Vialli did not agree that he was giving up the title too soon, as Chelsea were only seven points behind Manchester United with a game in hand. 'Realistic,' was his answer to that.

MONDAY, 15 MARCH

Vialli called a team meeting at training to thrash out the reasons behind the successive home defeats which had punctured morale. After back-to-back defeats at their Bridge fortress, William Hill reduced the Blues to 8–1 outsiders for the championship and a distant 22–1 to land two trophies.

Flo said: 'We have had a chat and, to be honest, we needed to talk after losing two matches in a row. We've talked about those games but also looked forward. Hopefully it will help us regain our edge, but we have to stay positive because we are still in a good position and we don't want to waste all the good work we've put in over the last six months. We have to stay focused and concentrate until the end of the season because nobody knows for sure how far we can go.'

To clear the air, Luca took all the staff to Robbie's restaurant Friends for dinner. 'It was a good meeting,' said Williams, 'and a good little night out with Luca, followed by a few speeches and the odd sing-song.'

TUESDAY, 16 MARCH

The team's thoughts turned to Europe. Chelsea's last visit to Norway had turned into an Ice Age farce in the Arctic circle outpost of Tromso, seventeen months earlier. Vialli scored twice in the last five minutes on that occasion to save them from complete humiliation in a snowstorm as the Viking part-timers skated to a 3–2 win. Chelsea steamrollered the Norwegians 7–1 in the return, but Vialli was grateful for the first-leg lead over Valerenga as temperatures in Norway were once again solidly sub-zero. The match was not in any doubt because the Ulleval stadium has undersoil heating. It would take at least a foot of snow on the day of the game to cause a postponement. Vialli planned to use the return with Egil Olsen's underdogs to relaunch Chelsea's season. 'It's up to my players now to show what they are made of. They are professionals and I expect them to respond positively and to show that we are still confident.'

Poyet, out since Boxing Day, was still waiting for the all-clear. Williams said: 'He is running, but he hasn't done any football work yet. He's still a long way off. He won't be ready for Valerenga or for next weekend either.' Despite being sidelined for two and a half months he was in second place on the club's scorers list with eleven goals in just twenty-seven appearances. Desailly's hamstring was also a concern.

Chelsea successfully persuaded the FA to move their home match against Leeds should they reach the semi-finals. They were due to face Leeds at Stamford Bridge on Monday, 5 April, just three days before the first leg of the Cup Winners Cup semi takes place. The Leeds game would be switched to 5 May. The away match at Wimbledon was also moved from Saturday, 10 April to Sunday the eleventh. If the Blues missed out in Norway, then the Leeds and Wimbledon matches would be played as scheduled.

Talks between Vialli and Desailly seemed to resolve any problem the Frenchman had, and the club's key defender would be staying.

Morris signed a new four-year contract to keep him at the Bridge until 2003, quadrupling his wages to around £10,000 a week.

WEDNESDAY, 17 MARCH

Chelsea left for Oslo without the heart of their defence; Vialli put Duberry and Lambourde on stand-by. Vialli admitted: 'We have a big match on Sunday at Aston Villa and want to make sure we can get our best possible team out for that.' Flo said: 'If it was a final then obviously Marcel and Frank would be with us here. But there is another big important game on Sunday and we want to have a strong, experienced side for that. We have Michael Duberry and Bernard Lambourde or Andy Myers to take their places here, so we shouldn't have a big problem.'

Flo was the centre of attention in his native country. He said: 'I think perhaps that a lot of people will want to talk to me, but I don't think it will be like Brian Laudrup, who was followed everywhere in Copenhagen. I am perhaps not as famous as he is. There will be a lot of Norwegians to see us in Oslo, but they will be more interested in the whole team. English football is very popular in Norway and they will be there to see all our famous players, not just me. Also, the Valerenga fans are well known for being the most passionate in Norway, so they will only be interested in me if I am on the losing team!'

Agreement was reached over an extension to Flo's contract to 2004 at £1.2m a year after talks between Hutchinson and Flo's agent, Martin Kjenner. Kjenner said: 'Both parties agreed after a half-hour meeting. There is no real speed to sign anything, so we will wait until the end of the season.' Flo had two years left to run and had attracted interest from continental clubs, but Vialli gave assurances that he would be used more frequently. The new five-year contract increased his salary by almost fifty per cent. It was third time lucky for Chelsea after talks before and after the World Cup to extend his contract. Flo said: 'I couldn't be happier right now. I'm getting back to fitness and my girlfriend is expecting our first child. We're happy and settled in London. It is true that we have agreed a new contract, and although there are a few more things to discuss, I will sit down in the summer and sign it.'

Flo had agonised over whether or not to make the trip to Oslo with his girlfriend Randy due to deliver within a fortnight. Tore said: 'Her mother's with her, but if I get the call I'll rush back. If it's a boy, maybe I'll call him Luca – if I get picked!'

Olsen was at it again, criticising Chelsea's treatment of Flo. 'I believe he should play more. Tore is a star player in Norway and so it is a little bit surprising so strong a player isn't used more. I believe a footballer needs to play, if not every week, then quite often, if he is to reach his full potential. But I'll be pleased if he's on the bench against us because I think it'll improve our chances.' Olsen felt Tore's laid-back approach didn't help. 'Tore is very humble and he doesn't say very much. I talked to him a lot when I was in London. I can say what I feel about the way Chelsea use him, but I can't do anything about it.'

Vialli was going to take a few risks, as he explained: 'We cannot relax. If we do, we get into trouble. We are out to win the game. We will not sit back and play counter-attacking football, there is no point. We will take the game to Valerenga and try and score an early goal to kill off the tie. A couple of goals would be good for our morale. If that means playing myself, then fine; even though I have not played for a couple of weeks I still feel as if I've got the experience to cope. The conditions will not be a problem – the pitch so far is playable. If it is not we will play another day, it shouldn't be a problem.'

Bates wandered down the aisle of the club's charter flight and chortled. 'Tomorrow we will find out if our squad system is up to it.'

When the team arrived, there was snow piled high around the Ulleval stadium and a stuffed polar bear in the lobby of their hotel.

THURSDAY, 18 MARCH
Valerenga 2   Chelsea 3 (agg. 2–6)

Vialli lost his rag again on the pitch, but preferred to highlight the return of English clubs as a force in European football. 'It's obviously a very good thing for the Premiership to have two sides in the last four of major European competitions. Not only will it raise English football's profile, but maybe Premiership clubs now realise they can still succeed. When Liverpool were European Cup holders, English clubs used to be absolutely unbeatable, and I hope Chelsea have gone some way towards regaining that reputation. The four teams left in the Cup Winners Cup are probably the four strongest sides who set out last year. I don't care who we get, but it would be nice to have the second leg at Stamford Bridge this time.'

The Ulleval has not always been a happy hunting ground for the English – this is where Graham Taylor's turnip seeds were sown six years ago – but tonight's mission was accomplished in the opening fourteen minutes as the holders raced into a two-goal lead. Vialli had gambled by leaving Ferrer as well as Desailly and Leboeuf at home and Zola on the bench, but Valerenga defended woefully. When teenage understudy Terry, deputising impressively for Ferrer at right-back, bent a low cross towards the far post after eleven minutes, Vialli miscued his first attempt but hoofed his second into the roof of the net from point-blank range. Valerenga left another space for Lambourde to volley the second from a half-cleared set-piece. Kjolner's header punished the holders for a momentary lapse in concentration, but Flo went on to collect a much-needed near-post header from Petrescu's cross. Flo is regarded as something of a country bumpkin in the capital because he comes from outside Oslo, and the acclaim of Chelsea's 1000-strong force was drowned out by guffawing Vikings until Carew skipped round de Goey to make it 3–2 four minutes before the break.

That put an end to the scoring, but such was Chelsea's manifest superiority that Vialli could afford to withdraw three more automatic choices – Wise, Babayaro and Flo – at the interval. In a practice-match atmosphere after half-time, only the player-manager himself appeared to retain any appetite. Although perhaps it was a little too fiery. He was fortunate to get away with swatting Walltin with his hand under the nose of the Belgian referee Amand Ancion, and he appeared to give Tran a dig in the ribs with his elbow in passing. Vialli had to wait to find out whether his luck would hold at a UEFA disciplinary commission in Switzerland. A UEFA spokesman warned: 'If a player wasn't booked, it's not necessarily the end of the matter. We have to take the referee's report and those of the match observer and UEFA delegate into consideration. Video evidence would be a last resort if we received a complaint about a player's behaviour.'

In the early hours of the morning, the plane carrying the Chelsea party, media and fans was involved in a mid-air scare as the jet was forced to abort its landing – because there were no baggage handlers waiting at Heathrow. They were just twenty-five seconds from touchdown when the Air 2000 Airbus charter jet suddenly lurched steeply back into the sky. The captain said they were being diverted to Gatwick. No one knew what was happening as, on the point of landing, the plane went into a steep climb. Some thought the undercarriage had failed. Bates called it a 'very worrying moment' and demanded an investigation. 'I spoke to the pilot, who was still as white as a ghost when he landed at Gatwick. He told me he had been in continual radio contact with Heathrow from thirty minutes out, but was then suddenly ordered to abort his landing. I intend to find out exactly what went wrong. We are not happy about it, to say the least.' Air 2000 launched an internal investigation. A spokesman said: 'The handling facilities, applied for three days earlier, were not available.' Airport operator BAA claimed there was a mix-up between Air 2000 and baggage handlers British Midland Airways – and the captain was told thirty minutes before the plane was due to land. A British Midland spokesman said: 'We understand a fax requesting handling facilities was sent to us, but we never confirmed receipt of it.'

Much earlier in the day, the new England boss announced his first squad with a message that he planned to sort out Le Saux and Fowler because of the need for harmony in the camp during the build-up to his first match in charge against Poland in the vital Euro 2000 qualifier at Wembley. Keegan said: 'They've got to in some way repair the damage that's been done. The last thing we want is any friction or bad feeling between two players who are playing for the same cause. I'm going to get the two of them in a room when I meet the players on Sunday night and I'm going to spend five, ten or fifteen minutes with them. I'll let you know what happens in that meeting, and that will be very important for the two players as well as for me. I've got to solve it now to my satisfaction, and that's what I'm going to do. But I'm pretty sure that if I get the two lads in a room with no outside influences then it can be solved. It's not something the FA have asked me to do – they've not interfered at all – it's something I feel I have to do. I want a nice atmosphere round the England camp – that's the least you should expect. Everything should be channelled towards getting a result against Poland.'

FRIDAY, 19 MARCH

Vialli landed a trip to a sunshine isle as Chelsea were paired with Spanish dark horses Real Mallorca; lucky Luca had avoided the long haul to face Lokomotiv Moscow and the short straw of Serie A leaders Lazio.

Mallorca, one-time leaders of the Primera Liga in Spain this season, were currently fourth in the table, and Vialli's assistant Williams was planning to watch them against Deportivo La Coruña at the weekend. Their star players are goalkeeper Carlos Roa, the Argentinian who broke English hearts in the World Cup shoot-out in St Etienne, and £5m-rated striker Dani Garcia, who had been tracked since Christmas by Arsenal. Mallorca had reached the last four with a comfortable 3–1 home win against Barteks of Croatia after a goalless draw in the first leg. It was the highest point in the club's eighty-three-year history, yet only 16,000 fans were in the stadium. Coach Hector Cuper said: 'Chelsea are brimming with talent. I've seen them on television this season and they are very good. But I stress one vital factor: Mallorca is very positive in every game we play and our defensive record speaks for itself.' Asked if Mallorca were approaching the matches with trepidation, he replied: 'And Chelsea too.' He added: 'I'm absolutely confident we will reach the final. Otherwise we wouldn't even bother turning up. We'll try and seize the initiative and score first.'

Club spokesman Malachy Kerrigan said: 'We are expecting thousands of Chelsea fans when the second leg is played on April twenty-second. The weather should be splendid – beach in the morning followed by the match.' But therein lay a potential problem. Chelsea had been offered just 2000 tickets; if the Spanish club came under pressure they would agree to allocate a further 1000. A minimum of 5000 Chelsea fans were expected to travel to the sunshine island for the second leg, which would leave at least 2000 ticketless fans on the streets of Palma. Fears of black-market chaos and crowd trouble loomed as UEFA reduced the capacity of the Luis Sitjar stadium to just 14,000. Real Mallorca spokesman Juan Frontera said: 'UEFA have stopped us using our 8000 standing places for European matches, and with segregation that means just 14,000 will be able to watch Chelsea. And the people of Mallorca will want to go to this one. We will wait for the arrival of Mr Colin Hutchinson, the Chelsea managing director, on Tuesday with the English police, security and travel people. Normally we only have about 100 police in the stadium, even for the bigger matches. But if they say we need 400 for this match, that's what we will get.'

Bates said: 'It is a great draw for us and the one we wanted, but it is unfair to start talking about unwanted fans travelling. The trip will be carefully planned by us and monitored by the authorities. I am sure most of the hotels in Spain will already be booked and we are looking forward to the match in every way. We want to do what Arsenal did and reach two successive European finals. And then go one better and win it. What we are achieving in Europe is just part of our progress. It was amazing that at the end of last week people were talking of a crisis. That was rubbish.'

Vialli hauled his squad in for training after only a few hours' sleep, ahead of the vital clash at Villa. Gregory declared he would 'put the boot in' on Chelsea's championship chances. Villa's own hopes of landing the title were long gone, destroyed by a dismal run of six defeats in seven games. Gregory said: 'We fancy our chances against Chelsea. We definitely owe them one, particularly since they plastered us in the Worthington Cup when we sent a deliberately weakened side to Stamford Bridge.'

Babayaro was to stand trial. He appeared at Feltham Magistrates Court, west London, accompanied by an official from Chelsea and pleaded not guilty to an indecent assault at his home. He was bailed, along with his two friends, to appear for a committal hearing.

SUNDAY, 21 MARCH
Aston Villa 0   Chelsea 3

Flo's goals and the impending return of Poyet gave new impetus to the title challenge. Vialli knew how important Flo and Zola were to his own bid. 'It is vital to have someone to stick the ball in the net. We create a lot of chances with our passing football. Tore has struggled, and that is normal after injury, but we were not too worried about him. He has responded very well and now he is fully confident, and along with Gianfranco he can help the team.'

Vialli's clever comments after the defeat by West Ham had lessened the weight of expectation, and Gregory's caustic pre-match claims that they were not good enough to lift the title blew up in his face as Chelsea swept back into third place, just three points behind Arsenal with a game in hand, and two on leaders United.

The only surprise was that it took Chelsea so long to translate their superiority into something tangible. It wasn't until the thirteenth minute of the second half that Flo collected his tenth goal and maintained his record of scoring against Villa in all three of their meetings. Ferrer supplied the pass for him to outpace Barry and deceive Southgate before lifting the ball beyond Bosnich. Bosnich went on to prevent an embarrassing glut of goals. Any thoughts of tiredness following the mid-week trip were dispelled in the final minutes, when Chelsea gained the just rewards for their performance as Villa crumbled: Flo became provider to set up Goldbaek, who drove in his fourth goal, and Morris rounded off a brilliant performance of his own with a beautiful chip to connect with Flo's run from deep. The Norwegian's control and finish were exquisite.

The only downside was Wise's involvement in a slanging match with Villa physio Jim Walker that saw him collect another suspension. Wise would miss his fifteenth game against Wimbledon, joined by Desailly, booked after a minor skirmish with Stan Collymore at the end of the first half. Perhaps Wise's outburst was out of frustration at not being able to produce the goals that the actions of himself, Goldbaek and Morris deserved.

Vialli now cranked up the psychological warfare in the title race, although he conceded it would take a slip-up from both United and Arsenal to completely open the door. 'I think we are still in a great position to finish the season. We will play our remaining games like World Cup finals. It's not up to us because Manchester United and Arsenal are winning games week in, week out. But we can't do any more than we are doing at the moment to try to win the title.' Flo also believed they were right back in the picture. 'We still want to fight for the title. It was a good win and we'll keep fighting. Maybe we've put some pressure on the people above us and we have to hope they drop some points.'

Flo was a pleased man. 'I feel I'm back in form now as I was certainly struggling. My confidence is getting better and I felt much better after getting the goal in Norway. I really needed those goals. You worry when you go a long time without scoring, especially when the team has been struggling to create goals. In training we talked about this and about how I have got to get in the box more with Gianfranco. It's always hard when you come back. I feel the tempo in my body is not as sharp as it was, but you just have to play more matches to get it back, and today I felt very good.'

Manchester United followed up Chelsea's morning game by destroying Everton 3–1 in a second-half blitz, while Arsenal won 2–0 at home to Coventry on the Saturday, so Vialli's side were still seven points off top spot, with a game in hand on the two sides above them.

The England players met up at 9.15 p.m. after Keegan had helped resolve the dispute between Le Saux and Fowler. They had shaken hands at their Buckinghamshire HQ and held a twenty-minute clear-the-air session with Keegan, who said: 'I'm delighted Graeme and Robbie were able to shake hands even before I asked them to come to our meeting. It was important for them to be able to do so in private, rather than publicly. I'm satisfied our preparations for such an important game will not be disrupted either as a team or with them as individuals by what may have happened in the past. As far as I'm concerned, the issue is over and done with.'

Keegan had threatened to send the pair home from his squad if they didn't patch things up. 'We were in the room for twenty minutes and both players were able to talk at ease with each other. Straight away I said that's good enough for me, as they both desperately want to play for England. That was what came out most strongly as I'd said I didn't want players fighting and squabbling and ignoring each other. One of them, I can't remember which one, said to the other it would be a shame as they both deserved to be here – and they do.'

MONDAY, 22 MARCH

Zola eagerly awaited Poyet's return. 'It will be a huge boost for us to have him back. It could be a crucial factor. I only hope it won't happen too late. When you are playing against a team with ten men behind the ball, it's so tough to break them down. That's when a player like Gus can make all the difference. He is so powerful in the air and makes great runs into the box.'

Vialli hoped to snap up Garcia for a cut-price fee before Thursday's transfer deadline, but Barcelona took up an option to extend Garcia's contract for another two years – even though he did not want to stay. Garcia fumed: 'They sent me a letter to tell me, although the manager, Louis Van Gaal, has not said anything to me. Seeing how little I feature in their plans, I don't know what to think. I don't know why they have done it.' Garcia was now contracted to Barca until June 2001, sending his transfer valuation up to £5m. That was far more than Chelsea were willing to pay, especially as Flo was fit and back in form.

TUESDAY, 23 MARCH

Zola believed Keegan should give Wise an England recall. 'Dennis, in my opinion, is a really great player. He's one of our most important players because you know you can rely on him all the time. He's experienced and in my opinion it's a pity he doesn't play for the national team.'

Bates wanted the Cup Winners Cup final switched from Villa Park to Wembley. A request to UEFA president Lennart Johansson was made when he visited England. Bates said: 'We think Wembley would be the perfect stadium to end the Cup Winners Cup. The UEFA president knows how we feel and the rest is up to him.' But Bates's wish was rejected out of hand. A UEFA spokesman said: 'The stadium for the final was decided on in October. There is no chance of moving it.'

WEDNESDAY, 24 MARCH

Flo refused to play for Norway in a vital Euro 2000 tie in Athens because of the imminent birth of his child. The Norwegian FA put a private jet on stand-by at Heathrow to whisk Flo over to Athens if Randy gave birth ahead of the game.

Flo was involved in a new row over his ankle operation, with the hospital demanding payment of the £1500 bill. Flo considered the dispute 'silly', as he explained: 'It's difficult to pay a bill when I haven't received one yet. I'll pay the bill as soon as it comes.' Hospital chief Jan Stadass was 'very angry' with the surgeon who said the bill would be paid following the operation in January. Stadass said: 'It is a disgrace if Flo has not paid, but, of course, I will have to check who has actually sent the bill, and if not, why not.'

Le Saux broke his silence in his *Evening Standard* column to insist that he didn't want to add to Keegan's statement, other than to say: 'I am professional and we're all united in a common cause this week. I would say, though, that the last few weeks have been difficult, with so much media attention focused on me and some inevitably negative reaction from fans into the bargain. There was one match, the FA Cup tie up at Manchester United, in which I just felt that one mistimed tackle, one accidental challenge, would bring everything crashing down. For that match, I will admit, I just concentrated on keeping out of the way, which is not my normal way of doing things.'

Transfer deadline day was imminent, but there was no movement, although Hughes secured an extended loan earlier in the week. Le Saux was linked with Paris St Germain, but it would take at least a £6m bid to prise him away, and that would be a major stumbling block.

THURSDAY, 25 MARCH

Wilkins remained tight-lipped over whether he would replace Rix. He insisted he had used Harlington to get fit for the Masters tournament, but conceded that he also took 'warm-down' sessions with the Chelsea players. He said: 'I haven't been offered a coaching appointment, so at the moment any job with Chelsea is purely hypothetical. At the moment there aren't any vacancies anyway.'

FRIDAY, 26 MARCH

Rix was sentenced to a total of twelve months' imprisonment. He looked shaken as he was sentenced by Judge Timothy Pontius at Knightsbridge Crown Court. Rix was also told by the judge that he would have to remain on the sex offenders register for the next ten years. He would be released after serving half the sentence, after which he would remain subject to the terms of licence.

The judge said that the girl had regarded Rix as a kind man and had trusted him, and 'therefore was willing to go at your invitation to your house and your hotel bedroom'. He accepted the girl made no strong protests to Rix's advances. In court, it was revealed that the victim's family lived near Rix in London and are Chelsea supporters. The judge pointed out that Rix had a pornographic movie on the television in his hotel room, and that he had refused to use a condom despite the girl's specific requests and his knowledge that she was a virgin at the time.

Judge Pontius told Rix: 'These offences took place when she was only weeks short of her sixteenth birthday, the age of consent. Yet at the time of the offences she was plainly a girl who was fascinated and flattered by the attentions of a man who was to her knowledge a celebrity, attended by the glamour of fame and success.' He added: 'There is no evidence in this case at all to suggest this girl herself deliberately set out to seduce you, no evidence that she was the one who made all the running, and no evidence of her initiating any sexual activity, merely a response of a teenage girl to your words of flattery.' Rix's QC, Desmond de Silva, had said that the girl had lied about her age, pursued Rix by phone, and led him on. The judge dismissed this as an 'unjustified attack'; jailing Rix would be an 'important deterrent'.

Bob Wilson had been called as a character witness, telling the court Rix was an 'inspirational' coach and the backbone of Chelsea's success, adding that the case had had a 'devastating' effect on Rix and his family.

After the hearing, Hutchinson said: 'He is probably unemployable in football, but the job will be kept open and he will return to his post. That is the wish of the club, the wish of the manager Gianluca Vialli, and the wish of the players. Chelsea do not condone what Graham Rix did, but he is paying a very, very high price for one mistake. He will serve the sentence and the stigma will stay with him for the rest of his life.' His agent, Dennis Roach, agreed: 'It's a severe sentence for a moment of weakness.' Rix sent a message of thanks to Bates, and to his wife, Gill, 'for her loyalty'.

Chelsea became the subject of condemnation for not sacking Rix. League Managers Association chief executive John Barnwell said: 'What Chelsea have decided is their prerogative as a football club. It's debatable as to whether that's the right thing or the wrong thing. As for the LMA's position, if that is Chelsea's stance and with their being close to the situation, then you have to respect their position. They would not have gone into it lightly.' The FA issued a statement: 'This is clearly a serious matter. We will be in consultation with Chelsea FC. Another statement will be issued when our consultations are completed.'

Despite the outrage in some quarters that Rix was not dismissed by Chelsea, the players were very supportive. Zola, who was having a short break in Sardinia, said: 'I am very pleased that Graham Rix will still have a job with Chelsea when he comes out of prison. That is something I think all the players will be glad to hear. He is a very good coach. The results we have achieved prove that. It is good to know we will benefit from his professional abilities in the future.'

Rix spent his first night in jail in a segregated cell at one of Britain's toughest prisons. He was sent to Wandsworth Prison, south London, and, as a convicted sex offender, was immediately sent to the Vulnerable Prisoners Unit where inmates on Rule 43, which protects them from attack by other prisoners, are housed. There are more than 300 sex offenders in the VPU at Wandsworth, and Rix rubbed shoulders with about seventy-five of them on his wing.

MONDAY, 29 MARCH

It was Wilkins's first day at work. 'I thoroughly enjoyed the session, although obviously I would much rather it had been under different circumstances. The fact that I have been able to get friendly with the players over the last three weeks made things easier for me. People watched me one day standing next to Zola as he was practising free-kicks and assumed I was coaching him. How absurd! Franco is such a great example to any kids coming into the game. He is first on the training pitch, doing some drills between cones, then he stays behind to practise his free-kicks. Funny how many goals he scores from them, isn't it? The more he practises the luckier he gets. His example has rubbed off on youngsters like Jody Morris.

'It was a comfortable session and a good first day at the office. Gianluca just concentrated on his training and allowed me to get on with things. I have to say that he trains very hard. Luca still works himself into the ground, and he is extraordinarily fit. The players here have a tremendous rapport and an excellent team spirit. They're a lovely bunch of lads. Luca's very much the boss; it's just up to me to organise it and get the session on.

'From here on in it's got to be hard work, hard graft, and I'm sure then we can achieve success. It's pleasant to be back. I enjoy working with players on the training field rather than anything else. These guys at Chelsea are fantastic footballers and I've been so impressed with them. Coaching them will not be hard because they are such great professionals.'

TUESDAY, 30 MARCH

Leboeuf agreed an extension to his contract to keep him at the club until 2002, ending all concerns over his future. It would be signed in the summer because it missed Thursday's deadline, which is for the registration of new contracts as well as for transfers. The £30,000-a-week deal closed the gap on the £2m-a-year top earners at the club.

De Goey was offered a two-year extension to keep him until 2003, while Morris was celebrating his recently signed four-year extension with a £70,000 Porsche.

WEDNESDAY, 31 MARCH

In-demand Mallorca keeper Carlos Roa was considering quitting at the end of the season, according to club coach Cuper. The Argentinian World Cup star, in outstanding form and determined to shut out Chelsea in the Cup Winners Cup semi-final, had attracted interest from a host of European clubs, including Manchester United, who had him earmarked as a possible replacement for Peter Schmeichel.

April...
April...
April

*Poyet back with a goal ... top three
separated by one point ... then out of
Europe and three successive draws wreck
last chance of title*

THURSDAY, I APRIL

Boys-only nights out were on the menu for Luca. Jody Morris explained: 'There have been a few times when we have had to bomb out our wives and mates. We all go out to dinner and have a chaps night out. It's a Chelsea thing. The women may not always be that happy, but I think Gianluca is a good geezer. He has created an amazing atmosphere and spirit at this club in the hope that it rubs off on the pitch. When a player is good friends with a team-mate, he is more likely to run that extra few yards to help someone out.' Luca's assistant Gwyn Williams tipped the twenty-year-old to be a candidate for player of the season for his progress. Morris said: 'I'm delighted to have been getting a good run in the team, particularly with all the fantastic players in the squad. We are looking for a place in the Champions League.'

Gus Poyet was back on the bench for the start of the vital Easter programme after three months out and a week of full training. 'Having Gustavo back will be a big boost for the squad,' said Eddie Newton. 'We need all our best players available at this stage in the season.' A measure of his influence was that, despite his absence, he was to be offered a new three-year contract.

Petrescu, with just one more season left on his contract, wanted talks on a new contract to extend his career at the Bridge, but Gullit was monitoring the situation. Petrescu said: 'I hope to still be at Chelsea next year, but the club have not made me an offer.'

Desailly dismissed the notion players earned too much when he said: 'You can't say a footballer earns too much in relation to an electrician because there's no comparison. A lot of people could be electricians and I do respect them. That doesn't alter the fact that footballers have a special talent. Yet Ronaldo doesn't even earn ten per cent of what's made by the best boxer, Formula One driver or American footballer. So don't come to me and ask if it's decent a footballer should earn so much. It really kills me when people reproach us with that.'

Desailly felt that young English superstars such as Beckham, Owen, Campbell, Morris and Scholes needed to leave the Premiership and play in Italy to progress. He explained: 'Psychologically, you need to improve in this country, but that is happening with Chelsea and Manchester United doing well in Europe. You have to be more open, and maybe you can see that with Steve McManaman going to Real Madrid this summer. I think you need a few more players to go away and learn the Italian and Spanish way of playing and come back with that experience. The tactical side is so important and the foreigners can give you new views on this. I see it happening at Chelsea. You can see Jody Morris, Mark Nicholls and Michael Duberry learning from Luca. Even Graeme Le Saux has learned a lot from him. Michael Duberry is a typically English defender. He is strong, he is bold and he doesn't give anything away at the back, but he doesn't mind giving the ball away. Now he is looking at how we are training and realising that the tactical side is important, that you can man-mark or play zonally in a line, that you don't have to throw the ball away. They are all learning. Graeme Le Saux is a great player, but he used to play the diagonal low ball all the time. Now he is trying to pass it.'

Old boy Graeme Stuart, a record £1.1m signing from Sheffield United, was ready for his debut for Charlton on Saturday, but John Barnes was out with a groin injury, while Alan Curbishley opted to play Yugoslav keeper Sasa Ilic despite the war in the Balkans. Whatever the outcome, Stuart was ready for a champagne reunion with Williams, the man who took him to the Bridge at the age of fourteen. 'If we lose, anything will taste like flat beer, but if we win I'll happily buy Gwyn champagne. I trained with Wimbledon and Arsenal, but once Gwyn took me to Cheslea there was no other club for me. I enjoyed every minute at Chelsea, but I've lost touch with Gwyn a bit over the years and I'm looking forward to meeting him again. There have been so many changes at Stamford Bridge since I left six years ago that I think Gwyn is the only survivor.'

FRIDAY, 2 APRIL

Bates warned Manchester United and Arsenal, in his usual modest style, that Chelsea had the easier of the run-ins. 'All the signs are that this is going to be the most successful season at the club since I've been here. I know we won two cups last season, but hopefully we will win the Cup Winners Cup again and also get into the Champions League despite all the horrendous injuries we've had, which we don't tend to talk about the way other clubs do. United have got injuries and they've also got a very heavy fixture schedule. Let's hope they draw their FA Cup semi-final against Arsenal which would give them more of a fixture congestion. The problem with Arsenal is that they never concede any goals, but we're still there. It's tense, but we should enjoy it. It's really important that we go into the new millennium as one of the top clubs in Europe – then, of course, the challenge is to stay there.'

Bates recalled the last time Chelsea went into the Easter programme with thoughts of the title. Successive heavy defeats in 1989 should have made the chairman wary of counting his Easter chickens. Bates said: 'We lost four-nil at home to West Ham and then six-nil at QPR. That was a very hard Easter – ten goals without reply – and Eddie Niedzwiecki was injured. We should have signed another great goalkeeper immediately, but John Hollins didn't, he kept prevaricating. That's what really cost us then, but this season is a bit different: we only have one game over Easter.'

Bates felt his team were far too strong for struggling Charlton. 'We know Charlton won't be easy because they are fighting to stay up when we all thought they would be dead at the start of the season, and they've spent a bit of money in their terms, but class should tell and I think we've got more class than them. Then we ought to beat Mallorca, although nothing in life is certain, and reach the Cup Winners Cup final at Villa Park, where we have a good record. If it was a Chelsea–Lazio final, that would be a real measure of our progress. Mind you, I said that about playing Real Madrid in the Super Cup and we beat them, which technically made us champions of Europe.'

Joe Kinnear, recovering from a heart attack, was an interested observer as the Wimbledon team prepared to play a key role in the destiny of the title, first at home to United, a week later playing Chelsea, and then Arsenal. He said: 'It's staggering that all three clubs have only lost three games this season, and Arsenal are still unbeaten at home, but other statistics stand out. For United and Arsenal, it's about goals: scored in one case, not conceded in the other. In thirty Premiership matches Arsenal have conceded just thirteen goals, only four at Highbury. Remember people questioning the age of their defence, the oldest in the Premiership? But we are renowned for spoiling a few parties, so it's going to make the next few weeks interesting. We've got quite a say in the championship.'

SATURDAY, 3 APRIL

Charlton Athletic 0 Chelsea 1

Three points snatched in a tough derby nudged Chelsea right back into the title race, five points behind Manchester United with a game in hand. But Luca refused to get excited: 'We are third and the two in front of us are two great sides. They are more experienced, and I can't see them throwing away the chance to win the title. United may have drawn today, but I don't think they'll lose their way.' Vialli insisted it was not a psychological strategy. 'I always say what I think. If we only had one team in front of us we might make it.' Only when pressed did Vialli add: 'If we win our game in hand. If, if – but it is difficult. We're not talking about poor teams, we are talking about Arsenal and Manchester United. They may have only drawn their games today but they have not lost the chance to win the championship. You can bet they will win again next time.'

Di Matteo admitted Rix's absence was striking a blow at a crucial time in the campaign. It was a matter Vialli pointedly refused to talk about. Di Matteo said: 'Graham was a vital part of the team and it has been strange and difficult not working with him at the training ground. We miss him. Ray Wilkins has replaced him, though, and he wants to be succeessful like the rest of us. He is a good person. Hopefully we can keep Graham cheerful by winning. It would be nice to visit him. All the players want to see him, but we cannot. He can see just one person every two weeks and it is up to him who he sees. That is sad. Our thoughts are with Graham and we wish him well in prison.'

Di Matteo had plundered the untidiest of winners in the twelfth minute, courtesy of some dreadful faffing around by Charlton's goalkeeper and defender Carl Tiler. Desailly and Leboeuf then calmly thwarted all Charlton's attempts to get back in the game after Chelsea switched off for the second half. Vialli said: 'Marcel showed his commitment to Chelsea. He was in the right frame of mind. He'd played two matches for France and had only been back for two days. He did very well. I thought in the first half Charlton were a bit afraid of us, but they came back, and although it was not pretty they made it hard. Obviously we were the better team, but I think they can stay up.'

The gritty win had settled the nerves jangled by that uncharacteristic blip against United in the FA Cup and the Hammers at Stamford Bridge. Di Matteo was more upbeat than his manager about Chelsea's title hopes: 'Of course we can still win the title. What would be the point going out there if we didn't think we could? We have got this far and this near, and we are definitely not going to give up now. Look at the table: we are just five points behind United and one behind Arsenal. We have a game in hand on both of those teams and there are a lot of points up for grabs. United are in pole position, but this win has kept us on their heels. We are not really in a different position to the one before the game, although you'd have to say that our chances have increased slightly. Yet it's still up to Manchester United and Arsenal. They are both very, very strong and tend not to lose many games. All we can do is win our games and see what happens.'

Alan Curbishley described Chelsea's winner as a 'howler'. He said: 'Sasa called for it but Carl Tiler decided to go for it, and that's what decided the match. If Chelsea had finished off one of their great moves early on we'd have perhaps had no complaints, but the goal that beat us was down to bad play on our part.' Ilic, a Serb, had defied a call from the Yugoslav FA to boycott domestic matches, and wore a black armband throughout the match.

De Goey had come off after the first half with an attack of migraine, exacerbated by the incessant drum beat behind his goal throughout the first half. Physio Mike Banks said: 'He felt so ill at half-time. He was complaining of feeling faint and of light-headedness. It was too risky to let him continue. He rested the remainder of the weekend.' It was a rare chance for Hitchcock. Wise said: 'So Hitchy reappeared in the Chelsea goal and I saw one of the funniest things I've ever seen in football: he fell over after just thirty seconds on a pass back. It was as if someone had shot him. Then a crane came over and picked him up and he booted the ball away.'

The skipper also welcomed back Poyet. 'It was great to see him back when he came on as a substitute. We've missed him. He's such a big personality in the dressing room.' Poyet said: 'Once again my season has been interrupted by injury but, unlike last year, I still have a chance of playing a big part in trying to win some trophies for Chelsea.'

SUNDAY, 4 APRIL

Bates was preparing his programme notes for Thursday's game after more adverse publicity over Rix. Convict no. CW7290, in cell K49, was indirectly criticised by club patron Ruth Harding. Matthew Harding's widow said: 'We cannot have this kind of thing in football clubs.' And Labour MP Claire Ward was unimpressed with the then Minister of Sport Tony Banks's reply to her question in the House, 'Does he agree the decision by Chelsea to keep open the job for Graham Rix after his conviction is a cynical disregard for the views of the family and a step back in making football accessible to all?' Banks had replied: 'Some may feel the club has erred in its judgement so soon after the sentence, but it's a matter for them to decide and Rix will suffer his due penalty as he should.' The MP pointed out that Banks's response contrasted with his haste in calling for the head of Glenn Hoddle.

The chairman described his notes as 'Churchillian', but they did not receive a good press – naturally enough, with so many references to the 'gutter press'.

'Let me make it quite clear,' he wrote. 'I have no sympathy for Graham Rix, nor do I condone his behaviour. But he is neither a pervert or a paedophile. I have no sympathy for the girl involved, but I have a great deal of sympathy for Rix's four innocent children who can now look forward to a childhood of vilification and persecution. We have been criticised for announcing our decision so quickly to keep Rix's job open, but the punishment for Rix's offence was appallingly harsh. Chelsea have no intention of adding to it. He will resume his duties upon release. He is not being paid in the interim, although his family will be provided for. Chelsea look after their own.'

He was adamant he would not be influenced by the media: 'Unlike some clubs, the gutter press will not be allowed to run Chelsea football club. That is the duty of the board, including the chairman. We must make the decisions, as we see them in the best interests of justice and Chelsea football club irrespective of media-manipulated so-called public opinion. Popularity is rightly for others, such as players and coaches. Directors must not be swayed by the hysteria whipped up in the media of the day within their short attention span. We have been criticised for announcing our decision so quickly to keep Rix's job open by the very same people who have been pestering me for a statement on his future since his arrest.'

Bates also delved into the detail of the case, firstly fighting the indecent assault charge. 'This consisted of dancing and french kissing, to which the girl willingly responded. The girl admitted that she had indulged in such actions before, including having her breasts fondled. For that Rix got four months. Secondly, between 8 January 1998 and 27 February 1998 the girl phoned Rix using her mobile no less than nineteen times. Rix did not phone her once. Thirdly, the girl lied about her age on two occasions, saying she was two months short of her seventeenth birthday, and she had admitted that she lied. Her father accepted that, as recorded on his tape. Fourthly, the girl told Rix she was on the pill – why? Fifthly, the girl consistently lied to her parents as to her whereabouts, claiming she was staying overnight with friends. Sixthly, the girl, having told her sister that she was visiting a girlfriend, of her own volition made a journey across London from Fulham to Kensington, went to Rix's hotel room after ten p.m. and participated in the acts which Rix was charged with. There was no force used. It was by consent, and the girl was used to drink. Afterwards, the girl refused to go home because she had told her family that she would be out all night (if your fifteen-year-old daughter had told you that, would you not make further enquiries?). For that the judge gave Rix eight months in jail. Where's the justice?'

Gaby Shenton, of children's charity Kidscape, branded Bates's comments 'repellent, repugnant and horrific', adding: 'It seems Chelsea are willing to sacrifice morality for the sake of a good coach.' NSPCC head of policy Liz Atkins said: 'Chelsea's efforts should be directed towards protecting children and young people rather than protecting a man who has been convicted of a serious sexual offence against a child.'

MONDAY, 5 APRIL

So much for being a long-term successor to Schmeichel: Carlos Roa's contract expires in two years, but he won't negotiate a new one because he believes the dead are merely sleeping while they await the resurrection with the 'second coming'. He said: 'The earth is going to end in 2001. There is no point accepting a new contract. In fact, I am considering packing in football at the end of the season and preparing for everything that is going to happen.'

Coach Cuper said: 'It's true. Carlos is thinking of retiring at the end of the season. On current form he is the best goalkeeper in the world, and there's simply no one better at saving penalties. He practises, and there is no harder trainer in Spain. He is crucial to our team. If Chelsea want to beat Mallorca they will have to do well to beat Carlos Roa. Chelsea are technically very good, but that won't intimidate us. I'd never regard an opposing team as one we cannot beat. As far as I'm concerned we are always the favourites.'

WEDNESDAY, 7 APRIL

Vialli selected himself to partner Zola up front, leaving Wilkins in charge on the bench, and not for the first time opted to avoid the press conference. The last time Wilkins was in charge on the touchlines Fulham had scraped into the Second Division play-offs despite losing 2–1 at home to Watford; he was sacked the following week by Keegan. Now Vialli asked him to help coax the holders through a tricky semi-final first leg. Wilkins said: 'I've been asked to do this role by Luca and I feel happy doing it. During my time out of the game I've watched a lot of Italian and Spanish football and I've been doing my best to keep up with it. It would be difficult for Luca to assess everything that's happening on the pitch, so I will look after things on the sidelines – and, hopefully, make the right decisions. Since I came back to Chelsea I've been out to dinner several times with Luca and I believe I know his way of thinking in relation to football matters. Being in the dugout with him for the first time on Saturday was a good experience, and I'm ready for the challenge if the decisions are down to me this time.'

In his *Evening Standard* column, Le Saux wrote: 'We know we're on the brink of achieving things at the club yet no one is talking about it ... The only difference has been that Ray Wilkins has replaced Graham Rix, but even that was a gradual process. Ray had already been at the club for a couple of weeks in case the worst-case scenario became a reality with Graham – as it so proved. I intend to write to Graham in the near future, as do most of the squad, but in the meantime Ray's arrival has been almost seamless. The players at the club really are a good bunch and they've all readily accepted him.'

Mallorca had beaten mighty Barcelona four times this season – twice in the Primera Liga, then home and away in the Spanish Super Cup. Ferrer warned:

'Maybe they don't have any superstars, but Mallorca are difficult to beat and dangerous on the break. I can remember us losing to them by five goals once when I was at Barcelona, and they have been challenging for a UEFA Cup place for the last three or four years despite selling some of their best players. It's all about confidence at Mallorca at the moment. Cuper has got them believing they can beat anybody, so they will come here without any fear. I think they were very happy to get the away game first because they will feel they can get a result on their own pitch. It is not the best surface, because it is so dry there the grass can be very thin. I have played there a couple of times and the surface does give them an advantage. The fans can be noisy, too, but it is not an especially intimidating place to go.'

Poyet had played alongside Dani at Real Zaragoza. He warned: 'He is a skilful player who can play just behind the front two or, as he is now, as an out-and-out striker. He joined Zaragoza from Madrid and did well for us, sometimes playing up front and sometimes linking the attack and midfield, depending on what formation we played. When he went back to Real Madrid he didn't play a lot and so he was there just one year and moved on to Mallorca. I think he is now playing the best football of his career. His anticipations are very good and he uses space very well. I think he will give us problems if we allow him too much time on the ball, or if we leave too much space behind the defence. He is very quick and we must close him down.'

Vialli, in his programme notes, envisaged a tough tie: 'I think the two clubs are quite similar in the way we are contending with the giants: Real Madrid, Barcelona, Arsenal, Manchester United. We are both playing good football, getting results and winning trophies. There's a feeling of enthusiasm, optimism, enjoyable football and great spirit in the team plus a good relationship with the supporters. Both clubs have got a very charming and fascinating style. So I have to warn our supporters who think it might be easy for us to beat Mallorca. They are a very good team with the best defensive record in the Spanish League, and up front they've got quick, sharp, skilful, deadly strikers, so I presume that they will defend deep and try to play counter-attack. It is important for us not to concede. That is the priority.'

He also asked the supporters to get behind Wilkins: 'Because of what happened to Ricco, you'll see on the bench a very familiar face to all of you, Ray Wilkins. He's come in to help us out in Ricco's absence for the next few months, and he'll give his all to his old cause to make things better. It's a pleasure and a privilege to work alongside such a gentleman and a very good manager. Give him applause, but don't forget to back the team as well. This is Europe and there's no tomorrow. It is the last time you will see us at home in Europe this season.'

THURSDAY, 8 APRIL

Chelsea 1   Real Mallorca 1

During the warm-up to the Liverpool game Zola had cracked a ball into the Matthew Harding Stand, hitting Philip Copper from the Isle of Wight and breaking his glasses. Franco invited the eight-year-old into the dressing room tonight and showed him around behind the scenes.

Wilkins made his debut in the Bridge dugout, although Vialli picked the side and made the crucial substitution at half-time. It was clear that the boss was not happy in the dressing room during the interval. Flo said: 'Gianluca Vialli was very angry at half-time. He wanted us to fight harder.' Within minutes of Flo emerging from the bench he had preserved the holders' forty-one-year unbeaten home record in Europe. It was an exceptional volley by Flo, especially as he had come on cold.

The eccentric Roa combined natural brilliance with some divine intervention to underline the Spanish team's reputation as the Arsenal of the Primera Liga with only twenty-one goals conceded in twenty-eight League games. Roa might be tagged the 'vegetable' in Spain for his vegetarianism and off-beat beliefs, but he made the most of his talent. He produced some orthodox handling, catching every cross and pushing away long-range shots from Wise, Morris and Babayaro. The Nigerian seemed hypnotised in front of an almost open goal, crashing his shot into the ground and allowing Roa to scramble back and save.

Chelsea paid dearly for that miss when Dani strode intelligently on to a through-ball from Veljko Paunovic and skipped around the advancing de Goey before cracking his shot into the far corner of the open goal with Leboeuf unable to recover.

Desailly scraped the outside of the post with a header from a Petrescu cross five minutes before the interval, and after the break Flo came on to rescue his side. One of Leboeuf's weighted long-range passes was superbly controlled first time by Petrescu, and when the Romanian crossed to the far post Zola won the header. The ball bounced off Marcelino and Flo reacted instantly, whipping it away from the defender first time and slamming into the roof of the net. After an hour Poyet made his entrance in place of Zola, and it wasn't long before he headed just wide from a Petrescu cross. Again a Petrescu cross gave Vialli his first and only chance, but his close-range header produced another save.

But with so little to choose between these teams a penalty shoot-out in Majorca was a distinct possibility. This was Chelsea's biggest test in Europe, confronting a team of similar technique who gave little away at the back, so Wilkins was not too despondent about the draw which left Chelsea needing to score on the sunshine isle. 'We still have a very good chance. We are the type of side that is always capable of scoring goals away from home. Another higher-scoring draw is all right for us with the away-goals rule.'

Wise was captured on TV taking a bite out of Marcelino after the defender had scored his face with his nails. Dirty Den escaped only because the referee missed it. Marcelino said: 'Wise tried to bite me and provoke me into a reaction.' The two squared up after sixty-one minutes when the Spanish defender caught hold of Wise and twisted his ear. Marcelino added: 'I had to be cool and quiet not to get involved. I know the TV shows he tried to bite me, but I didn't feel anything. We knew a lot about Wise; we've seen him on television in the Premiership and we know what he is like – good player, but with an intense character. I'm not going to make an official complaint to UEFA about what he did. That's his way of playing, it's his problem.' Wilkins said: 'I never saw it. We'll have to look at the video and see what the situation is.' Wise had to wait for UEFA delegate Sajn Vlado of Slovenia and match observer Bjorck Lars-Ake of Sweden to file their reports before learning whether or not his bite will leave another scar on his disciplinary record. Renowned joker Wise refused to talk about the incident after the match, saying with a grin: 'No, I'm not talking to anybody about anything.' Wise told team-mates and management that his action was only a retaliatory gesture which did not inflict physical damage and was never intended to do so.

Mallorca's Argentine coach Hector Cuper claimed: 'For twenty-five minutes we were completely in control of the game. But the referee wasn't on our side and there were clearly a few things that went against us. But we won't change our style for the second leg because it worked so well here.'

Later, Vialli talked about the significance of the tie and how it would affect the second leg. 'The Real Mallorca team had a good attitude. They came here with a very organised, very disciplined way of defending and they held us out for all of the ninety minutes, except when Tore volleyed so wonderfully into the back of their net. We know we have to score there. Until we score, Mallorca are the favourites, but we can live with that. We will be patient. One goal will be enough to begin with.'

FRIDAY, 9 APRIL

Le Saux emerged tight-lipped from a two-hour meeting with the FA's disciplinary commission. He dashed out of St Andrews and jumped straight into a taxi just after one p.m., refusing to speak as he left the hearing accompanied by Hutchinson. Le Saux's defence, conducted by one of the country's top legal experts, was based on 'gay' taunts, not covered by the FA rule book.

Fowler was hit by a six-match ban and found guilty on two misconduct charges. He was also fined £32,000 for his cocaine-sniffing miming against Everton. Some way to celebrate his twenty-fourth birthday! Fowler's anger was increased by the FA's more lenient view of Le Saux's punch, which earned a one-game ban and a £5000 fine. His solicitor, Kevin Dooley, declared: 'Robbie is deeply disappointed over what he regards as an unjust and disproportionate sentence.' The FA's acting chief executive, David Davies, warned: 'Any appeal would have the power to increase Robbie Fowler's sentence, as well as reduce or remove it.'

Davies, who refused to answer further questions on legal advice, added: 'Le Saux spoke of being subjected to a torrent of abuse from a fellow professional about being gay. Mutual respect between players should be a minimum requirement. Highly paid internationals are role models, although we must also accept that as human beings they can occasionally make mistakes. Both Fowler and Le Saux admitted all charges. Graeme made no attempt to excuse what happened. But equally he believes he was subjected to considerable provocation.' As for Fowler's heavily criticised line-sniffing antics, Davies said: 'The FA are pledged to fight drug abuse. Our stand on that issue is well known and well received throughout Europe. We are pleased that Robbie has agreed to help Liverpool police in their anti-drugs campaign.'

Ferrer cleared fears of a major injury worry after limping off against Mallorca – it was only a bout of cramp – but he was being left on the bench for the vital Premiership derby at neighbouring Wimbledon. Lambourde replaced him. Wise and Desailly were replaced by Duberry and Di Matteo as they served one-match bans for five yellow cards. Forssell and Goldbaek were Cup-tied and were back in the squad.

Wilkins said: 'I don't think we'll have a problem concentrating the players' minds on Sunday's match. It will be quite a different sort of game I am sure, but they are a good bunch of lads here and they will be back up for it. Nights like the one against Mallorca are a real bonus. It was like chess out there at times, but Sunday will be back to the more traditional English type of tussle.'

With United and Arsenal contesting their epic semi-final, a win would put Chelsea two points behind United and one adrift of Arsenal, who would have played one extra.

Leboeuf, never a lover of the Dons style, said: 'It is a tough game on a rubbish pitch, but hopefully we'll take three points. It is always a battle against them. You have to fight. There is never a good time to be playing Wimbledon. It is always special for them to play us and they're always up for it. They try to ridicule us. After a tough European game this is not a fixture I would have picked for us. European football is more technical and enjoyable. We know Wimbledon will try and play the ball in the air. They have tall players and it suits their style. But they also have quality players. It is a tough run-in to the end of the season, yet if we want to be champions we must get used to it.' Caretaker coach Dave Kemp, standing in for Kinnear after his heart trouble, reacted to Leboeuf's comments: 'If he's saying he wants a battle that's good, we'll give him one. But it's disappointing that he feels he has to bring up the old cliché that Wimbledon can only win by fighting. I think everyone knows how far this club has moved on and we are now a very good footballing side, hopefully good enough to give Chelsea a tough test.'

SUNDAY, 11 APRIL
Wimbledon 1   Chelsea 2
Chelsea came away from Selhurst Park with the best away record in the Premiership. Victory at Middlesbrough on Wednesday would now take them back to the Premiership summit while United and the Gunners re-ignited their FA Cup war of attrition, a draining distraction to Chelsea's advantage.

Wise missed his fifteenth game of the season through suspension, so Poyet made his first full start since 26 December, with five other changes to the side held at Stamford Bridge by the Spaniards. Poyet was soon in the thick of it, failing to connect with an ambitious bicycle kick and then flashing a near-post header wide from Zola's whipped free-kick in the opening ten minutes. Chelsea scored with their first shot on target. Perry dithered in his own half, Goldbaek scampered unmolested down the left flank, and his low cross was planted beyond Sullivan by Flo for his fifth goal in as many games – a timely return to form.

Marked by Leboeuf, whose first instinct against Wimbledon is usually to duck, Hartson's ample physical presence created barely a ripple of disquiet in the Chelsea defence. There was a tame volley which de Goey could have gift-wrapped before falling on it, and one snap shot which Poyet hoofed to safety without blinking.

Duberry headed wide from Zola's cross, then the little Sardinian's far-post volley was blocked magnificently by Cunningham. Indeed, Wimbledon were in such a languid mood that they never threatened remotely to make a game of it, and eight minutes after the restart their pacifism was duly punished again. When Zola picked out Poyet, arriving late in the box, Sullivan didn't have a prayer.

Petrescu, Zola and Goldbaek all queued up to squander chances as the contest became embarrassingly one-sided. By the time complacency got the better of Chelsea, and Gayle converted Ainsworth's cross right at the end, there was only enough time for a ritual late siege of de Goey's goal. But it would have been a travesty if Wimbledon's flurry had robbed Vialli of his chance to regain poll position at the Riverside.

Not for the first time in recent weeks, Vialli opted out of the post-match debriefing, leaving it to Wilkins to assess the ever-changing situation. 'We're absolutely thrilled with the way things have gone today and our performance merited a bigger winning margin. The players have clawed their way back into contention through sheer hard graft, and this is now a massive week for us. Middlesbrough will be tough because they're having a mini revival, but we're back on the tails of Arsenal and United and there's a marvellous mood of optimism in the camp considering all the different nationalities in our dressing room. The fitness of the players at the end of such a massive week is as good as it ever was at any point in the season.' Wilkins also had words of praise for Poyet: 'Having Gus back is like signing a new player. But even when he was in plaster, he's always been around the dressing room as a positive influence on the other lads. He's a terrific guy to have in the team. I think it's a testament to all the hard work he's put in that he should come back and play so well for a full ninety minutes after such a long lay-off.' Di Matteo echoed the sentiment: 'Morale has been high throughout the season, but it is even higher now that Gus is back. He is such an important player and in many ways is an extra weapon we can call on.'

Apart from his sparkling form on the pitch, Poyet was also playing his part in persuading Dani – who had played with Poyet at Zaragoza – to consider the Bridge as his next move. Dani shares Poyet's agent and was being seduced by the glowing reports from his former team-mate about life at Chelsea.

MONDAY, 12 APRIL

Old Trafford old boy Bryan Robson insisted: 'We can have a say in where the title goes. It's looking tight at the top. If we can beat Chelsea, then United will be two points in front with a game in hand and a better goal difference. That would be one hell of an advantage. I'm sure everybody at Highbury and Old Trafford would be delighted, even if we take Chelsea to a draw. Our next two home games are Arsenal and United. If we beat Chelsea and Arsenal, and then lose to United, Alex Ferguson might buy me a drink! But seriously, Vialli has done a tremendous job. In Desailly and Gianfranco Zola he's got two of the best players in the world, and the return of Poyet is vital. Their run-in looks easier, too. I think it's fair to say that both sets of fans at the semi-final replay will be keeping a close eye on the score at the Riverside.'

TUESDAY, 13 APRIL

Vialli took a vow of silence. He had no intention of speaking to the English media for the rest of the season. His stance was given full club approval. He was fed up with the constant refusal to accept his insistence that Chelsea were behind Manchester United and Arsenal as title favourites, sick of the mundane questioning, and a touch insulted by a reference in a *Times* article to his command of English being 'fractured'. Apart from a brief and evidently involuntary appearance at Charlton, Vialli had left Wilkins to handle media obligations.

But in Blake's Hotel in Kensington, under contract to an Italian TV station, Vialli suggested the title was possible: 'Having seen Manchester United and Arsenal in their most recent outings, I think we can catch and pass them. We refused to give up and were rewarded with some good results. At this point, they don't look so far away, do they?'

Wilkins refused to defend Wise, who had a UEFA hearing hanging over him, but praised his form: 'Dennis has really impressed me. He has been playing some smashing football and has this desire to win which is infectious. There's nothing wrong with wanting to win, and sometimes if you take the animal out of the guy, you lose the player. It's a bit like the Roy Keane situation, and perhaps Patrick Vieira at Arsenal is a little bit like it. You have to understand these players, but obviously they have to learn to control themselves too. It's a balance.'

Vialli finally launched a £1.5m libel case against AS Roma coach Zdenek Zeman over his allegations of doping. Vialli was absent from the Rome court but was represented by his lawyer. As usual in Italy, the first audience was devoted to technical aspects of the case, which became inevitable after attempts at mediation failed. The next session, before Judge Lucia Fanti, was scheduled for 12 November.

Vialli gave the Roma coach something else to think about by confirming his interest in the Italian club's £6m striker Marco Delvecchio. Fearing Casiraghi's absence would extend beyond next season, he was very keen on the sixteen-goal striker. 'Delvecchio is an outstanding player,' he said, 'with all the skills and qualities we need to complete our strike force. The problem is simple: the price we're being quoted is just too high. So for the time being we'll sit back and wait.'

There were new fears that Casiraghi might not play again until the autumn of 2000 after he revealed that his other leg had come close to an amputation on the operating table the night he was rushed to Princess Grace Hospital from Upton Park.

Casiraghi's specialists in Bologna believed the problem with the left leg – during marathon surgery on the right knee, the left leg was raised and developed internal bleeding – had even brought him close to death on the operating table. Casiraghi had been taken back to his private room after surgery, but the alarm was raised the following day when his left leg began to swell. Another surgeon was called and Casiraghi was rushed back to the operating theatre. Both sides of his left leg were slashed open to relieve the haemorrhaging. There would soon be a round table conference with all the medical experts before it was known precisely how long Casiraghi would be out.

Hutchinson said: 'We are monitoring the situation, but we have always said that it would be after the start of next season rather than at the start of the season.'

Hutchinson had no official confirmation that it might be far longer than the club anticipated. He said: 'We shall have to face that situation if and when we are told by the medical staff. The players are mindful of Gigi's problems and concerned for him. He is very popular at the club. If they do win anything this season he will be one of the first people they will think of. All we are concerned about right now is the player's health and welfare, rather than how much we have invested in him.'

Poyet was fired up to face Boro, who have only lost once at home all season. 'It is a difficult game, but we shall try to do the same as we did at Aston Villa and win away. They are a good team with a difficult striker to mark, but we try to do our best. The most important is the winning of the three points.' For the first time for much of the season Vialli had a full-strength squad to chose from, with Wise and Desailly back from suspension.

WEDNESDAY, 14 APRIL

Middlesbrough 0   Chelsea 0

Zola collapsed in a heap at the final whistle on a bitterly cold night on Teesside.

He had missed a chance normally he would bury; Schwarzer's superb save prevented the team creeping up on the blind side of the two FA Cup semi-finalists and into top spot. Boro felt they should have had a seventy-fourth-minute penalty when Cooper and Flo collided inside the Chelsea box. Instead, Chelsea broke clear and Wise sent Zola on a clear run to goal. Schwarzer stuck out a foot to block Zola's shot and ensure that his side held on to a well-deserved point. 'The first thing that popped into my mind,' said the keeper, 'was, I've done nothing all game, I might as well do something and earn my money. Fortunately enough, I got some part of my foot to the ball and pushed it away.'

Prior to Zola's one on one, Chelsea had failed to trouble battling Boro.

Wilkins conceded: 'I can only hope that Manchester United and Arsenal find it as hard coming here as we did. All credit to Middlesbrough because they are unbeaten at home this year and they made it tough for us. Gianfranco is very disappointed at missing his chance. But, to be fair, I think it would have been unjust if he had scored. Put it down to the save.'

Luca sat in Robson's office, watching the end of the Manchester United v. Arsenal replay. 'I must admit I was hoping the game might go to a penalty shoot-out with no serious injuries but with one or two limping, forlorn-looking players at the end. A few more red cards would have been enjoyable for Chelsea fans too. But what was most enjoyable was what Bryan said about our game. He thought that with the bombardment Middlesbrough gave us, especially the aerial bombardment, that Chelsea sides of the past would definitely have lost. He recognised the improvement that has taken place here. Now we must work to keep that improvement going in our remaining games.'

THURSDAY, 15 APRIL

Mike Reed was the one referee no one would have anticipated for such a vital match with Leicester City. Two years ago Reed was attacked in his car as he drove home from the Bridge after awarding a hotly disputed penalty in an FA Cup replay between the teams. He was replaced as referee at the subsequent League meeting seven weeks later by FA chiefs, who feared for his safety. But Reed drew a line under past squabbles. 'I've refereed four games at Leicester this season without any recriminations, and the same goes for Chelsea. What happened two seasons ago is water under the bridge, and I won't even be giving it a second thought on Sunday.'

FRIDAY, 16 APRIL

Wise was in danger of missing the return leg at Mallorca. 'I didn't bite him. That's the answer,' Wise said after being asked by UEFA to submit a written statement. 'There was no complaint from the player, Mallorca, the UEFA official or the referee. Even the player afterwards said I didn't bite him. I would like to thank the papers and others from the media for doing a great job. My gesture to bite him was only shown on TV and everyone jumped on the bandwagon. You asked him after the game if I bit him and he said no, but the papers went on. That's all I've got to say.'

Wise was supported by Wilkins. 'You have to analyse the action of the other gentleman in the incident. I've no idea what will happen. All I've been told is Dennis has been charged. He gets butchered. If he tackled someone in the way he gets tackled they would writhe in agony. All Dennis does is get up and get on with the game. Since I've been here I reckon the discipline of Dennis and the players has been superb.'

Chelsea were about to play the first of four home games from six to decide the championship. Duberry said: 'The title is in our hands. We're ready to battle. In the past, when the going had got tough Chelsea were found wanting. Not now. This is the best title race for years.' Wilkins, again deputising for Vialli in the media conferences, added: 'I've never known a fitter Chelsea side than this one. I'd be disappointed if we are not there or thereabouts at the end. We expect a tough game against Leicester and we will need to bring the ball down out of the air and play our game. Our new surface will help us do that.'

Vialli was proud of the 'chaps': 'Every single player has done us proud this season. Here we are with just six games left and we have lost only three. But they know that it is these six games and the remaining European Cup Winners Cup matches which will decide how our season is remembered.' He insisted his team must win, but warned: 'We have found out time and again since I came to Chelsea that Leicester are a very hard side to beat. We must battle as we battled at Middlesbrough, but we are at home and we must add goals to our excellent performance up there. Chelsea have never qualified for the Champions League, so we have six games left to make our own little bit of history.'

SATURDAY, 17 APRIL

For Sky TV's live coverage Vialli broke his vow of silence. It was ill advised.

Luca discussed the title and gave his public support to the club's decision to stand by Rix. 'Listen, this is the first time I have talked about that, I have always been reluctant, but I love Graham Rix. He has been punished for something which he has done, and when that finishes there is no reason why he should be punished again. When he comes back, he will be made welcome – especially by myself.' Bates had received numerous letters of support from fans who had apparently backed his decision to stand by Rix by a ratio of six to one.

Vialli again indicated that he thought his side could win the title. 'I'm proud of my players. When you look in the dressing room, see all these players' CVs, with that experience they still have that great desire, which is the most important thing. There is no point having great players if they feel they are on holiday at a charming club in a beautiful area of London. They want to be successful, they are still hungry. We hope the most important week of the season will be the last one. We want a good finish to the Premiership and want a second time in a row to win the Cup Winners Cup. That would be amazing.'

Vialli also explained his decision to keep a low profile. 'Sometimes you need a break because I don't know what to say, and it is not only football questions which are asked as people ask about the Graham Rix situation and the Dennis Wise incident.'

SUNDAY, 18 APRIL

Chelsea 2   Leicester City 2

Vialli blew bubbles with his gum throughout the match, but the bubble burst with a tactical error that was one of the defining moments of the entire season. It was painful as Vialli and Wilkins watched in anguish as Chelsea spectacularly blew their chances, throwing away a two-goal lead in a disastrous last eight minutes leaving them with a near-impossible task to catch Manchester United and Arsenal.

Vialli took most of the flak after a tactical substitution which horribly backfired. He replaced the small but efficient Ferrer with Duberry to counter the aerial menace of O'Neill's decision to bring on big Ian Marshall. But still Chelsea collapsed under the bombardment, conceding two goals in a five-minute spell, ensuring that the club would be chasing shadows rather than titles for this year. Vialli was inconsolable, with Le Saux, left on the bench until the start of the second half, warning: 'Do not interview him under any circumstances.'

In the glorious sunshine it seemed Vialli's original strategy of switching to three at the back, leaving Le Saux on the bench, was working. Ferrer played on the right side of the back three – a position where he had excelled for Barcelona for a decade. It gave Chelsea a sound defensive formation against a side that tried to play the passing game at the outset rather than just hoofing it forward more in hope than expectation. Not for the first time they squandered a host of missed chances, but still looked to have secured victory when they went 2–0 up. Within the half-hour Zola raced through on to Di Matteo's stunning chipped pass over the top of the Leicester defence and coolly lobbed advancing keeper Keller. Defender Robert Ullathorne was stretchered off with a suspected broken leg after injuring himself in his attempt to stop the Italian. Zola was in his element, tormenting the visitors with a deft range of trickery, but Flo should have done better than head just wide of the post from one of his strike partner's accurate crosses. Di Matteo orchestrated attacks with more freedom after Vialli's surprise switch in tactics. Wise and Morris provided the platform for Di Matteo to probe forward menacingly, and he had a header cleared just off the line before placing a shot just wide. Morris also threatened with a couple of long-range efforts, while Flo headed straight at Keller. Little did Chelsea know at that point how costly those misses would eventually prove.

Chelsea took time to get back into it at the start of the second half. After de

Goey pulled off a stunning parry to deny a rifled volley from Savage, they started to get their act together. Petrescu miscued a shot on the turn just wide, Flo fired over, and Keller matched de Goey's agility to acrobatically tip a far-post header from Wise around the upright. Di Matteo again opened up the defence with a lobbed through-ball. Petrescu also lobbed Keller from the tightest of angles, and although his shot hit the post, Elliott directed it into the roof of the net in his attempt to clear. Substitute Poyet just failed to connect with one cross when he had a clear sight of goal, and Elliott only managed to put off Di Matteo at the last second as the Italian again burst through himself.

The brilliance of Zola, dominance of Di Matteo and excellence of de Goey should have been enough to increase the pressure on the top two, but at the end Leicester pumped old-fashioned route-one high balls into the penalty area and all those old frailties, those jitters at the back, returned. A cross from Elliott into a packed penalty area was unwittingly deflected into his own net by Duberry in the eighty-third minute. With three minutes left, Guppy beat Petrescu and cut in from the left flank to curl a tremendous strike into the far corner past the despairing dive of the Dutchman. Guppy said: 'I thought we were on top towards the end. I went to cut in and the space opened up. I've scored a couple like that this season so it couldn't be a fluke. Ian Marshall gave us an extra dimension up front and I went out to try and get the crosses in. We got the two goals at the right time to give us a chance. But they've had a great season, and just because they've dropped a couple of points at home it doesn't make them a bad side. We didn't come here to ruin anyone's chances but to do something for ourselves.'

Wilkins tried to explain away the worst setback of the season, refusing to blame Vialli's decision to substitute Ferrer as the catalyst which ruined Chelsea's entire season. 'No, it did not have a massive effect. Albert had a super game but our problem is with either very small or very big, and in that period we needed sturdy defence. We felt the situation merited the chance when Marshall came on, especially at set plays. They went a bit route-oneish towards the end and we didn't cope with that at all.'

There was an immediate dressing-room inquest, but there was little Vialli needed to say to the players that had surrendered the title chase. Wilkins said: 'I don't think he needed to say too much to the lads. They knew what he was feeling in that situation – bitterly disappointed. Let's be honest, we never defended a two-goal lead, and with the quality in our team we should have been three or four up. Give Leicester credit for their never-say-die attitude. Guppy struck his goal superbly. In the end we just couldn't cope with Marshall and his aerial ability. We had the quality to do that but made the mistake of dropping far too deep, and that always gives you problems. But there is a big European game coming up on Thursday and we will concentrate on that.'

O'Neill was in his usual belligerent mood. 'We destroyed the game, the savages destroyed the game. But we were terrific against the team going for the championship when, according to the media, we had just come here to make up the numbers. We came out of it with a well-deserved point because we were terrific. Marshall caused them problems because he's good in the air, but my main concern was to try and get us to believe we could compete against Chelsea's world-class

players. Steve Guppy was sensational, and Neil Lennon was magnificent. I'm proud
of them. We were highly competitive. Someone asked me whether Chelsea had
taken their foot off the pedal. They are going for the championship – nobody takes
their foot off the pedal.'

Did the substitutions change the course of Chelsea's championship? O'Neill
said: 'You'd have to ask Gianluca about that. I'm sure they will consider this two
points dropped against a supposedly inferior side. I don't mean to be sycophantic,
but Chelsea are an exceptionally good side. They deserve to be where they are, but
there is no point us coming down here to make up the numbers. I hope they get
through against Real Mallorca on Thursday. That will keep European football alive
in this country.'

Zola looked completely distraught as he received the Man of the Match award.
He said: 'We are very very disappointed. We couldn't control the game in the final
minutes. They put pressure on us by putting the ball in the box, as many balls as
possible. Unfortunately we couldn't handle it.' Le Saux conceded the Blues were
facing a lost cause. 'At this stage of the season, to have been so close yet lose – or
rather, draw – a game in the last ten minutes could prove very costly. We will
continue the way we have done all season, not looking at anybody other than
ourselves. We know we're a strong side and we have to play with as much
confidence and enthusiasm as we can. It's been a long season and we want some
sort of reward for it at the end.' Le Saux pinpointed fatigue and a failure to keep
possession or convert chances at important stages as reasons for their collapse.

Chelsea's title odds lengthened from 4–1 to 5–1 third favourites, behind Arsenal
at 5–2 and Manchester United at 1–2.

Eight months of hope all but ruined in just eight minutes.

MONDAY, 19 APRIL

Leboeuf believed the team must share responsibility for letting Vialli down.

'Of course he's got big pressure because he's young, he's a new manager and he
plays for Chelsea, and everybody knows you don't forgive any mistakes for a club
like Chelsea. He knows how hard the job is and he just wants to do it professionally.
The club is going well, is growing up very well, and we just support him and try
to give him the best. But that wasn't the case on Sunday, and we are sorry for that
because Luca deserved to give the League to the club. But if it is not this year it
will be the next. Manchester United are not the best team in the country, but they
will win the championship. We can make up for that by winning the Cup Winners
Cup and then go on to build from there. I have won a World Cup medal, but I still
need a championship medal and a Champions League medal before my collection
is complete.'

UEFA decided to take no action against Dennis Wise, though they admitted:
'The player's unsporting gesture warrants clear disapproval.' Chelsea had faxed
their detailed observations on the incident to UEFA headquarters over the
weekend, and it was believed they included the legal implications of Wise being
punished for the bite which left no teeth marks.

TUESDAY, 20 APRIL

De Goey was absent from training, but was expected to play on Thursday despite his wife miscarrying and a broken little toe being X-rayed in hospital.

WEDNESDAY, 21 APRIL

Chelsea were about to embark on a mission to avoid the end of their season. 'We are good enough to look at the match with confidence,' Vialli said, but he conceded the odds were 'forty to sixty' against, although that was weighed against the proven effectiveness of his psychological games. 'Reaching the final would be great for the players and the supporters,' said the Chelsea boss, 'and we want to keep the Cup. Not beating Leicester was a blow, but we have experience and spirit in the squad and I'm sure we can respond in the right way.'

Leboeuf remained positive and buoyant. 'I'm expecting them to play almost the same game as they did in the first leg. They will try to sit back and play on the counter-attack. They're well organised, but we're very good playing away – probably better than we are at home. We know we're capable of winning.' But the season was taking its toll; the match against Real Mallorca would be his forty-seventh of the season. 'We've only lost three games this season and we haven't done a lot wrong. But for the last twenty minutes on Sunday I felt so tired I couldn't run. I couldn't give one hundred per cent to the team and I was ashamed of myself because the supporters pay good money every week and I feel as if I let them down. It wasn't all my fault. The PFA say they will try to help, but it's about money and television wanting more and more games. My body tells me it is getting fed up with football. I have asked the PFA and the FA for help. You cannot expect us to play fifty games a season. It is impossible. They are asking too much of us. In Germany they have a two-month break. It is not right.' His holiday started on 10 June after France's end-of-season internationals, and he was due back for Chelsea training on 7 July. 'Just over three weeks. I will ask the club for an extra week off.'

Cuper was keeping the grass long and the diameters of the pitch to a minimum at the Luis Sitjar stadium, his purpose to create a congested, exhausting arena. 'Nobody beats us at running,' Vicente Engonga, his midfield player, said.

Black-market tickets were exchanging hands at almost five times face value. The local authorities described things as 'highly charged', and 800 policeman were drafted in to control Chelsea's 5000 fans.

THURSDAY, 22 APRIL

Real Mallorca 1   Chelsea 0 (agg. 2–1)

Vialli faced the awful reality: no silverware. Wise's last-gasp headed miss with a gaping goal before him ended the Blues' interest in retaining the Cup Winners Cup. As Zola's cross arrived at the far post a minute from time, from no more than five yards Wise's downward header bounced wastefully wide. Inconsolable, Dennis apologised to his team-mates in the dressing room afterwards.

Vialli said: 'I think we've done our best and there's nothing I can blame on the players if we don't win anything this season. We are still in a good position in the League, we've reached a semi-final in Europe, and it's been a good season, although it could have been better. We will keep improving and the future will be even brighter, but you can't be a great player or manager if you're unable to live with triumph and defeat. The chaps gave a great performance tonight. We knew we had to play attacking football and, despite that, we restricted Mallorca to only a couple of chances. But they won, and in the end the result is all that matters. Perhaps last season we won the trophy with the help of a little luck and, this time, fortune has gone the other way round, but we can live with that. There's no way I'll blame Dennis, he did very well and he was up and down the pitch all night. At least he was in the right position to have the opportunity, and I can't ask anything more than what he did out there tonight.'

De Goey had needed a pain-relieving injection before kick-off, just in case someone stood on his foot. Petrescu also played on with a broken toe, picked up weeks back in Romania. Morris, too, had a big toe injury. Chelsea strived hard during the match – Di Matteo's left-foot volley smacked the bar, denying him the chance of a reunion with his former club Lazio in the final, and Roa's flying save thwarted Flo – but this was a performance which summed up the season: since the autumn watershed when they lost Laudrup and Casiraghi, the attack had lacked penetration. All that defeated the holders, in the end, was Leo Biagini's powerful near-post header after fourteen minutes.

In a gripping climax, Desailly was riled by an off-the-ball punch from Olaizola. The Frenchman spent the last three minutes hunting down his assailant, but only caught up with Olaizola after the final whistle, by which time he was too dejected to administer anything more than a severe ticking-off. Wise was also targeted: he was pelted with missiles, including wooden staves once employed as flag poles, in the pre-match warm-up, and provocative Spanish fans also unfurled a banner denouncing him as 'a cannibal'.

Poyet emerged from the dressing room after the match to be surrounded by both Spanish and English media. 'Everybody's very disappointed. It was a final for us today. We tried to do our best, we played the best we can, but sometimes when you go on and can't score it's very difficult. I don't know really what I can say now. There's a danger we could end up with nothing and miss out on the Champions League. We cannot afford to let that happen, so the game in Sheffield is an absolutely vital one for us. It's the biggest game of the season so far. After this defeat we have to change the chip in our head. We have to try and forget this defeat as soon as possible. We still can't believe we lost to Mallorca. We had about forty shots in the two games against them and had only one goal to show for it. It's going to be much tougher for us to win the Champions League or UEFA Cup in future, so we knew this was our best chance of winning another European medal.'

Vialli concluded: 'It's a difficult moment, but as long as we keep working hard like we have done so far, in the end we can be successful. We have got plenty of winners in the side. I know some players might be down physically and mentally, but tomorrow is another day, as they say in Italy. We have improved our Premiership position from last year, which was our most important target, and we still have five matches left to try and get into the Champions League. We will give it our best shot, and if Manchester United and Arsenal lose, anything is possible. I would like us to be where Manchester United are, but even if we don't qualify for

Europe we can't be seen as a failure.' Vialli had been rightly impressed by United's 3–2 triumph over Juve in Turin. 'We watched United on TV and they taught us a lesson. When things seem to be impossible you need to perform out of your skin. They were fantastic. We want to be as good as them, even better than them if possible, in the future. It was good to watch such a great match.'

There was silence inside the away dressing room. Some players changed quickly, others sat in stunned silence. Wise said: 'We played well and just missed chances. I tried to be too precise with my header, I tried to place it in the corner. I headed it well, but just wide.' Di Matteo added: 'You can imagine how depressing it is. It was our last chance to win a trophy and this chance has gone so now we have to fight hard again in the championship. It's crucial we don't let things slip now and try and finish the season on a high.' Zola said: 'We had good chances. Unfortunately the ball didn't go in and the goalkeeper made a couple of fantastic saves. There is nothing you can say, because when you lose playing like that you cannot complain too much. You have given your best.' He shook his head. 'That's all I can say.'

By the time the coach pulled into Harlington, it was 2.15 a.m. On board, all was silence.

FRIDAY, 23 APRIL

Vialli had arrived at the crossroads of his playing career. When he took over from Gullit, he was given a mandate to see out the remaining eighteen months of his contract as player-coach, with an option for a further two years as manager only.

As he sifted through the wreckage of the end-of-season collapse, Vialli – thirty-five in July – struggled with the twin demands of management and sharpness in front of goal. 'I definitely want to play next season. I've got no problem carrying on with both jobs. Sometimes it's difficult, sometimes it's demanding – but it's always exciting. And I will carry on doing both jobs as long as the club has no problem with that, although if you want to be a good manager you have to realise that it's difficult to be part of every game as a player. I have to be in the right frame of mind before I pick myself, but I love playing, I love managing and I love the responsibility of making all the decisions. I know I can't play for ever, and I won't be doing it in three or four years' time, but at the moment I would like to carry on.'

Vialli carried the can for a series of costly blunders. When he opted out of naming himself among the substitutes against Mallorca, he deprived Chelsea of a recognised goalscorer on the bench – an astonishing oversight. He claimed: 'I don't like being a substitute. I'm not the sort of player who can come on and turn a match. In my mind I know I have to be on the pitch for ninety minutes because I rarely score as a sub. I don't think I have scored more than two or three times as a substitute.'

If he needed any reminder of the perils of trying to play and manage beyond his sell-by date, he needed to look no further than sacked predecessor Gullit, or Rix's temporary replacement in the dugout, Wilkins, who became a victim of his own workload at neighbouring QPR.

Vialli ordered his team to 'do an Arsenal' and recover from the bitterness of losing a cherished Cup prize by showing they still meant business in the Premiership title fight. Arsenal had bounced straight back from their shattering FA Cup semi-final exit at the hands of Manchester United by thrashing Wimbledon 5–1 just five days later. Vialli challenged his side to make Sheffield Wednesday feel the backlash.

Luca was back in action on the training ground just a few hours after the retreat from Spain preparing for his nineteenth appearance of the season alongside Forssell, as Flo reported for international duty ahead of his country's Euro 2000 qualifier against Georgia. If Manchester United slipped up at Leeds a few hours before the Hillsborough clash, Chelsea could draw level on points, even though Ferguson's team would still have a game in hand and a massive goal-difference advantage. So, the last, last chance!

SUNDAY, 25 APRIL

Sheffield Wednesday 0   Chelsea 0

After lunch at Arkles, the Bateses settled down to watch the match on their big screen. At the end, Ken was almost in tears after the final rites of his club's 1998–99 Premiership challenge.

After the misery in Majorca, this was a game Chelsea simply had to win, but a third successive failure to collect maximum points left them four points adrift of leaders Arsenal and three behind United, having played a game more, and with Leeds breathing down their necks for the final Champions League qualifying slot. A win was the very least Vialli and his stuttering team had to achieve.

Vialli raced to the tunnel as soon as the final whistle sounded. He finally threw in the towel, and tipped Arsenal to retain their title. 'It was not the best game we have played. We had to win the game, but we did not do enough. What we have to do is take our chances. Yes, that is one thing we have learned from this season, definitely. United may become distracted with so much going on so I see Arsenal being a little bit out in front. As for our chances, I really think it is all over now. It is about the other two teams, and the aim now is to stay in third place and make sure we can try for the Champions League.'

Leboeuf admitted the whole camp were demoralised after watching their season collapse. 'We are definitely out of the championship now. To win the title we would have needed to win our last five games, and I don't think we'll catch the others now. It's difficult to keep your head up after the sort of week we've just had. But there is still a Champions League place at stake. We know where the problem lies and I am sure we will resolve it by next season. It's a huge disappointment because we have all worked so hard to win something this season.'

Shot-shy Chelsea never really tested Wednesday, despite knowing it was win or bust for their title hopes. The decision by Vialli to start the game as one of six changes (Hitchcock was given his first start of the season) did little to inspire as he tried to inject some fresh life into a season that had disintegrated spectacularly over twelve days. Even the prospect of facing the Premiership's friendliest team was not enough to lift them. Their initial refusal to offer even token resistance twice in the opening three minutes should have been just the encouragement Chelsea required. Ferrer ran forty yards without the hint of a tackle, before Forssell, preferred ahead of Zola, was allowed the luxury of time to turn and shoot over the crossbar from inside the area. Goldbaek, who had also earned a starting role, was then presented with an open invitation to test Srnicek, but dragged his effort wide.

Vialli rang the changes again during the interval in a desperate search to find the spark to re-ignite his title bid, turning to Zola in place of the ineffective Forssell.

Zola needed just two minutes to deliver a tantalising cross, encouraging Srnicek to come racing off his line. He failed to reach his target ahead of Poyet, but the Uruguayan's brave header narrowly failed to find the top corner. Carbone, so often the source of Wednesday inspiration in a miserable season (although this point assured Premiership survival for the club), was faced with the responsibility of ending his close friend Vialli's championship challenge. He came close ten minutes into the second half, brushing the top of the bar with an impudent twenty-five-yard chip that sent Hitchcock scrambling backwards, but the game nevertheless drifted towards a goalless outcome. Srnicek was not forced to make a single save in the entire game.

Carbone was fortunate to escape punishment as tensions frayed, following a clash with Wise. The volatile Italian was incensed when Wise removed the hairband which restrains his flowing locks. He clearly hit out at Wise, right under the nose of referee Steve Dunne, who saw no reason to produce a card of any description.

Defiant Vialli promised his squad would be transformed from title nearly-men into champions. He maintained the campaign had not been a disaster as his squad would learn valuable lessons despite finishing the season without any silverware. 'We have to learn from Arsenal and Manchester United. The players of Chelsea have done their best and I have a great squad and great players. I am very happy with them but we have to learn valuable lessons from this season. The main thing is to be more clinical. Neither can we let a lead slip like we did against Leicester. These are things that make a great team a winning team. Lifting silverware gives you a great feeling and we'll not be doing that this season, which makes me sad. But I will remain quite happy and positive for the future, and next season I believe we can improve again. I also believe that as long as you improve as a team then you are doing well. It means you will reach the top sooner or later. That's why I believe we can become the best team in England.'

A crumb of comfort: this was the twenty-third clean sheet in fifty-two games, which was a record.

Casiraghi had to have yet another operation in Bologna: surgery was necessary to try to regain flexibility in his right knee. Chelsea reopened negotiations for a replacement for him. Simone Inzaghi and Marco Delvecchio were targets, but priced beyond Chelsea's means, while Spain's left-back Sergi had been recommended by Ferrer.

MONDAY, 26 APRIL

Luca met Hutchinson – it was time to firm up plans for next season. The MD said: 'Hopefully the summer will be busy. Homework and research on new players has been going on for several months. We had a three-hour meeting reviewing the season and planning ahead. Unlike five years ago we are competing for the short supply of quality players who can take their pick of the top European clubs. We are often battling against the likes of Milan, Inter, Lazio, Barcelona and Real Madrid for big names. On stadium capacity we are at a huge disadvantage, not only with the continental giants but domestically. Chelsea is competing in handcuffs. Delayed planning permission is not only restricting saleable capacity to 34,700, but is costing the club over seven million a year in income. This is at a time when Manchester United are to up capacity to 67,000, Liverpool, Aston Villa and Newcastle are to top 50,000 and Arsenal are looking to achieve 60,000. It is a big challenge. The success of not only Chelsea FC but Chelsea Village is essential if we are to continue progressing.'

TUESDAY, 27 APRIL

A report published by accounting firm Deloitte & Touche that Vialli's team earn an astonishing £27m a year placed them as the highest earners in domestic football, followed by Manchester United's £26.9m, Liverpool's £24.1m and Newcastle United's £22.3m. Chelsea's wage bill had jumped by an enormous eighty-one per cent, although this included the business travel payroll for the club which has nothing to do with the players' salaries. The influx into the League of overseas players commanding huge salaries contributed to the wage explosion.

The PFA fended off criticism of their members' massive overall forty per cent increase in wages. Gordon Taylor defended claims of greed among players, saying: 'The fact is that these wages are paid by clubs who demand success and the game has never enjoyed as much income from gate receipts, television and sponsorship in particular. If the game is hoping to try and attract the best players from all over the world, it is inevitable that they must offer the best wages, and that will include other players in the team who will want to be upgraded and not left too far behind. There is this emphasis on the top level and the demand to stay in the Premiership. In the top flight the game is about players, and players' wages are, for the most part, covered by gate receipts alone. Every labourer is worth his hire and it is not as if the player is putting the club's arm up its back. It is up to clubs to balance budgets, and it is only fair that players should share in the income the game is getting now from many sources.'

FRIDAY, 30 APRIL

Vialli confessed that the final ten minutes against Leicester was the defining moment of the club's season.

He also pinpointed the arrivals of Desailly and Ferrer as key moments, but promised at least three more in the summer. 'I think United will sign at least three new players. The last three years before I took over here the idea was that there will be three new players each season – it just helps to mix it up sometimes and that's what we hope to do here. We shall certainly be looking at a striker, but the competition from other teams to sign players will be intense. We are very close to the teams, but there is still obviously a difference. We have got money to spend, but there will be no point going out and spending, say, thirty million because teams in our position in the past have done that and then finished fourth or fifth the following season. It is not always the answer.'

The budget for next season depended on qualification for the Champions League. Vialli continued: 'This is why the game with Everton is so important. If we can win this game then the spirit will be so much better for the last three games. To get a place in Europe is worth quite a lot, so we want to qualify. We will have money to spend in the summer.' It sounded as if Luca already knew the budget would not be more than the £12m he had last year, even after qualification for the Champions League. Equally, there was only so high the club could go in terms of salaries. 'The ideal player is a player on a free transfer who doesn't earn too much and who plays really well. That isn't easy, but sometimes it happens: Gus Poyet on a free transfer, Tore Andre Flo for a small price, and Marcel Desailly a lot cheaper than many thought he would go for. They were all bargains, but you then have to pay higher wages. I think they are two great examples of the way Chelsea are moving. We try to be always aware of what happens not just in England, but in Europe. We have got money, but obviously the less you spend the more happy the chairman is. We don't want to throw money away.'

Vialli added: 'There will be a spirit of revenge next season because we have done so well but ended up winning nothing. We have to improve in terms of personality, and also be more clinical when we have to kill the opposition off. Overall we have been quite consistent, which is important because this has always been a problem for the club. The season hasn't quite finished yet, but I don't like the way people are talking about Chelsea now. It seems to me that some are underestimating what we have achieved this season so far. We are third at the moment, and obviously we will try our best to improve that position. But I think anyway it's not shameful to come behind Manchester United and Arsenal. Even though it's hard to admit as a Chelsea supporter, over this season they still have something that we need to catch up with to compete with them until the last match of next season.'

Fanatics who fancied recreating golden Stamford Bridge moments in their own gardens got the chance when the club sold off the old pitch: one square foot of turf for a tenner, making £200,000 from the sale of 20,000 square feet. The two penalty spots, the centre spot and the four corners were auctioned to supporters on the club's internet site.

May...

May...

May

*First ever place in the Champions League
... a record three defeats in the entire
season*

SATURDAY, I MAY
Chelsea 3   Everton I

In a white shirt and a big, knotted, blue-striped tie, Vialli presided over sunshine football at the Bridge. 'This was our best performance at Stamford Bridge. It was very professional and gives us the chance to finish the season in our best possible way.' Chelsea produced a phenomenal thirty-one attempts at goal. With an out-and-out goalscorer it could have been double figures by half-time.

That must be Vialli's priority for next season. They cannot rely on little Zola all the time. A rare headed goal with a textbook leap from the little Sardinian put his forwards to shame. Leboeuf's shot on the run was pushed out, and there was Zola with a pinpoint cross for Petrescu to make it two. But with Leboeuf limping, Jeffers scored, and there were nightmarish visions of a repeat of Leicester, when Chelsea's jitters surrendered a seemingly unassailable lead. This time a Zola free-kick special finished off Everton. Vialli admitted: 'There was a sense of relief when we scored the third goal. We were in control of the match, started well, creating chances and playing well, but against Leicester it went quite badly in the last ten minutes and they got a point.' De Goey observed: 'We just haven't been scoring enough goals lately, but that's football, it happens sometimes. Whether we need to buy another striker is not my problem, it's down to Vialli. I don't worry about that. I've got enough to do stopping them at the other end.'

Don Hutchinson was complimentary about Chelsea. 'Poyet had a lot of room and Zola was different class, as usual. It was not just down to us, Chelsea were excellent. They started so well. It was hot out there and we were always chasing after them. I'm not sure they are as good as Manchester United or Arsenal, but I'm sure Mr Vialli will go out and buy some players.' Vialli said: 'This club will keep improving, and you can't improve if you sell your best players. You build your team around them. We have had a lot of offers for Tore, Robbie Di Matteo, Jody Morris, Michael Duberry and Marcel Desailly – everybody. The offers have come from England and abroad, but they are not for sale. We want to improve the squad, not weaken it.'

What about Super Dan? The fans' favourite was nominated as one of the big names on the point of departure. When Vialli was asked about the banner proclaiming love for Super Dan and begging him to stay, he said: 'It's been there the whole season. It means Dan Petrescu is loved by the supporters.' Asked whether such affection was reciprocated, he carried on drinking water and smiled. 'Dan has done exceptionally well, played forty-odd times this season even though he's been injured. He has been very good. He has a contract for another year, but if I had an offer for ten or twelve million I'd think about it.' The point Vialli was making was that the top players at the Bridge are not going unless he receives over-the-top offers.

But to keep players of the calibre of Desailly interested and content, the club had to reach the Champions League. The French defender said: 'The minimum goal for us this season is to qualify for the Champions League. We showed we are a good team all season then lost it in the last four games, and we owe it to the fans to show we can play at a high level.' Desailly was still unsure as to whether or not he enjoyed English football, but Vialli surely cannot contemplate losing a player like him.

Vialli began to set the scene for Wednesday's momentous third-place-Champions-League showdown with Leeds United. 'I hope it is a great game. Leeds are in quite good form and that makes it more difficult for us. We are in a very good position, but it depends on our result with Leeds and the last two games after Leeds because anything can happen. Our future is in our hands, which is good. We are five points ahead and that is a good advantage – they have to come here and win the game. For once a team will come to us and try to win, and that will be a different game than we are used to here. It will be nice to finish the season with an important game, it keeps up the concentration levels.' When Vialli was asked whether a win would conclude the race for third place, he smiled. 'Mathematically, yes. I know I am not very good at maths but we would be eight points ahead of Leeds with two games to go.'

SUNDAY, 2 MAY

Arsene Wenger branded Chelsea 'cheats', suggesting that they had falsified figures to their accountants to arrive at a wage bill at Stamford Bridge of £26.4m.

Bates was furious: 'Mr Wenger must think he is the manager of Chelsea because he seems to know where our money is coming from in terms of our income, where it's going and how much we pay our players. Since he is the manager of Arsenal, it is none of his bloody business. What's more, he doesn't know our financial position and I'm pretty sure he's not a financial consultant. He is an idiot for calling us cheats and he's also out of order, because as I recall he was coach at Monaco and somehow they survived on gates of three and a half thousand because they were funded by Prince Rainier. Italian clubs spend an awful lot of money and they don't need Mr Wenger to worry about their income either. Is it cheating for Lazio to spend fifty million in one season, or for Barcelona or Real Madrid to spend the amount of money they do? In any case, don't you think they pay big money at Arsenal for their players? Is it not true that they pay their Dutch players big money? Is it true that the Dutch players are also paid secondary contracts? As we know, the Inland Revenue are looking very closely at image rights deals. Some of the big clubs in Europe are funded by individuals; others such as Eindhoven are financially supported by multinationals like Philips. Arsene Wenger has made some stupid remarks, and in view of these comments, and also in view of Jerry Boon's false figures, we shall be consulting our lawyers.'

Boon's error was to include all the employees of Chelsea Village in the final account. 'Mr Boon is some sort of self-appointed expert. He is not an official voice of the Premier League or the FA and he will have egg all over his face because of this. The Chelsea Village shares dropped three per cent after the figures were released and they are not true. The basic wage for our players is £20.6m and according to Mr Boon's figures that puts us below Arsenal. It's typical of Mr Boon that he didn't ask anybody at our club to comment, otherwise he would have found out that last year we trebled our members of staff because of our expanding Chelsea Village. He has got it wrong, and he will have to put it right. I will be demanding that he circulates to everyone in the game the correct figures.'

Vialli handed over responsibility to Williams when asked to justify the supposedly exorbitant wage bill. Williams pointed out that it included 400 employees at Chelsea Village as well as almost seventy people employed by the travel company.

Wenger came up with a new way of describing the outspoken chairman, calling him 'a very sensitive boy'. The Arsenal manager said: 'I didn't mention Chelsea at all in what I said – or maybe once when I was asked about them and I answered that I did not know if they had an extra income. I also said that if clubs spent more than they can afford then that is nearly cheating, but I didn't mention any particular club. If Ken Bates is thinking of suing me then he must be a very sensitive boy, but I am not worried about what he says.'

The Chelsea chairman chuckled mischievously when told of Wenger's response. 'Yes, Mr Wenger is perfectly correct. I am a very, very sensitive soul – I thought everybody knew that. I get hurt very easily, and so does my lawyer.'

Bates continued the saga in his programme notes: 'Boon sets himself up as an authority on soccer finance and should therefore have higher standards, though in truth I suspect that the work was done by some junior articled clerk and Boon just wrote the review. You may remember one of Mr Boon's previous reports on the top twenty richest clubs in the world. Man Utd was given pole position. Mr Boon used sales or turnover as a yardstick. On that basis Chelsea is the richest club in the world with sales last year of £88.3m (Man Utd £87.9 m), but we are not by a long way yet, which simply demonstrates the foolishness of such reports. However, we do have the second-highest net assets of all quoted soccer clubs at £65.4 million, and our salaries/sales ratio is thirty-one per cent, the same as Man Utd, and the lowest in the League.

'Funnily, we have had brushes with Mr Boon's firm, Deloitte & Touche, before, in 1993, when the insolvency partner tried to bankrupt Chelsea. It took two High Court cases before Mr Christopher Morris was thrown out. The fact that there were full statements and legal representations did not deter him. The judge awarded Mr Morris his costs. He never claimed them because I would have challenged him in court. At one time I planned to sue all 2000 partners in Deloitte & Touche for damages, but we won anyway. That would have been fun.'

MONDAY, 3 MAY

Goldbaek conceded Chelsea's season would have been a waste of time if they lost to Leeds. 'The game against Leeds is a massive one for us and we cannot afford to slip up if we want to be totally sure of a place in the Champions League. If we slip up we will have nobody to blame but ourselves.'

David O'Leary generously insisted Vialli's side would keep hold of their Champions League place. 'I still feel that the three teams in the top three places will finish there – and deservedly so. They have the strongest squads. It didn't take a rocket scientist to predict, at the start of the season, which three sides would be occupying the top positions at this stage. When you look at the wage bills and the players of the quality Manchester United, Arsenal and Chelsea have, you would expect them to be leading the way. What has delighted me is that we have won the "other league", because there are some excellent sides who will finish below us in the table.'

TUESDAY, 4 MAY

Vialli thought that Leeds currently had the best form in the Premiership. He told the supporters: 'Fasten your seat belts because this is going to be a cracker.'

Wise said: 'We're prepared for a difficult game, but we're good enough to beat them. Each year we've been progressing, getting higher and higher up the table. Last year we finished fourth, the highest since I've been here. If we win tomorrow we'll be third and into a competition we've never qualified for. That's progress, even if we won't lift a trophy at the end of this season.'

Jody Morris was also upbeat: 'We have been a bit down recently because we feel we threw away the chance of the Premiership title, but personally it's been great for the last half of this season because I've played as much as anyone. Michael Duberry and I are the only home-grown players who have really established ourselves this season.'

WEDNESDAY, 5 MAY

Chelsea 1   Leeds United 0

Third place – Chelsea's best finish for twenty-nine years – and entry to the Champions League guaranteed. Zola was relishing a crack at Europe's premier competition after a wonderful season. 'I'm really looking forward to the Champions League because for me next season is going to be, maybe, one of my last. You never know. I will be thirty-four after next season and you have to consider everything. At the end of next season I'm going to make a decision. For me, it's very important to give the best; if I can't give something to the team, it might be the right moment to give up.' Zola, who cost £4.5m from Parma in November 1996, played in every Premiership game this season and made a total of forty-eight appearances in a hard-fought campaign at home and abroad. 'Physically speaking I've coped, considering I'm thirty-two. I handled it very well, but some players like myself who played all the games maybe needed a bit of a rest.'

The goal that secured the Champions League place came in the sixty-eighth minute when Le Saux rampaged down the left before delivering a deep left-wing cross to break down the Leeds defence and Nigel Martyn's resistance. Poyet, Chelsea's lucky talisman, rose above everyone to power home his thirteenth goal of the season. Vialli said: 'Poyet is a great player, a real danger. He gets forward and scores goals. But to say we lost the championship because we didn't have him would be unfair on the likes of Di Matteo and Dennis Wise. We could have done with him, but injuries happen in football. He is a crucial player for the team but we were still on top of the League without him.' Poyet said: 'It could be the most important goal of my career. The dream has become a reality and we will play in the Champions League next season. It is magnificent for me. I feel very happy. We know if we finish third we still have to play the preliminary round, but next season we will keep improving.'

There was a bust-up between O'Leary and Leboeuf after the Frenchman was accused of getting Woodgate booked. O'Leary accused Leboeuf of feigning injury five minutes into the second half when the Frenchman charged into the Leeds half with the ball before being upended by Woodgate. O'Leary said: 'One moment Leboeuf was limping and the next he was running around as if there was nothing wrong with him, so I'll let you decide what I think. My player said he never touched him. As he came off afterwards he told me that he had got a World Cup winners' medal, but I told him that I'd got a few medals of my own from my eight hundred or so games. Centre-halves used to be made of different stuff in my day.' Vialli did not want to enter a war of words. He simply said: 'I couldn't care less. I respect his opinion, but I don't really care.' Leboeuf was not happy to stay silent. 'I have a scar on my ankle to prove I was not faking. He also accused me of raking up the old "I won the World Cup" joke. If O'Leary wants a war I will quite happily get my lawyers, the Football Association and my club involved.'

Wise also had a go, clashing with Bowyer in an ugly twenty-third-minute challenge right in front of the Leeds bench, who immediately sprang to their feet in anger. Wise planted a playful kiss on O'Leary's assistant Eddie Gray. Then he was booked.

In Le Saux's opinion, Chelsea's title chances had vanished 'in the three home games against Blackburn, Leicester and West Ham where we picked up two points from nine. If we had won two games and drawn one that would have given us seven extra points and put us top of the League. These are the small margins of error within which we have to work.'

Bates announced that 'renewals of season tickets and executive areas now exceed twelve million pounds, a club record'. The fans expected that to be spent on new players.

THURSDAY, 6 MAY

Vialli was well advanced with his plans for next season, eyeing £3.5m-rated Sheffield United whiz-kid Curtis Woodhouse, one of the best young English talents around, hailed as the next Paul Ince. Vialli wanted to buy a couple of top home-grown players to join his multinational squad.

Di Matteo was linked to four Serie A clubs willing to pay £7m. 'He's under contract,' said Bates.

Zola's home-town club Cagliari wanted him back. His announcement that he would consider a return to Italy at the end of next season caused a flurry of activity at the Italian club. The Sardinian-based side had always longed for the day of Zola's homecoming. Team manager Gianfranco Matteoli described Zola at the start of the season as 'one of us, someone who has made it and was raised in Sardinia. We're waiting for Zola. If he still has the desire to play after England, he has to end his career with us.' Now the club believed it would come true. Technical sports director Liandreo Landinin was taken aback by Zola's revelation that next season might be his last at the Bridge. He said: 'This has caught us all unawares. I have not had any contact with Zola just yet. However, I'm not really that surprised to learn of Gianfranco's statement. It would be fantastic for the club and the fans if we could lure him back here. He has always had a great nostalgia for Italy, and in particular for Sardinia.'

Bates announced that he did not want to play Champions League games at Wembley. 'I actually think that by going to Wembley it cost Arsenal their place in the knockout stages of the Champions League. They certainly lost that home advantage because Highbury has one of the smallest pitches in the country, which is why they have got such a good defensive record – they know how to exploit it. It was not quite the financial success that some people may have portrayed it as. They were more or less giving tickets away towards the last match because they could not fill the spaces.'

Chelsea spent £2m to secure the leasehold of Richmond Athletic Ground, which is to be turned into London's first state-of-the-art soccer training facility. Richmond was one of three potential sites considered for a youth academy and training centre. Chelsea are four years into a ten-year lease at Harlington, but it shares pitches with Imperial College hockey matches on Wednesday, Saturday and Sunday afternoons.

Forssell took his driving test. He passed. A few days later he celebrated by driving Flo's car to training.

FRIDAY, 7 MAY

Tottenham's season had tailed off since their Worthington Cup triumph, but despite three consecutive defeats against West Ham, Liverpool and Arsenal, Ginola insisted Spurs would be giving their all against Chelsea and United – for their own sakes rather than for Arsenal. Spurs hadn't beaten Chelsea in the League since 1990, and the Blues triumphed 6–1 at White Hart Lane last season.

SATURDAY, 8 MAY

The biggest cheer at Tony Banks's House of Commons dinner, which raised £20,000 for survivors of Chelsea's 1955 championship-winning side, was when a Ruud Gullit greeting was read out.

MONDAY, 10 MAY

Tottenham Hotspur 2   Chelsea 2

An hour before the game Vialli reviewed the season and looked forward to the next. Players mischievously jostled him as he gave a Sky TV interview on the pitch.

He said: 'Yeah, I've got a few ideas. Obviously it is quite difficult to find better players than the Chelsea players at the moment because they are top-quality players. They've shown this season that they can do a great job. So it is gonna be difficult, and very expensive. We have a few grand to spend, but we want to be really careful, so let's play the last match of the season and we will sit down and obviously do our best to improve and strengthen this team.'

He analysed his team's weaknesses, pointing to the number of leads they had let slip. 'Sometimes we should have been more clinical. Attacking football is fine, but sometimes, as a team, we've got to be able to hold a result.' He admitted he had much to learn. 'I've made a lot of mistakes but I'm still quite inexperienced. But you keep learning – if you want to. I want to become a better manager and I want to do something important with this club. So I will have to start concentrating on the managerial side of the job.' His days as player-manager, already dwindling, looked as good as over.

Even with the slimmest of chances Vialli's side were determined to keep the pressure going on Arsenal and Manchester United, and they scored after just three minutes with their first attack. Poyet headed on for Flo, who showed nice control until his shorts were tugged by Carr. From Wise's short free-kick Zola's curling cross was met by Poyet leaping ahead of Iversen and Walker. The Chelsea fans began to chant 'We want seven' and 'You might as well go home', but Poyet's fourteenth goal of the season didn't bring the overwhelming win on a ground that Chelsea had dubbed 'Three Points Lane'. For this was a vastly different Tottenham under Graham's guidance, made of sterner stuff.

Leboeuf was forced to concede a corner while he waited for stand-in keeper Hitchcock (de Goey had hurt his hip during morning training) to come and collect the ball, and off Ginola's delivery into the penalty area Iversen flicked out a shot past Hitchcock at the near post to score, despite Armstrong being in an offside position. Three minutes later Poyet put Flo in position. The big centre-forward flicked his way round the back of the defence, but his angled shot deflected off Walker over the bar. Vialli substituted the ineffective Zola for Forssell after fifty-four minutes. Ten minutes later Leboeuf over-elaborated while trying to dribble out of defence and was caught by Ginola, who scored a typical goal with a shot that left Hitchcock standing.

Vialli then made a double substitution, bringing off Morris and Petrescu and sending on Di Matteo and Goldbaek. Petrescu headed straight down to the dressing room.

Goldbaek cracked a wicked twenty-five-yard angled dipper into the top corner after seventy-two minutes.

'I thought it was an exciting game for the supporters,' said Vialli, 'but we didn't give our best performance. In the end, a draw was a fair result, but I'm not totally happy.'

FRIDAY, 14 MAY

Vialli was amazed at the competitive spirit of English football after three years in the country. 'Anything can happen in England. When Forest beat Blackburn I was not surprised, but it was something which would be impossible in Italy or in Spain. In those countries teams without motivation will always lose without a fight, but I think it is much fairer over here. Everyone always tries their best in every match, which makes it very enjoyable in this country. The English League is one of the most difficult and exciting there is.'

Vialli tipped Manchester United to win the Premiership, praising them as one of the best European club sides in living memory. 'We lost only three games all season. That is good, but not good enough to win the title. Arsenal and Manchester United have been exceptionally good. Ten days ago I thought Arsenal would win the title, but now I think it will be United, and they are still in two finals. If they win two out of the three, they will go down as one of the best club sides of recent years, up there with Milan, Juventus and the Liverpool side of the 1980s. They are one of the best sides I've ever seen, and they will continue to improve. Both Ferguson and Wenger know what they must do to improve and they have the mentality to do it. But we have an advantage because we can improve more. We are younger in terms of success, and the manager, squad and organisation can all get better. We can only get better after this year's experience.'

SUNDAY, 16 MAY

Chelsea 2   Derby County 1

Vialli rounded off his first full season with a win and his first Premiership goal of the campaign, his tenth in all. Vialli had awarded himself a rare place in the starting line-up, and with his thirty-fifth birthday less than two months away, he still possessed flashes of class as his reshuffled side put on a display of assurance to treat the fans at the end of a season of outstanding progress. Vialli made six changes including leaving leading scorer Zola on the bench, just where he had started the season at Highfield Road.

The first half epitomised much of the campaign, with Chelsea utterly dominant without scoring the bag of goals their superiority merited, suffering a fatal lapse of conviction at the edge of the box. Babayaro put Chelsea ahead, then Luca scored in the second half after an exquisite chip from Flo had carved out the chance. Carbonari produced a late reply with a twenty-yard free-kick that crept just inside the far post.

Wise said: 'Luca's done well in his first full season as a manager. He's had to get used to it, but sometimes I think he knocks himself too much, blames himself when it's down to the players. It's not for me to tell him his job, but I think in situations like our semi-final away to Mallorca we could have done with his experience as a sub.'

Vialli said: 'It was the best way to finish the season. We got three points even though we knew there was nothing on the game. We showed good professionalism and enthusiasm and we made our supporters happy.' Of his future, he said: 'My first concern is to become a better manager. If this means I've got to hang up my boots it's something quite sad, but that's what will happen. But I've got a few weeks to think about that.' Of the season as a whole, he observed: 'Seventy-five points is usually enough to win the title. We have improved a lot. We've improved our consistency since last season, and also our determination.'

And it was a good season, a record-breaking one on eight counts. Firstly, the club recorded the least number of defeats in a season, beating the previous four from the Second Division in 1984 and the eight in the top flight in 1970. Secondly, along with champions Manchester United they became one of the few to go through an entire campaign with only three defeats (the others were Preston, 1887–88; Leeds, 1968–69; Forest, 1977–78 and 1978–79; Liverpool, 1987–88; and Arsenal, 1990–91). Thirdly, they set the record for the longest unbeaten run in all competitions in the top flight of nineteen games, and the longest unbeaten League run in Europe of twenty-one games. Fourthly, they qualified for the Champions League for the first time in the club's history. Fifthly, although trophyless over the season, Chelsea won the Super Cup for the first time. Sixthly, they broke the club's best defensive performance over a season, having conceded just twenty-nine goals; the previous lowest was thirty-four in 1906–7 and 1911–12 in Division Two, and forty-two in forty-two games in 1970–71. Seventhly, they achieved a record number of clean sheets. And finally, for the first time Chelsea fielded a team of eleven internationals.

MONDAY, 17 MAY

It was time for reflection as the team sped off to the Far East to earn some money, despite feeling jaded after an enhausting season.

Latin and Gallic emotions were overflowing with regret and recrimination. In the final analysis it was one of the club's greatest seasons, yet perhaps the most disappointing. Chelsea could have been, indeed should have been, champions. The final distance between Manchester United and second-placed Arsenal was marginal. The reasons for failure were numerous; injuries to key players, suspensions (mostly to Wise) and Laudrup's defection were all major contributions. Three defeats should be good enough for the title, but there were too many draws. And perhaps the main defect was the failure to secure a new top-class striker once Casiraghi was crippled.

Vialli's assertion that he didn't want to disrupt the harmony of his dressing room as the reason for not making a new signing disguised the real problem. The two or three targets he wanted collapsed for various financial reasons, either extravagant loan demands from Barcelona for Oscar, or Premier League strugglers Everton being ready to pay more for Kevin Campbell than title-chasing Chelsea. Filippo Maniero might just have triggered an upsurge in goals to secure a few more wins instead of draws.

Casiraghi had at least ditched his crutches after six months; he wore a plaster cast and walked with a heavy limp. He said: 'It's getting better all the time and I was allowed to walk on my own for the first time at the weekend. After my latest examination the doctors say I am doing pretty well, which has given me greater confidence. I can't rush anything, but I'm hoping to be playing again in England at the end of the year. I had only three months in England before I came back home and I enjoyed my time in the Premiership. It was a great experience, and

I'm looking forward to going back. Chelsea were pretty unlucky to finish third, but Manchester United played extremely well and deserve everything they get.'

Marseille stepped up their interest in Desailly. President Robert Louis-Dreyfus and coach Rolland Courbis met Desailly's agent, Pape Diouf, for talks on Saturday, and the player linked up with his adviser in Paris two days ago. He still owns a sumptuous villa at nearby Aix-en-Provence, and loves the region and its climate, and has repeatedly criticised the style of play in this country. Marseille had made him their number one target to replace Inter Milan-bound central defender Cyril Domoraud – pairing him with national legend Laurent Blanc. Club director Marcel Dib said: 'If our president can come up with a deal, you never know.' Desailly insisted his meeting with Diouf was a long-standing arrangement, and that he had been in Paris to sort out some private matters.

Newton was being chased by Atletico Madrid and Feyenoord after announcing that he had played his last game for Chelsea. Newton, twenty-seven, was available on a free transfer after failing to agree terms at Stamford Bridge. West Ham were following his situation closely, but he relished a move abroad. 'What I want most is first-team football, and if I have to go abroad to get it, I will do. It would be exciting to play in another country and it's flattering to hear big clubs are interested. I've loved my time at Chelsea and I've won a lot of medals with them, but I can see that it's time to leave. I have been here since I was a schoolboy and now I am not in the manager's plans. I've tried to change his mind, but I can't. Now I have to think of my career.'

Wise was in reflective mood at the end of the season. 'This is the best Chelsea team I've played in. If we improve next year like we have in each of the last few years, we'll be up with Manchester United and Arsenal again and hopefully above them. Next year we've got to aim for seventy-nine points and we can win the League. If we play the way we've played this year we'll not be far off. I'll tell you how far this club has come: we're disappointed at finishing third in the League a few points behind the champions. It ain't that bad.'

Bates concluded: 'Looking back, we have achieved so much and made a great deal of progress. Two Cup quarter-finals and one semi-final is a record that many clubs would be proud of. It is a measure of how much Chelsea has changed that we regard it with a degree of disappointment. The championship itself was within our grasp, but in the end we threw it away. We know that, and the players know that, and they are more disappointed than the supporters.

'Within eight weeks, for varying reasons, we lost Laudrup, Casiraghi, Flo and Poyet, and the guts were knocked out of the team. It is a tribute to the squad's character that they continued to win so many matches. But in the end we must reflect on too many silly goals given away by world-class defenders, and too many open goals missed by world-class strikers. I still thank the players, though. They have given us some disappointments, but over the season we have seen some outstanding football too, and some of the games have been as good as, if not better than, any I have seen in my seventeen years as chairman.'

Afterword

When the season ended, the players flew to Hong Kong for two matches, and then took a well-earned break before reporting for three weeks' intense training on 5 July. Before Vialli took his holiday in Sardinia, he met Bates to discuss strategies. The chairman observed: 'Luca is such a good man that he kept saying, "I don't know whether I'll be a good enough manager for you." But when was the last time you heard of a manager who holds his hands up and says, "It's my fault we didn't beat Leicester because I made the wrong substitution"? That's not the sign of a bad manager, it's the mark of a great man. Luca is very quiet, but everything he says gives a clear indication of what he is thinking. Ruud Gullit was a footballing genius, but the difference is that Luca is a painstaking one. He works everything out in fine detail and leaves nothing to chance.' Bates also told of the players' continuing hunger for success: 'The players came to us, the management, and said they wanted to be paid big bonuses for success, but nothing for failure. There aren't many clubs where players would say that. It's all or nothing, and it's very encouraging.'

Despite this optimism, it had threatened to be a disappointing summer for Chelsea. The club declared its ambition to make new signings before the 1999/2000 season got underway, and offered Roma £16m for Italian international Luigi Di Biagio and striker Marco Delvecchio, but both deals were blocked by incoming coach Fabio Capello. Hutchinson said at the time: 'It's been a frustrating summer. Delvecchio has been particularly disappointing. The player and club reneged on what had been agreed. Obviously, he used Chelsea to get a better contract, but that's part of modern football.' Vialli immediately turned to Nicola Ventola, and his £10m bid was accepted by Inter Milan after they completed the world-record £30m signing of Lazio striker Christian Vieri. But Ventola was determined to stay in Serie A.

With Casiraghi struggling to play again, Chris Sutton once again became a leading target. Chelsea initially refused to match relegated Blackburn Rovers' £12m asking price, but, after more behind-the-scenes negotiations, on a sunny late afternoon early in July Vialli introduced the new £10m centre-forward at a press conference at the Bridge. After all his continental acquisitions, here, at last, was a blunt touch of British bulldog. Vialli said: 'I am not saying we are soft, but you need to be physically and mentally tough. In England, sometimes it is a tough game, and if you are not tough enough you can be turned over. Chris is a tough competitor, and we missed that last season. He has the right combination. Chris is a player with everything. He can help us become the best team in the country. We did not score enough goals last season, even though we played some great football, and Chris has the ability to do that for us. We have a better equipped squad now.'

Sutton wanted to become a Chelsea hero in the Peter Osgood mould. 'There have been many cult figures over the years,' he observed, 'and I just hope I can emulate those who have come here. This is a new start for me. I couldn't have come to a better club. I'm looking forward to getting started.'

Sutton, twenty-six, signed a six-year deal worth £30,000 a week – certainly the sort of salary the best overseas stars have commanded at the Bridge. To join Chelsea, he exercised a clause in his contract enabling him to leave Ewood Park after four years if the club was relegated. He added: 'It is a really good move for me. When I knew of the interest I was always going to come to Chelsea. Chelsea are a club well capable of winning things, and I want to be part of it. People in the past have said that foreign players are not committed, but Chelsea have a bunch who are well equipped and up for the task. It is a physical game, and sometimes you have to dig in when things are not going that great. But part of the reason I wanted to come here is the sort of football they play – they have so many great players. Obviously, if I can do well here then I hope it will help me get back into the England team.'

Ken Bates revealed how Sutton had snubbed Manchester United and Spurs in favour of Stamford Bridge: 'Alex Ferguson was in contact with his agent and didn't want him to talk to anybody until he had a chance to do so himself. United made their move at the weekend, and right at the last minute David Pleat at Tottenham did exactly the same. Chris simply didn't want to talk to them because he'd made his mind up he wanted to come to Chelsea. We've arranged Italian and French lessons for him so he can understand team talks!'

With a record 17,100 season tickets sold and £15m banked, Bates was in a position to authorise this spending spree for Vialli, and the most significant signing alongside Chris Sutton was Didier Deschamps. Luca brought the influential thirty-year-old midfield ace from Juventus for just £3m, although he became one of the most highly paid players in the Premiership. The French World Cup captain's decision was partly made as a result of Marcel Desailly's announcement that he would stay at the Bridge: Desailly and Deschamps started their careers together at Nantes, each is the godfather to the other's children, and they are the best of friends. 'The fact that my international colleagues Frank Leboeuf and Marcel Desailly play at Chelsea will help me adapt,' Deschamps said. 'I was close to Vialli at Juventus, too. But now he's the manager, so it will be different. It has to be.'

But, after signing a three-year contract, he was under no illusions about the task ahead: 'I'm not looking for an easy life. The most important thing for me is to play in the best team in England. I've won the World Cup with France and the Champions League twice. I've won the French title with Marseille and Serie A with Juventus. Now my goal is to win the Premiership with Chelsea.' Deschamps was once famously described by his fellow countryman Eric Cantona as 'nothing more than a water-carrier'. 'I don't see any shame in being a water-carrier,' Deschamps retorted. 'It is the job I have done at two big clubs and it has helped me achieve a lot of success. I am not a star; I am a defensive player, a hard worker. I work for the team. It is my job to get the ball and give it to the other players. I know what I can do well.' And former Juve coach Marcello Lippi recognised those qualities – he described the Frenchman as the player he would never sell.

Deschamps also insisted that London was the place for him: 'Manchester United are a great team, but I would always choose Chelsea above them because I would prefer to discover London than Manchester. My wife and I have a little boy. It's a very important factor for me and my family. It's a fantastic city and I am looking forward to discovering it.'

Another exciting signing, on a Bosman free transfer, was that of Ajax youngster Mario Melchiot. Chelsea beat off a determined challenge by Rangers to land the Dutch Under-21 star, who has already made over a hundred appearances for Ajax, agreeing a three-year contract worth £11,500 a week. Melchiot said: 'I don't like to lose, so it's great to sign for Chelsea. They bought me for my versatility, although my best position is in the centre of defence.' Yet another Italian, twenty-five-year-old Carlo Cudicini, signed from Serie 'C' Castel Di Sangro as cover keeper, and Danish centre-half, Jes Hogh, signed from Fenerbahce for £300,000, as Vialli spent £13.3m, but recouped £7.85m in sales, a net outlay of just under £5.5m.

Eddie Newton departed for no more exotic a destination than Birmingham City, who had also tried to sign Bjarne Goldbaek for £1.5m. Andy Myers left for Bradford City for £800,000, Dmitri Kharine went on a free to Celtic, and Michael Duberry was sold to Leeds for £5m. Vialli was also resigned to losing Roberto Di Matteo, who wanted to return to Italy. Vialli said: 'Roberto is convinced he must play in Serie A to get recognised at international level again. I wish him luck, and we'll have to congratulate the club that buys him as they are getting a very fine player.' There were contented smiles, though, when another strange decision from Brian Laudrup – this time to quit FC Copenhagen – gave Chelsea a £1.75m windfall under the sell-on clause in his contract.

Tore Andre Flo signed a new five-year contract to end speculation about his future. He said, 'I had no doubt in my mind. I like it at Chelsea. It's a good club with good players, and I like to be in London.' There was also an accolade for Gianfranco Zola. He won the Golden Chair award for being the best Italian player outside Italy, beating Sheffield Wednesday's Benito Carbone into second place, and his own manager into fifth place. But Vialli would not be up for the award in future because after 499 games, sixty-nine of them in a Chelsea shirt, he finally decided to hang up his boots and concentrate on management. He said: 'From now on I will be a manager and only a manager. I have had enough of training with team-mates, all those five-a-sides and kickabouts. It is time to become a more traditional manager, an Italian-style manager. I need to go further and deeper as a boss. Every time the realisation that it is all over hits me, my heart tightens a little bit. I hope I leave behind good memories of me as a player, and I hope the supporters understand that behind my actions and eccentricities there is a lot of sincerity, sensitivity and, most of all, a sense of humanity.' Luca pledged the next two years of his life to making Chelsea one of the top sides in Europe. 'My contract with Chelsea runs through to June 2001, and unless they sack me I intend to honour it.'